Global Soundtracks

Global Soundtracks

WORLDS OF FILM MUSIC

MARK SLOBIN, EDITOR

WESLEYAN UNIVERSITY PRESS

Middletown, Connecticut

Published by Wesleyan University Press, Middletown, CT 06459

www.wesleyan.edu/wespress

© 2008 by Wesleyan University Press

Printed in the United States of America

5 4 3 2 1

Library of Congress Cataloging-in-Publication Data

Global soundtracks : worlds of film music / Mark Slobin, editor. — 1st ed.
    p.   cm. — (Music/culture)
  Includes bibliographical references and index.
  ISBN 978-0-8195-6881-6 (cloth : alk. paper) — ISBN 978-0-8195-6882-3
(pbk. : alk. paper)
  1. Motion picture music—History and criticism. I. Slobin, Mark.
  ML2075.G55 2008
  781.5'42—dc22   2008010984

Contents

·◉·

Part Three: Comparative Vistas

Preview of Coming Attractions

Mark Slobin

·◉·

When viewers saw the very first film in 1896, they also heard a musical accompaniment. No surprise here; music had always flowed around entertainment spaces. In the nineteenth century, mass culture spawned more and more visual attractions. People expected some kind of soundtrack for the dance, melodrama, comedy, acrobatics, magic, and animal acts that they paid a few pennies to see. Film offered just one more come-on in the carnival of entertainment. For the next three decades, colorful music continued to circulate in the air around the black-and-white moving pictures. Without on-screen dialogue, these stereotyped sounds gave viewers clues to the movie's locale, storyline, character types, and emotions. Starting around 1915, the musicians would turn to page seven or twenty-seven in their handy tunebooks and pull out something for war, death, Indians, Chinese, storms, cowboys, or whatever was coming up in the next scene.[1]

Finally, American technology and business figured out how to blend sound and image into a single reel of film. In 1927, the tide turned in a musical, with a singing superstar, Al Jolson as *The Jazz Singer*. The idea of the "talkie" spread quickly around the world. Everywhere, people discovered that they could not only import tuneful and brassy American movies, but also create their own sight-and-sound products. These fast-growing world cinema systems spoke in the language and musical dialects of local audiences. As in the United States, producers realized that music and dance powerfully attract paying customers, so from the start, music drenched the soundtrack.

In "Hollywood," the code name we all use for the American film industry, somebody had to define what a built-in soundtrack would be like. The studio heads turned to experienced stage and variety show composers, mostly immigrants from central Europe. Led particularly by Max Steiner, this group created the filmscore as we know it, with its basic styles and philosophy. The point was to make moviegoing a totally integrated, comfortable experience, unlike the once jerky and fragmented feeling of going to a picture show. Burch calls this the Institutional Mode of Representation, a suitably portentous term for a commercial conspiracy to consolidate a corporate image (1990). It is more stable, respectable, and profitable to offer folks a seamless viewing experience, in the dark with popcorn, in which dialogue and music alternate, overlap, and blend in an absorbing story carried by proven stars and terrific sets and costumes.

The filmscore as it developed in the 1930s is like a rushing river fed by basic tributaries, the available streams of musical thought, symbols, and actual units of sound from several sources: (1) nineteenth-century symphonic music, opera, and operetta, both German and French; (2) early twentieth-century French and German cabaret and music hall; (3) American popular entertainment, from the blackface minstrel show of the mid-nineteenth century through vaudeville acts and the Broadway musical. As film composers combined these sources, they muddied the waters and flooded the world with a sonic wash that has accompanied all films, everywhere.

No matter where or how you turn to filmmaking to tell a story, there's a set of standard practices and devices that you can expect viewers to understand. Nobody questions the threatening chords that comes right before the villain appears, or the swelling strings that signal love. The heroine's theme song glides in and out under the dialogue so we know how she's feeling. When somebody falls or slides, the music moves with them, in the imitative technique called "mickey-mousing." Music signals genre, such as comedy, horror film, western, or thriller, even before you grab your first handful of popcorn. This system relies on well-known codes attached to specific musical instruments, orchestration, special effects such as synthesized or electronic sounds, and a whole set of expectations about what makes music happy, sad, threatening, nostalgic, scary, tearful, or ethnic that come out of the older sound-culture sources listed above. This entire, really complicated system of signs and subtexts goes down easily, so fluidly that it infiltrates virtually all the cinema systems of the world, regardless of local ideology. Around the world, audiences understand the musical codes for sad and happy, menace and mirth. They expect action sequences to pulsate with sound and romance to throb with feeling, even if the resources for the scene might differ locally in terms of instrumentation pacing or melody line. Music operates on the brain with incredible speed. A recent French study shows that both trained and untrained listeners agree very strongly in connecting selected pieces of music to specific emotions, even at exposure times of less than a second: "250 milliseconds of music may suffice to distinguish happy from sad excerpts" and subjects agreed strongly on their responses to short excerpts, grouping a large sample of pieces in terms of four emotional clusters of "happiness, serenity, fear and anger, and sadness" (Bigand 2005). No wonder it is easy to construct dominant codes of film music in Western society and export the resulting products worldwide.

Even "alternative," "indie," or "auteur" filmmakers go along, or, with their experiments, show that they know the system so well that they can avoid or undermine its conventions.

Within the feature film world, the genre called the "musical" has received the most critical attention (Feuer 1993, Altman 1981, 1997), but separate studies could analyze the many other genres that place music at center stage or that rely heavily on music for their impact. Each has its own founding fathers (never mothers) and heroes. For example, our sense of what a horror picture should sound like largely was shaped by one Herman Stein, who doesn't get the attention that major feature-film composers garner. In dozens of films such as *Creature from the Black Lagoon* (1954), with its indelible "creature-theme," Stein set the standard. In another domain entirely, Gene Autry, whose first full-length biography only appeared in 2007, mastered the cultural image of the singing cowboy so thoroughly that he made a fortune by understanding how commercial synergy works. As film historian Jeanine Basinger (2007) concisely summarizes the strategy, "he used his movies to sell his radio show, his radio show to sell his recordings, his records to sell his sheet music and the covers of his sheet music to sell his movies." Autry understood that all his films should star him as himself, not some invented persona. Other genres also center on apparently authentic musical lives. The musician biopic puts musicians' lives on display, ranging from classical composers (Mitchell 2004, Raykoff 2000) through pop, jazz, country, and rock artists.

Many other music-based films await ethnomusicological analysis, for example those connected to another form, dance. The dance-lesson film cuts across cultures from white, immigrant, and interethnic couples in the United States to Mexican, Irish, Australian, and Japanese gyrating hopefuls looking for love. The invention and evolution of each new film genre only strengthens the indelible impression that the dominant system makes on the minds of filmmakers, critics, and audiences alike. It is rare for a convention to fade away entirely, as film music is just another popular culture form, and they all depend on both reliability and novelty to keep their consumer base, just as every supermarket has familiar products and a significant percentage of items that say "new!"

The accepted tradition of film music extends its sway way beyond feature films into cartoons, nature shows, history channel shows, industrial film, even into documentary and ethnographic film, genres supposedly beyond entertainment value. It spills over into the newer forms of moving pictures, including television, computers, and all the emerging media that can be squashed into a cellphone window (Cook 1998).

All of this musical manipulation always has been attached to a well-entrenched, self-assured, capitalized American music-marketing system that has interacted with the huge range of cinemas found within the United States and around the world, over the nearly eighty years of sound film. This anthology looks at some of the ways that filmscore practice, developed in the United States, was adopted and adapted by a wide variety of cinema systems, ranging from the "subcultural cinema" of American minority groups through the national cinemas of countries around the world and the emerging, multi-sited, transnationally targeted movies made for an ever more complex and sophisticated global audience. The first section surveys "Hollywood," that nickname for the age of classic American cinema. The book then turns to subcultural cinemas and broad comparative approaches to film music studies that crosscut individual and localized traditions. Then a parade of case studies follows, each author going into depth about specific film places, times, and situations around the world.

The purpose of this introduction is not to lay out a template that all the authors will follow, since the demands of each of their film domains and their own interdisciplinary backgrounds lead each to find his or her own way of locating broad film music issues in specific settings. Rather, the following sections present some general issues and begins by surveying the types of cinema systems the book covers.

A Typology of Global Cinema Systems

Subcultural cinema. Within large multicultural societies, small groups may take the camera into their own hands and make movies for internal consumption only. In the United States, twenty years into the history of film, Jewish Americans and African Americans were the most agile in finding openings for a cinema of their own. Yiddish-language film (beautifully surveyed in Hoberman 1991) and "race film" (first anthologized in Diawara 1993, then in focused monographs like Bowser 2000 and Green 2000) offer a rich repository of expressive statements by those on the margins of the mainstream. Most of this material vanished, being low-budget and ephemeral, a kind of undocumented cinema. Enough has been reclaimed and reissued to give us a tantalizing set of snapshots of subcultural fiction film. In these shoestring stories, music plays a critical role in marking off ethnic boundaries and simultaneously entering into dialogue with the mainstream, as we shall see below.

Although they reveled in the rich variety of available musical expression, early subcultural film lacked the financing and audience base to remain a credible cultural force. Cripps (1993) reveals ways in which Hollywood weakened black film by skimming the talent and the concepts of representation of subcultural artists. Yiddish film fell prey to the lack of new immigration after 1924, the destruction of the language's homeland in the Holocaust, and the assimilationism of Jewish Americans. Without really knowing about these earlier subcultural models, new countercinemas sprang up in the United States in the 1970s, under the more favorable social conditions of minority empowerment and multiculturalist agendas, including Chicano (Noriega 1992), Asian American (Foster 1997, Xing 1998, Hamamoto and Liu 2000), Native American, feminist, and a "queer" gay and lesbian body of work and criticism (Rich 1998, Dyer 1990). Independent African-American cinema resurfaced in the 1980s as film-school graduates learned from older masters. The studio-controlled, yet Black music-driven, Hollywood "blaxploitation" movies of the 1970s also acted as a stimulus for subcultural expression.

Eventually, the defining of an "independent cinema" movement began to fold minority filmmaking into a broader category in the 1990s, located on sites such as Independent Film Channel or Sundance, and most recently in the new spaces opened up by internet filmmaking. The works and themes of ethnic filmmakers weave in and out of an "indie" cinema system that is designed as a showcase for innovative work. It is also meant to serve as a farm club for the major-league film teams. For subcultural film, the line between opposition and co-optation remains blurred. As always, music in film is both a great pull and a great sell (Smith 1998). Since film is an industry, if subcultures should happen to make money and choose to spend it on movies, they can actually set the agenda, as is currently happening with Native Americans: "Indians have gone from the stereotypical impoverished noble savage to the stereotypical Mr. Money Bags," so Indian financing of films puts them in the power position for the first time: "both the Oneida of New York and the Mohegan Tribe of Connecticut turn down about a dozen script submissions a year." As Sonny Skyhawk, an Indian producer says, "how are we going to overturn the image of the American Indian if we don't do it ourselves? Hollywood sure won't" (Ulmer 2005). Musically, one wonders whether the results will be conservative or innovative.

Even though such subcultural film entrepeneurs have emerged to take charge of image and marketing, their job is not easy. Moctesuma Esparza, who is developing a chain of Latino multiplexes called Maya Cinemas, says "to do it right, it's very tricky. The Latino market is not a homogeneous group that feels the same way about music or movies or even the actors they like" (Bernstein 2005).

Other societies have spawned subcultural cinemas, notably India and the USSR. In part two below, Greg Booth reports on the music studio system in India's film headquarters, now dubbed Bollywood, while Balasubrahmaniyan and Joseph Getter focus on the Tamil industry, which produces hundreds of films annually but remains less known, keeping its subregional and, in some sense, subcultural status.

European cinema. European cinema is—and isn't—part of the same sphere as the dominant American system. European émigrés created it, and European writers and directors have critiqued and revised it. Many European films follow standard Hollywood practice; still more use it in part. A significant subset, sometimes critically acclaimed, offer local variation and counterpractice. The traditional film-studies fascination with "auteur" theory stresses the individuality of directors, sometimes including filmmakers' distinctive approaches to music. I am less interested in auteurs than in the idea of European national or regional cinemas, a late topic in film studies beyond the masterworks approach or the histories of particular movements, such as French Nouvelle Vague. Dyer and Vincendeau's 1992 volume on *popular* European cinema marked a helpful departure, but only included one music article. The work of Caryl Flinn (2004) and Roger Hillman (2005) on German film point the way to studying the intricate connections between history and music in a European national cinema. Then there are overarching trends, such as the values assigned to classical music as a source, that might mark a general European sensibility, as opposed to that of Hollywood.

Europe itself falls into subgroupings with particular musical tastes and tendencies, both regionally and nationally as well as aesthetically and historically. If you spend some time watching a particular grouping of European movies, say the "golden age" of Central European films of the socialist era (ca. 1948-1989), you notice a crosscutting orientation toward music, as part of an historical moment. The role of the popular song as nostalgia, of classical music as the voice of authority, and of American pop music as forbidden fruit—these and other themes resonate in the work of numerous directors and decades. Internal variation is not hard to find, since Poles, Czechs, Hungarians, and Yugoslavs had different outlooks and histories.

Regional Cinema Centers. At some times and places, local cinema systems turn out to be powerhouses whose products might even rival Hollywood within certain neighborhoods. This was the case for Mexico in the 1930s to 1950s: "in 1938, the film industry was the second largest industry in the country after oil," and was "the major exporter of films between Latin American countries" (King 1990:47).The genre that drove this engine was the *comedia ranchera,* based on deeply local songtexts, instruments, melodies, and character types, all the while drawing inspiration from American models, particularly the singing-cowboy movies of Roy Rogers and Gene Autry. The *caberetera* genre added a darker urban layer to local production. Partly, Mexican film flourished in a period of more nationalist assertiveness and lesser Yankee control, just one example of the lively interactive pattern between American and regional entertainment systems. In part two below, Marilyn Miller's essay on a single Mexican film illuminates how much music can inform us about the complex interplay between a national cinema and its neighbors, in both the Caribbean and the rest of Latin America.

It was not just Mexico that turned local inspiration into marketable styles: Both Brazil with its carnival-based *chanchada* and Argentina with its tango films based success on indigenous musical forms (Burton 1990:17) In the same period of the 1930s to 1950s, music-driven Egyptian cinema was the local center, dominating the Arab world. Music was the engine that pulled the train. It is no accident that Egyptian film became "the most profitable industrial sector after the textile industry" exactly when "50 percent of all films belonged to the genre" of the musical (1944–1946), the overall figure for 1931 to 1961 being one-third of the 918 feature films the country produced (Shafik 1998:12, 103). Martin Stokes's article on one Egyptian star, Abd al-Halim, evokes both local nationalism and the wider regional perspective.

Indian cinema is another obvious candidate for regional center status, as Greg Booth and the team of Joseph Getter and Balasubrahmaniyan tell us. The term "Indian" covers a huge space of several national cinemas, where Hindi film serves as the pace-setter. The Indian system has projected its power in places as culturally and geographically separated as the Soviet Union and Africa, the latter detailed by Abdalla Uba Adamu's article in this volume. Today, with distribution on videoforms that turn the world into a "region" of intense diasporic networks, Indian films arrive in a local grocery store, chopped up with advertisements for businesses from New Jersey to Singapore. Even the scanty literature on Indian film music mentions the creative tension between local and mainstream musical sources, beginning in the 1950s: "formulas became rigidly established when storylines proved successful at the box-office. Producers plagiarized foreign films, just as music directors adapted foreign music" (Arnold 1991:27). The fluctuation of influence and innovation that marks Indian film emerges strongly in its music, in a system where the music director might well be the key member of the production team. Just in the last few years, the visibility of "Bollywood" in Europe and the United States has risen significantly. Now you can see the latest Hindi film on the marquee at multiplexes along the freeway in Connecticut.

Soviet cinema also functioned as a regional power from 1917 to 1991, spread across eleven time zones and some two hundred nationalities, creating a gigantic, truly captive audience. Foreign films were excluded almost entirely, and limited resources meant that audiences would see a handful of hit movies over and over and over, indelibly marking dialogue and, particularly, songs into the consciousness of all citizens. Soviet products also flooded central and eastern Europe and were exported widely to Asia and Africa. Internally, this Russian-dominated system had its own mainstream-subculture side, in a hierarchy from Moscow and Leningrad to provincial studios, where fledgling national cinemas and filmmakers in places like Uzbekistan, Kazakhstan, Armenia, and Georgia operated in the shadow of a dominant system of training, technique, and advancement. Their emergence from subcultural status to post-soviet independent national cinemas in the 1980s and 1990s marks a regional turning point that has produced wonderful local films.

South Korea is fast becoming the newest regional center; "from well-packaged television dramas to slick movies, from pop music to online games, South Korean companies and stars are increasingly defining what the disparate people in East Asia watch, listen to, and play." So popular are its products that one travel agency estimates that "eighty percent of travelers to South Korea pick television theme tours, visiting spots where their favorite dramas were filmed" (Onishi 2005). This bundling of media has emerged with the new intermedia complexity, embedding film music within a dense set of entertainments that share the same brand.

To sum up, no hard and fast distinction can be made between national and regional cinema, since films can play multiple roles, internally and for export. But national roots still bind cinemas to their home soil.

National cinemas. Everywhere, local cinemas sprang up in the shadows of American film, from the earliest decades of film history. In Brazil, "from 1900 to 1912, Brazilian films dominated the internal market"; this "fostered a public habit of frequent movie going [and] intense filmmaking activity"

(Stam 1997:20). In 2007 in Bhutan, a similar process of national identity creation is unfolding, through the once-isolated country's emerging film industry: "Cinema already has a strong influence on the culture and behavior of the general public . . . it is creating new heroes and new values," says newspaper editor Kinley Dorji (quoted in Chopra 2007). And national cinema does not need a nation-state, as Edward Said pointed out about Palestinian cinema: "Palestinian cinema provides a visual alternative, a visual articulation, a visible incarnation of Palestinian existence in the years since 1948 . . . these films represent a collective identity" (Said 2006).

National cinemas remain largely unchronicled until the 1990s, with the appearance of early surveys like Lent's (1990) for Asia, Diawara's (1992) on Africa, and scattered studies such as Heider's (1991) and Sen's (1994) on Indonesia, with China attracting significant attention due to its successful exports of the Fifth Wave filmmakers (e.g., Chow 1995). For any national cinema that is not also a regional exporter like India, building dikes against the flood of Hollywood products has become very, very hard, even in Europe. Small systems in places such as Thailand and Indonesia have flourished or declined over the past several decades of independence, giving viewers a sense of local color and melody that sometimes switches between home-grown and American or Indian sources and styles. Below, articles on the output of huge nations like Indonesia (Sumarsam) and China (Sue Tuohy) appear alongside the small-scale energy of the Caribbean country of Martinique (Brenda Berrian) as examples of the film music of national cinemas.

That term is not without its problems, since it assumes some "nation" as a unifier, either as producer or audience. But we know for sure that music speaks—or rather sings—to larger issues, since it runs like a scarlet thread through everyone's film histories. Almost every study on a national cinema mentions the foundational role that music has played since 1930 in the blossoming of local cinema sensibilities. This is only natural. Despite the uneven playing field of production and distribution, people like to hear their own vernacular language and genres, to see local bodies in motion. So they still come to movies that are at a lower level of technical excellence. In the Nigerian Hausa context discussed below by Abdalla Uba Adamu, video-forms make possible an entire production and distribution system of locally loved movies and musical reference systems that could not make it to trendy film festivals or art-house circulation. It comes as no surprise that this national cinema will get labeled, now emerging as "Nollywood," once the Western media notice a national cinema system, and touted as "one of Nigeria's positive cultural contributions to the international community" (Ogbechie 2005).

Today's national cinemas stand in a very different relationship to their own societies in conditions of transnationalism, ranging from local-response world-market pressures to the unfolding regional story of European film in the age of the European Union. Nestingen and Elkington's recent study of Nordic cinema supplies good insights (2005). They point out adjustments from older national projects to the newer conditions of globalization, while still singling out the durable popularity of domestically produced movies for local audiences. Language seems much more important than music as a survival strategy, except in Iceland, where the fame of performers like Bjork and Sigur Ros allows for a greater range of possibilities. Their general conclusion about the Nordic context holds true for the whole topic of national cinemas today: "at a millennial juncture characterized by globalization, national cinema takes shape on a crisscrossed economic, political, and cultural terrain" (Nestingen and Elkington 2005:2).

India's ambitions to displace Hollywood's dominance grow stronger by the year. One director, who set his latest film in London, says: "If we are serious about Indian films we should be getting them seen all over the world. The way to do that is to reach out not just to British Asians and Indian Americans but beyond even the diaspora" (Mansoor 2007). This has possible implications for the tried-and-true film music formulas that floated Bollywood movies for decades.

Supporting a national cinema can still be a point of honor in a country seeking its twenty-first-century identity, such as Russia. There, in 2002, the government decided to subsidize one-third of the film output, as long as filmmakers submit the scripts for approval and stick to patriotic, historic, or children's movies (Walsh 2005). This impulse to create a centralized cinema based on domestic production, harks back to the world of Soviet film, and doubtless affects the type of music that creators choose. In Indonesia, as Sumarsam argues below, the government has a long-term interest in shaping a purely national message for the media, including film. The authorities urgently feel the need to create a national cinema in a postcolonial country that is ethnically diverse and geographically vast, and they have the market size to match their ambitions.

In the end, what is national is what people think is national. In Tamil cinema, the Hollywood "leitmotif" system, where the filmscore tags each character with a distinctive theme, has begun to dominate only recently (Getter and Balasubrahmaniyan, below). Local writers trace this practice back to the ancient Indian aesthetics laid out some two thousand years ago in the *Natya Sastra*, though an outsider may imagine that long exposure to Western film music practice also might play its part.

"Third" and "accented" cinema. Clusters of cinema production can be the work of small, specialized groups or individual creators. They blur the edges of any system of cinema classification. In the late 1960s, Latin American filmmakers and cultural critics sparked an effort to invent a countercinema that would avoid the ideologies and industries of the dominant practice, in both its industrial and ideological power. Cuba supported this movement through its national film school, which offered guidance. Brazil, Argentina, and other countries came through with directors who exemplified this trend, eventually called Third Cinema. Glauber Rocha and Fernando Solana acted as theorist-exemplars (see Pines and Willemen 1989). The Argentine Solana had this to say in 1979: "Third Cinema is an open category, unfinished, incomplete. It is a research category. It is a democratic, national, popular cinema. Third Cinema is also an experimental cinema . . . there are 36 kinds of Third Cinema" (quoted in Willemen 1994:182). This deliberately provocative idea of an open-ended, liberatory cinema emphasized both the local and the global. The concept expanded as African cinema came into the picture and innovative subcultural systems like Black British filmmaking emerged in the 1970s. Musically, the resulting films sidestepped the mainstream and tried innovative ways of introducing local sounds. Often, filmmakers restricted music as a way of focusing attention on other parameters of presentation and avoiding Hollywood's idea of score.

"Third Cinema," then, was an international, ramified, and ambiguous term that acted more as a call to redefine standard cinema thinking than as a coordinated practice. But by the mid-1990s, "Third Cinema" and "Third World" cinema were merging with a body of independent work being done by nonaffiliated, individual artists. In 2001, Hamid Naficy grouped all these creative spirits together under the heading of "accented cinema: exilic and diasporic filmmaking." He sees this work as "less polemical than the Third Cinema"; still engaged, but "less with 'the people' and 'the masses' as was the case with the Third Cinema, than with specific individuals, ethnicities, nationalities, and identities, and with the experience of deterritorialization itself . . . every story is both a private story of an individual and a social and public story of exile and diaspora" (Naficy 2001:31). Naficy makes a sharp statement about the importance of music and sound in these films: "they . . . stress the oral, the vocal and the musical—that is, accents, intonations, voices, music, and songs, which also demarcate individual and collective identities" (ibid.:24–25). But in his film analyses, like earlier Third Cinema critics, Naficy doesn't actually detail music's crucial contribution.

New ways of thinking about globalization can create networks that blur the lines of categories such as "subcultural" and "accented." Take the case of "first nations" film, highlighted by a 2005 event that brought together unlikely partners: the Museum of Modern Art and the National Museum of the American Indian:

First Nations\First Features celebrates an emergent world cinema in filmmaking, the most recent innovation in indigenous storytelling. The directors of these award-winning films draw viewers into alternative cultural worlds through their compelling narratives and distinctive aesthetics. This is the first exhibition to focus on the feature filmmaking "firsts" of indigenous directors.
(FirstNations\FirstFeatures 2005)

The organizers' language makes full use of buzzwords—"emergent," "innovation," "alternative," and "firsts"—to link films that go back as far as 1991 and that are said to reflect old patterns of "storytelling." Part of what connects this innovative edge to older Third Cinema approaches is the urge to do things differently, and this might affect music. For *Atanarjuat: The Fast Runner* (2001, directed by Zacharias Kunuk), the first-ever Inuit feature film and an international success, the decision was to make natural source sounds more important than the filmscore: "*Atanarjuat* probably has one-third as much sound track music as any other feature film recently released and relies much more heavily on the actual sounds of the Arctic action . . . we view the audio landscape of the Arctic as a soundscape, and try to convey the same emotional impact normally reserved for violins and drums by the sounds of winds, foosteps on frozen snow, and silence" (Cohn 2005). New forms of accented film will continue to stretch the borders of "film music."

Transnational Control, Global Opportunities

The global cinema system is in a state of real transition in the early twenty-first century. True, old structures of control in all sectors of filmmaking are still in place: financing, marketing, and distribution. These remain in Euro-American hands to a considerable extent. The situation makes it very hard for small cinemas to find their audience, as a recent African lament makes plain: "Getting African films to African audiences is still the big hurdle, said [director] Zeze Gamboa. "There is no means to get it to theaters, and some countries don't even have theaters" (Polgreen 2005). So a report from the major annual African film festival tells us that "here in Ouagadougou signs for American blockbusters were hastily plastered over in favor of homegrown films on the festival roster. But as soon as Fespaco ends, people here say, the blockbusters return" (ibid.).

This capitalist control system is not just American. "For Tunisian filmmakers, the key source of external funding is France . . . creating [what Raphael Millet calls] 'filmic deterritorialisation'" (Armes 2005:182). As

Cameroonian director Jean-Marie Teno points out, "African filmmakers have always been dependent on European public monies for their productions," and while that used to be primarily French money, as in the Tunisian case, increasingly it is the European Union that makes decisions. Since the EU demands that "film projects must be presented by African government officials, not filmmakers," local powers are working hand in glove with transnational ones to limit the creativity—including musical content—of independent directors (Teno 2005). To compound the difficulties, neither European nor African establishments care much about whether the finally funded films are actually distributed and seen, either in Europe or Africa.

On the other hand, transnational opportunities beckon to even small cinemas, sometimes holding out hope, but most commonly inflecting the way that people project their film futures. Anyone trying to sell a local cinema has to consider the world market, as for any commodity: Thai film is "an industry looking to measure global ascendancy not by festival prizes but by international deal making." As Thanit Jitnukul, director of *Bang Rajan,* put it at a panel of local filmmakers: "Our movies must talk to non-Thai audiences" (Lim 2005). Globalization changes film music in ways that we are only starting to hear, but certainly involves both an increasingly standard approach and more local color. The essays below will take up these changes.

Further debate within the filmmaking and film-studies communities will refine, extend, and redefine the types of cinema systems presented above as film evolves in a world ever more tightly linked by cybercultures and transnational traffic. Any category offered here can be contested and reconsidered. For example, the work of North African directors living in France combines several categories, as a recent survey explains. The French nationally funded cinema brought these filmmakers into the system as immigrants and outsiders, but also as French directors, so "it is better to talk not of an accented cinema but rather of a cinema of integration or assimilation," which nevertheless makes subcultural points (Armes 2005:187). The point is that cinema systems have been fluid and interactive, across time and space, and that music shapes and defines film, globally. It would be a huge effort to make even a general map of this shifting terrain of cultures and commerce. What this book tries to do is offer a flexible and multilateral approach to interpreting the cultural cues that soundtracks send out to audiences, as a vital part of exquisitely crafted industrial/artistic products. We do this in two ways. Case studies bring you right into the action, talking to the makers of the film product and cutting to the chase of characters and cultures, with music at the center. But we also want to try out comparative approaches, which have been singularly lacking in film studies. Around the world, filmmakers reach for many similar musical strategies. A focus on "Hollywood" vs. "national" obscures the threads that bind the film world together, as a global fabric of feeling stitched together locally, regionally, and transnationally.

Overall, *Global Soundtracks* covers the main ways of writing about film music: individual film analysis, directorial or star specificity, genre studies, production methods, cultural siting of scores, and patterns of U.S./non-U.S. interaction. To look at a particular Pedro Infante film from Mexico (Marilyn Miller) or the work of Abd al-Halim in Egypt (Martin Stokes) is to zoom in on a particular setting, in all its complexity. Eric Galm dissects the interplay between Disney and Brazilian musicians in the 1943 film *The Three Caballeros*. Brenda Berrian listens to Martinican director Euzhan Palcy's way of defining herself and her region, Sumarsam digs into Indonesian historical films' choice of musics as part of national identity, while Joseph Getter and Balasubrahmaniyan focus on recent Tamil film, a branch of the huge Indian cinema complex.

To examine the evolving strategies of Bollywood studio work (Greg Booth) or the ways that Chinese films comment on themselves (Sue Tuohy) musically requires different lenses. Abdalla Uba Adamu maps the unfolding of Hausa videofilm music in a single region. My own sections largely draw on the earlier decades of sound film, to provide grounding for the exuberant expansions and remodelings of film today as media and markets proliferate, entailing shifts in production, distribution, and reception. In many ways, today's film musical resources and strategies all belong to a new era of negotiation as compared to earlier decades.

We hope you'll enjoy this viewing experience. It is built along the lines of the shows I went to as a kid in Detroit, with cartoons, newsreels, short subjects, and a double feature. Or you might think of the old French system of usherettes hawking ice cream in the aisles, or any of the many culturally colorful ways that people go to the movies globally. As editor, I have not specified a format for the authors, either in topic or style, so the essays offer a sampling of individual approaches, which seems to match the material. Gratefully, I've noticed that some contributors parallel my terminology, such as Miller's interest in "simulation" and "erasure," but such coincidental convergences are not driven by editorial mapping.

Opening Credits

I am enormously grateful to the film scholars who have taken the time to tutor me over the years, starting with Richard Slotkin (who also provided helpful comments on my chapters), Jeanine Basinger, and Catherine

Portugues on the East Coast and continuing with Julianne Burton, Bill Nichols, and Seymour Chatman in California. Graduate student work has been very helpful, including an M.A. thesis on Tamil film music by Anuradaha Mohan, as well as seminars at Berkeley, NYU, and Wesleyan, where groups of undergraduate and graduate students kept coming up with great case studies. Thanks to Faye Ginsburg for access to a key interview, Tom Lehrer for invaluable issues of *Film Music,* and to Srdjan Karanovic for talking about his work. As always, Wesleyan's frequent sabbaticals helped enormously. Joint viewings with Greta, particularly of the Soviet cinema to which she is native, have combined pleasure with insight, and my daughter Maya's professional film vision is always acute. I owe a debt to Tom Radko for accepting this project at Wesleyan University Press, and to Suzanna Tamminen, his successor, for honoring that commitment.

Note

1. The recent literature uncovering the amazing variety of accompanying sound to early cinema (Abel and Altman 2001) lends an ethnomusicological quality to a situation that seemed all too limited, in the tunebook, post-1915 way referenced here. But it still scants the ingenious ways that people made sense of early cinema in different societies, such as the *benshi* figure in Japan who stood next to the screen and explained the action. We probably will never know how many kinds of music accompanied early movies in the scattered cinemas of the world.

Works Cited

Abel, Richard, and Rick Altman, eds. 2001. *The Sounds of Early Cinema.* Bloomington and Indianapolis: Indiana University Press.

Altman, Rick, ed. 1981. *Genre: The Musical.* London: British Film Institute.

———. 1987. *The American Film Musical.* Bloomington and Indianapolis: Indiana University Press.

Armes, Roy. 2005. *Postcolonial Images: Studies in North African Film.* Bloomington and Indianapolis: Indiana University Press.

Arnold, Alison. 1991. *Hindi film git: On the History of Commercial Indian Popular Music.* Ph.D. dissertation, University of Illinois.

Basinger, Jeanine. 2007. "Back in the Saddle: A Cowboy Tycoon." *New York Times,* April 6.

Bernstein, David. 2005. "A New Multiplex Is Aiming to Capture a Bilingual Audience." *New York Times,* August 1.

Bigand, Emanuel. 2005. "Multidimensional Scaling of Emotional Responses to Music: The Effect of Musical Expertise and of the Duration of the Excerpts." Paper delivered at Musée de l'Homme, May 23.

Bowser, Pearl. 2000. *Writing Himself into History: Oscar Micheaux, His Silent Film, and His Audience.* New Brunswick, N.J.: Rutgers University Press.

Buhler, J., C. Flinn, and D. Neumeyer, eds. 2000. *Music and Cinema.* Hanover and London: Wesleyan University Press.

Burch, N. 1990. *Life to Those Shadows.* London: British Film Institute.

Burton, J. 1990. "Towards a History of Social Documentary in Latin America," in *The Social Documentary in Latin America,* ed. J. Burton, 3–30. Pittsburgh: University of Pittsburgh Press.

Chopra, Anupma. 2007. "Is That a Lama Behind the Camera?" *New York Times,* October 14.

Chow, Rey. 1995. *Primitive Passions: Visuality, Sexuality, Ethnography, and Contemporary Chinese Cinema.* New York: Columbia University Press.

Cohn, Norm. 2005. Interview with Faye Ginsburg on email, July 22.

Cook, Nicholas. 1998. *Analysing Musical Multimedia.* Oxford: Oxford University Press.

Cripps, Thomas. 1993. *Making Movies Black: The Hollywood Message Movie from World War II to the Civil Rights Era.* New York: Oxford University Press.

DeCurtis, Anthony. 2005. "The Unlikely Greek Chorus Singing the Enron Blues." *New York Times,* April 17.

Diawara, Manthia. 1992. *African Cinema: Politics and Culture.* Bloomington: Indiana University Press.

———, ed. 1993. *Black American Cinema.* London and New York: Routledge.

Dyer, R. 1990. *Now You See It: Studies in Lesbian and Gay Film.* London and New York: Routledge.

Dyer, R. and G. Vincendeau, eds. 1992. *Popular European Cinema.* London and New York: Routledge.

———. 2000. "Strategies of Remembrance: Music and History in the New German Cinema," in Buhler, Flinn, and Neumeyer 2000, 118–41.

Feuer, Jane. 1993. *The Hollywood Musical,* 2d ed. Bloomington and Indianapolis: Indiana University Press.

First Nations\First Features. 2005. "About the Showcase." http://www.firstnations firstfeatures.org.

Flinn, Caryl. *The New German Cinema: Music, History, and the Matter of Style.* Berkeley: University of California Press.

Foster, Gwendolyn. 1997. *Women Filmmakers of the African and Asian Diaspora: Decolonizing the Gaze, Locating Subjectivity.* Carbondale: Southern Illinois University Press.

Green, Ronald J. 2000. *Straight Lick: The Cinema of Oscar Micheaux.* Bloomington: Indiana University Press.

Hamamoto, Darrell, and Sandra Liu, eds. 2000. *Countervisions: Asian American Film Criticism.* Philadelphia: Temple University Press.

Heider, Karl G. 1991. *Indonesian Cinema: National Culture on Screen.* Honolulu: University of Hawaii Press.

Hillman, Roger. 2005. *Unsettling Scores: German Film, Music, and Ideology.* Bloomington and Indianapolis: Indiana University Press.

Hoberman, J. 1991. *Bridge of Light: Yiddish Film between Two Worlds.* New York: Museum of Modern Art and Schocken Books, 1991.

King, John. 1990. *Magical Reels: A History of Cinema in Latin America.* London and New York: Verso.

Lent, John A. 1990. *The Asian Film Industry.* Austin: University of Texas Press, 1990.

Lim, Dennis. 2005. "Play it Again, Siam." *The Village Voice,* March 9, 56.

Mansoor, Sarfraz. 2007. "Love and Social Commentary." *Guardian Weekly,* March 30–April 5, 22.

Mitchell, Charles P. 2004. *The Great Composers Portrayed on Film, 1913–2002.* Jefferson, N.C. and London: McFarland & Co.

Naficy, Hamid. 2001. *An Accented Cinema: Exilic and Diasporic Filmmaking.* Princeton: Princeton University Press, 2001.

Nestingen, Andrew, and Trevor G. Elkington. 2005. *Transnational Cinema in a Global North: Nordic Cinema in Transition.* Detroit: Wayne State University Press.

Noriega, Chon A., ed. 1992. *Chicanos and Film: Representation and Difference.* Minneapolis and London: University of Minnesota Press.

Ogbechie, Sylvester. 2005. "Nollywood Rising: Global Perspectives on the Nigerian Film Industry," www.nollywoodconventionusa.com.

Onishi, Norimitsu. 2005. "Roll Over Godzilla: Korea Rules." *New York Times,* June 28.

Pines, J., and P. Willemen, eds. 1989. *Questions of Third Cinema.* London: BFI Publishing.

Polgreen, Lydia. 2005. "Africa Makes Fine Films. Of Course, Projector May Fail." *The New York Times,* March 10.

Raykoff, Ivan. 2000. "Hollywood's Embattled Icon," in *Piano Roles: Three Hundred Years of Life with the Piano,* ed. J. Parakilas, 329–58. New Haven and London: Yale University Press.

Rich, B. Ruby. 1998. *Chick Flicks: Theories and Memories of the Feminist Film Movement.* Durham, N.C.: Duke University Press.

Said, Edward. 2006. "Preface," in *Dreams of a Nation: On Palestinian Cinema,* ed. Hamid Dabashi, 1–6. London: Verso.

Sen, Krishna. 1994. *Indonesian Cinema: Framing the New Order.* London: Zed Books.

Shafik, Viola. 1998. *Arab Cinema: History and Cultural Identity.* Cairo: American University in Cairo Press.

Slobin, Mark. 2000. *Subcultural Sounds: Micromusics of the West,* 2d ed. Hanover and London: Wesleyan University Press.

Smith, Jeff. 1998. *The Sounds of Commerce: Marketing Popular Film Music.* N.Y.: Columbia University Press.

Stam, Robert. 1997. *Tropical Multiculturalism: Comparative History of Race in Brazilian Cinema and Culture.* Durham: Duke University Press.

Teno, Jean-Marie. 2005. Interview on www.newsreel.org/articles/teno.htm.

Ulmer, James. 2005. "Indians Investing, but Carefully, in Hollywood." *New York Times,* April 15.

Walsh, Nick Paton. 2005. "Return of the Cold War." *Guardian Weekly,* May 13–19, 25.

Willemen, Paul. 1994. *Looks and Frictions: Essays in Cultural Studies and Film Theory.* London: BFI Publishing.

Xing, Jun. 1998. *Asian American through the Lens: History, Representations, and Identity.* Lanham, Md.: Altamira Press.

PART ONE

·◉·

AMERICAN WORLDS

·◉·

MARK SLOBIN

The Steiner Superculture

·◉·

This chapter makes a short tour of "Hollywood," focusing on the earlier, foundational decades. I will use the term "superculture," which is adapted from my earlier work on the global music system (Slobin 2000). There, the term refers to the dominant, mainstream musical content of a society, in effect, everything people take for granted as being "normal," such as the singing of the "Star-Spangled Banner" at sports events; "Auld Lang Syne" at New Year's Eve; children's songs such as "Old McDonald Had a Farm," often taught in schools as "official" American music; the canon of popular music, with its Graceland and Halls of Fame; the idea that country music is more patriotic than city music; and so on. The music superculture has ideological underpinnings and strong control systems. In Europe, the state did much of this work traditionally, through centralized radio and television broadcasting (think BBC) and support for the arts, including their "national heritage" side. In the United States, the state is traditionally less interventionist, leaving much of the definition of the social order to commercial forces through popular culture.

In this chapter, the supercultural force is film music as it developed in the studio era, when a handful of enterprises controlled the production and the worldwide distribution, exhibition, and marketing of American film. This system spawned the integrated filmscore in the early 1930s, an extremely effective technical and aesthetic practice that spread to the rest of the world as, simply, the way that film music works. The central figure will be Max Steiner, who largely is credited with making the filmscore work. The next chapter turns to his successors in the 1950s and beyond.

This story has been told in many other books as part of the history of Hollywood. The particular angle of vision advanced by the present study is to offer analytical approaches that are more ethnomusicological than biographical or musicological. From this point of view, *every film is ethnographic, and every soundtrack acts like an ethnomusicologist.* Since any movie presents the viewer with a human society (or something similar, in animal-based films), the job of the composer is to offer sonic substance to the housing, clothing, language, and customs of the place. It doesn't matter whether the action takes place on a sci-fi battleship, an idyllic small town in Iowa, or the mean streets of Hong Kong. Placing people in motion means you have to construct an integrated and logical society, music and all.

Cinema is different in this respect from, say, opera, one of the main sources of Hollywood film music. One approach to the composer as ethnomusicologist adopted below is to examine the "exotic" in filmscores. The nineteenth century is full of operas set in exotic locations, with composers finding ways to depict the staged society. But these shows, set in the Middle East, for example, "do not claim . . . to represent objectively . . . the Middle East as it really is. Rather (or also) they presnt themselves as fictions, objects intended to provide entertainment or invite aesthetic contemplation," says musicologist Ralph Locke (1998:105). This is similar to many light films, transparent in their use of pseudo-ethnographic settings and musical materials. For example, in the "Road" series of Bing Crosby and Bob Hope, which tend to take place in faraway places, we don't expect *The Road to Bali* to show us authentic Balinese society and music. But most films want the viewer to be drawn into an everyday world—mean streets of Brooklyn, the spaceship Enterprise—that will seem coherent and credible in all ways. The old movie studios had libraries where a film crew could find out how everything looked at the time the movie was set, and the composer, say Max Steiner, could look up the available music of the period.

This sense that the filmed domain shows an authentic society is far from other photographic norms established in the nineteenth century. For example, when commercial photographers took pictures of the Parthenon in Athens or the Colosseum in Rome, they "strove to remove from their pictures any unseemly intrusion from the present day that might disrupt the viewer's contemplation of the ancient world," which meant that "the modern residents of the country are often kept out of sight" (Szegedy-Maszak 2005:14). Such an anti-ethnographic position is diametrically opposed to the proliferation of ancient-world movies, for which entire fictitious worlds with huge sets of pyramids, temples, or the Roman forum were built to look convincing, including, as in the case of Miklos Rosza scoring *Ben Hur,* "authentic Roman music," despite our nearly complete ignorance of what that might have sounded like.

The composer doing this work of ethnographic grounding is one manifestation of the unseen figure who lurks behind every film, the narrator who, as Robert Stam says, "has been variously called 'le grand imagier' [Albert Laffay] and the 'meganarrator' [Andre Gaudreault]. The filmic equivalent of Wayne Booth's 'implied author,' this figure can be metaphorized as an orchestra conductor who takes charge of the various 'instruments' of cinematic expression" (Stam 2005:35). How nice that Stam instinctively applies a musical metaphor itself to describe the film narrator, the one who sets out a coherent storyline, cast of characters, and setting. As part of his job of making sense of the viewing experience, this narrator marshals music materials to describe how a human community lives, and has two ways of serving them up: as music the people actually sing, play, and listen to—source—and as music that somehow suffuses the scene from outside the space of the action—score. It is often literally the symphonic sound that "orchestrates" what the narrator has to say. The interplay of source and score can be very complicated. Together they structure a musical ethnography.

The implied narrator acts as an ethnomusicologist in three ways: (1) by inventing an imaginary community beyond the viewer's everyday experience, such as an exotic locale; (2) by reworking a well-known genre setting, like the western; or (3) by visiting a contemporary or recent familiar setting, such as American urban life. This chapter mines Steiner's work for the first two, while a close reading of a city film emerges from considering "the sons of Steiner," in the next chapter.

If the Steiner solution to fulfilling music's mission had not become the industry and world standard of how to integrate music into narrative, it could be seen as just another eclectic experiment in film music accompaniment. When sound film came in after 1927, people tried all sorts of ways to package music that had been performed live for the first thirty years of cinema. Steiner started as a Viennese theater composer who emigrated to Broadway, and he mostly drew on what he knew to cobble together a new tradition. Those materials were very Eurocentric and, by the 1930s, kind of musty. As Richard Taruskin points out, "Hollywood, it might seem, had provided a haven for a musical style that had become outmoded in the concert hall and the opera house" (Taruskin 2005:550).[1] Steiner's range of references, at the beginning, was pretty narrow. Only later did he branch out to bring in more Americanisms and innovations. He himself belonged to a popular music tradition with deep roots in Vienna, home of Mozart, Beethoven, Johann Strauss ("the waltz king"), and the postromantic modernist Mahler. His family ran the Theater an der Wien, where Beethoven worked. His grandfather is credited with convincing Johann Strauss to write in the new operetta style for the popular theater, while Richard Strauss, another postromantic, was Steiner's godfather. His inventory of styles ran from Richard Wagner's vast, melodramatic German operas through French impressionism to the jaunty modernism of the European cabaret tradition. America of the 1930s allowed him to create a dramatic cosmopolitanism of castles and chorus girls, melodramatic soundscapes, psychological tone-painting, folksy frontiers, and canny showmanship. Our interest in Steiner extends beyond his well-studied success in underscoring narrative structure and providing psychological insights into character development (Daubney 2000). In thinking about film music globally, as culture, this foundational figure also needs to be seen as an ethnomusicologist.

Early Steiner Ethnographies

Among Steiner's earliest assignments were films with exotic locations and characters. In these settings, ethnography literally can go wild. Already in 1932's *Bird of Paradise*, a South Seas romantic adventure, Steiner mixed an orchestral score with depictions of indigenous music-making, tossing in generalized colorful music that drew on the Hawaiian music craze. A pre-code movie, *Bird of Paradise* stars a nearly nude Delores Del Rio—a Mexican actress posing as a Polynesian—who turns the head of all-American Johnny, a sailor, with predictably dire results. One way to reveal the workings of a filmed ethnography is to inventory all the kinds of music that the soundtrack holds. By laying out the tool-kit of the implied narrator, we can see not only what is included, but what is left out, replaced, or redesigned. The superculture needs to *describe* a community's music culture, but also wants to *exert control* over it.

Here is Steiner's inventory of musical resources for *Bird of Paradise*:

Symphonic. Score for the sea, drawing on Debussy's impressionism (*La Mer*) and featuring the harp; some dramatic underscoring.

Jazzy. Music for a school of flying fish; recorded music on a gramophone used as barter for a native canoe.

Hawaiian. Hawaiian-inflected score for the main title; Hawaiian hula dancing and choral chanting; ukulele music.

Indigenous islander. Drumming and dancing for native rituals.

This is quite the ethnomusicology of an imaginary community. Even the fish need to be typecast (shades of Disney films to come). It's about as authentic as Del Rio playing a Pacific Islander, yet at moments, the score tries to sound accurate, particularly when the camera focuses on Hawaiian-looking singers and dancers engaged in chants and hula dances. That these are mixed with purely fictitious, generalized "tribal" drumming styles is significant. I would like to distinguish between music understood to be *vernacular*, belonging to the group we get to know, and music that represents an *assumed vernacular* approach. Calling this "assumed" vernacular music draws attention to both senses of that word: assumed as "taken for granted," and assumed as "pretending to be something," as in "assumed identity." Even this early, groping Steiner score reveals a complex relationship with ethnography that is hard to analyze systematically. The islanders, though not shown as Hawaiians, carry Hawaiian culture, which is then translated into an orchestral version that acts as a frame around the picture. At the same time, they drum and dance like screen Africans or American Indians, a move away from the specific to the general.

Despite the apparent discrepancies here, most of the musical materials of *Bird of Paradise* would have looked and sounded perfectly reasonable to an American audience that was entirely trained to generalize the exotic, in the music they played on their pianos, their recordings, and also the dances and games they did at home and in public (Lancefield 2004). They were also completely cozy with the live musicians in moviehouses, who churned out something like Steiner's melange of sources, so there is nothing really new about his choices or his methods of mixture.

In this early experimental period of the filmscore, what draws the attention is the tentativeness with which the orchestral music itself appears, compared to its dominance a few short years later. The ease with which the score took over directly parallels the studios' eagerness to produce the ultimate integrated product that allowed for few questions: indeterminacy was slowly phased out. As Stam puts it, "the fact that dominant cinema has largely opted for a linear and homogenizing aesthetic where track reinforces within a Wagnerian totality cannot efface the equally salient fact that the cinema [is] infinitely rich in polyphonic potentialities" (Stam 2005:21–2). In short, a silent competition goes on between the need for certainty and the inevitability of indeterminate interaction of a movie's elements. Do the "possible contradictions and tensions between tracks become an aesthetic strategy, opening the way to a multitemporal, polyrhythmic art form" (ibid.:20), or does the filmmaking team desperately try to limit the free play of the elements? The answer is, predictably, both. Music inherently acts sometimes simultaneously, but certainly sequentially, to settle down *and* to unsettle the audiovisual experience of moviegoing. In the early period now under discussion, the control freaks were on the rise. Writing about the way that screen comedy was ironed out in this period, Henry Jenkins could just as soon have been talking about music: "an aesthetic based on heterogeneity, affective immediacy, and performance confronted [a] primary emphasis upon causality and consistency, closure and cohesiveness" (Jenkins 1992:278). In musical terms, the strictly ethnographic and the invented vernacular both yielded sonic space to the supercultural symphonic.

Musical symbols such as the ones just discussed for *Bird of Paradise* long have been discussed as a branch of *semiotics,* the study of sign systems. Musicologists talk about two main options that the classical period—just before and after 1800—evolved for composers, resources that remained the core of how to build meaningful music well into the twentieth century. As Richard Taruskin recently has summarized the situation, one choice was *extroversive semiotics:* "whereby music could represent the sights and sounds of the natural worlds and the moods and feelings of the human world . . . this included the sounds of other music, hunting horns, courtly dances, quotations of famous pieces, whatever—and their built-in associations" (Taruskin 2005:539). This symbol system is the main subject of these introductory chapters, which detail the way that composers like Steiner and his successors combined an offscreen symphonic matrix with onscreen music performance to represent natural and social worlds, based on conventional associations.

As for the other approach, "there was the newly important domain of *introversive semiotics* ('pointing inward')—a sign system made up of sounds that pointed to other sounds or musical events within the work itself," such as how keys and themes relate to each other, in purely musical terms. Film music does rely on listeners picking up on internal relationships among musical cues, such as having the same theme come back in major or minor, or be played by another instrument, and Steiner developed that discipline very effectively as a way of revealing characters' psychology or shifts in the plotline. For example, for *Mildred Pierce* (1945), Steiner immersed the viewer in a memorable "main title," the music heard over the opening credits, then kept bringing the main themes back throughout the film in different musical clothing, one form of "introversive semiotics."

Putting these two techniques together, in classical composition as well as in filmscores, "we are dealing then, with a mode of instrumental discourse capable of very subtle shades of allusion and irony" (Taruskin 2005:539–40). In the analyses below, advancing an ethnomusicological perspective will lead to greater stress on the extroversive elements of the soundtrack, since they signal and interpret most of the cultural and social content, as opposed to the psychological portrayal and narrative underpinning that a great deal of traditional film-music studies concentrates on.

Having groped toward these technical solutions just a couple of years into the sound film era, already by 1932 Steiner had expanded his control of the film's effectiveness in offering an integrated experience. He wrote a sensational score for a pioneering monster movie of 1932 called *King Kong,* the film that really drew attention to the composer's contribution to a movie's success. This score repeatedly has drawn the attention of film-music scholars

(Kalinak 1992, Franklin 2001), as well as the producers that keep funding remakes of this durable vehicle. Featuring a gigantic gorilla who fights for dominance with dinosaurs on a mythical island, this lively entertainment spanned locales from tropical cliffs to Manhattan canyons, ending in a shootout atop the Empire State Building. More than the restricted island world of *Bird of Paradise, King Kong* offered Steiner scope for any and all conventions he could dream up and deploy to tease and thrill an audience. He had to find ways to place sound-tags on drum-beating "natives," prehistoric monsters, hardy American good guys, and a leading lady who would be ape-napped. The genius behind the movie was Merian Cooper, an explorer/ethnographer type himself. Ten years earlier, he had produced *Grass,* a semifictional account of the nomadic migration of the Bakhtiayari, an ethnic group in Iran. Back in the 1920s, Cooper had to rely on whatever a local theater pianist or pit orchestra could imagine as a soundtrack; now he had the services of a highly trained composer. The resulting filmscore not only made Steiner's reputation, but strongly influenced his central European immigrant colleagues, such as Erich Korngold.

Dissecting a slice of the music for *King Kong* can identify principles that would become supercultural, accepted without question in thousands of filmscores and by billions of ticket-buyers worldwide, down to the present. The work of immensely successful creators like John Williams in adventure vehicles (*Indiana Jones, Jurassic Park*) flows naturally from these devices. We will look just at one pivotal scene. Ann, the heroine, has been captured by the "natives" of the mysterious island that she and her adventurer colleagues have sailed to in hopes of getting some good copy. They end up with more of a story than they bargained for. The intrepid American guys rush off to save her, after brushing off the Chinese cook's interest in the rescue. The islanders blend theatricalized elements of Africans and Polynesians. They are dark-skinned and brutish, which in the 1930s also would have signaled the menace that white Americans felt about the African-American presence, an overlap fraught with musical significance for years to come.

Steiner's immediate task was to write music that would supply the viewer with an ethnography of an indigenous society. This falls into the category of *verisimilitude,* an ornate term that collapses into "imitation of truth," which is what Hollywood is always aiming at, at least nominally. Articles previewing forthcoming films often report how much time and money goes into replicating specific surroundings, like getting the precise place settings used in an upscale Victorian household, or getting the actual cars, helicopters, and firearms for war and action movies. Only occasionally does the journalistic spotlight turn to the musical preparation. Some film composers write about the work they do in period music, as Miklos Rozsa does about his Roman-empire score (1982), but the musical masterminds mostly stay in the shadows, helping the implied narrator with the ethnography. Others talk about their role as actually being that of an unreliable narrator, as Bronislau Kaper does, in connection with a Civil War film of 1951: "Sometimes I bring phony emotions into the picture to wake the audience up" (quoted in Chatman 1990:94).

Natalie Zemon Davis, an eminent historian, has spent a long time thinking through "film and historical vision," and has devoted an entire book to how films depict slavery, from the Roman version in *Spartacus* to the American variety in *Beloved* (Davis 2000). She glancingly mentions that someone was assigned to the music, but the idea of musical authenticity is a mere sidelight for her. This neglect of music is not in the least surprising. However, Davis does cite the music for *Spartacus*. The director, Stanley Kubrick, "urged the composer Alex North to learn what he could about Roman music; failing that — and given the state of knowledge about Roman music at that date, failure was certain — he should seek inspiration from Prokofiev's score for *Alexander Nevsky*," an epic about medieval Russia (Davis 2000:25). For members of the community of artists — painters, writers, composers — their colleagues' accomplishments loom large. In influential essays, the director of *Nevsky*, Sergei Eisenstein, boasted about Prokofiev's impressive achievement. This trumps Kubrick's concerns about the musical gap between first-century Rome and fourteenth-century Russia.

In recent decades, someone called the "music supervisor" makes the composer's job easy by simply pulling period pop songs off the shelf and pasting them on to scenes to authenticate time, place, and character: "1950s small-town American teenagers" or "1990s inner-city Black youth." But commercial-film ethnomusicology starts back with Steiner. The natives in *King Kong* have their own music, as does their habitat, ominous Skull Island, and the music does most of the work of building a believable ecology. Most movies, even today, make indigenous peoples blend in with nature so thoroughly that they are practically part of the landscape, not set off from it. In products such as a Betty Boop cartoon of the same era as *King Kong*, the Polynesian-looking savages who want to cook her in a pot appear first as bushes, using the natural camouflage of their shape and clothing to hide their evil intentions. This way of thinking was authorized back in the eighteenth century by views of the "noble savage" — children of nature who might be noble, but were usually "savage" — who lived in isolated surroundings. This attitude lives on today in some of the rhetoric of the ecology movement's view of indigenous peoples as always being in harmony with nature. Viewed this way, why distinguish different peoples and traditions? Conceptually, ideologically, politically, dramatically, and musically, all natives are the same, and that includes the Skull Island savages of *King Kong*.

In creating a hair-raising cinematic scene—the capture of the heroine, Ann, and her abduction by the giant gorilla, Kong—Steiner harnessed the energy of a musical medium, the symphony orchestra, and the power of musical conventions. Much of the description below is well known to film studies, but it needs to be restated here as a kind of base camp for this book's expeditions to ever more remote filmmaking settings.

The symphony orchestra. Why did Steiner choose the full-blown symphony orchestra, deploying dozens of troops in this campaign for clarity? It would be more economical to have just a handful of expressive musicians, or, nowadays, just a couple of electronic players on synthesizers and drum machines. Music also was layered last into the film, so saving time and money in making the soundtrack was high on the list of commercial priorities. After a film was finished, only the music kept it from getting out to movie theaters where ticket sales would pay the studio bills. Music directors like Steiner worked—and still work—under extreme pressure. So the orchestra is a luxury, but also a necessity in the 1930s. To understand why, we have to look back to its history. As Taruskin summarizes the situation, "from the very beginning the orchestra—the most complex of all musical ensembles—was often explicitly . . . regarded as a social microcosm, a compact mirror of society. The orchestra, like society itself, was assumed to be an inherently hierarchical entity" (Taruskin 2005:290). So to introduce an orchestra as the main voice of the implicit narrator is to set up a power relationship. The symphonic filmscore is a small version of the social order, so acts as the true definer, regardless of what the onscreen characters do musically. Also, the increasingly dominant symphony orchestra—with its sisters, ballet and opera—became a sign of upward mobility. Every town of any size in Europe and the United States had to have one, and the idea spread around the world. This attitude is truly supercultural: The social role of a musical structure is entrenched, with deep roots in the past, and remains unquestioned.

The longevity of the orchestral principle is amazing. In the energetic Soviet cinema that ran parallel to Steiner's early work, marxist ideology might have dictated dumping the elite orchestra for humbler, worker-and-peasant-based ensembles. Yet the idea of the symphony prevailed, since the leadership saw it as the most advanced form of musical workforce, hence suitable for "progressive" societies. The ethnic republics of Soviet Central Asia had to have orchestras to show they were now modern, and that model was exported to places like Egypt, to which Soviet advisors flocked. Today, the symphony orchestra still evokes a value system that overarches national economic, demographic, and ideological divides and just keeps on going, from Hollywood to Bollywood to Beijing. At the beginning, in the 1930s, its power was just the engine the Hollywood studio heads needed in their drive to make their products dominant, and Steiner was only too glad to oblige.

With the full range of instruments of the largest orchestras—strings, woodwinds, brass, percussion—Steiner had a huge musical instrument that he could control with absolute precision. He pioneered the "click track," a nonstop pulse that he could hear while he conducted as a huge screen rolled the edited film in a soundproofed studio. Second by second, he led his exquisitely professional musicians through the sudden changes of tone color, rhythm, melody, and harmony that it takes for music to match visual action, dialogue, and sound effects. In the integrated filmscore, the music's mission is to make everything perfectly plain. Film is just a bunch of short takes, pasted together for an illusion of continuity. Film editors work hard to make sense of the jumps from shot to shot, scene to scene, but coherence is still hard work. The camera focuses on one thing, place, person, and moment, then flicks to another relentlessly, for an hour and a half at the least. Music is glued to each take, both to specify and to smooth over the cracks.

But the social power and cultural resonance of the symphonic score goes beyond its utility as an integrator, as remarks by Howard Shore tell us (in an interview on radio's *Opera News,* 2 February 2005). His twelve-hour score for the blockbuster *Lord of the Rings* trilogy describes an evolutionary arc that parallels the social development of Tolkien's imaginary communities. The first film details the setting's tribal cultures with simulated vernacular, folk instruments and themes. In the second film, he insinuated hints of more classical styles, including operatic voices, particularly the signature sound of diva Renée Fleming. By the third installment, Shore gave the symphonic-operatic sound full sway to show a progression toward "higher" states of living. This up-from-Skull-Island mentality would seem to be—but is not—highly anachronistic seven decades after Steiner's methods emerged, not only as film technique, but as a philosophy of how to do ethnography.

Whatever range of sounds you draw on, from the orchestra to today's samplers, you have to pour it all into a set of familiar molds, cozy, accepted *musical conventions,* and this is where ethnography enters. People have to be able to match sight and sound, and you don't want to make it hard. They already have the clues, from advertising jingles, school songs, popular music, and, of course, many movies they already have seen. You can go against the grain, be ironic, put a comic sound behind violence, but that move also relies completely on the viewer appreciating the emotional gap. In the case of the *King Kong* scene, a handful of conventions goes a long way.

Drumbeats. Only some of the world's indigenous societies thought of skin-covered instruments as their basic sound symbol, but in Hollywood's mind, they all do. Drumbeats could be of any kind: multilayered and sophisticated, with fascinating layers of overlapping complex rhythms, or repetitive, thumping, and monotonous. Real societies might have one, both, or many in-between ways of making music from drums. But film ethnography recognizes only the latter type. Not only is a heavy, brand-name beat universal, but very often it falls into a DUM-dum-dum-dum DUM-dum-dum-dum pattern that suits mythical Skull Islanders, supposedly real Africans, and, most commonly in American films, Native American groups. Steiner already had used this rhythm in *Bird of Paradise* for Polynesians. In an insightful article, Claudia Gorbman shows that as an emblem of "Indians," this drumbeat dates to the work of early twentieth-century American classical composers of the "Indianist" style, and it probably goes back even earlier, though American Indians do not favor this rhythm traditionally (2000). Why, then, does Viennese-trained Max Steiner import this throbbing, pounding motif to Skull Island? Again, all "savages" are the same in the Western mind. Let me stress how important it is that this locale is mythical, yet needs a coherent ethnography. In the age of anthropological exploration that perhaps reached its peak at the time *King Kong* came out, Americans and Europeans were flooded with articles, books, photo essays, and documentary films about many parts of the world that were under Western rule, which meant almost anyplace in this last flowering of colonialism, a system that controlled over two-thirds of the world's landmass. Drumbeats make a convenient way to simplify the huge and confusing range of body types and cultural practices the West had to confront and control. Since America's colonial holdings were small, the imported descendants of slaves and the subjugated indigenous people—African and Native Americans—were (and still are, to some extent) the internal Others that could be generalized and, in current terms, "profiled."

Drumbeats are not the only all-purpose exoticism the superculture spawned. John Mowitt has skewered the "Me Tarzan, You Jane" locution, which involves what he calls "copular suspension," emphasizing "the degree to which the 'foreignness' linked to copular suspension is not only 'universal,' that is, it is used indiscriminately for the 'foreignness' of Africans, Indians, and as we shall see, aliens, but that this linkage is intimately linked to the cinema" (Mowitt 2005:70). In other words, these supercultural tools are found nowhere else but in the movies.

Pentatonic scale. If you pick out the black keys of a piano, you get one kind of scale that music specialists call "pentatonic." The song that Americans sing at New Year's Eve parties, "Auld Lang Syne," is a good example. Try this out, and you will stumble on a "primitive" tune that someone like Steiner could paste onto the inhabitants of a rainforest, desert, or tropical island. In Hollywood ethnography, it suits Chinese, African, or Native American societies just fine, as well as Scots and Irish. This is partly because, in fact, this scale type appears all around the world in many cultures, so film composers found it very handy to use. Like the drumbeat, the pentatonic patterning is a grid that you can lay across the social structure of a storyline.

This peculiar positioning of a scale type lasts long. In a recent review of world music albums from Morocco, the author wonders why Gnawa music has been so successful in the West, starting with rockers Brian Jones and Jimi Hendrix way back. Perhaps it's because "it's pentatonic music, which means that it doesn't sound so weird and extraterrestrial to us aurally challenged Westerners as other forms of Arabic music do" (Morgan 2003:60). This is a truly supercultural statement. It generalizes, it stresses how Westerners avoid difficulty when confronting the musical content of the Other, and it marginalizes, making most "Arabic music" (a generalization) seem like the product of non-humans, or, at best, "weird." Apparently, we haven't moved much beyond Steiner's worldview, despite our vaunted "globalization."

Chromaticism. If you play all the black and white keys of the piano sequentially, you get a line of small equal steps. Skip a few, go back and forth, using notes next to each other, then jumping, and you'll end up with a "chromatic" line. If you do this smoothly and fluidly, the melody will be sinuous and slinky, and if you make the rhythm recognizably repeating, you'll be on the way toward the type of tunes that Steiner and company preferred for certain social circumstances. In our *King Kong* scene, the chromatic nod goes to the heroine, not the natives. This brings us to gender as a musical construction. All screen societies, apart from location, skin color, language, and other cultural categories, need to be gendered as well. The supercultural system does this in various ways. Sometimes it's a choice of instruments: In older Hollywood movies, a saxophone sneaks and snakes its way to show the temptation that a woman offers a man. The cavalry, pirates, and any action hero is more likely to have brass support from horns and trumpets. But melodic line can do just as much as instrumentation to gender-tag a scene. The suggestiveness of the chromatic line goes a long way back in Western music, but was particularly pronounced as feminine in nineteenth-century opera, such as the theme for the sensational seductress in *Carmen* (McClary 2002). It is no coincidence that the character Carmen is also a gypsy, an outcast minority ethnic group of the West. Often the old opera melded the native and the female for double danger and drama. In *King Kong,* we feel Ann's horror and shock as she is dragged and tied to a stake, through the chromatic theme that appears when the camera turns to her.

These three components are ethnographic, in the sense that they locate and describe human groups sonically. Other conventions that Steiner & Co. rely on come from the classical music world more generally. They are so commonplace that you have to think to notice them.

Instrumental tone color. Here we move into an ethnography of the Western world itself. Why should certain instruments have associations of emotion, structures of sensibility? Even in folk societies with a narrow range of instrumental choices, each one has its social as well as acoustic resonance. For example, across much of Eurasia, women simply don't play stringed instruments. Where there are drums, women might play only one kind, as in the Middle Eastern tambourine tradition. In Melanesia, tradition kept women away from the long, hollow-log ritual percussion, with punishments for infractions. In the West, until recent shifts in gender roles, the borders were sharply patrolled. No young women used to play the brass and percussion, being limited to winds—flutes, oboes—and the harp. The cello was often off limits due to its playing position between the legs. The piano and its sacred cousin, the reed organ, spread through Europe and America as instruments of what was being defined as the feminine space, the home, just as in Japan the koto zither became a girls' specialty, a "social grace." In short, instruments are just as typecast as scales.

Tone color—or, more technically, timbre—never fades away as a conventional fallback in film. The oboe, or its darker cousin, the English horn, continue to make scenes poignant or reflective. Trumpets and horns still stir up action, gongs are still exotic, drums signal the savage or the melodramatic, and so on down the list. Even the switchover to electronically produced sounds did not crack the old code that much, since they may remain rooted in the older acoustic space of the world of Steiner and his audience. Newer layers of sound referencing may pile up—jazz and hip-hop stylings, for example—but it's hard to kill off conventions. Every cinema system has its own version of timbral expectations, for example the equation of *sarangi* = sadness or flute = pastoral in Hindi film.

The scene of Ann's captivity on Skull Island puts these various conventions into play:

1:00. medium shot of the islanders drumming and dancing. They are playing a large assortment of hand drums, usually called "tom-toms" in the trade. Some look mildly ethnographic, while others are clearly imaginary, a visual parallel to the sound of "native" music, which may blend local sounds and Hollywood inventions. Steiner's melody is in a pentatonic that is both universal and familiar to Americans—think Irish—that is also a sign of cultural distance, due to its very generality.

As the islanders swarm up the ladder to the top of the stockade, we get a rising sequence, a form of musical mimicry known as "mickey-mousing" in honor of the Disney cartoons just emerging at the time. We see the chief in front of the fantasy gong. Don't ask who is doing metalworking on this "stone age," if not prehistoric, island. Viewers know subconsciously that eventually the gong will be struck at a climactic moment—why else is it there?

Finally in this minute, there's a quick cut to Ann being dragged, set to what will be her theme: chromatically feminine and anguished, a combination of gender-typing and emotional mickey-mousing.

2:00. The stockade gates swing open, we get the delayed gong stroke, which signals "Orient," a generalized non-Western space located somewhere beyond Los Angeles. Till now, we might have mistaken the islanders for Africans, due to their dark skin and stereotyped behavior, particularly drumming, but the island locale and the gong bring a Pacific tinge to the sight and sound. This curious overlap is part of the supercultural blurring of the "Other" that Steiner supports with the drum-gong mixture.

A drumbeat of doom strikes up in rising sequence for the altar steps, yielding to the chromatic melody as Ann comes into main focus. Her theme becomes the center as she is tied up, helpless. The drumbeat shifts from the chaotic multirhythm of the islanders to the fateful footfall of nineteenth-century romantic and postromantic symphonic music, from Beethoven through Wagner and Mahler. This is exactly the takeover of native sensibility that is so typical of the supercultural approach: The drum changes hands and achieves far greater authority in the grip of the symphony than of the "savages." Yet both are Steiner's invention as the puppet-master of the film's expressive universe. This easy control over point of view and resources is what makes the superculture strong.

3:00. The islander theme disintegrates as the warriors run away from the altar, the music miming their panic; they have been stripped of whatever narrative authority they have, which soon will shift to Kong. The orchestra weighs in with its heaviest voice, the low brass of trombones and tubas, another high-romantic symphonic move, with the counterpoint of the ululating islanders, who have lost their theme and their social control. The upward-step mickey-mousing returns.

4:00. The gongstrokes intensify, and after ever more dissonant chords, sound is suspended as the chief summons his personal authority as the mediator between the human race and the giant ape. The gong alternates with Ann's whimpering; she too has lost her "voice," the chromatic theme. All is now ready for the film's hero to arrive.

5:00. Kong's footsteps are not exactly covered by the term "mickey-mousing," so gigantic are the shuddering chords. The footsteps act as a synchronized drumbeat for the demonic low brass, with long tones and hints of earlier themes, and now it is Ann's screams that act as punctuation. Kong's roars are well timed. We hear how source sound (screams and roars), sound effects (the symphonized footsteps are meant to be "natural sound"), and soundtrack (the brass) all blend to make a single scene work, blurring the lines among the various categories of the soundtrack. Today, of course, synthesized effects would replace everything Steiner could deploy, but the familiarity of the cultural conventions, including animal, savage, and gender-typing, have barely changed.

6:00. Ann regains her voice and attempt at authority as she struggles. The chromatic line moves into the brass as Kong picks up Ann and faces the islanders. This blending of girl and ape "voices" foreshadows the intimate relationship of the film's two main characters.

Our selected scene is rich in ethnographic detail, but it's not just a description of any real people. The film composer is building paragraphs of narrative, using a vocabulary that is soaked in exoticism and eroticism. Audiences knew it well from nineteenth-century European composition, twentieth-century popular music, and the stock accompaniment to pre-sound-era film. This supercultural control over real and imaginary worlds is ethnographic itself, revealing layers of assumptions and authority that are so entrenched and engrained that everyone took them for granted. This is what anthropologists look for: basic patterns and structures, what Pierre Bourdieu (1979) called a *habitus,* a kind of cultural cocoon. The early Hollywood film world created such a habitus, in its own social world of the studio, and its music is the soft lining of that cocoon. So effective is this scene from *King Kong* that the 2005 remake of the movie brings the Steiner music back, transposed to Kong's vaudeville moment on a New York stage, in an act of homage to the old master.

Having twice referenced a Betty Boop cartoon that overlaps with *King Kong* musically, a closer look is called for. *I'll Be Glad When You're Dead, You Rascal You* (1932) confirms and extends the discussion, both in terms of analysis and genre, by adding the cartoon to the story of the supercultural system's rise.

You Rascal You puts Betty in the beleaguered position of *King Kong's* Ann, and the music is just as stereotypical. As in *Bird of Paradise,* the early Steiner Polynesia film, a convenient volcano sweeps away the natives and lets the white people get on with their lives. This would be helpful enough for analysis, but there's much more. Over this basic scenario, literally, looms the figure of Louis Armstrong. Armstrong's hot jazz band acts as main title to the movie at the cartoon's opening. This cartoon forms part of a series of jazz-based Betty Boop features dreamed up by her creator Max Fleischer, who worked out a trick of tracing live-action figures onto cartoon characters. At a critical juncture, Betty's clown and dog sidekicks Koko and Bimbo escape the savages, and as they run, the stereotyped DUM-dum-dum-dum beat of the native drums fades into the jazz band's rhythm section. Floating over the hapless duo in place of the sun, Satchmo's monstrous round head jeers them, cackling "I'll be glad when you're dead, you rascal you." Should there be any doubt about the equation of Black American = savage, physically and musically, the equal sign turns positively neon when the native chef, stamping in his cauldron, morphs into the live jazz drummer, beating his skins. Rarely does one get so literal a glimpse into the potent power of film music not just to confirm, but also to create the ethnic and racial stereotypes that suffuse American society. What is hinted at in *King Kong* is spelled out in the cartoon, making one long for a serious ethnomusicological inquiry into the music of animated film, which not even the present volume can supply.[2]

From Skull Island to "Texas, 1868"

King Kong was a genre all to itself, and Betty Boop was in a league of her own. Next, we'll extend the politics of island savagery to a broader horizon, the American West, with a tried-and-true panorama of realistic-looking settlers, soldiers, and Indians that fueled thousands of short serial movies, feature films, and the early TV top-ten shows for decades. The

Figure 1. Max Fleischer turns Louis Armstrong's drummer Tubby Hall into a cannibal in *I'll Be Glad When You're Dead, You Rascal You* (1932).

Central European sensibility of Steiner and company ran headlong into the need to underscore American history, ideology, and mythology. Among the dozens of fine filmscores the western engendered, none is more wide-ranging in its musical means than Steiner's work for *The Searchers*, an epic 1956 film directed by the great John Ford. This soundtrack combines the composer's orchestral subtlety, the source music of the warring parties, and an extra "western" theme song that opens the film. Dismantling and sorting out all these sounds on the workbench allows for a more comprehensive reading of the generic version of supercultural film music. *The Searchers* is perennially on all-time best American film lists, and John Wayne's image from it was included in 2002 for a set of American hero clips as an emblem of post–September 11 resolve. In 2006, a film critic for the *New York Times* went so far as to say that "all American cinema" comes out of this much-admired western (Scott 2006).

The Searchers goes deeply and tragically into ethnic conflict in a violent, postcataclysmic frontier setting just after the Civil War: "Texas, 1868" is the first frame after the opening credits. The production team assumes the responsibility of ethnography: placing us in the space and time in all its detail. As usual, we have no choice but to believe the sights and sounds, assuming that speech, clothing, locale, architecture, and music are accurate. We know that director John Ford cared a great deal about credibility. For this film, he personally recast the novel and screenplay brought to him, heightening the fierce tension of the plot by sharpening the characters and the action. This puts the populations in extreme conflict. He imported dozens of Navajo extras to the wilds of the Four Corners region of the Southwest, instructing them on how to be Comanches, and put white actors in redface, imposing a typically single-minded social order.

Here is the plot in a somewhat simplified version: Ethan, the monomaniacal hero played by John Wayne, is searching for his niece Debbie, who survived a deadly Indian raid on his brother's frontier farm. His side-kick is Martin, a quarter-Indian the family had taken in. The Comanches killed Debbie's younger sister, along with her mother Martha, the sister-in-law whom Ethan illicitly longed for. Ethan is totally obsessed with finding, then murdering Debbie, whom he sees as being racially defiled by the Indians, but Martin intercedes, and they bring her home at film's end. Ethan, always the outsider, rides off rather than merge back into the community. Other types include Mose, a half-witted settler deranged by time spent with the Indians; the Jorgensens, the Swedish settler neighbors whose daughter Laurie is meant to (and eventually does) marry Martin; and George, a foolish guitar-playing rival for Laurie's hand. *The Searchers* is basically in three acts: (1) Ethan's arrival at the settlement and the destructive raid by the Indians; (2) the long search for Debbie; (3) the return with Debbie and the reintegration of the white community.

The Searchers is an unusually complex film, from the viewpoint of musical ethnography, with its layers and intersections of race and gender. The pairing of a major composer and filmmaker, both active shapers of the supercultural system, turned out to be very fruitful. As an epic, it offers a wide range of music to match its panoramic sweep in time (several years) and place (the search party's odyssey). To cope with this variety, a survey follows of the types of music that the film provides in its effort to cover its territory. Most film-music studies concentrate on the themes that tag main characters, noticing their development as the action unfolds, or look at key moments to analyze and admire craft. But to move toward a more ethnomusicological understanding, we turn again to inventorying *all* the ethnographic kinds of music that a given film packages for the viewer. This sketches out the whole range of possibilities that a production team approved, setting each individual musical type and moment in the larger context.

VERNACULAR MUSIC

"Vernacular" is music that apparently arises from within a particular group, but can be introduced either by the score or as source music. This segment of the soundtrack is a key to the "authenticity" that viewers absorb, the presumed accuracy of the filmworld. Unlike the imaginary world of *King Kong*, here Steiner has to ground the vernacular in the better-known, but still imaginary 1868 Texan soundscape, which comes in two types:

"*American.*" Three items are associated with the "Americans": "Shall We Gather at the River," a hymn, performed twice, communally, at a funeral and a wedding; "Skip to My Lou," played by Laurie's unsuccessful, guitar-playing, un-macho suitor; and "Yellow Rose of Texas," done as a dance.

Of these items, the hymn deserves a closer look. Was "Shall We Gather at the River" in fact available to Texans in 1868? Possibly. It first appeared in 1864, which isn't much time for it to go way out to the frontier. For the settlers, then, this hymn might have been a recently acquired expression of faith, rather than an ancient affirmation, as it sounds to the viewers. Issues like this get at the heart of verisimilitude's nagging nature. Timelessness is important in terms of values, and this hymn gives us a bedrock sense of who the settlers are. We imagine these people grew up with "Shall We Gather," as did their forefathers. After all, they use it all the time, both at the funeral of the massacre victims and at Laurie's wedding. The question of whether "Shall We Gather" would have been used at a funeral, at a wedding, or at both by the same group of settlers is hard to establish. It certainly seems unlikely that they would have sung it for such disparate occasions, but maybe it is the only hymn they know.

Why does the soundtrack create this ethnographic "fact?" Two reasons come to mind. One is that Ford liked the hymn, and used it in other films as a stick-on label for frontier faith. The other is that its dual appearance is extremely handy as a structural marker within the film's architecture: It marks the end of the first "act" and the beginning of the third. The entire distribution of music in *The Searchers* serves structural, ethnographic, and emotional needs simultaneously. This combination of framing, feeling, and flexibility helps explain why films have music at all, an implicit question this book raises. Celluloid communities provoke ethnomusicologists to the same questions as do live groupings: What is music for?

Beyond the folk and hymn content of settler music culture, another category of "American" music appears regularly in John Ford's work: cavalry music, often the march "Garryowen" or another Irish-identified tune. Throughout his cavalry films, Ford's fondness for seeing the U.S. Army as an Irish enterprise recurs, and music, like accent and "stage Irish" mannerisms, is a prime indicator. For one hundred years before *The Searchers,* American audiences were used to seeing stereotyped Irish figures march across the stage, appear on the covers of sheet music, and cut through the scratchiness of early recordings. Ford wanted to bypass the image of drunkenness, serving girls, and Irish mother songs to show how his ethnic group made America strong. "Garryowen" was in fact the theme song of the Seventh Cavalry, which, like "Shall We Gather," had just been turned to this purpose in the 1860s. Again, we hear a "timeless" musical-social pairing that was in fact newly minted. In *The Searchers,* the march blares somewhat longer than needed if it were merely to establish the horse soldiers' presence. Their ordered ranks stand as a contrast to the lonesomeness of the searchers and the misery of the white women captives being brought to the fort after having been liberated from the

Figure 2. Would settlers in "Texas, 1868" sing the same hymn for a funeral and a wedding? *The Searchers*, 1956.

Indians. From a horseback sound, the march seamlessly merges into a full-throttle orchestra setting, lending the tune and the soldiers the automatic authority of the symphony, here equivalent to the power of the state.

Finally, what about "Skip to My Lou," a children's song played by the grown-up suitor? This is actually pretty accurate, if you think about the "play-party" tradition. In conservative American communities until rather recently, couple dancing was considered immoral among teenagers, and was replaced by gatherings where young folks acted like little kids, dancing to "London Bridge" and tunes like "Skip to My Lou" to avoid flirtation and contact. A settler community bent on singing hymns for all occasions might well have cut courting to a minimum this way.

To summarize, the "American" music culture that the film sketches out is one in which the inhabitants know only one hymn and a couple of play-party tunes, and the cavalry is resolutely Irish. It is this musical core that the other vernacular styles extend and oppose.

But wait: What about the Jorgensen family, Swedish settlers who speak with an almost comic accent? Why does Steiner not give them some folksy music to reinforce their foreignness? A question like this never comes up in classic film-music studies, but sticks out like a sore thumb if you're scanning the ways of the superculture. Following the melting-pot doctrine, John Ford wants the Jorgensens to assimilate fully into the majority English-speaking Protestant population of the settlers. The screenplay shows them as staunch, Americanizing supporters of the dangerous, possibly doomed effort to hold onto the Indians' land. Their daughter Laurie's eventual marriage with the mixed Indian-Anglo character Martin offers a dream scenario for the melting-pot model. It also turns *The Searchers* into what Doris Sommer has called a "foundational fiction," a work that deploys romantic alliances of mixed racial types to anchor the myth of the emerging nation (1991). But for our purposes, the Jorgensens also can serve as a prime example of the principle of *erasure,* an aspect of film music that is just as important as inclusion. Who gets soundspace and who gets silence carries major cultural meaning.

Consider another example of erasure, applied to a non-American. Within the dead-serious narrative of *The Searchers,* a moment of levity arrives with a "squaw" who Ethan and Martin name "Look," who thinks she's married to Martin. She is played entirely for laughs, and the music joins in, trademarking her. Her point of view, and her eventual death, are totally irrelevant; as both a woman and an Indian, she is deprived of the great poignancy lavished musically on the white women's fate. She belongs to a Hollywood stereotyped character, "the Indian Maiden," recently analyzed by M. Elise Marubbio (2006), whose contact with white men is usually lethal in this period. Her music is not even Indian, but rather generically comic, effectively X-ing her out as a full human being. Suppose we line up the ethnics who don't get ethnic music: the Indian woman on one side and the Swedish settlers on the other. Juxtaposed to the Jorgensens' lack of music, the squaw's ethnic erasure seems even more final, since she cannot even blend—as they do—with their group's music culture at a funeral or wedding. It is only on the warpath that male Indians perform ethnicity, and it is there that they get a full balance with the "Irish" whites. Look's music points in various directions, and shows how the choice of presence and absence, as well as precise means of expression (here the orchestra's authoritative voice), collaborate in a multidimensional way. Her status as non-American moves us to the next general type of music in the film.

"*Non-American.*" Beyond the stereotyped settlers, two other groups of aliens are tagged musically: Indians and Mexicans. As mentioned above, Claudia Gorbman has laid out elegantly the history of Hollywood's stereotyped musical ways of grounding the appearance of Native Americans (2000). She points to the way that Indians' musical agency—their ability to control what they sing—increases as American ideology allows for a more even-handed treatment in the later, liberal westerns, through *Dances with Wolves* (1990). For *The Searchers,* before cultural generosity set in, what is really glaring is the fact that the hired Navajo extras are asked to sing in Plains Indian style. Our standard image of Indians, with feathered bonnets and descending-line melodies, comes not from the Southwest, but from the Midwest. As we saw with the Skull Islanders, musical leveling of very disparate ethnic groups and nations is among the deepest instincts of supercultural film music. Whether what we hear is how 1868 Texas Comanches actually sang is not a question anyone seems to care about: John Ford, moviegoers, or film critics. The orchestra drives home this standardization through its drumbeat and heavy-footed pentatonicism. Strikingly, Steiner and Ford ignore the early liberal western *Broken Arrow* of eight years earlier (1948), the first to allow Indians pointedly to sing their own songs. In this respect, *The Searchers* looks like a throwback.

The terms *displacement* and *replacement* can condense just what is going on here, and in many similar situations. Displacing the possibility of Navajo music—which verges on the *erasure* suggested earlier for the film's Swedes— shifts our attention from ethnography to stereotype. The resulting replacement substitutes one kind of ethnic music or group for another, and is a common enough feature of everyday American life, as when a Haitian "becomes" a "Black" on a city street, or a Christian Arab becomes a "Muslim" threat. Trying to specify how film music collaborates in these processes is part of the aim of this book. Replacement remains a bedrock of film music, and can sometimes unwittingly cause viewer confusion. Rarely do we learn about how film's consumers respond to a composer's choices, but occasionally, sentiments surface, if only in published reviews, like this one for a 2005 remake of the old frontier classic *Little House on the Prairie:* "The woods surrounding the Ingalls' cabin are deep and snowy, but the music—chanting that sounds like an African tribal song—does not quite fit the picture. Could this be 'Little House on the Serengeti'?" (Stanley 2005). Alessandra Stanley's fear of replacement conveys a deep-set comfort with stereotype as a viewing cushion.

Continuing on the quest for *The Searchers'* strategies, the appearance of "Mexican" music, while much more fleeting, reinforces this approach. In the midst of their odyssey, exhausted Ethan and Martin stop at a Mexican inn for dinner and information. Suddenly, a señorita flashes her long skirt, off-the-shoulder blouse, and castanets at Martin, who gives her a brusque brush-off while shouting to her mother "Mamecita, mas frijoles!" (more beans, Mom).

Ah, the usual erotic ethnic woman, we muse. So happily do viewers accept whatever the film's implied ethnomusicologist dishes out that they probably don't notice that it is *Spanish* señoritas, not Mexican, who flash castanets. In the same time period of the 1950s, there are Mexican films that show flamenco, with its clangy castanets, as an exotic form, imported to Mexico. But for Hollywood, it's all just "Latin": displacement and replacement strike again. A one-minute appearance of so-called Mexican expressive culture plays into the film's outlook. In American frontier society, Mexicans figure as bystanders and mediators in the fierce rivalry between Anglos and Indians, as Charles Ramirez Berg points out in his thorough survey of Latino stereotypes. In his extensive chapter on John Ford, Berg says about the female Mexican characters that "they are frequently stereotyped as sneaky and untrustworthy" (Berg 2002:136). The flamenco señorita strays far from

Figure 3. The flamenco señorita in the frontier cantina: Martin shrugs off the erotic exotic. *The Searchers*, 1956.

this stereotype—she is completely up-front, another sign that music adds extra dimensions to the system, even in its briefest appearances.

Looking across cinema systems for comparative examples helps clarify how the superculture works, and it is time for a first example of this working method. *The Searchers* does more than *displace* Mexican music; it actively *rejects* it in the form of the spurned señorita. In the French film *Le Pont Des Arts* (2004), director Eugene Green whips up a surprising example of rejection that parallels the frontier scene. In that film, whose soundtrack is composed completely of baroque music, a plaintive, foreign female voice intrudes on the audio world of the self-absorbed hero. He has fallen in love with a dead classical music singer whose album he owns, and is stalking mournfully through the deserted Paris streets. Suddenly, he runs into an exquisite Kurdish woman who is dressed in full ethnic attire. She is singing a presumably authentic song, and says enigmatically that she has been singing to attract someone—him, since he appeared. She appears not to be a streetwalker, but an embodiment of otherness, a stylized alternative to the hero's obsession. But he stays loyal to his phantom love and turns away decisively. The Kurd's attraction and disappearance is just as momentary as the señorita's. This scene parallels Martin's rejection of the Mexican girl in favor of his quest for the elusive Debbie. We are seeing that film music can deal with the temptations of the exotic, erotic female in a standardized way that highlights the severe difference in relationship between settlers and Mexicans in Texas, 1868, and the French and the Kurds in Paris, 2004. We also could read both scenes as one of countless variations on the musical overlap of race and gender in so many films.

To return to *The Searchers*, what we are really hearing in the señorita scene is not so much vernacular music, but *assumed vernacular* music, of which there are several kinds, introduced both as source music and underscoring.

In the classic Hollywood era, starting in 1927 with Al Jolson's blackface songs in *The Jazz Singer,* "white" Americans continued a long theatrical tradition of directly imitating the music of minority and foreign peoples. This is part of the superculture's paradoxical combination of democratic inclusiveness and relentless stereotyping. This mimicry goes on repeatedly in many American movies from the 1980s on, when white characters act out Motown songs for moments of bonding or celebration. They gain strength and energy by simulating somebody else's vernacular.

The Searchers not only shows communities singing and dancing apparently authentic items, like the hymn and the cavalry march, but also invents music that can be passed off as the genuine item. The sound evocation of white settlers is loaded with ingenious "Americanisms" that emulate, even fetishize, a mythic musicality. This gambit starts right at the beginning of the film. There is a surprise package in what is called the "main title music," a carefully crafted piece that supports the opening credits and often foreshadows the narrative. In the early days of the filmscore, and to some extent even today, the composer unfolds a small symphony with theme, countertheme, and recap of the opening theme. It's the Viennese valentine to the sonata form that dominated classical music. This format has the virtue of attuning the viewer—who is slouching into a chair, juggling popcorn—to the film's genre. For male-oriented movies like the cowboy, pirate, or adventure films, the main title often combines manliness with romance. Kathryn Kalinak dissects Erich Korngold's pioneering swashbuckling score for *Captain Blood* (1935) this way (1992:66-112). As a frontier epic, *The Searchers* ought to go heavy on the macho battling between settlers and Indians. Surprisingly, the soundtrack withholds the comfort of main-title mundanity. After a brief dramatic flourish signals that the movie is a western (brass drama over Indian drumbeats), we hear a song called "The Searchers," which asks "What makes a man go wandering?" a question amply answered over the next two-plus hours. This opening gambit is cast in cozy campfire style. It relies on yearning close harmony, with guitar and light string backup. I call this "assumed vernacular" because, like all "western" songs, part of the "country and western" labeling, the song called "The Searchers" has little to do with the real musical life of cowboys. Those hard-working, underpaid, and lonely men often played the fiddle, and mostly sang by themselves in their long nighttime vigils, like shepherds everywhere. The "western" song arose and spread with the movies, particularly through the work of the "singing cowboys," Gene Autry and Roy Rogers (Stanfield 2002). So by 1956, a movie-driven image of male musical bonding, despite all its hokiness, easily scattered crumbs of versimilitude to a fable-hungry audience. A manufactured genre like the singing cowboy slides into familiarity and passes as musical ethnography. Viewers can settle down into their seats and also sink comfortably into this folksy style, ready to follow the adventures of tough but true and tender men in rugged settings. In a way, this version of main title represents its own type of displacement, of Steiner himself and European symphonism in general, as part of Ford's deep Americanism.

The guitar and strings of "The Searchers" song blend directly into Steiner's filmscore. The lettering of "Texas, 1868" follows the credits. Out of blackness, a door opens onto the prairie, and a frontier woman gazes pensively into the distance. We hear a lovely violin theme with an intense yearning feel backed by the folksy guitar chords. Emerging from the men's campfire harmonies, "Lorena" tracks the camera's women's-eye view of the prairie. On first hearing, I was sure this was a prize example of Steiner's skill in transforming his Viennese background into an American sensibility. The tune's upward-sixth motif can be found easily in the works of Gustav Mahler or Steiner's godfather, Richard Strauss. The great historian of the American myth, Richard Slotkin, kindly informed me that the melody is in fact a true American vernacular product, a song called "Lorena," that dates to just before the stated setting of the film. "Lorena," a favorite of Confederate troops, was sung on both sides of the Civil War, which ended just three years before 1868. Coupled with the just-written "Shall We Gather at the River" and the just-adopted cavalry march "Garryowen," the Civil War song "Lorena" completes a trilogy of brand-new songs meant to evoke a legendary time.

We know Steiner liked "Lorena," since he had used it earlier in *Gone with the Wind* (1939), where it accompanies a pre–Civil War charity ball, played by a Black orchestra, itself an interesting bit of ethnography. Since the song had not yet been written, we know that precise authenticity was not Steiner's concern. "Lorena's" appearance in *The Searchers* references the Confederacy in two ways: through the earlier film's view of the mythic South and as something Ethan might have sung as a Southern soldier. The moviegoer would have seen *Gone with the Wind*, so that reference might have worked, but would have no access to the history of the song's appeal to Civil War troops. All films are *intertextual*, meaning any given viewing evokes memories of earlier moviegoing. All horror films bounce off earlier ones, and any star turn, from Humphrey Bogart or Audrey Hepburn to Julia Roberts, evokes the actor as much as the character. *Musical* intertextuality is not much discussed in film studies, but when you listen to a durable master like Steiner or John Williams, with a huge body of work, you can hear the echoes and even the quotations from film to film. These resonances multiply, leading the critic Gerard Genette to prefer the term *transtextuality* "to refer to all that which puts one text in relation, whether manifest or secret, with other texts" (Stam 2005:27). Genette's term is a good one for crosscultural borrowing, which involves a huge range of possibilities across space and time.

Music's basic nature of being composed of many different elements—rhythm, tempo, instrumentation, melodic line, tone color, etc.—allows it to comfortably control levels of transtextuality, from the very hidden to the most blatant quotation. Recently, the scores for Quentin Tarantino's *Kill Bill* films kaleidoscopically rotate musical motifs from obscure films that the director likes, in a kind of postmodern riot of references. Steiner's quotations embody his personal musical preferences—sometimes he cites his own scores—but mainly they reference conventionality and privilege predictability.[3] Like drumbeats or scale types, specific citations, like "Lorena," which do not even emerge from the characters themselves, locate the viewer culturally as well as sonically.

The simulation that Steiner's symphonic "Lorena" introduces can stand in for countless examples of the ways that filmscores deal with vernacular source material. The ethnomusicologist aspect of the implied narrator takes a rest while the real boss stands up to conduct. So many cases of this kind of musical manipulation occur that it is tempting to make a typology, or at least to offer up a set of terms that sketch out the possibilities. The substitution of orchestra for onscreen vernacular source music sometimes appears as *amplification,* a sort of loudspeaker effect that happens when the supposed fife and drum of the cavalry's "Garryowen" fade into a full-score version, seamlessly. Ford and Steiner want the viewer to be overwhelmed by this first appearance of the mighty army in the midst of the rude frontier skirmishes we have seen up that point. The soldiers actually have accomplished what Ethan and Martin have failed to do: rounded up and reclaimed a group of white women prisoners of the Indians. At other times, in other films, the effect is more of *taming,* or at least *gentrifying* the common people who are singing.

There is more simulation, sometimes very subtle. I already have mentioned the imitation of Native American music, which here, as usual, includes the DUM-dum-dum-dum rhythm, parallel fourths, and so on. Ford offers an extra added attraction in *The Searchers:* imitation of simulation. The character Mose is a half-wit settler who perhaps has been damaged by time spent with the Indians. Twice he imitates them when he sees and hears them. By whooping while the settlers are defending themselves against an Indian onslaught, he temporarily switches sides, and quickly stops when it is noticed. Mose's mimicry adds an extra shading to his slightly darkened skin. Ethan, who is what Slotkin calls "The Man Who Knows Indians," would never stoop to this form of emulation. He can track Comanches and speak with them, but never joins their chants, nor does this tend to happen in other westerns. People's music, like their "blood," is supposed to stay within their community in Hollywood's world-view, unlike the real world, where folks constantly trade musical inspiration and insight.

In the early 1930s, starting with *Bird of Paradise* and continuing with *King Kong*, we see Steiner struggling with techniques that he will polish and perfect over the two decades that led him to the mature mastery of *The Searchers*, across dozens of scores and Oscar nominations. Along with colleagues such as Korngold and Waxman, Steiner shaped a central European, classical-music-based sensibility that comes from, and ends up strongly reinforcing, a supercultural sensibility that has left an indelible mark on film-music practice. No matter how much musical materials shift in the next decades, incorporating ever more assumed vernacular styles such as jazz, rock 'n' roll, and eventually hip-hop, the basic approach never really changes, with its twofold mission: to produce economically an musical ethnography of a given community, as part of the necessary authenticity of the filmed world, and just as concisely to use conventional markers of feeling to target and guide the viewer's journey through the narrative. Both needs are deeply cultural. A commercial elite of producers takes on the responsibility of defining both the expected and the novel with a confidence and authority that overarches all the variety, confusion, and turbulence of both the filmed and the real-world societies. The way that American composers, music supervisors, and producers have done this work has been so efficient and effective that all the cinemas of the world have had to learn, emulate, and, in some cases, resist or supplant this supercultural system.

Cracks in the Pavement

Joni Mitchell's famous line "they've paved paradise and put up a parking lot" would seem to describe what the integrated filmscore did to the open-ended vistas of early film. All choices are foreclosed and every experience seems predetermined. Yet that is not the way of supercultures. If they were simply authoritarian and totalizing, they wouldn't work half as well as they do, since people would tune out or be turned off. The system has built-in cracks, like any pavement, the result of inefficient or lazy contractors, weather, and the wear and tear caused by the very vehicles the asphalt is built to carry. Pedestrians take this further, cutting trails across the grass and ignoring sidewalks altogether as they make their own choice of routes to a destination. Both producers and consumers create indeterminacy in the product; a movie is a less predictable industrial product than a Snickers bar.

In the case of classic Hollywood films, composers were under the thumb of producers or studio heads who had their own ideas of how much and what kinds of music a given film should have. All films are collaborative, so even Max Steiner's shadow went only so far in covering the film's musical choices. This is most telling in terms of extra music, often performed by the characters themselves in little scenes that give us an extra cultural charge. *Mildred Pierce* (1945), one of Steiner's best-known and analyzed scores, offers a couple of moments that seem like cracks in the pavement. Much of Steiner's strategy in *Mildred Pierce* is analyzed tellingly in Claudia Gorbman's groundbreaking study of supercultural technique, appropriately titled *Unheard Melodies* (Gorbman 1987). She clarifies concisely how, in the supercultural system, music works best when heard least. She concentrates on the motif-system, which attaches melodic units to each character like yellow stickies. Not only do we recognize each character—often stereotypically—but we know who to pay attention to in a given scene. In *Mildred Pierce*, one character has no motif: the Black maid, whose high-pitched, almost hysterical voice is a sonic signature. As we saw with the squaw and the Mexican girl in *The Searchers*, by and large, classically, minority characters get their own music only when it's meant for comic effect. Unless they merit star status, "non-American" characters tend toward caricature or silence. One of the great exceptions was Carmen Miranda, a Portuguese-born Brazilian songstress who rode the wave of Latin American friendship known as the Good Neighbor Policy in the 1940s (see Galm, in this volume). U.S. foreign policy tilted to protect our southern flank, and Miranda's sprightly shapeliness, terrific stage presence, and eccentric outfits, including her trademark fruit-basket hat, made her a standout star. She was "Latin," with her Portuguese somehow standing in for Spanish. Her film career is worth a long musical look (Solberg and Meyer 1996). Its impact is crystallized in the surprising cameo appearance of this hyperbolically ethnic film figure in *Mildred Pierce*. Mildred (Joan Crawford) has two daughters, the good girl Kay and the bad girl Veda. Kay dies off, leaving the stage entirely open to Veda's machinations and crimes, but before Kay departs from the scene, she has her musical moment. Mildred has just been working with the Black maid on the pies she has started to sell, a first step on her road to becoming a successful businesswoman in World War II America; when the men are away, the girls can rise to power. Mildred hears odd music in the living room. As a single mom, she has been working herself to

Figure 4. Carmen Miranda invades Mildred Pierce's living room: a subcultural breakthrough denied. *Mildred Pierce,* 1945.

the bone, and she thinks this sacrifice should include splurging on ballet and piano lessons as part of girls' training for proper womanhood. We have heard Veda play Chopin. But when she steps out of the kitchen, mom finds Kay wearing makeup and a homemade outfit, singing "Down South American Way" like Carmen Miranda, in *That Night in Rio,* 1941. Horrified, Mildred grabs Kay and tells her to wipe off the lipstick and go upstairs; meanwhile, bad-girl Veda smirks, enjoying the subversion that she will push to extremes as the film unfolds

The Miranda scene marks the only reference to non-white America (beyond the maid) in a movie resolutely dedicated to the white woman's problems in a changing society, the terms in which *Mildred Pierce* usually is discussed. Like Kay herself, certain angles of women's experience are expendable. The appearance of Miranda, brief as it is, substantially fills out the filmscore's musical ethnography of war-time America lushly insinuated by Steiner's themes. Popular culture, with its destabilizing potential for women, permeates every living room. Even the sacred parlor piano can be an agent of erotic exoticism.

Miranda was both safe and scary; the Hollywood code forced costume designers to come up with a navel-covering panel for her sensuous South American look. But every script fiercely domesticated her into the American space, such as providing her with an acceptable Latin mate. Musically, her production numbers are double-edged. In *The Gang's All Here* (1943), she follows Benny Goodman onto the bandstand. He has just done "Don't Pooh-Pooh Paducah," a hymn to heartland American values, and while Miranda latinizes the song, she also blends right in, following the melting-pot model of assimilating the best of your heritage into an emergent U.S. culture. Presumably, little Kay has seen some of these movies, and is imitating them as good clean fun. Miranda's crossover from one Hollywood film to another gives yet another example of how music, and musical icons, spill over and offer supplemental pleasures in movies. For Berg's survey of Latino stereotypes, Miranda is one of a set of standard images, the "female clown." He sees her figure as "exaggeration to the point of caricature, another way to elicit derisive laughter and belittle the Latina Other" (Berg 2002:75). While one can't argue with this basic outline, it seems to leave out the power that Miranda shows here to seriously destabilize the American home. Mildred's severe response goes beyond what reaction to your little daughter's imitating a "female clown" would require. Musically posed, a caricature has more carrying power.

This mini-scene also resonates with other plot elements in *Mildred Pierce,* so we have to integrate it into the rest of the narrative to figure out its narrative value. As always, it is Veda, the bad daughter, around whom everything rotates. Kay flirts with popular culture but dies before she can grow into it, but Veda will move deeply into the world of commercial song after rejecting Chopinism. The classics offered her a good-girl façade, but the psychological trumps the social in "women's films," and Veda spins out of control as part of her endless war with her mother. Stuck on her own, she briefly makes a living by singing in a dockside dive for sailors and riff-raff, owned by Wally, a central, shady character in the film, who is always after Mildred, but never gets her.

Veda's brief cabaret career is another musical component of *Mildred Pierce* that escapes Steiner and the domineering symphonic score. Just as Kay's Miranda number seems to prefigure Veda's move to musical seaminess, so the bar itself already has made an appearance, right near the film's opening. For reasons still unexplained to viewers (there's a murder mystery built into the film), Mildred is wandering by the harbor in a total daze. She seems to contemplate suicide, stopped only by an alert cop. As she wanders off, faint music creeps in. As Mildred approaches a sleazy nightspot, Wally taps on the window and invites her in for a chat. Dazed, she accepts and they sit down. The camera then pans to the small stage space, where we now focus in on a woman singing "You Must Have Been a Beautiful Baby, 'Cause Baby, Look at You Now," and lingers for a few seconds, leaving our principal characters alone at the table. Almost tangentially, we see sailors and other viewers. This is one of the few moments of real community life the film contains, since it so intensely about the psychology and claustrophobic behavior of its main figures. In fact, the only other communal scenes are in Mildred's restaurant, where we hear faint, cheerful background music. These are the moments that draw attention to what music is doing in film: Very often it conjures up community, effortlessly and without need of explanation. It's as if the film simply satisfies a human need for music to bring people together. Of course, there is a narrative logic to including the nightclub stage, since later, Veda herself will be up there sing-ing, and the lyrics about "a beautiful baby" let Steiner layer irony onto the wayward daughter. This is filmscore craft at its finest and fully justifies pan-ning the camera for a few seconds of relief from Joan Crawford's endlessly tortured cheekbones in half-shadow. For just a few seconds, *Mildred Pierce* has become a musical, the film genre that evokes—and tries to structure—community (Feuer 1982).

This move goes back to the earliest sound films, notably René Clair's *Sous les toits de Paris* of 1929 (see Gorbman 1987 for a detailed analysis). Clair distrusted the new power of the synchronized soundtrack. He felt deeply that the banality of hearing clocks tick and people talk would detract from the established "art of film." In response, he found ways to give each appearance of sound a special resonance. *Sous les toits de Paris* (Under Paris Roofs, 1929) opens with a long pan down from the rooftops of the title to the enclosed street space of a working-class Paris neighborhood. As the camera descends, the volume comes up on a song-seller. He has gathered a crowd to hawk his wares, and they are all performing the latest hit under his direction. As they sing, the camera tracks various characters, offering hints about the plot. A musical ethnography begins the film, and Clair makes a strong statement about the power of music to conspire in the crea-tion of both a celluloid and a viewing community. After the first verse, the audience is ready to sing along with the Parisians. This doubles the power of the soundtrack, one of the only components of film that can reach out beyond the screen and grab the viewer, as recognized in post-classic 1980s musical movies such as *Purple Rose of Cairo* (1985) and *Pennies from Heaven* (1981) that have characters move from their seats into the framed image to sing and dance. Lars von Trier's powerful *Dancer in the Dark* (2000) allows star singer Bjork to live out cheerful musical fantasies in her darkest moments. Film noir movies of the 1940s and 1950s often stop the action in its desperate tracks to linger on a singer in a sleazy bar (*Detour*, 1945), or a Latin band in a crowded club (*Criss Cross*, 1949). These mo-ments combine pure entertainment, a heightened sense of community be-yond the usually isolated obsessions of the main characters, and some sug-gested storyline support to justify their inclusion.

When Max Steiner builds even the slightest song performance into a women's melodrama, he is not just filling time. In both *The Searchers* and *Mildred Pierce*, Steiner is a master motif manipulator, but also a field-worker who artfully articulates a music culture. Only when his audience is fully grounded in a multidimensional celluloid society can the story—and his music—touch their hearts. No wonder people look not only to nineteenth-century opera, but also early twentieth-century German cabaret as sources for film music. In Wally's dive, Wagner and Brecht share a few seconds of fellowship: sentimental identification, ironic alienation, and pulsing melodrama take over the screen.

Musical erasure, inclusion, and outright manipulation remain privileges of the producers, so are deeply supercultural. But music also provides many moments when the grip is loosened. The many onscreen performances that interrupt action and narrative in films open up spaces of relaxation and a certain indeterminacy even within a Steiner-scored film. As American society changed in the 1950s, composers came up with new solutions to the mixture of entertainment and control that mark the filmscore. The "sons of Steiner," began to reconfigure elements of the system at the same time that the old man wrote *The Searchers'* score: the mid-1950s. The next chapter reveals some of their strategies, and also tiptoes into the territory of film music beyond Hollywood, anticipating the global thinking of the essays to follow.

Notes

1. Taruskin has a concise account of Steiner's distinguished colleague, Erich Korngold, in the monumental *Oxford History of Western Music,* where he commends Korngold for commanding "the full panoply of Wagnerian and Straussian resources with a routined virtuosity that exceeded Wagner's and Strauss's," singling out the love scene from *Anthony Adverse* (1936) for special praise (Taruskin 2005:551).

2. Daniel Goldmark's *Tunes for 'Toons: Music and the Hollywood Cartoon* (2005) advances the topic considerably.

3. A fascinating example appears early in *The Searchers*. Ethan has an emotional moment with Debbie, later to be the object of his quest and hatred. The score plays with the rising sixth taken from "Lorena," quietly converting it into an almost exact quotation from the fourth movement of Mahler's Fourth Symphony. That movement presents a song text that describes a child's-eye view of Paradise. I have to read this as an insider reference by Steiner to the thematics of the scene; the music is keyed very low and the quotation is unreadable to almost any moviegoer. In a sense, the moment ethnographizes Steiner himself.

Works Cited

Berg, Charles Ramirez. 2002. *Latino Images in Film: Stereotypes, Subversion, and Resistance.* Austin: University of Texas Press.

Bourdieu, Pierre. 1979. *La Distinction: Critique Sociàle du Jugement.* Paris: Minuit.

Chatman, Seymour. 1990. *Coming to Terms: The Rhetoric of Narrative in Fiction and Film.* Ithaca, N.Y.: Cornell University Press.

Daubney, Kate. 2000. *Max Steiner's* Now, Voyager: *A Film Score Guide.* Westport, Conn.: Greenwood.

Davis, Natalie Zemon. 2000. *Slaves on Screen: Film and Historical Vision.* Cambridge, Mass.: Harvard University Press.

Feuer, Jane. 1982. *The Hollywood Musical*. Bloomington: Indiana University Press.

Fischer, Lucy. 1980. "*Applause:* The Visual and Acoustic Landscape." in *Film Sound: Theory and Practice,* ed. J. Belton and E. Weis, 232–246. New York: Columbia University Press.

Franklin, Peter. 2001. "*King Kong* and Film on Music: Out of the Fog," in *Film Music: Critical Approaches,* ed. K. J. Donnelly, 88–102. New York: Continuum.

Goldmark, Daniel. *Tunes for 'Toons: Music and the Hollywood Cartoon*. Berkeley and Los Angeles: University of California Press.

Gorbman, Claudia. 1987. *Unheard Melodies: Narrative Film Music*. Bloomington and Indianapolis: Indiana University Press.

———. 2000. "Scoring the Hollywood Indian," in *Western Music and Its Other,* ed. G. Born and D. Hesmondhalgh, ed. Berkeley and Los Angeles: University of California Press.

Jenkins, Henry. 1992. *What Made Pistachio Nuts? Early Sound Comedy and the Vaudeville Aesthetic*. New York: Columbia University Press.

Kalinak, Kathryn. 1992. *Settling the Score: Music and the Classical Hollywood Film*. Madison: University of Wisconsin Press.

Lancefield, Robert. 2004. *Hearing Orientality in (White) America*. Ph.D. dissertation, Wesleyan University.

Locke, Ralph P. 1998. "Cutthroats and Casbah Dancers, Muezzins and Timeless Sands: Musical Images of the Middle East," in *The Exotic in Western Music,* ed. J. Belman, 104–36. Boston: Northeastern University Press.

Marubbio, M. Elise. 2006. *Killing the Indian Maiden: Images of Native American Women in Film*. Lexington: University Press of Kentucky.

McClary, Susan. 2002. *Feminine Endings,* 2d ed. Minneapolis: University of Minnesota Press.

Morgan, Andy. 2003. "The Songlines Guide to Gnawa," *Songlines* 18:58–61.

Mowitt, John. 2005. *Re-Takes: Postcoloniality and Foreign Film Languages*. Minneapolis: University of Minnesota Press.

Rozsa, Miklos. 1982. *Double Life: The Autobiography of Miklos Rozsa*. Tunbridge Wells: Midas Books.

Scott, A. O. 2006. "'The Searchers': How the Western Was Begun." *New York Times,* June 11.

Slobin, Mark. 2000. *Subcultural Sounds: Micromusics of the West,* 2d. ed. Hanover and London: Wesleyan University Press.

Solberg, Helena, and David Meyer. 1996. *Carmen Miranda: Bananas is My Business*. Documentary film.

Sommer, Doris. 1991. *Foundational Fictions*. Berkeley and Los Angeles: University of California Press.

Stam, Robert. 2005. "Introduction: The Theory and Practice of Adaptation," in *Literature and Film: A Guide to the Theory and Practice of Adaptation,* ed. R. Stam and A. Raengo. Oxford: Blackwell.

Stanfield, Peter. 2002. *Horse Opera; The Strange History of the 1930s Singing Cowboy*. Urbana and Chicago: University of Illinois Press.

Stanley, Alessandra. 2005. "Pa, This Prairie Looks Dark and Scary." *New York Times,* March 26.

Szegedy-Maszak, Andrew. 2005. "Introduction," in *Antiquity and Photography: Early Views of Ancient Mediterranean Sites,* ed. C. Lyons, J. Papadopoulos, L. Steward, and A. Szegedy-Maszak, 2–21. Los Angeles: J. Paul Getty Museum.

Taruskin, Richard. 2005. The Oxford History of Western Music, vol. 2. New York: Oxford University Press.

MARK SLOBIN

The Superculture Beyond Steiner

·◉·

In the mid-1950s, the Hollywood sound system suffered a series of shocks.
The rising dominance of television and the breakup of the studios allowed
for huge fissures, not just small cracks, to open up. A younger generation of
American-born composers kept the conventions of the filmscore, but
plugged in new energy sources to keep their product lively. This was the
post–World War II way: target young couples and, a bit later, teenagers
with cash in their pockets. The new styles of advertising, the creation of the
45-rpm record, FM radio and other pop forms slanted marketing toward
youth culture, and the building of studio devices to cash in on the songs in
movies, all are detailed in Jeff Smith's *The Sounds of Commerce* (1998).
These and other trends pushed film music out of its cozy routine.

Even as old man Steiner was writing the symphonic score for *The
Searchers,* the young lions of film music were searching for untapped vernacular sources. Elmer Bernstein (*The Man with the Golden Arm,* 1956) and
Leith Stevens (*The Wild One,* 1954), helped to create the early "jazz score."
The Wild One became famous for Marlon Brando's indelible image as a California biker gang leader. Stevens said the jazz of the filmscore reflected the
feelings of "exhibitionistic . . . confused and wondering" youth (Stevens
1954). Perhaps it does, but in thinking through musical ethnography, it
seems fair to ask whether the score grows out of the musical vocabulary of
California bikers of the early 1950s. In fact, the music of the displaced
Southwestern migrants who became the backbone of rural California
towns was country music: "for the migrants, country singing stars such as
Gene Autry represented the triumph of their way of life over the corrupt
ways of urban America" (Shindo 1997:208). Not only did this group not
produce rebels, but "they became part of the conservative movement that
elected Ronald Reagan governor of California in 1966 and 1970" (ibid.:4).

Even if we grant the displacement of the storyline from the original novel's California setting to Anywhere, U.S.A., not only would Brando's real-life counterpart have had little familiarity with big-city jazz sounds, but might well have scorned them. Stevens's re-creation of reality outdoes Steiner's version of simulated ethnography by a country mile. This *displacement* of a population's musical taste helps solidify structures of feeling about subcultures that ripple out into the real world. The film helps to sideline country music, reinforcing its always marginal standing in America's self-perception. By not identifying country with the crude biker crowd, that style can remain rural but cheerfully downhome or patriotic. Only in Robert Altman's *Nashville* (1976) could a cynical view of country creep into Hollywood sideways, in the work of an offbeat director. But it is not only country music that is refashioned in *The Wild One*. The urban, popular jazz that Brando and his buddies savor was not written by or for Leith Stevens's "confused exhibitionistic youth," but rather was the mainstream dance music enjoyed by a broad cross-section of Americans. In short, Stevens produced a customized score not unlike the elaborate bikes and hot rods of the characters: fantasy on a solid American chassis.

The immense influence of movie-made imagery extends way beyond how Americans think about themselves, modeling what world societies think the U.S. is like. Those images then reshape the local sense of self. Both producers and consumers of global soundtracks soak up supercultural information as fact, not fantasy. The music for black-leather-jacket-wearing, rebellious bikers has roared across countless screens and streets worldwide. The ominously circling motorcycles around a helpless woman that we might see in an Indian film have a single source: *The Wild One*. So well known is this image that it can even be parodied, as in the Tamil film *Mouna Ragam*'s take-off on *Singin' in the Rain*, using middle-class schoolgirls splashing merrily through a production number. Suddenly, they are surrounded by guys on bicycles—not motor scooters—and although first alarmed, they flippantly knock the boys' hats off and go on their way. This type of displacement plays with what Part Four below identifies as a figure of film music, a narrative-musical stereotyped scene.

Case Study: The Man with the Golden Arm

Like Leith Stevens, Elmer Bernstein felt the need to underscore dramatically the turbulence of postwar American life, but he was assigned to a film about big-city angst, not small-town bikers. He wrote a jazz-based musical ethnography about a white inner-city community for *The Man with the Golden Arm* (1956), a portrait of a white Chicago drug addict. Here is what Bernstein had to say about his approach: "There is something very American and contemporary about all the characters and their problems. I wanted an element that could speak readily of hysteria and despair, an element that would localize these emotions to our country, to a large city if possible. Ergo,—jazz" (Bernstein 1956:3).

This social situation of jazz, geographically and emotionally, already assumes an ethnomusicology of contemporary America that could well be questioned. The bebop of 1956 does not readily bring hysteria and despair to mind, and in other films, it is rock 'n' roll that does this job, as the moral panic music of the day. Rock 'n' roll, most noticeably in *Blackboard Jungle* (1955) already was muscling in as the sound symbol for rebellious youth. Despite standard references to the film having a "rock 'n' roll score," the only rock moment comes in the main title—Bill Haley's "Rock Around the Clock." Much like the avoidance of country music in *The Wild One*, the rest of the film steers away from rock 'n' roll in favor of different forms of jazz-based pop music as the sonic reflection of the war between the generations. The fact that the one rock song stuck in the mind of the public and the industry as the main motif of *Blackboard Jungle* shows just how restless everyone was to move on to the newest shock-value music. It was a quest that mirrored not so much surging youth, but rather the pop culture industry's frenetic search for new forms of marketable trends.

When Bernstein chose jazz, rather than rock 'n' roll, as his language for urban "hysteria and despair," something else was going on, and it might have to do with an attitude towards Blackness, as refracted through the jazz musician (Gabbard 1996). Certainly *Golden Arm* offers a remarkable example of social and cultural erasure and displacement. To fully fathom its methods, we need to view it not just as a free-standing filmscore, but also in terms of a larger issue: music as part of adaptation, a frequently scorned Hollywood practice that is finally receiving its due, in movies such as *Adaptation* (2002) and most cogently in Robert Stam and Alessandra Raengo's remarkable three-volume survey of the subject (2005). Let's go back to the film's source: the novel of the same name.

The Man with the Golden Arm, Nelson Algren's 1949 novel, won the very first National Book Award. Lurid, sensuous, and deeply ethnographic, its cadences would still have been hanging in the air at the time the film was made. At first, Algren was tapped to do the screenplay, but a major fight with director Otto Preminger left him on the outside. No wonder: the dream factory redid virtually every aspect of the novel, except for the Chicago setting, the name and problem of Frankie Machine, the drug-dependent protagonist, and a few supporting characters. Just to cite one shift, Frankie Machine, a tall Polish blond, and his sometimes mistress, Molly-O, a petite brunette, ended up being played by Frank Sinatra, a slight brunette, and Kim Novak, a statuesque blonde. More seriously, in the novel, Frankie kills his drug dealer and ends up committing suicide, while his wife Sophie goes mad. In the film, Frankie is a reformed drug addict whose wife kills the pusher, leaving Frankie and Molly to literally walk off into the sunrise.

For our interests, the important remodeling comes in the competing ethnographies of the novel and the screenplay. As Stam says, "the issue becomes one of *comparative narratology*, which asks . . . what events from the novel's story have been eliminated, added or changed in the adaptation, and more important, why? Many adaptations eliminate specific *kinds* of materials . . ." (Stam 2005:34). Ethnography goes beyond events to the whole human setting. As Algren himself said about the adaptation, "I was sorry that it was a Chicago story that had nothing to do with Chicago. Some of the people were dressed like old Vienna and some like old San Francisco. The book very specifically took place at a certain time, at a certain locale, and the movie took place nowhere. It was unframed, it was very murky, and there were just plain idiotic things in it" (Donahue 1964:123). To start with, the denial of the demographic is severe. Algren's Chicago slum is populated principally by Poles, with a Jew or two and a few Irish, adjacent to an African-American area. In a bold sweep of ethnic cleansing, the film presents ethnically unmarked white Americans and virtually no African Americans. This approach leads to serious musical erasure, displacement, and replacement that play directly into the methodologies of this chapter. A whole sector of possible musical associations simply has been eliminated by the fact that it is only unaffiliated whites who live, love, fight, shoot up, and make music in the world within the film. Although Stam points to ways that music can help an adaptation become persuasive, he does not tend to isolate musical shifts from source novel to film. Since Algren's implied narrator is a very meticulous ethnomusicologist, comparing the two versions of the story sheds real light on supercultural practice. The erasure part is easy enough to summarize: The book's copious descriptions of Black music-making simply don't make it to the screen, any more than do the references to Polish music.

The musical filtering-out is more subtle. Throughout the novel, the characters sing and quote lines of popular songs to each other as part of daily conversation. Indeed, this pop music coding of communication stands out as one of the original and colorful parts of Algren's style. Here are some examples, first from Frankie's fake-invalid wife Sophie:

Her reply was simply to weave her hands in front of her face like a Hawaiian dancer and to sing saucily:

> *Hello, Aloha, how are you?*
> *I'm bring you kisses from over the sea.*

A few lines later:

She watched while he cut everything into small cubes for her and then sat weaving her hands instead of eating.

> *Others you've met*
> *May call you coquette . . .*

[*Frankie*] "Quit yawpin' 'n scoff," he told her, "you sound like a lost orphan in a rain barrel."
  For now she fancied herself a vocalist with an all-girl band. Over the sausage she smiled faintly at the unseen players, encouraging one with a nod here and another with a nod there. There was something really distracted about her smile.
  "What the hell are you—a bird?" But his eyes were clouded with concern for her.
  "Evelyn 'n her magic violin," Sophie explained easily, "I can do magic too."
  "Well," he sighed, realizing he was in for a long, long night, "here we go again."
  mean to me

she sang.

> *Why must you be mean to me? (Algren 1949:249)*

Not just Sophie, but also Molly-O tries to engage Frankie with snatches of song:

[she] picked up some song or other in her hoarse, wise, taunting voice, letting her eyes remember the one night they had danced together.

Molly-O can even parody songs, as in the case of "one of her little sing-song taunts: *"Let me be your little sweetheart, I'll be much obliged to you,"* an ironic version of "Let me be your sweetheart, I'm in love with you." (Ibid.:111)

This substitution of lyrics for conversation among estranged or intimately connected couples forms just one way that Algren orchestrates the community. At the neighborhood New Year's Eve party, he carefully notes that "in the middle of the *Switeczyna Polka* the younger couples began jitterbugging" (ibid.:160). In a long, nightmarish, drug-confused scene, Frankie sits in the grotesque Black bar where the emcee Mr. Floor Show's entire spiel reaches him through his fog; then "the three-piece band began beating it out while Miss Mite took over.

I wonder who's boogin' my woogie now. (Ibid.:303)

With ethnographic accuracy a bit later, the narrator even dates the music:

In one corner somebody sniggered.

I want the frim-fram sauce,

the war horse went into some two-year-old novelty tune,

With the aussenfay
And cha-fa-fa on the side. (Ibid.:305)

How could the filmmaking team sidestep the opportunity to drench the diegesis similarly with this colorful array of musical citations, a novelist's methodical way of marking the territory? Preminger was not interested in this type of ethnography. He prized the novel's shock value only in terms of its possibilities for exploring the forbidden and thrilling topic of drug addiction, causing *The Man with the Golden Arm* to be banned by the Catholic Code and panned in the press. To achieve this singlemindedness, Preminger wanted only the sonic impact of a new type of score, not a rich ethnomusicology of an actually existing Chicago neighborhood. Maybe the sensationalism of the score is what moved Algren to say one approving thing about the adaptation: "I like the music" (Donahue 1964:123). Composer Elmer Bernstein understood his assignment to be the creation of a score entirely based on the lead character: "there are only three themes which are exploited in a compositional manner in the development of the score: . . . 1) Frank's relationship to his general environment; 2) Frank's relationship to his home environment. . . ; 3) Frank's relationship with "the other woman" (Bernstein 1956:3). Of these, only the first would allow for the implied ethnomusicologist to enter, but he is denied entry, in the psychology-centered approach the filmmakers are fixated on.

Rather than "go ethnographic," Elmer Bernstein turned to musicians close at hand. The dominant sound comes from the work of Shorty Rogers, a West Coast white jazz band leader, with solos by drummer Shelly Manne. Bernstein is drawing on the novel's depiction of Frankie Machine as a wannabe jazz drummer, the one salvaged musical element in the screenplay. Shelly Manne's frenetic drumming is the heroin theme. Considering the common portrayal of drug-addicted jazz musicians as Black (down through *Bird,* Clint Eastwood's 1988 bio-pic of Charlie Parker), *Golden Arm*'s whiteness seems almost glaring. Drummers, perhaps even more than sax players, once were indexed Black and savage, as seen in the Betty Boop cartoon's visual linkage of the cannibal and Louis Armstrong's

Black sideman. The 1940s big band era, with stress on white drummer heroes like Gene Krupa, may have made a character like Frankie Machine more plausible. Indeed, shortly after *Golden Arm,* in 1959, *The Gene Krupa Story* revisited the problems of a white drummer getting hung up on heroin: Here filmed life imitates film art in a complex intertextual move.

Shelly Manne and Shorty Rogers were logical choices from the ethnographic point of view, as they would have been Frankie Machine's role models. It is in this way that ethnomusicology emerges: in the filmmaking team rather than the adaptation. Manne, also a drummer, and Rogers were Frankie's contemporaries. Both broke in with white bands in the 1940s and were established figures on the West Coast scene. Manne ran his own night club, wanting to have "a friendly place" where "my men could play all the time," a set-up Frankie would have loved. Footage from 1962 of Manne and Rogers's bands (from the television program *Jazz Scene USA*) opens the camera's eye onto almost identical collectives of white men of varying ethnic origin with white shirts and narrow ties, slicked down or crew-cut hair, and a very precise, controlled manner of playing. In this context, the "urban hysteria and despair" that Rogers and Manne are supposedly supplying for Elmer Bernstein's music direction seem more comforting and cosmetic than titillating and terrifying, a reading that the film's happy ending bears out. Later, Manne would parlay his Hollywood success into television work. Figure 1 shows the album cover for *Daktari,* a mid-1960s Africa-based show for which he wrote in an early version of world music fusion style. The album's photo of the white drummer amid the African animals, who stand in for African society, offers a disturbing parallel to the displacement of the filmscore for *Man with the Golden Arm.* Not that Algren himself is immune from such cultural misconnections: in the novel, the Black bar just described features a group of monkeys in a cage looking down on the frazzled humans.[1]

Before we leave *Golden Arm,* two musical interpolations need highlighting to extend our interpretive range. Beyond the substitutions and erasures, scores also add significant elements to round out their ethnographic instincts. One comes in two strategic spots. The first, visually faithful to the novel, shows us Frankie on a fire escape in an early Sunday morning, after a hard night of card-dealing, the talent for which he has earned the sobriquet of the title: the man with the golden arm. Here is Algren's sound cue for the moment: "From where the narrow alley ran a child's cry, high-pitched, brief and cut off sharply, came up to him like the cry of a child run down in the drunken driver. A cry that held no hope of help at all, a cry that pitched the very darkness down" (Algren 1949:281). Nothing could suit the bleakness of the author's Chicago more. In place of this lone, helpless outcry,

Figure 1. Shelly Manne and his animal band: the survival of "savage music" into the television age. *Daktari*, 1966–69.

Elmer Bernstein wrote music for the people that the film places in Frankie's line of sight: sober, god-fearing community members walking to church, backed by clearly Coplandesque orchestral music. Much like the church-going congregants of westerns, where orderly community stands against the anarchy of gunslingers, *Golden Arm* sets up a stark contrast of the sinner and the saved, despair and redemption. Unlike the novel but more like the western, the Chicago film saves the hero from destruction. The second time we hear the uplifting cue comes when Frankie and Molly head off into the sunrise at the very end of the film. This music was not Elmer Bernstein's first choice; he explains that here "I had my only serious disagreement with the producer. I lost. It seemed to me that the only honest way to end this film was on a 'downbeat' note . . . Mr. Preminger felt that the audience would have taken enough by the time . . . in any case . . . we have Frank dutifully walking into a better life . . . and we are sent from the theater in a state of euphoria" (Bernstein 1956:12). Bernstein describes the theme as having "the same blues motif which had started the film with Frank's walk down the same street," but he understandably glosses over the basic lone-trumpet sound as being a Copland quotation.

Why Copland? In the 1930s and 1940s, Aaron Copland constructed a symphonic sound that ended up as the accepted ideal of how to paint America in sounds. Particularly in the ballet scores *Rodeo, Appalachian Spring,* and *Billy the Kid,* the Brooklyn-born Copland created a formula for wide open spaces. It stressed simulated vernacular music often based on folksongs, and the suggestion of an inherent goodness of the vast American social and physical landscape, all based on a vaguely defined white population with hints of nearby Mexicans, though not many African Americans. All this is very similar to the world of *The Searchers* or even the Chicago of *The Man with the Golden Arm*. Copland's limited work as a film composer notably includes *Our Town*, a darkly sentimental survey of a white small-town community that nicely complements his simulated vernacular style. By the mid-1950s, that composer's sonic vision of America had etched itself deeply into the ear of both composers and the general public. The way he imagined the striving and goodness of the nation left an indelible mark on film and television composition, down to the network news lead-ins that reassure us about the bad news we are about to hear. In *Golden Arm*, evoking Copland's customary soundscape and idea of a communal moral center foreshadows Frankie Machine's redemption. It is only natural for this musical element to triumph as Frankie goes off with Molly, heading toward a new life at the film's close. Perhaps they will join the white church-going couples that the music previously accompanied. The absence of jazz here erases even the distant presence of a Black sensibility that Rogers and Manne had provided.[2]

An interpolation that pays tribute to Copland's canny Americanism seems far from Algren's point of view, but perfectly understandable from Hollywood's perspective. But there is another, more striking intervention in the soundtrack of *Golden Arm*. It underlines the pointed poignancy of the missing African-American musical role. Frankie Machine's attempt at rehabilitation is interrupted by a brief imprisonment, and he is dragged to an underground city prison cell. His sidekick and other tiresome characters carry on noisily.

In the novel, Algren obligingly fills out the music for the moment:

To the tune of some old frayed song, offered over and over again by Applejack Katz in his horribly fifty-four-year-old squawk

I'm a ding-dong daddy from Duma
'N you oughta see me do my stuff

Till the other cots would howl him down. (Algren 1949:209)

This Jewish wino's raucous display simply doesn't fit the adaptation's needs. Instead, beneath the cellfolks' chatter, throughout the entire scene, a plaintive Black voice that could only be Paul Robeson's can be heard singing something sounding like a Black spiritual, specifically "Sometimes I Feel Like a Motherless Child." The voice remains disembodied, but is placed precisely in the filmspace by its echo-tinged resonance. Both the scene itself and discussions of Elmer Bernstein's pioneering jazz soundtrack ignore this moment. Its racialized pathos rounds out the film's stubborn silence around Blackness. How does the Robeson sound resonate ethnographically? Paul Robeson burst on the American social scene dramatically in the 1930s, as a bigger-than-life, charismatic African-American male who was an athlete, intellectual, actor, and concert singer who broke color barriers constantly. His progressive politics brought him into conflict with the establishment. By 1956, he would have been fully associated in people's minds with both the powerful sound of Blackness and with political controversy, so his presence in *Golden Arm* might have something to do with a very thorny set of issues in the ethnography of Hollywood's own blacklist-era culture wars. At the same time, the civil rights movement was beginning to crest, with positive connotations for the music of African-American uplift. The sound of the spiritual inevitably conveyed a soulfulness and striving that was understood to be part of American bedrock identity. It appeared in the early 1940s films that Hollywood produced as part of an effort to make Black Americans feel more included in supercultural entertainment (Cripps 1993).

None of this would seem to have anything to do with the world of Frankie Machine, whose life, like his name, seems programmed by his slum environment. Robeson's appearance is surprising and isolated within the film's enclosed music culture, particularly given the absence of any Black musical role models for Frankie's jazz. There is no easy answer to the impact of this moment, but one thing is clear: the only time that Black music occurs, it is placed in a significantly subordinate space—the confines of a prison cell—as a troubled accompaniment to the hero's hard times, even as it is blatantly absent from every scene of streetside vitality and drama. The scene offers musical *erasure* and *replacement,* in that it eliminates Applejack Katz's squawk in favor of other cellblock singing, and introduces an element of *displacement* by repositioning the acoustic space that belongs to the tenement houses and night spots of Algren's African Americans in their Chicago slum. Make of it what you will; this chapter aims at laying out methods, not interpretations.

Let me summarize the difference between Algren's and Preminger/Bernstein's views on the world of Frankie Machine, and how music fits the contrasting patterns. The literary critic Carlo Rotella's fine analysis of *The Man with the Golden Arm* incisively identifies the past-oriented, future-dreading, claustrophobic quality of the book: "the novel's prematurely aging, childless, for the most part unemployed characters move through the once-familiar, once-sustaining neighborhood terrain with the regretful nostalgia of people twice their age" (Rotella 1998:76). This explains Algren's insistence on the constant exchange of scraps of music, mostly salvaged from the past. The Hollywood stake in the neighborhood lies in a more general anxiety about growing urban danger, and suggests that personal responsibility and American opportunity can break the spell of blighted city life. This move toward sermonizing calls for a more top-down, managed approach to music to keep the themes clear and the contamination of America's actual musical complexity and confusion far away from the film's need to organize the neighborhood. So we are not so far from Steiner's *Searchers;* it is just that the terrain of violence, regeneration, and ideology have shifted from the Western to the urban frontier. Indeed, the superculture has taken away, rather than yielded to, the vernacular in this celebrated example of the "jazz score."

The Survivability of the Superculture

Space does not allow for a full exposition of film of the last forty years, from the ethnomusicologists' viewpoint. Still, it can be said that not that much changes over time. Supercultures thrive on predictability and reliability, even more than on novelty. The need for a steady-state cinematic universe has only become more pronounced with the growing trend toward sequels and blockbusters. This section touches on just a couple of the ethnographic methods of the foundational period as they keep marching through time: the erasure of the African-American presence and the role of simulated vernacular music.

More than thirty years after *Man with the Golden Arm,* 1989 saw the release of *The Fabulous Baker Boys,* starring Michelle Pfeiffer and the Bridges brothers (Jeff and Beau), she as a hooker turned cabaret singer and they as contrasting brothers who are stuck with working together as a cocktail-lounge piano duo. Jeff, tall and attractive, wishes he were a jazz piano artist, while Beau is a chunky family man. The plot is paper-thin: The brothers hire Suzie Diamond (Pfeiffer), she and Jack (Jeff Bridges) have a fling, he discovers the artist within and goes off on his own. One type of music dominates the movie from end to end, several versions of what is broadly called "jazz" in recent American music classification: (1) offscreen lightly orchestrated cool jazz for exterior scenes and a couple of mood moments; (2) source recordings of Duke Ellington for Jack and Suzie's growing intimacy; (3) the lounge style of the brothers, pre-Suzie; (4) Suzie's jazz vocals; and (5) the "art" jazz of a Black-run club that is Jack's spiritual home, and that he visits twice. There are no stingers, suspense music, classical allusions, popular music as commentary or source sound, or any other type of familiar underscoring of the narrative. It is in this sense that the blanket—and contested—term "jazz" can cover a range of styles that otherwise might need genre distinctions. The screenplay tells us that all this music is trivial, and that only African Americans can be authentically expressive, but it methodically leaves them out of the score and the action.

Take, for example, the audition scene. This is one of those generic plot moves, a familiar narrative unit that crops up in a variety of works that I call a "narrative knot" below. This particular knot features bored producers watching a chain of hopeless wannabes until they find the future star. In *Baker Boys,* the first tryout gets some time, but then the audition breaks down into two-second snippets to convey the range of candidates, keeping viewers from enjoying the prospect of attractive forms of kitsch and camp. There is exactly one African American in this microsurvey—a stereotypical husky, hyper, woman. All the grotesques need to parade past us so that Suzie Diamond can sparkle when she turns up, late, foul-mouthed, and seemingly incompetent, only to wow the brothers.[3]

Despite its obvious interest in displaying Michelle Pfeiffer, who did her own singing in the film, most notably sprawled across a grand piano in a sultry red gown, *Baker Boys* wants Jack to be the central figure. One of the many Hollywood tropes about American music is the desire of the white musician to be "Black." It is the driving force of *The Jazz Singer* of 1927, and carried the momentum of the later fascination with the Jolson character. The *Baker Boys* seems to borrow directly from a scene in *The Jolson Story* (1946), which marks a figure of inspiration and influence. There, young Al, toiling tediously in a large minstrel show troupe, visits a Black club and picks up new styles that will offer him substance for the desperate urge towards individuality that will earn him a solo career. These inspirational Black-run clubs, including the one in *Baker Boys,* are usually downstairs; the metaphor needs no explanation, and might remind us of Paul Robeson's location in the jailhouse of *Golden Arm.* However, unlike Robeson's invisibility, and the lack of Black presence in *Golden Arm's* nightclub scene, in *The Baker Boys* of over thirty years later, it is the Black club manager who holds the power. At his first visit, the repressed pianist Jack Baker disses the young Black prodigy pianist holding forth, only to have the manager put down Jack by saying that the boy has been a regular at the club for a year—"where have you been, Jack?" Jack's second visit (which thus structurally marks off the whole film into two acts), comes at movie's end, after he has broken with both his brother and the singer Suzie. As he performs moodily at the same piano after hours, the manager pops up from nowhere and offers him Tuesdays and Thursdays, ending the film on a hopeful note. In neither club scene do we get to hear an extended performance; what we do hear of Jack's Black-approved music is nothing special, and is about as generic at the lounge music that Jack is leaving behind. It seems that the authenticity of Black music, with its promise of true originality, trumps the power of the music itself. It is hard to imagine Jack's future music being anywhere near as potent as the Ellington interpolation that plays behind the growing erotic attraction between Suzie and Jack.

The Fabulous Baker Boys can stand in for films that have no real vernacular to simulate, but need standardized musical mythology and musicology anyway. At the same time, the 1980s and 1990s also saw a mini-trend of movies that pay enormous attention to the ethnographic point of view in sometimes exquisite detail. A bushel of bio-pics—film biographies—about country and rock singers (*Coal Miner's Daughter, Sweet Dreams, Great Balls of Fire, The Buddy Holly Story, La Bamba*) stressed the vernacular by revisiting the lives of powerful vocal stars, often falling into familiar patterns and ruts of how to do a movie about a legend. Far more interesting are fiction films that take place in the Appalachian region, the presumed homeland and heartland of old-time American culture and music. The Coen Brothers' *O Brother, Where Art Thou* (2000) even started a boomlet of traditional music covers and reissues. Two contrasting, pre-*Brother* ways of making musical ethnography define John Sayles's *Matewan* (1987) and Maggie Greenwald's *Songcatcher* (1999). The latter actually introduces an ethnomusicologist as the main protagonist. As independent films, neither is burdened by studio or genre expectations, and both make a personal statement about the mythology of mountain people. This would seem to move the discussion away from the studio system, but it is important to see how cultural values spill across easy categories like "industry" and "indie," particularly where music is involved.

Appalachia is the home of the "mountain music" that became "country music" after its discovery and diffusion by records and radio in the 1920s. Outsiders naturally turned toward upland sounds as a way of defining America, through its oral traditions. The first serious fieldwork and publication was done by an Englishman (Cecil Sharp, in 1912) looking for supposedly unsullied versions of Anglo-Saxon balladry. From then on, the metaphor of "roots music" crept into America's sense of itself. The symbolism was badly needed in a country sustaining waves of south-north migration and torn by social strife. The folklorists' 1930s expeditions to country cabins and chain gangs, from Kentucky to Texas, have been well documented, resulting in the impressive archives at the Library of Congress. The work of pioneering collector John Lomax and his entrepeneurial son Alan laid the foundations for both the documentation and the marketing that would end up as the "folk revival" of the 1950s and 1960s. The export of star performers—Black and white—accompanied this rural to urban movement of roots music.

Early sound cinema largely disregarded this heritage-building potential of Southern "folk music," save for carefully orchestrated, progressive documentary, particularly in two filmscores by the composer Virgil Thomson for Pare Lorentz's nonfiction films, *The Plow that Broke the Plains* (1936) and *The River* (1937). The studios paid lip service to downhome sentiments in *The Grapes of Wrath* (1940), the story of the uprooted emigrants of the Dust Bowl period. These works were cousins—sometimes deliberately, usually unconsciously—of Soviet or American leftist "cultural front" attitudes toward "people's music." The older 1930s ideologies filtered through the folk revival of the 1950s and 1960s as part of counterculture sensibility. By the 1970s, independent filmmakers could rethink Appalachia, not in any predetermined way, but as a region full of local color and social struggle in fiction films like *Norma Rae* (1979) and *Matewan* and documentaries such as *Harlan County, USA* (1976). As the maker of *Matewan*, John Sayles, says about his story set in West Virginia coal country, "all the elements and principles involved seemed basic to the idea of what America has become and what it should be. Individualism versus collectivism, the personal and political legacy of racism, the immigrant dream and the reality that greeted it, monopoly capitalism at its most extreme versus American populism at its most violent . . ." (Sayles 1987:10). All this—and the romance of location and colorful characters—could draw in the committed filmmaker. From the 1920s on, Americans strongly equated Appalachia with "old-timey music," the choice of vernacular elements as building blocks for a filmscore became inevitable. *Matewan* and *Songcatcher* are radically different films, but share a passion for local setting and sounds.

John Sayles has long had the freedom to sculpt his own cinematic vision and to be rewarded with the mantle of maverick. He wrote his own book on the making of *Matewan*, which tells the story of a bloody encounter in the 1920s that pitted ethnically diverse, unionizing miners against a homogeneous and brutal band of mine-owner enforcers. Although the book is called *Thinking in Pictures*, it helpfully includes an exact account of music's contribution. Sayles starts with a conventional summary of music's role—it is "added to the images" to "reinforce, underline, counterpoint or deny what is happening on the screen." Like any conventional director, he thinks that "when it works, movie music is like a natural voice, like the only sound the picture up there could possibly make" (Sayles 1987:109). The *Matewan* team was dedicated to aesthetic understatement in matters such as color selection, and the music had to match. But the film's precise ideology dictated distinctive sound choices: "nonverbal musical fusion is the first step in forming a union out of people initially suspicious of each other . . . integration of musical groups has always been a factor in the spread of new musical forms" in America, so each instrumental sound in *Matewan* carries the heavy baggage of ethnography, even as it sprays a mist of mood over the hills and towns of West Virginia.

Sayles avoided the most "obvious" choice, the banjo, because "we felt its bounciness and attack were inappropriate to the mood of the story and kept it out of even the upbeat musical cues" (ibid.:111). *Matewan* tells a tale too dark for this ethnographically correct instrument to carry. Setting aside the question of whether the banjo really was the most popular instrument in mining camps in 1925 (probably not), Sayles let the harmonica and dobro do the work of "underscoring to help set a mood or punctuate a transition from scene to scene." John Hammond, not a local musician, carefully calibrated a vernacular-like harmonica sound that "is sometimes a kind of editorial comment, sometimes the sound of a character's emotional state, sometimes the mood of the shot made into sound. Working with John was similar to working with an actor" (ibid.). Each musical choice came out of painstaking experimentation; for one scene, the composer, Mason Daring, made a number of suggestions, but they were rejected: "a standard fiddle song seemed too jarring, and mixing a guitar in with it gave a buckboard-and-calico feeling we didn't want. The harmonica was too evocative of the deep South and another try with something slower on the fiddle was too lugubrious and menacing. Finally Mason got hold of a dobro . . . a little less southern and bluesy sounding than slide guitar, the dobro turned out to be the right voice for the scene. The notes have a clean liquid attack but bend into a question at the end, sort of a *boinnnng!* What gives here? Who are these people? What happens next?" (ibid.:113). This rejection of the fiddle, like Sayles's other pronouncements, gets to the heart of the methodology of simulating the vernacular: It arises from the filmmakers' assumptions and prejudices. The fiddle is at once "jarring," "lugubrious," and "menacing." Wouldn't that versatility, and the genuine popularity of the instrument in the time and place, make it particularly useful? Eventually, Sayles settles on the fiddle as the voice of the white miners, unintentionally continuing a long tradition of denying Black musicians the instrument as part of their heritage, yet another instance of erasure.

I've quoted Sayles at length because of his precision, which offers illuminating insights into the world of the creative collective. It is usually hard to dig into the minds of the filmmaking team in such technical musical ways. Essentially, the writer-director has provided an unusually candid and detailed account of how a thoughtful filmmaker acts as an ethnomusicologist while really trying hard simply to simulate vernacular music for the purposes of mood and narrative. Usually the solutions are automatic, like a fast-food chef picking the right ingredients from the freezer to make an acceptable lasagna or chocolate-chip cookie, allowing for the cook to add special "secret" spices. How this will be consumed is always a gamble, but it has to satisfy the creative team first and foremost.

Sayles's frank account combines preplanning with intuition, forethought about future audience response with the filmmaker's momentum. This is far from the classic Hollywood studio set-up: summoning a house composer at the very last minute of production and making him cut a score to order. Yet the very cogency and minimalism of Sayles's maverick musicality allows for the kind of standardized cueing that the superculture relies on. If the mandolin stands for Italian workers, harmonica for African Americans, and fiddle for whites, and you select specific "typical" tunes, then the instruments and melodies can become metaphors for social melding: "as the movie progresses, the instruments try to stretch. A country fiddle plays [the Italian worker's song] 'Avanti Populo,' a harmonica bends notes around an Italian mandolin melody, the players move closer to each other, all trying to pick up phrases of a new musical language" (ibid.). At this level, the time-honored Hollywood motif system is extended, not eliminated, as the basis of a filmscore. Even specific moments seem stock, like the singing of a hymn at graveside (cf. *The Searchers*). Just how far an independent filmmaker can crack open the supercultural framework is an open question, especially when it comes to ethnography, perhaps the mostly deeply held of elements, both for the production team and the audience.

Maggie Greenwald's *Songcatcher* offers an almost complete complement to *Matewan*. Together, the two films define the full spectrum of musically manipulating Appalachia, and also reveal the hidden conformities within independent filmmaking. *Songcatcher* takes place a generation before *Matewan*, around 1900, so the future nastiness of mountain life is just over the horizon. The central figure is a self-indulgent ethnomusicologist, Lily, who is miffed at her subordinate role as a woman academic and mistress to a married man, so lights out for the hills to visit her sister Erna's settlement school. Erna is ensconced in a lesbian relationship with a fellow teacher. Thickheadedly, Lily finally learns how songs get the mountain folk through their hard life, literally lets down her hair for a romp with a local singer-songwriter, and gives up her academic life to go off with him to market cylinder recordings of ancient Appalachian ballads to city folk, all this being catalyzed by the mountaineers' violent disapproval of the lesbian couple. *Songcatcher* is highly anachronistic, even as it unfolds unorchestrated folksong in its homespun setting of cabins and dances. Wearing its sisterhood on its sleeve, the film is more about self-fulfillment than the life of the "folk." Much of the perceived ambivalence comes out in the DVD voice-over commentary by the film's director and musical advisor. On the one hand, they take great pains to document the lengths they went to make the music authentic, usually by hiring consultants who are well-known folk revivalists. On the other hand, they talk delightedly about how the young actress Emmy Rossum, from New York, had to be coached thoroughly to approximate a vernacular style.

As always, details and erasures are telling. The filmmakers reduce the immense shaping force of African Americans in mountain music to a tiny cameo appearance. Taj Mahal, a fine blues revivalist and world musician, appears fleetingly as a Black man strumming the banjo beside the guitar-wielding hero. Lilly's main informant, the young girl played by Emmy Rossum, is startled; she claims never to have seen a Black man. Even odder than the near-erasure of Black musicians from the record is the film's conclusion. Lily and her new boyfriend decide to leave the mountains and start a record business based on "hillbilly" styles, at least two decades before talent scouts from the city actually stumbled on the mountain music market in the mid-1920s. Even then, the sales were for rural buyers, not for northern big-city folk, who took until the 1950s to flirt with the idea of a "folk revival."

Like many an independent film, *Songcatcher* skitters nervously between supporting and flaunting convention. Its ethnographic credentials come largely from its extreme care in allowing solo singing to emerge from daily-life contexts. Despite the inevitable staginess of the folksong scenes—even the villain can sing movingly in old-timey style—real pathos emerges when the locals try to sing their way out of hard times. So it is all the more jarring when a stock orchestral filmscore weighs in at moments of danger and eroticism. This distrust of the power of ethnography goes to the heart of recent American film's reluctance to rely on the vernacular, unless it is a Motown song.

The opening and closing musical moments of *Songcatcher,* framing the entire narrative, neatly summarize cinematic ethnomusicology. We first see Lily at a lovely square piano in a finely appointed academic apartment, singing that most studied of all old-time English ballads, "Barbara Allen," in the way she would have learned it: with harmonic accompaniment, sung as a genteel song about olden times. The entire balance of the film follows Lily's awakening to the true nature of ingenuous, unadorned ballad singing; she even briefly hears "Barbara Allen" performed in an old-timey way. After Lily goes down from the mountain with her lover to start her record business, "Barbara Allen" reappears for the closing credits, now in the voice of none other than recording star Emmylou Harris fronting an upbeat instrumental arrangement that helps make a commercial soundtrack album possible for *Songcatcher.* The entire film, then, unfolds as a huge parenthetical clause between a century of marketable versions of "Barbara Allen."

The point of stressing the many ironies of well-made, sympathetic independent films like *Matewan* and *Songcatcher* is not to show the futility of "authentic" musical ethnography in cinema, but rather to uncover the many layers of paint and wallpaper that cover the filmed walls of our musical homes, wherever they are in the world. Extending some of the foregoing analysis to films made elsewhere can move this chapter toward the coming global, crosscultural survey. Two parallel moments in films based on folksongs, from the Soviet Union and China, move the discussion abroad: *Shadows of Forgotten Ancestors* (Sergei Paradjanov, 1964) and *Yellow Earth* (Chen Kaige, 1984). Both come from state-dominated cinemas. We tend to think of Paradjanov and Kaige as auteur directors with their own strong vision, and that is true enough. What interests us here, however, is the way underlying supercultural methods infuse the work of even very original filmmakers.

Shadows came out in the "thaw" period of Soviet culture when directors teased more leeway out of the stubborn socialist system. *Shadows of Forgotten Ancestors* made a splash, both at home and abroad, when it suddenly surfaced. Cultural liberalization under Khrushchev had made it possible for filmmakers to try new techniques and messages that were impossible before. Paradjanov's flair for visual flamboyance (including nudity), surrealism, and ethnic settings with mythic storylines set him off from the state-controlled feel-good youth movies or earnest social statements that echoed past concerns. *Shadows* is set among the Hutsul mountaineers of Ukraine in an unspecified period. Paradjanov's later work moved to the setting of his native Caucasus (he was Armenian), but here he is essaying the ethnography of a people to whom he has no connection. This might say something about the complex relationship among non-Russian peoples in the Soviet Union. The plot is simple enough, and allows for broad strokes of folklorism to paint a wash of peasant grittiness and magical realism over the narrative. Ivan and Marichka try to overcome their families' enmity, but she dies accidentally while rounding up a stray lamb. He is driven nearly mad by grief, is seduced by an earthy nympho woman who cuckolds him. He ends up killing himself. All this is set in a natural and human landscape of extreme pastoralism and dizzying camerawork, with liberal doses of the local folk music. All the instruments make their appearance, from soulful flutes and portentous alphorns to buzzy jew's-harps and scrapy hurdy-gurdys, along with many solo and choral songs.

Paradjanov mixes musical gestures. The lovers get a flute motif, longhorns tend to signal disaster, the hurdy-gurdy is ominous, the jew's-harps are playful, and the songs are either evocative or directly support the action (weddings, for example). In short, we have a careful collection of well-organized sound that conveys a coherent Hutsul ethnomusicology. But

Paradjanov is just as involved in simulating the vernacular as Max Steiner. The question of whether three husky Hutsuls really play jew's-harp trios doesn't come up, or whether they would play the *trembita* horns for so many different occasions. It's rather like the settlers in *The Searchers* singing an all-purpose hymn. The hurdy-gurdy is never physically grounded, appearing much more as a timbre than as an ethnographic presence.

Finally, what do we make of the filmscore, for there is one, even in this countercultural, village-based folktale? It enters at dramatic junctures or, almost randomly, to evoke a mood, and is written in pure Soviet symphonic style, which is to say there are faintly folkloric gestures. The voice of the controlling narrator falls back into its accustomed authoritative mode despite the entire thrust of the film, much as it does in the American film *Songcatcher*. Sometimes the folksong blends into the filmscore, giving two voices to the message. These moments are intriguing for trying to work out the meanings of ethnographic music: When do the locals get their say, in their own context, and when does the voice of authority channel them? We might add to our terminology by talking about *ventriloquization* as a special form of displacement. The authorities may have had a hand in this process, beyond the filmmaker's choices. At a festival of 1960s Soviet film, I asked a director about his interest in vernacular and popular music. He replied that for one of his films, he would have much preferred to use only music familiar to the characters. But in the Ukraine studio that Paradjanov also worked in, the management tended to thrust a composer and a style on the director. Perhaps Paradjanov had no choice.

Paradjanov, even if constrained, was breaking the mold, since his folk are not singing just to support an upbeat Stalinist view of progressive peasantry building the future. His relentlessly naturalistic view of the Hutsuls, which combines sympathy and stereotyping, is novel, and not much seen in the West either at this time. Other late Soviet filmmakers tried out social themes in exotic settings. Since musical ethnography remained a fuzzy zone, individual approaches abounded. One film about the Kyrgyz of Central Asia, *The First Teacher,* allows little local color to seep into the gripping story of an early communist teacher establishing himself in a remote village. A certain socialist/realist/puritanism can curtail an excess of visual or audio display, the opposite of Paradjanov's splashiness. The director finally yields to the collective power of music as the village begins to accept the teacher. We see a bustling marketplace and a community for the first time, and music marks the moment. Once musically defined, the villagers can rally around the hitherto distrusted teacher and the ideology he stands for. Another Kyrgyz-based film of the Thaw period, *July Heat,* bounces off live, local music-making (the local *komuz* lute) against canned

Radio Moscow music to symbolize the tensions around modernization. The action largely takes place within a single, claustrophobic yurt-ful of isolated workers who represent competing ideological tendencies. One character smashes the radio, while the *komuz* player has to leave the tent to stand up for his cultural heritage. The slow experimentation with these themes by Russian filmmakers creating the fictional Other represents one type of non-American exploration into musical ethnography.

A similar transition period in China offers counterpart examples. The films of the 1980s by Fifth Generation directors, who moved from their Chinese training into the Western critical limelight, also play with folk music themes, sometimes in awkward ways. In Chen Kaige's *Yellow Earth* (1984), set in a remote and barren region of China in 1939, Gu Qing, a communist soldier, has embarked on ethnomusicological fieldwork. His task, at which he ultimately fails, is to convert local music sources into communist song fodder. He comes up against the reality of a miserable family in a desolate countryside. "The people" is localized into individuals, particularly a striking peasant girl, Cuqiao, looking for her place in a tense, volatile society. Gu Qing teaches Cuqiao a communist song, which she sings as she defiantly crosses a huge river, intending to escape the fate of a country girl by joining the communists. The river drowns out the song; we do not know her fate.

Rey Chow has written an absorbing and subtle critique not only of *Yellow Earth,* but also its reception (Chow 1995). She sorts out the complex ways that folk music complicates any simple analysis of the film's politics. Chow observes that when we hear Cuqiao's songs, we do not see her singing them: The light is low and her head is averted. The music seems to resound from and through the landscape. This suggests a tension between the girl's interiority and her emblematic ethnographic presence, to put it in my terms rather than Chow's. This strategy is not unlike Paradjanov's way of handling the Hutsuls. Chow also raises the issue of the invisible symphonic accompaniment that overlays Cuqiao's lonely songs. As she says, "the orchestrated backing functions rather like an ideology that tries to subordinate her story to a false—because artificially produced and amplified—sense of harmony with the community" (Chow 1995:100). This cuts close to the bone. Chow is revealing the rather mixed motives of the Fifth Generation filmmakers, who brought new expressive resources and storylines to Chinese film, but stayed within conservative political bounds. In this, their musical approach parallels the Thaw period work of Soviet filmmakers, which both critiqued and supported the dominant cinema system. This short look at musical ethnography helps tease out common threads among late-communist cinema systems. It also speaks to how elements of the old

Steiner world, such as symphonic dominance and musical stereotyping, might help toward building a crossculturally sensitive methodology for film music studies.[4]

Before we leave the work of the superculture, one more trick in its bag needs some comment. In recent decades, the "compilation score" often supplants the older filmscore model. The power of musical ethnography shifts from source or symphonic sound to the popular song, dragged in from its life outside the movie theater.

Some writers think that this practice gives viewers more room for musical pleasure and open-ended interpretation. Anahid Kassabian argues for a radical shift in the way that viewers "identify" with the films they watch. She flags a number of technical ways in which this newer style of fitting music to narrative is looser, so offers more indeterminacy: "pop soundtracks have an aleatory quality—the songs have only a very loose fit with the visuals. These loose matches contribute further to the larger range of identifications possible with pop soundtracks than with classical scores"(Kassabian 2001: 80). She sets up an opposition between filmscores of "assimilation"—the oldtime approach of tightly controlled underscoring—and of "affiliation," where the viewer has more agency, more room for personal fantasy and connection with the characters.

How would you back up this claim? Empirical research would be the way to go, along the lines of a controlled experiment with two types of filmscores and follow-up interviews, but this approach is still foreign to film-music studies. There are hints in secondary sources to gauge how "identification" works on the ground. A random movie review might help. In the *New York Press* in 2001, Armond White is contrasting the pop soundtracks of two new films, *The Royal Tenenbaums,* directed by Wes Anderson, and *Vanilla Sky,* a film by Cameron Crowe. White spins out positions of "identification," along Kassabian's lines:

Crowe's disgrace of his pop music background contrasts with Wes Anderson's felicitous use of pop . . . Crowe uses pop for self-aggrandizement (like a snide rock critic) but *The Royal Tenenbaums'* pop subtext is unusual and special for defying such cynicism . . . [it] pays homage to peculiarly articulated personal visions. Crowe ransacks the rock 'n' roll catalog like a sycophant flattering the economy's key players (and their ugly psyches). That's the ultimate betrayal in a film that sentimentalizes betrayal. (White 2001)

"Peculiarly articulated personal visions" sounds like Kassabian's "affiliation." Certainly, the films he cites offer more openness than, say, John

William's controlling score for *Star Wars*. But as White goes into ever more detail over matters like why *Ruby Tuesday* is or isn't apposite to the dramatic situation of a given scene, I fail to follow the logic. His positions come from a very particular generational and demographic stance different than mine, and he is writing for insider New York readers whom he thinks will come from a similar background, whether they agree with his opinion or not. Pop soundtracks belong to a target market mentality. Like the music for commercials, they are tracking niche groups to whom they can sell a product. Reaction to pop songs tends to fall within demographic lines: Certain consumer groups have ready responses to song types when they have been of the heavily marketed type. This is at its most nakedly posed in commercials that try to link product—say, a car model—with possible buyers by using a song that some target market might like. While the range of identifications may seem broadband, it is in fact more narrow-casted than Kassabian allows. *Star Wars,* on the other hand, was designed for a vast, all-purpose global audience, so it is hardly surprising that it leans on tried-and-true sets of identifications and musical conventions.

Perhaps the compilation score does imply a shift in the methods of the implied ethnomusicologist. Some of the work of ethnography changes hands. The singer—say Ray Charles in *Sleepless in Seattle*—chips in by commenting on what the characters are up to, in a well-known voice and attitude. Scholars seem to know what is going on here, but they disagree. Ian Garwood faults Claudia Gorbman for deciding that "Somewhere over the Rainbow," as sung by Charles, corresponds to the character's feelings. For him, there is a disjunct between Charles's version "sung in the style of aspirational soul," and the "deportment" of the characters (Garwood 2003: 116). This scholarly discourse goes right by the viewer, who probably personalizes a response by deciding how the singer and song work with the images and action. The five voices of the songwriter, the singer, the music supervisor, the viewer, and the critic set up a certain polyphony. All this interpretive activity does seem less authoritarian than the tight control of the Steiner score. To switch to a painting metaphor, the compilation score can be seen as adding additional layers of ethnography onto the prepared surface of the filmed community.

But is it really that different? Listened to another way, the compilation score might even echo the old-fashioned soundtrack. Take this review of a 2005 film, *The Ballad of Jack and Rose:*

The film opens in 1986 with the image of richly hued red flowers seemingly bopping to the music flooding the soundtrack, Screamin' Jay Hawkins's singularly creepy song "I Put a Spell on You." This first version is by Creedence Clearwater Revival and is all growls and lugubriously plodding beats. Sometime later . . . neck-deep in melodrama, we hear the song again, only this time the voice prowling the soundtrack belongs to Nina Simone, a singer whose unhurried phrasing and heat bring the song to a slow boil.   (Dargis 2005)

"We hear the song again" sounds a great deal like Steiner's way of manipulating materials. The song's placement reinforces this impression. It seems to function like a main title, opening the film, so that it conveniently can reappear later to signal a narrative shift. Sometimes compiling just seems like a cheap and easy way to avoid the composed score, without losing the benefits of the tried-and-true system of narrative support and cultural meaning: One could riff on the contrast between the white maleness of Creedence Clearwater and the "prowling" Black femininity of Nina Simone, who brings things "to a slow boil." Steiner might have just switched from trumpet to sax to achieve a similar effect though a comparable cultural coding. To take an even more stolidly supercultural sense of how to interject pop songs, take *Herbie: Fully Loaded* (2005), starring a lively Volkswagen who "muzzles up to a sleek yellow sports car . . . to the sounds of Lionel Richie's 'Hello,'" and who "makes a sudden leap to the sounds of Van Halen's 'Jump'" (Holden 2005). Not much room for viewer identification here.

This strategic sowing of songs crosses genre lines, extending to nonfiction film seamlessly. Even the feature-length documentary has turned to the compilation scheme, for example in 2005's *Enron: The Smartest Guys in the Room.* Director Alex Gibney says this about the film's compilation score: "I wanted it to be like a toe-tapping Greek chorus that would comment on what was going on, even as it exemplified the mood." In citing the Steiner approach to music's way of both underscoring and psychologizing, Gibney offers the example of Billie Holiday's classic "God Bless the Child" for a re-enactment of the suicide of an Enron executive: "Like many aspects of the film, the song has two sides. There's a beautiful melody and then these dark lyrics about power and exploitation" (quoted in DeCurtis 2005). The journalist, De Curtis, waxes eloquent on the possibilities of the pop song in film: "popular music—with its shimmering promises of happiness and everlasting love countered by a fascination with such troubling human instincts as lust, pride and greed—proves an apt medium for the story of Enron's rise and fall" (ibid.). It seems that Wagner's and Mahler's takes on these topics—as filtered through Steiner and his supercultural system—no longer apply.

This short survey of the post-Steiner decades needs to acknowledge the work of some younger film composers who seem to have taken new approaches to adapting non-Western musical resources. The emergence of the world music score in the 1990s reveals the continuing restlessness of composers, always on the lookout for new resources. Mychael Danna's career can act as a guidepost here. Growing up in multicultural Toronto's soundscape and studying some ethnomusicology in college there, he turned naturally to nonsymphonic alternatives in his filmwork. His choices both reinforce and break the mold of the older system. For example, Danna worked on *The Ice Storm* (1997) with non-American Ang Lee, a director with a flair for off-center takes on Western culture. Quietly, Danna's score alternates an Indonesian gamelan sound with the orchestra, giving the viewer a fresh angle on suburban Connecticut wife-swapping and adolescent despair. But convention is not far below the surface. The gamelan slowly yields to the symphonic sound as the film turns toward a tragic conclusion, ending with an orchestral set-piece. Then there is the matter of the American Indian flute. Danna says he wanted "to remind the viewer in a subtle way about nature," an ice storm being the plot's turning point as well as the film's title, and "the sound of a Native American flute was just the perfect sound for that, for me." Below, we will see how Native American directors handle their flute tradition; here it is worth noting that for Danna, "the gamelan ensemble is the same thing. It's a music that, to our Western ears especially, seems more closely related to nature, a natural elemental [sound] almost" (interview on www.MychaelDanna.com). Perhaps this grandson of Steiner is not that far from the older system of "exotic" musical values after all.

Danna is writing the book on how a freelance, globe-trotting composer can experiment with the whole treasurehouse of world musical sounds these days: "Danna's aural adventures have taken him around the globe, and modern technology has allowed him to venture to exotic locales independently." For a film by his regular collaborator Atom Egoyan, the Armenian-Canadian director, Danna says "we're using a studio that's in Armenia, but I'm bringing all my own stuff . . . In Morocco, I ended up setting up in a big empty hotel room and I brought my own power and everything. That's where I end up a lot, looking for these less-traveled paths as music sources" (interview on MychaelDanna.com). Offbeat as he may be, and often working with "accented" directors" like Egoyan and Mira Nair, Danna operates as a personal, portable, plug-in, whole-earth film-music system.

This chapter has exposed just a few weapons in the supercultural system's accumulating arsenal as it battles for audiences. Many more need identification and description, but it is time to summarize and move on:

1. To help ground film narrative and make the filmed human community coherent, the dominant approach to filmmaking relies on music to homogenize and often stereotype ethnographically. Soundtracks also *replace, displace, erase, reject,* and *ventriloquize* the ethnomusicology of the individuals and groups that they depict.

2. Methods, techniques, and even specific items last a long time. The return of the Steiner score in the John Williams era (beginning in the mid-1970s) came as a surprise; some critics decried the film music's "corny romanticism" (Kalinak 1992:198). As Kalinak notes, "for Williams using a late-romantic sound was 'a conscious decision . . . music should have a familiar emotional ring so that as you looked at these strange robots and other unearthly creatures, at sights hitherto unseen, the music would be rooted in familiar traditions'" (ibid.). This combination of the new techno-visuality of special effects and the time-tested musical underpinning has stuck with the blockbuster for thirty years now, as witnessed by Howard Shore's remarks, cited above, about his own trilogy score, for *Lord of the Rings.*

3. Approaches, images, and stock set-ups from the American superculture also spread rapidly and durably to other global cinema systems. As Stokes says below for the Egyptian films of Abd al-Halim, "the conventions at play here are rooted in [the local concepts of] *tarab* and *turath,* but they also assume a familiarity with the American dance styles and genres of the 1940s and 1950s . . . a listener with some knowledge of the rhetorical flourishes of nineteenth century Western orchestral art music also seems to be assumed." Stokes's inclusion of both the popular and classical components of the supercultural system is significant.

4. The superculture is neither monolithic nor omnipotent, even in a state-run cinema system. Stray and systematic cracks allow for variation and even subversion, and this itself is part of the system. It needs variety and novelty, as well as uniformity, to survive. As we turn to the subcultures sometimes embedded in mainstream national cinemas, we will see how a complex interplay of sometimes dissenting voices breaks up movie monologism, within even a single society.

Notes

1. Shelly Manne's music for the *Daktari* soundtrack is worth listening to for its proto-world-music-soundtrack qualities. At the same time, *George of the Jungle,* a television cartoon Tarzan spoof that ran on Saturday mornings in 1967–1968, fused "jungle" drums, "Indian" parallel fourths, and jazz elements to create a familiar, encyclopedically stereotypical, effect. The 1997 big-screen version of *George* features numerous scenes of gorilla drummers. A single unit of

music-cultural caricature can run for decades in mass entertainment. Hiring a white South African pop artist, Johnny Clegg, for the film's songs and adding Latin music touches helps to move the soundtrack away from the heavy black stereotyping of the visual track.

2. Since writing this section, I became aware of Krin Gabbard's *Black Magic: White Hollywood and African American Culture*, which extends issues of Black erasure and invisibility in Hollywood down to recent films. He highlights the unacknowledged Black voice of Sarah Vaughan as the clincher for the romantic ending of the film *Wonderland* (1998), which "continues a long tradition of concealing the achievements of black people . . . the film relies upon the magic of Vaughan's voice but discards the rest" (Gabbard 2004:5). The subtle overlaps and differences between the Vaughan appearance and the Robeson interpolation indicate the complexity of analyzing this type of filmwork. I also am not sure that Gabbard's term "colonizing" adequately covers the ethnomusicology of Frankie Machine's white jazz milieu, either in the novel or the film. Gabbard echoes my interest in scenes like the Black nightclub's transforming presence in *The Fabulous Baker Boys*, discussed below, pointing out that "African Americans radically transform the lives of white characters, usually providing them with romance and gravitas" (ibid.:6).

3. How to read Suzie Diamond as a figure is not immediately obvious. We can see a kind of *Pretty Woman* upward climb of the talented hooker, but any social meaning seems a stretch. Suzie's life remains a vacuum; we know as little about her at film's end as we did when she first walked in. Nevertheless, the film's performance moments are crafted perfectly to make her singing body the centerpiece of a ramshackle film. Part of a complete history of film music would pay considerable attention to the ethnography of gendered music, particularly when performing women take over the screen. Surprisingly, the enormous interest over the last twenty years of the "new musicology" in opera as gendered drama has yet to transfer to a more important modern medium, film.

4. Another way to think about the films discussed in this section would be to tackle the score versus source issue relationship more comprehensively. Nowhere is this more sharply posed than in the attempt by the renowned sound designer Walter Murch to retrofit Orson Welles's musical intentions for *The Touch of Evil*, forty years after Universal Studio's 1957 decision to take artistic control of the film, including installing a Henry Mancini score. Murch (2003) describes how he worked from Welles's 58-page indignant letter where the director reveals that for the opening sequence, he wanted nothing but overlapping Mexican and American vernacular music coming out of the bars and streets of the border towns depicted. Mancini's score incorporates a certain hip Latin edginess effectively, but viewing the scene both ways, as DVD now makes possible, strikingly condenses the visual, sonic, aesthetic, and dramatic difference between an authoritative score and a simulated vernacular source-music approach.

Works Cited

Algren, Nelson. 1949. *The Man with the Golden Arm*. New York: Doubleday.
Bernstein, Elmer. 1956. "The Man with the Golden Arm." *Film Music* 15, no. 4: 3–13.
Chow, Rey. 1995. *Primitive Passions: Visuality, Sexuality, Ethnography, and Contemporary Chinese Cinema*. New York: Columbia University Press.
Cripps, Thomas. 1993. *Making Movies Black: The Hollywood Message Movie from World War II to the Civil Rights Era*. New York: Oxford University Press.

Dargis, Manohla. 2005. "A 60's Holdout and His Daughter, Living on an Island, Searching for an Epic." *New York Times,* March 25.

De Curtis, Anthony. 2005. "The Unlikely Greek Chorus Singing the Enron Blues." *New York Times,* April 17.

Donohue, H. E. F. 1964. *Conversations with Nelson Algren.* New York: Hill and Wang.

Gabbard, Krin. 1996. *Jammin' at the Margins: Jazz and American Cinema.* Chicago: University of Chicago Press.

———. 2004. *Black Magic: White Hollywood and African American Culture.* New Brunswick: Rutgers University Press.

Garwood, Ian. 2003. "Must You Remember This? Orchestrating the 'Standard' Pop Song in *Sleepless in Seattle,*" in *Movie Music: The Film Reader,* ed. Kay Dickinson, 109-18. London: Routledge.

Holden, Stephen. 2005. "Lord Love a VW Bug that Knows Its Mind." *New York Times,* June 22.

Kalinak, Kathryn. 1992. *Settling the Score: Music and the Classical Hollywood Film.* Madison: University of Wisconsin Press.

Kassabian, Anahid. 2000. *Hearing Film: Tracking Identifications in Contemporary Hollywood Music.* London: Routledge.

Murch, Walter. 2003. "Touch of Silence," in *Soundscape: The School of Sound Lectures, 1998–2001,* ed. L. Sider, D. Freeman, and J. Sider, 83-102. London and New York: Wallflower Press.

Rotella, Carlo. 1998. *October Cities: The Redevelopment of Urban Literature.* Berkeley: University of California Press.

Sayles, John. 1987. *Thinking in Pictures: The Making of the Movie "Matewan."* Boston: Houghton Mifflin.

Shindo, Charles J. 1997. *Dust Bowl Migrants in the American Imagination.* Lawrence: University Press of Kansas.

Smith, Jeff. 1998. *The Sounds of Commerce.* New York: Columbia University Press.

Stam, Robert. 2005. "Introduction: The Theory and Practice of Adaptation," in *Literature and Film: The Theory and Practice of Adaptation,* ed. R. Stam and A. Raengo. Oxford: Blackwell.

Stevens, Leith. 1954. "The Wild One." *Film Music* 13, no. 3: 3-7.

White, Armond. 2001. Review of: "The Royal Tenenbaums," *New York Sun,* October 21.

MARK SLOBIN

Subcultural Filmways

·◈·

Subcultural cinemas are the work of insiders who take the camera into their own hands with the firm intention of telling stories about small groups embedded within larger societies. These artists know the power of mainstream moviemaking all too well, but also understand how to channel expertise, and possibly funding, into their own expressive flow. The range of subcultural film practice worldwide is too vast to encompass here, and even the overall story for the United States has yet to be assessed or written about in any thorough way. Specialized studies of the American scene date only from the mid-1980s, and not much has been written about anyplace else, particularly for music.

This chapter provides some grounding for subcultural film music through a short account of two pioneering traditions: the "race " film of African Americans and the "Yiddish" film of Jewish Americans of the 1930s. Then it moves to a consideration of two more recent films, about New York Puerto Ricans and Oklahoma Native Americans, to extend the chronological and ethnic frame of reference.

Both Jews and Blacks began self-representation in the 1910s. The inclusion of readily identifiable soundscapes enriched the meager possibilities of their films' budget and appeal. These two large and influential U.S. minorities had the drive and the audience size to represent themselves in ways that radically reformulated the stereotypes of Hollywood. American film had been offering lopsided and ludicrous images of both groups since the very beginnings (Bogle 1991, Erens 1984). We also can see and hear real differences within early subcultural cinema, and this individuality will mark the later flowering of their successor systems from the 1960s on, among them Asian American, Native American, Latino, gay and lesbian, and a revived African-American presence. The passion to set up both a counternarrative and a corrective to mainstream moviemaking marks all these enterprises. So does a tendency to be underfunded, overlooked, and, eventually, co-opted, once the audience or the stars register on the radar screen of the industry.

For race film, we will look at the most-studied and appreciated figure of the movement, Oscar Micheaux, now the subject of several book-length studies (Bowser 2000, Green 2000) and video reissues.

A case study of one of his classic sound films, *The Girl from Chicago* (1932) can move us into Micheaux's world and at least hint at the complexity of trying to understand early subcultural cinema. *The Girl from Chicago* opens in the South, among members of a small-town Black community called Batesburg, then moves to Harlem, along with two scenes on an ocean liner. Alonzo, a Black secret service agent, apprehends the evil Ballinger in Batesburg, falls in love with the local teacher Norma, and the couple moves to Harlem to start married life. Another local girl, Mary Austin, a talented singer, is also Harlem-bound, where she finds work in a nightclub. Alonzo saves Mary from a false murder charge that should have been laid to Liza, Ballinger's heartless mistress. The film features several on-screen shootings and a healthy number of performances of music and dance. Here is the total list of Micheaux's musical resources: Canned ballet music for the main title and opening; Mary sings and plays on the local parlor piano twice; Another Batesburg character, Wade Washington, sings at the piano; Canned ballet music for Alonzo and Norma's ripening love; Same theme used for Liza leaving Batesburg; Harlem nightclub music: chorus line, novelty number, Mary sings; Dramatic canned symphonic excerpt when Mary is charged with murder; Happy canned symphonic excerpt for closing shot of Alonzo and Norma in love.

Clearly, Micheaux is not following the supercultural model. The music is very sparsely and unevenly applied to the narrative. It "makes no sense" in conventional terms to have a throw-away character like Washington sing a whole song, have Mary perform two songs in Batesburg and only one in Harlem, bring in the same ballet excerpt for very different narrative moments, and omit music for every moment of tension or murder scene (not even a punctuating "stinger" chord). Either we have to judge Micheaux simply to be amateurish, or to conclude that he is following his own model. The "amateur" issue is not trivial, since it can be an easy critique of the subcultural arts. Like the music, the camerawork and editing are similarly way off the Hollywood norm, hinting at an overall aesthetic or lack of experience. Above all, the shoestring budget that Micheaux worked on gives us pause. As with much regional and subcultural film, the sheer financial impossibility of offering audiences high production values needs always to be taken into account, along with aesthetic and social issues. In a film documentary on Micheaux (Bowser and Cran 1994), one of his actresses recalls how his crew borrowed a fur coat from a visitor to use as a costume for a shot while the director kept the woman busy in his office. It was the only way he could get his hands on a quality coat.

Ronald Green has thought through some of these questions: "Since Micheaux was not able to deploy high production values as *signifiers* because he could not afford them, he deployed *signifiers* of high production values," he writes (Green 2000:77). Green compares this to a Japanese Buddhist aesthetic: if you can't afford to build a temple, placing a pebble piously will have the same effect. So Green thinks that Micheaux's decisions, such as not "wallpapering" an entire movie or even whole sequences with background music, "emphasized rather than papered over the real world outside the story . . . the threshold of entry into illusion is higher in Micheaux's films than is prescribed by the Hollywood standard." Part of this is purely logistical: "race film producers [lacked] capital or time to allow them to move cast and crew to shoot on location in Harlem" (Masood 2003:65). Creating authenticity the way the superculture does it, through attention to location and art direction, was simply out of the question. Green sees this dilemma of Micheaux's substandard production values as "an index of his own economic and ethnic predicament as a filmmaker at the time" and of "the high-and-low bracketing structure identified in the narrative positioning of the characters"(ibid.:76–77). In other words, the half-fulfilled mission to deliver a seamless and integrating narrative is a metaphor for both the characters' and Micheaux's social situation, as well as that of the moviegoers of race film.

This is an ingenious argument, if a bit forced. It leaves out the complexity of the musical choices. The parlor songs in *The Girl from Chicago* do not fit this model. Those performances seem to show small-town Blacks as having a comfortable music life that is neither mainstream American nor rough-edged urban Black. They break the rhythm of the already jumpy plotline deliberately, creating a particular pacing, and are shot in an intimate way. Arthur Jafa, a noted African-American cinematographer, expresses his response to Micheaux's practice more musically. Writing about *Ten Minutes to Live,* he gropes for a descriptive vocabulary, and ends up with a jazz analogy:

the shape of the thing is so amazing. That film—I understand it in terms of volumes that contract and expand, but I can't get too much more precise than this. It's largely felt. It's how he juxtaposes short sequences with long drawn-out sequences, then short, then long . . . it's all got this rhythm and timing that's completely like Thelonious Monk. Is it accidental? Perhaps. Is it aesthetically arbitrary? I'm sorry, I don't think so. (Jafa 2001:14)

Aside from the fact that Jafa turns to music—Monk's offbeat moves—rather than Japanese aesthetics as a metaphor for Micheaux's work, what is striking about his assessment is how it grasps at words like "volumes," "rhythm," and "timing" for the overall effect, which is "largely felt" rather than perceived as precise narrative architecture. Micheaux's musical sensitivity pulls in this direction as well.

I would prefer not to see Micheaux as an isolated, ethnic, idiosyncratic figure—a kind of Black rugged individualist, perhaps comparable to a Thelonious Monk. We need to locate Micheaux in his period of cinema history. Both *The Girl from Chicago* and *Ten Minutes to Live* date from 1932. This is a year when Max Steiner was only beginning to figure out what Hollywood's standard practice would be. As we have seen, his own earliest efforts from this period, for example *Bird of Paradise,* are tentative. His work on *King Kong* is uneven, just as its editing seems jumpy and its pasted-in dinosaur and gorilla figures clump clumsily, if endearingly, through jungle and urban landscapes. Kathryn Kalinak summarizes the state of Hollywood's filmscore progress this way: "Film music initially responded to the upheaval presaged by technology without generating a definitive model . . . lacking conventions for treating music, the industry often turned to what was expedient (Kalinak 1992:68)." Hollywood only got a grip on itself when technology allowed it to do so: "The classical Hollywood film score awaited the technological progress which offered the possibility of sound mixing . . . and the attendant changes in aesthetics and economics which stabilized the viewing experience" (ibid.). This stabilization process was unreachable for a subcultural figure such as Micheaux, who had to continue doing "what was expedient."

Within early Hollywood sound film, the work of a Micheaux contemporary like Ruben Mamoulian puts things into perspective. Mamoulian's 1929 talkie *Applause* has been cited by many (e.g., Fischer 1980) as a pioneering effort to integrate music into the emerging notion of soundtrack. For example, the director made a breakthrough by having a split-screen view of contrasting songs, simultaneously showing the mother's burlesque bawdiness and her daughter's "Ave Maria." For all that film's sophisticated interest in sound, today it looks as raw and jumpy as Micheaux. A scene in *Applause* where the innocent heroine arrives in New York nearly doubles the parallel moment in Micheaux's 1932 *Ten Minutes to Live,* complete with disjunct camerawork and awkwardly pasted-in street sounds. As Mamoulian himself put it, "in *Applause,* unfortunately, the traffic noises had to be made on the set. It was pathetic, and it still is pathetic when I hear it" (Mamoulian 1980:90). The way Mamoulian's crude burlesque stagings interrupt the narrative, with the cuts back and forth from the audience to the stage, reminds one of Micheaux's Harlem nightclub scenes. And both film-makers highlight the heroine's wavering between the immoral nightlife world and the solid, stolid man who offers the dream of stable gentility.

Of course, Mamoulian's mainstream audience would consume the sights and sounds of *Applause* very differently than the way Micheaux's segregated subcultural filmgoers responded to his offerings. In a sense, Micheaux's milieu was more stable. He deeply understood the taste and expectations of the poor Black audiences who came to see his films. Mamoulian, however, was fumbling for his footing in his first film, scrambling to revamp his training in Russian theater and Broadway shows for a demanding but undefined audience. But the medium that the technology and aesthetic of 1930 made available to both filmmakers evoked similar artistic strategies, ones that underscore music's new, if unpolished, potential and power as not just a storytelling device, but as an intuitive way to feel film.

Micheaux and his race-film colleagues chose to keep their films within a subcultural space, while allowing the music to reference both in-group and supercultural sounds and methods. As a result, they lost out when Hollywood took over the Harlem nightclub as a central scene, since mainstream moviemakers could afford to hire away the best talent and raise the production values (Cripps 1993). In the late 1930s, Jewish-American filmmakers who tried to float an in-group cinema faced issues that were both similar and different. Like Black artists, they had been trying for some time to sustain an in-group cinema in the shadow of the dominant system. This was perhaps ironic, and very far from the Black situation, in that the Hollywood studios themselves were dominated by the very same generation of Jews who were trying to make an indie cinema based in the Yiddish language and ethnic experience. During the short but intense heyday of the Yiddish film, its creative spirits sometimes chose to emulate the superculture, most notably in films set in New York or in musicals that carefully paralleled the tone and structure of Hollywood's approach. Unlike the African-American struggle for recognition, Jewish entertainers already had vaulted to the top of American pop culture, so they were not about to star in fly-by-night ethnic melodramas.

In trying to track the extremely intricate web of supercultural-subcultural reflections in the Jewish case, we will compare and contrast two films about sons of cantors, the sacred singers hired by congregations to make services seem transcendental, rather than everyday. One film is an earth-shaking Hollywood production and the other an obscure Yiddish melodrama. They date from the period now called "The Golden Age of the Cantorate," when immigrant congregations paid top dollar to lure the finest singers. Both movies draw on images of prayer shawl–clad men deep in religious observance, a visual trope that acted as a label for the Jews in many American and European media even in the silent film era. Being able to put sacred song and the figure of the cantor into the soundtrack became an attractive possibility. It found its place as part of one of the most striking events of film history, when in 1927 a shaky studio called Warner Brothers released *The Jazz Singer,* starring Al Jolson, the top-grossing American stage performer. The film's success became the engine that drove the irreversible dominance of the sound film, worldwide, and changed the whole idea of film music. Widely discussed in the American studies and film studies literature (e.g. Rogan 1996), *The Jazz Singer* also holds a special place in this chapter's concept of subcultural film music.

In trying to understand the complicated and intense relationship between the superculture and subculture, what could be more helpful than a movie starring an immigrant, dealing with the dilemma of ethnicity versus assimilation, and deploying both vaudeville and sacred song as musical resources? Add to this the star's own ambivalent status and you have a heady mix. In fact, Jolson was the son of a cantor, just like the film's hero, and the film pretends to be a biopic, even though it distorts the star's own life story. The film, based on a recent Broadway play, tells the tale of Jakie Rabinowitz, who leaves his doting mom and abusive dad to seek fame on the vaudeville trail. In the process, he learns to perform in blackface and to gain the love of a non-Jewish dancer. On the eve of his debut, the "ghetto" begs him to stand in for his ailing father, as it is Yom Kippur, the holiest day of the Jewish year and the moment to sing "Kol Nidre," the most eagerly awaited performed prayer of the year. True to the Hollywood musical's insistence on the inevitability of happiness, *The Jazz Singer* allows Jakie (now Jack Robin) both to sing in dad's place and to have a triumphant opening night. The film ends with him singing Jolson's signature song, "Mammy," in blackface at his real-life concert venue, the Winter Garden, while his Jewish mammy beams in the audience and his girlfriend watches in the wings adoringly.

Musically, *The Jazz Singer* doubly co-opts the cantor, an easy sonic and visual icon of ethnicity for film. Yossele Rosenblatt, the most important cantorial superstar and Jewish recording artist of the day, appears as the voice of the hero's father. Rosenblatt, who used to spurn non-sacred appearances, was forced by financial pressures to appear on the vaudeville stage and took a huge fee for the film. Next, we see Rosenblatt sing a non-liturgical number, a sentimental Yiddish song about holding fast to your Jewishness, on a secular stage, which Jakie/Jack listens to in an anguished daze of self-doubt, and finally we see and hear Jolson, American's most popular performer, singing in the synagogue in place of his ailing father.

The musical contrast of the two "Kol Nidre" performances, starring Rosenblatt's operatically tinged cantorial pathos and Jolson's pop crooning emotionalism, is fascinating in itself. *The Jazz Singer* also featured Jolson doing mainstream pop numbers, but it was the inclusion of not only down-home, but deeply sacred ethnic music, the sentimental storyline, and the prestige and pride of seeing the in-group star that drew Jews in droves to *The Jazz Singer* and helped to fuel its enormous, epoch-making success. A contemporary Jewish-American magazine describes the scene:

This is in effect "old home week" for the East Side at the Warner Theatre in New York, where the "Jazz Singer" is now being shown and probably will continue to be shown for many months. These are audiences who murmur joyfully at flashing scenes of congested pushcarts and tenements, who roar with glee over the screen captions of *shiksa* and *kibitzer;* who sob unashamed. (Popkin 1927)

It is not just in its heavy deployment of sacred song that *The Jazz Singer* straddles the subculture-superculture line. The mother-son romance that is at the heart of the plot cuts both ways, as it already had been a key theme in American popular song for decades, largely in the form of the Irish mother song. There is one of those on the film's soundtrack, written by Jolson himself. Sometimes unnoticed in commentary on this famous film, the orchestral score offers as many clues as do the few live-music segments: The film is actually "silent" most of the time, since putting in on-location music was extremely expensive and cumbersome. For the love story between Jakie/Jack and Mama Rabinowitz, the arranger selected nothing less than Tchaikovsky's music for *Romeo and Juliet,* a Freudian choice. To accompany the opening documentary footage of New York's teeming Lower East Side, he picked an Irish-based popular song, *East Side, West Side, All Around the Town.* This choice helps to generalizes the film beyond the Jewish case, making it a broader statement about immigration and assimilation. Much of the score, like the Tchaikovsky, brings the authority of classical music to bear, such as Lalo's *Symphonie Espagnole.* Its minor-key poignancy comes from another attempt at harnessing the exotic, the French craze for Spanish settings (think *Carmen*). The transfer of one orientalist fantasy for another—the Jews were understood as not just as East Side but also mysterious East—forms just one link in Hollywood's chain of musical free association.

There is little Jewish-labeled music beyond "Kol Nidre," except during an extended scene of the squabbling synagogue board, trying to figure out who could replace Jakie/Jack's incapacitated father. This tune is a Hasidic song, strongly marked by what listeners would have heard as comic orientalism, even though the board members are not black-hat ultra-Orthodox Jews. The scene, and the actors' performance, comes straight out of the

Yiddish theater tradition, with its broad comedy and in-group satires. The appearance of such a strongly marked cameo, so authentically done, signals the blurriness of the subculture-superculture line, particularly when an urban ethnic audience is a significant part of the target market. That market was paying attention. In 1931, Cantor Leybele Waldman, a popular performer, starred in a short Yiddish film called *The Cantor's Audition* (video title: *A Cantor on Trial*). It presents a synagogue committee like the one in *The Jazz Singer,* for whom a succession of cantors, all played by Waldman, trots out their special style, one more satiric than the next. The winner is the one who sings in American pop style, clearly trading on issues that *The Jazz Singer* raises.

While *The Jazz Singer* moves in and out of the subcultural scene, the directors of Jewish-American films often chose to remain completely within an ethnic musical world. After all, the only audience they had, as in the case of race film, was an in-house, small-scale, underfunded market. Keeping films in Yiddish meant they were even more restricted than African-American cinema, but there were nevertheless more possibilities of selling the product. Until 1939, when World War II and the Holocaust put an end to the possibility of a transnational ethnic cinema, Yiddish films could appeal to both the European and American diasporas. They had abundant musical resources and settings to draw upon. They even managed to film on location abroad, as in the justly renowned musical *Yidl mitn fidl,* for which an American cast joined a Polish one in 1938 to create a double-diaspora feature. Since the Depression was even deeper in Eastern Europe than in New York, costs stayed down, as *Yidl* did by shooting in the largely Jewish town of Kazimierz Dolny. To stage the long wedding sequence in mid-film, the crew simply told the hungry townsfolk to turn up and behave as at a real wedding, and then generously fed the locals. The resulting scene has left us with the only extended Polish-Jewish dance sequence on film. What was just a fiction-film segment ended up not only ethnographic, but deeply ironic and poignant in the light of the imminent destruction by the Germans of both the wedding guests and their entire culture.

In the United States, Yiddish-language films combined a spunky Americaness with a sentimental European sensibility targeted at an older audience who combined nostalgia with fears of assimilation. As a result, many of the great Yiddish films stand out for their intensely conservative acting style, narrative thrust, and musical expression. Deeply New York–centered, they stand as an island in a sea of Hollywood and Broadway products that lapped around their shores, particularly since the Jewish audience-driven success of *The Jazz Singer* brought the superculture so close to home. Like a national cinema in other lands, the Jewish-American film could rely on a vernacular language and down-home cast to keep itself locally viable. Eventually, the drive toward assimilation, the end of immigration, and the hurricane of the Holocaust eroded this cinematic sandbar, just as race film was also dissolving into the main current of American film.

A survey of one Yiddish film of 1940, *The Cantor's Son*, reveals a rhetoric of nostalgia that relies heavily on music. The movie's ethnography of genres, venues, and meanings is grounded in the subcultural setting. But the overall effect is to create a fantasy world of anti-assimilation and survival of Old World values. By its very title, *The Cantor's Son* offers a mirror-image to *The Jazz Singer*. The charismatic, multitalented Moishe Oysher, the Yiddish star of *The Cantor's Son*, was the worthy in-group foil for Jolson. Oysher radiated a certain sultry sensuality, even while singing virtuoso cantorial numbers. Sometimes arch-conservative congregations that hankered for his golden voice boycotted him anyway (Hoberman 1991). He starred in several films and, like the film's hero, was a hit both in live performances and on ethnic radio, an important venue of in-group expressivity. Florence Weiss, his co-star, was in fact a singing partner of Oysher's. The real life–film life parallels recall the loose biographical overlap of star and script that made *The Jazz Singer* vibrate. So does the question the plot poses of whether the hero will stay close to his cantorial forefathers or move out into showbiz territory. Here the similarity runs headlong into an ethnic boundary. The film affords just as few supercultural music or career possibilities for Moishe Oysher as he had in real life; he never became a cross-over star. The conflict is played out as a preference for Europe over America, as symbolized by the hero's choice of both women and song repertoires.

A quick summary of the narrative and musical types is in order. We meet the hero, Saul, as a boy back in Belz, the semi-legendary East European town about whom the most famous nostalgic Yiddish song was written ("Mayn shtetele Belz," "My little town, Belz"). In an opening scene that closely parallels the one in *The Jazz Singer*, Saul's cantor father will not brook departure from family tradition, threatening to whip the boy with his belt, stopped only by the mother's intercession. She had just dragged the boy home from singing with a traveling group of Yiddish theater actors. As in the Hollywood film, the father's beatings lead the youngster to run away to seek his future in show business. This section of the movie leaves room for some cantorial scenes and the very accurate rehearsal of the theater group in an early classic, Abraham Goldfadn's 1880s biblical opera *Akeydas yitskhok* ("The Sacrifice of Isaac"). But early in the movie *The Cantor's Son* parts company with *The Jazz Singer* by giving the hero a Jewish girlfriend, his childhood sweetheart Rifke. The supportive theater troupe figures as a loving substitute family. When the company moves to America, it is New York that disappoints, not the actors. Young Saul's surrogate mother dies and, fifteen years later, we find him alone and broke. The star singer Helen offers him a job as a janitor in a Jewish nightclub, from which he quickly rises to become her co-star. The cabaret music is decidedly conservative. When we meet Helen, she is rehearsing "Ikh hob dikh tsufil lib," a Yiddish classic torch song. The pianist wants to take it at up-tempo tango speed, but she waves him off: "this isn't jazz," she says, and proceeds to croon the song at an unusually leisurely pace. We are far from *The Jazz Singer* now. When Saul wins over the audience and is offered a radio contract, he insists on singing the deepest number imaginable for his broadcast debut: "Ov harakhamim," a Hebrew prayer chanted at funerals. The liveliest number of the film is the Oysher-Weiss duet based on the nonsense syllables of lively Hasidic dance tunes, a real Old World sound. Nowhere in the film do we hear Jewish big band music, the actual in-group pop sound of 1940, let alone "American" mainstream music. Saul doesn't swing.

Finally, the plot takes us back to Belz, where Saul makes a nostalgic visit. After some powerful cantorials in his father's synagogue, he reconnects to Rifke, whom he decides to marry, spurning the New Yorker, Helen, who has traveled all the way to Belz to win Saul back. She resigns herself to abandonment. Whether Saul and Rifke will go back to New York remains open, much as the original pre-Hollywood, 1925 Broadway version of *The Jazz Singer* left its hero poised between the synagogue and the stage. The balance probably tips toward Europe, as J. Hoberman notes: "the New World recedes to but an inexplicable interlude." This anti-Americanism continues director Goldin's thinking; in his "two previous features, America was associated with economic exploitation and the failure of community. Here it carries aspects of inauthenticity. 'I tried to find my real self but I couldn't,' Oysher tells [Rifke]" (Hoberman 1991:265).[1]

Filmscores like *The Cantor's Son* sit comfortably in a setting of in-house popular music. But the echoes of the *Jazz Singer* reveal how deliberately the filmmakers are creating a counternarrative, as mediated through the figure of the singing star. Across a wide range of subcultural film, the superculture has seeped so much into consciousness as to be taken for granted. For its part, the mainstream anticipates this dialogue with the subculture. *The Jazz Singer* itself might be seen as a way of gaining a foothold in the New York ethnic market. Table 1 compares and contrasts the two films.

The interactive pattern of mainstream and subculture by way of filmscore reached a milestone in the "blaxploitation" films of the early 1970s. After the defiantly subcultural rage of Melvin Van Peebles's *Sweet Sweetback's*

Table I.

Comparison of The Jazz Singer *(1927) and* The Cantor's Son *(1940)*

The Jazz Singer	The Cantor's Son
hero is a real-life Broadway star	hero is a real-life ethnic star
star's father was a cantor	star is a cantor
hero flees abusive, anti-show biz father	hero flees abusive anti-show biz father
hero becomes Broadway star	hero becomes ethnic star
hero has non-Jewish girlfriend	hero leaves Americanized ethnic girl friend for hometown girl
hero ends up as Broadway star and cantor	hero ends up as ethnic star and cantor

Baadaaass Song (1971) scored with a funky soundtrack, Hollywood hired musicians like Isaac Hayes to one-up the score in an attempt to appeal to both a Black and a white audience, with considerable success. In these exchanges, each side wins and loses ground in the constant cultural skirmishes that mark American film as a metaphor for the larger society, and music can often be a principal player in the game.

The rising power of "ethnic identity" since the 1970s has allowed new directors to ride this wave and create beachheads on the shores of the superculture (Noriega 1992, Berg 2002, Feng 2002). Either as immigrants or as part of heritage reaffiliation, these filmmakers have taken up a sweeping variety of positions and wealth of narratives to express their individual and subcultural stances. They deploy music strategically in more ways than we can take account of here; the subject merits a book-length study. A recent book on Asian-American cinema points to "a dynamic relationship between mainstream and marginal cinemas" where both sides may trade in positive and negative representations as part of an intense interaction that defies simple analysis (Feng 2002:5). We will consider just two, very disparate examples to show a range of possibilities: *Crossover Dreams* (Leon Ichaso, 1985) and *Doe Boy* (Randy Redroad, 2001). The two films share very little, in terms of setting, themes, or musical philosophy, beyond a strong drive to make a subcultural statement.

Crossover Dreams combines two Latino talents: Leon Ichaso, the director, is a Cuban immigrant and experienced director (starting with *El Super,* 1978), whereas the Panamanian star, Ruben Blades, came to the film as a first-time actor but a renowned New York–based musician. This allows the film to boast an insider sense about the ethnic and cross-over music biz while keeping an art cinema feel. *Crossover Dreams* lays out all the problems of trying and failing to make it in the mainstream, while it stays literally upbeat about music as a force for individual survival and cultural continuity.

In some ways it echoes the concerns of earlier Yiddish cinema, such as the cross-over predicaments of *Overture to Glory* (discussed below), where the nineteenth-century synagogue singer gains an opera career but loses his family, and *The Cantor's Son,* with its conflicted hero, who rejects the Americanization of his life and career. Rudy Veloz, in *Crossover Dreams,* fails in his dealings with the record industry, loses his woman to an American dentist, but manages to escape from the drug-selling world back to the barrio and return, chastened, to his work as a salsa musician. These parallels and overlaps only confirm the ways that subcultural films often reinforce certain basic patterns, including narrative, values, the appearance of music, and the destiny of the musician, as metaphors for a group's struggle to find its way in the United States. No wonder: all these films benefit enormously from the vitality of the in-group music-making and charismatic musicians, from Moishe Oysher to Ruben Blades. The resulting products can please critics such as Vincent Canby, who reports in his 1985 review of *Crossover Dreams* that the film has "moments of pathos, but [is] anything but melancholy. Its heart has the ebullient salsa beat" (Canby 1985). The fact that Blades could draw on his own experience as a New York musician offers true testimony to the power that *The Jazz Singer* unleashed by combining musical star power and subcultural soul-searching.

Crossover Dreams describes three musical worlds: (1) an older New York Latin style, written into the music and the figure of Rudy's mentor Cheo, which he rejects, then rediscovers; (2) inane supercultural pop music played by a rock group in a recording studio; (3) Rudy's own cross-over song, a one-hit wonder that leaves him stranded, which combines elements of 1 and 2. As in many subcultural films, a careful composed score occasionally interpolates to stabilize the reading of the narrative for themes like romance or city loneliness. It is hard to delete the orchestra completely, even from a movie whose moral is "stay in your own ethnic backyard."

Feel-good as the film is, it effectively erases the possibility of a viable cross-over music. This dates it to the 1980s, before the great Latin Wave swept into mainstream American commercial music, with its range of artists and styles from Gloria Estefan to Shakira to Ricky Martin and the glam couple of Jennifer Lopez and Marc Anthony. Blades, it seems, came too early to make this scene, or, as in the film, lacked the skill of a mediator. The instinct to move toward larger markets through music has only intensified in the two decades since. As David Gale, executive vice president of MTV Films says, "music is always the first crossover medium." MTV released the very successful hip-hop film, *Hustle and Flow,* since "hip-hop is universal right now . . . and that's a big foundation for MTV. In film, we just get the benefit" (Coates

2005). The film's main song won the Oscar, underlining the way that once-subcultural music can dominate the mainstream eventually.

Gale's approach to crossover shows how much distance has been covered from the tentative independent subcultural filmmaking of earlier eras, but each American ethnic group has to follow its own expressive trajectory. *The Doe Boy* (2001), represents the newest subcultural cluster of filmmakers, Native-American cinema. Chris Eyre, creator of the first successful Indian feature film, *Smoke Signals* (1998), supported the film, marking the start of an indie, in-group network. The film won an award at Sundance, though it did not reach large theatrical distribution. As director Randy Redroad says, "when an Indian makes a film, the act itself is so improbable that it is inherently a glancing blow against stereotype and a new page in American film history" (www.kadar.de/pages/freestyle/projects/doeboy _production.html). *The Doe Boy,* however, is not a feel-good ethnic film. Rather, it sets its characters in a complex mix of reservation and city, with multiple heritages and musics in play. "To really capture the essence of his story, Redroad wanted a mixed-blood, mixed-tribal cast . . . lead actor James Duval . . . is of mixed ethnic backgrounds, his mother being Vietnamese-French, and his father being Irish–Native American Indian" (ibid.) Not every ethnic film today needs to be "pure-blood," even though it will be read as belonging to a single subculture. Similarly, the music for *Doe Boy* blends a variety of American film sources. Set in Cherokee territory, the score draws on contemporary Indian music, including "full-blood" Tommy Wildcat, who has received a Native American Music award as best flutist. Like the film's grandfather character, the young musician Tommy Wildcat makes his own flutes (www.cherokeeproud.com /tommy.htm). In the movie, the troubled half-Cherokee, hemophiliac hero draws solace from his grandfather's flute playing, and that instrument becomes the main carrier of "tradition." From the 1980s on, the "native" flute passed from being a little-known Indian instrument played by only a few tribes to becoming a symbol of pan-Indian identity and beyond, as part of the branded sound of New Age music.

The Doe Boy also relies on contemporary Indian rock to bridge the reservation-town divide and to suggest generational layers. But the film-score itself comes from the pen of Adam Dorn (professional name: Mocean Worker), who, a website suggests, "is not to be pigeonholed." Having worked with Wim Wenders (*Million Dollar Hotel*) he is a versatile composer who also functions as a working dj, party-album creator, and producer of a jazz label with his father, a jazz musician. He apparently wrote the *Doe Boy* score in two weeks, long distance, but one reviewer finds that "it manages to evoke Native American melodies and instruments while avoiding the stereotypical flutes and tom-toms and, in fact, evokes much folk music from around the world" (www.filmmonthly.com/video/Articles /DoeBoy/DoeBoy.html). So Redroad assigns the "stereotypical " Indian flute to the ancestral grandfather and allows the composer to move the film from a small subcultural space to the larger world music scene. This approach suits the film, which has a layered, ambivalent take on its hero's difficult coming of age as a mixed-blood hemophiliac.

There is no easy way to fix the meaning of a film like *The Doe Boy*, in which the boy's angry, militarist American father is mistakenly shot down by his hunting buddies, while he himself comes face to face with a deer and refuses to kill it, despite bearing the heritage of legendary Indian hunters. He finds comfort in his Indian mother and girlfriend, but is left facing an uncertain future in a state of perilous health, always on the margins.

As a subcultural film, *The Doe Boy* offers a contrast to the clarity of *Crossover Dreams,* and this range of strategies points to an important principle: the flexibility of restricting or opening up a film's identity through musical resources. Subcultural filmmakers can choose the "ethnic" or the more general route in musical grounding for their narratives. The production team itself might not agree, as in the case of the film *Face* (2005), where the Chinese-American director Bertha Bay-Sa Pan, had this to say about the African-American composer she worked with: "I wanted the score to get away from the Chinese thing, but he put gongs in. I said, 'That's too obvious, that's a kung fu movie.' And he said, 'I like my gongs.' He kept trying to sneak them back in. He said on my birthday he was coming to my door with a gong ensemble" (Edelstein 2005). Certainly the choices are not all that simple for a film with a broadly international cast and crew that takes up the problems of a Chinese-American woman who has an African-American hip-hop boyfriend.

For *Atanrajuat: The Fast Runner* (2001), the creative team explicitly rejected a narrow identity. This was the first Inuit ("Eskimo") feature film, so the stakes were very high, and the stance explicit: "We don't accept the frame of reference to us as 'ethnic' first and filmmakers second. That frame reflects other peoples' expectations and often race-based assumptions" (Cohn 2005). The director, Zacharias Kunuk, deliberately avoided an Inuit-only score, hiring Chris Crilly, who wrote "pieces that reflect his own Celtic musical roots" (http://ctr.concordia.ca/2001–02/Apr_25/11-Crilly /index.shtml) and borrowing from other small-scale societies, notably the Tuvans of Siberia, the Aboriginal Australians' didjeridu horn, and percussion from India. The strategy worked: The film won Crilly a Canadian Genie award for best filmscore.

Yet appropriating other people's indigenous music can stir up unexpected anger, even if you are a subcultural filmmaker yourself. The Tuvan musicians who created the song that ended up in *Atanrajuat: The Fast Runner* were angry. For example, Sayan says: "what the film did was a cultural insult because of the context in which our music was used. That context mutilates the music. And it's not the first time that a film director has used 'Prayer.' There was a Bulgarian director who also used it. It was awful what he did: he put our prayer in the mouth of the devil, because to a simple listener, it sounds powerful and menacing" (Levin 2005:289). Yet Sayan concedes that *The Fast Runner* grasped the essence of Tuvan music: "you could say that our music touched that film director . . . and he chose a place where there's a kind of harmonization with nature . . . the person who chose that music didn't know the words, but understood that it was a deep and serious song, and that it would be appropriate for this situation. And it worked" (ibid:290).

By borrowing and moving out to a wide choice of sources, subcultural filmmakers redirect any audience expectation of a close fit between a film and the ethnic identity of its makers. A classic attempt at breaking down preconceptions comes in Julie Dash's *Daughters of the Dust* (1991), a milestone movie of recent African-American independent cinema, the first feature by a woman director. The slow-paced, chronologically irregular action takes place on the "exotic" Georgia Sea Islands. The narrative engages ethnographically with the modernization of an isolated Black family, around 1900. For this time and place, the filmmaker might well have relied on roots music. Excellent archival recordings are available, since folklorists and ethnomusicologists "discovered" the islands, from the 1930s on. Yet Dash went for an African-tinged-world-music/new-music score. When questioned at a screening, she admitted that she wanted to go around expectations rather than reinforce preconceptions. To some extent, this parallels her decision to write dialogue in a reconstruction of the local dialect, literally a simulated vernacular, rather than in the usual all-purpose Southern Black speech of Hollywood films. The film stands as an isolated effort to buck the superculture, drawing respectful comments but not enough audience to allow Dash to continue easily on her artistic path. In the United States, it is usually more successful to market hip-hop stars and scores or to trade in comfortable scenes of ethnic life (*My Big Fat Greek Wedding*) than to follow a personal subcultural vision. Either way, music always makes a decisive statement about the nature of a filmed community, even as it mediates between producers' plans and audience expectations.

The impulse to create subcultural cinema is not purely American. The brief flowering of Polish-Yiddish film in the 1930s is but one poignant example. More broadly, the Soviet Union and India offer a wide range of local systems nestling under the wings of large-scale supercultures. In every case, music shapes the identity of such microsystems, and a truly comparative approach to film music would try to generate enough data and insight to move toward broader patterns of superculture-subculture relations.

Note

1. Goldin's conscious conservatism coordinates with a broad stream of 1920s to 1940s Jewish-American popular music. In the period after the end of mass immigration (1924) and before the Second World War, older Jews allowed themselves to relax into nostalgia for the first time. As Jews rose economically, moving out from teeming tenements to the quickly rising suburban neighborhoods of New York and other big cities, they maintained an intensely ethnic lifestyle even while young people chafed at the family imperatives of observance. Already in the mid-1920s, a recorded vaudeville skit foreshadows the atmosphere of *The Cantor's Son*. In Solomon Stramer's novelty disc "A yidisher heym in amerike" ("A Jewish Home in America"), the jazz-loving kids are brusquely diverted from "Yes Sir, that's My Baby" to a cantorial number when dad recruits them as a backup choir to his vocalizing. At the same time, even a pop star like Sophie Tucker, who had made it big in mainstream entertainment, realized the value of putting out her greatest hit, "My Yidishe Momme," as a bilingual record, one side in English and the flip side in Yiddish, offering two somewhat diverging takes on cherishing one's lonely gray-haired mother. The English lyrics lack the self-punishment of the Yiddish version's stress on guilt.

Works Cited

Berg, Charles Ramirez. 2002. *Latino Images in Film: Stereotypes, Subversion, and Resistance*. Austin: University of Texas Press.

Bogle, Donald. 1991. *Toms, Coons, Mulattoes, Mammies, and Bucks: An Interpretive History of Blacks in American Films*. New York: Continuum.

Bowser, Pearl. 2000. *Writing Himself into History: Oscar Micheaux, His Silent Film, and His Audience*. New Brunswick, N.J.: Rutgers University Press.

Bowser, Pearl, and Bestor Cran. 1994. *Midnight Ramble: The Story of the Black Film Industry*. Documentary film.

Bowser, Pearl, Jane Gaines, and Charles Musser, eds. 2001. *Oscar Micheaux and His Circle*. Bloomington and Indianapolis: Indiana University Press.

Canby, Vincent. 1985. *Review of Crossover Dreams. New York Times*, March 29.

Coates, Ta-Nehisi. 2005. "The Color of Money." *New York Times*, July 10.

Cohn, Norm. 2005. Interview with Faye Ginsburg on email, July 22.

Cripps, Thomas. 1993. *Making Movies Black: The Hollywood Message Movie from World War II to the Civil Rights Era*. New York: Oxford University Press.

Edelstein, David. 2005. "The Clash of China's Generations, Set to a Hip-Hop Beat." *New York Times*, March 20.

Erens, Patricia. 1984. *The Jew in American Cinema*. Bloomington: Indiana University Press.

Feng, Peter X. 2002. *Screening Asian Americans.* New Brunswick, N.J.: Rutgers University Press.

Fischer, Lucy. 1980. "*Applause:* The Visual and Acoustic Landscape," in *Sound and the Cinema,* ed. Evan Cameron, 182–201. Pleasantville, N.Y.: Redgrave.

Green, Ronald J. 2000. *Straight Lick: The Cinema of Oscar Micheaux.* Bloomington: Indiana University Press.

Hoberman, J. 1991. *Bridge of Light: Yiddish Film between Two Worlds.* New York: Museum of Modern Art and Schocken Books.

Jafa, Arthur. 2001. "The Notion of Treatment: Black Aesthetics and Film," in Bowser, Gaines, and Musser, 11–18.

Kalinak, Kathryn. 1992. *Settling the Score: Music and the Classical Hollywood Film.* Madison: University of Wisconsin Press.

Levin, Theodore. 2006. *Where Rivers and Mountains Sing: Sound, Music, and Nomadism in Tuva and Beyond.* Bloomington and Indianapolis: Indiana University Press.

Mamoulian, Rouben. 1980. "Rouben Mamoulian, Director," in *Sound and the Cinema,* ed. Evan Cameron, 85–97. Pleasantville, N.Y.: Redgrave.

Masood, Paula. 2003. *Black City Cinema: African American Urban Experiences in Film.* Philadelphia: Temple University Press.

Noriega, Chon A., ed. 1992. *Chicanos and Film: Representation and Difference.* Minneapolis and London: University of Minnesota Press.

Popkin, Zelda F. 1927. "The Jew on the Stage and Screen." *B'nai Brith Magazine* 41, no. 2:18.

Rogan, Michael. 1996. *Blackface, White Noise.* Berkeley and Los Angeles: University of California Press.

Film Sources

The National Center for Jewish Film has restored and made available many classic Yiddish films, at www.jewishfilm.org. Some of Micheaux's films have been restored, although they go in and out of distribution; in late 2006, eight titles were available on www.moviesunlimited.com.

PART TWO

·◉·

GLOBAL FILM MUSICS

·◉·

Cinema Systems

GREG BOOTH

That Bollywood Sound

·◉·

In 2002, a British pop musician with whom I was acquainted and who knew
of my interests in India and its music, called to tell me he was leaving shortly
for Mumbai. He was producing a song for a local pop singer and wanted to
record the song using, as he described it, "that incredible string sound that
you hear in Bollywood movies." As we talked about it, I learned that the specifics of the sound that my friend sought involved large orchestras, especially
with large string sections playing unison melody lines and rapid passagework with impeccable intonation and ensemble, endless eclectic instrumental
combinations of Indian and non-Indian instruments, unexpected harmonies, regular and extreme use of electronic reverberation effects, an idiosyncratic mix of Western and Indian stylistic features, and a facility with electronic instruments and amplification. In terms of the recording process, my
friend sought a recording in which individual instrumental sounds did not
stand out discretely but instead formed part of a huge wash of sound, in
which the strings "bled" through on the horn parts and where the drums and
guitars sounded as if they had been recorded on a single microphone. Ironically, when my friend reached Mumbai, he found that the best place to get
"the Bollywood sound" was no longer in Mumbai, but in Chennai, the home
of another Indian film industry that produces films primarily in Tamil.

The Hindi-language film industry, which finally was located solely in
Mumbai (and which has come to be called Bollywood by the Indian and
international press), is—technically speaking—just one of India's many
language-based film industries. India has produced films in fifty-one languages since 1951; in addition to Hindi, the most prolific industries (in
rough order of size) have been those in Tamil, Telugu, Malayalam, Kannada, Bengali, Marathi, Gujarati, Oriya, and Punjabi. The Hindi industry
maintained the largest output until 1979, when the first three southern
linguistic industries all exceeded Mumbai's output for the first time.

Perhaps more important than sheer numbers, Hindi films were the only ones that routinely were released throughout India, from an urban center less tied to tradition or to a single-language ideal than those further south. Despite significant political and cultural opposition, Hindi has been the most widely spoken indigenous language in independent India and frequently has been referred to as the national language, giving Hindi films a similar, if less prestigious national identity. The ubiquitous songs of the Hindi film industry formed the staple of Radio Ceylon's immensely powerful shortwave broadcasts (such as Binaca Geet Mala) that were widely received (and loved) throughout South Asia from 1954 through the mid-1970s. Later, they acted similarly as the basis for All India Radio's popular broadcasts (on Vividh Bharati, etc.,) and still later, for those of Indian television. For all these reasons, Hindi film songs defined the mainstream that other directors and composers in Tamil or Bengali had to join. Musical and technical innovations in Mumbai were subsequently and routinely employed by their colleagues in what came to be called the regional cinemas.

From the 1930s forward, the musicians of the Hindi film industry led the integration of foreign influences (large orchestras, Latin and other popular styles, developments in background music). It is historically accurate, therefore, to identify the orchestral sound of commercial Indian films with the musicians, composers, and arrangers of Mumbai. Despite a contemporary reality dominated by increasingly careful fiscal management, computer-based recording, and music sampling, the sound tracks of films made in Mumbai from the latter 1940s through the first half of the 1990s testify to most of the characteristics that I list above.

The Tamil, Telugu, and other industries imitated musical developments in Mumbai, but routinely lagged behind new developments. The reason that my friend had to record in Chennai in 2002 was that by that time, the film and film music industries of Mumbai had shifted into a more explicitly transnational notion of sound, technical and industrial production, distribution, and so forth. Large orchestras in large recording spaces and a profoundly Indian filtering of foreign influences were things of the past in both aesthetical and industrial terms. The Chennai industry, on the other hand, had yet to embrace those changes fully and could still produce the sounds that were considered old-fashioned in the north. By 2004, however, even Chennai had shifted to the computer-based composition and recording processes that Mumbai had pioneered. A foreign producer seeking "that Bollywood sound" in 2005 would be sorely disappointed wherever he looked.

This study outlines the development of the socio-professional structures and musical features of "that incredible string sound," largely from the perspectives of the musicians and other professionals who were part of the

Mumbai film music industry before, during, and after what Ashish Virmani (2004) has called "Old Bollywood." Changes in cultural, economic, and political conditions—exacerbated at times by innovations in the technologies of film and music production—produced gradual change in industrial structures, professional practice, and musician identity. Despite numerous changes, however, the long hegemony of the Mumbai orchestral sound and industrial system stands out among the popular culture histories of the twentieth century.

From the beginnings of sound film production in 1931 through the mid-1940s, Mumbai film studios and their employees dominated the film industry and its music. World War II and Indian Independence (1947) were followed by the collapse of the studio system and a long period of unique creativity and cultural dominance from a film industry routinely described as "chaotic" (e.g., the 1949 Indian Film Enquiry Committee as reported in Raina 1983:12). This dominance lasted through the early 1990s and corresponds to the Old Bollywood period. Subsequently, economic liberalization, digital technology, and the increasingly international mind-set on the part of younger industry participants led to the rise of what must be called "New Bollywood" from the mid-1990s through the present. Although periodization is a dangerous tool at best in any cultural history, and although many internal stylistic divisions and alternative conceptualizations are possible, these three broad time-periods were each characterized by distinctive responses of the film-music industry to shifting combinations of industrial organization, orchestral make-up and size, recording technology, influential personnel, and dominant social groups. They are thus helpful in developing an understanding of how Bollywood's orchestral sound relates to these broader issues.

Early Developments in Mumbai Film Orchestras

A number of scholars, including Arnold (1988), have discussed the early history of Hindi film music and the dramatic antecedents whose music and musicians played an important role in musical composition and performance in early 1930s film music. Arnold also reports that in the mid-1930s, a "typical" orchestra consisted of approximately six violins, cello, bass, clarinet, saxophone, flute, and tabla. Although early ensembles were often syncretic, much of the music itself was copied directly from Indian stages. This was especially true for the products of Prabhat Studios, located in Pune. Master Kirshna Rao's score for the 1936 hit *Amar Jyoti* offers an example of the almost entirely Indian sound track played by a syncretic ensemble that includes perhaps two or three violins, cello, clarinet, flute, sitar, mandolin, piano, and jal tarang, plus tabla and pakhawaj.[1]

The song "Suno suno, ban ke prani," sung by Shanta Apte, appears about forty-five minutes into the film and is the narrative's third music scene.[2] The song is slightly less than three minutes long and aside from a very brief introduction (a three-second piano arpeggio) and two short instrumental interludes (both roughly five seconds) is all singing. The ensemble plays the melody with Apte in unison; there is neither harmony nor countermelody. Variety is achieved largely through quasi-improvised elaboration in the style routinely associated with Indian melodic practice and through timbral shifts as instruments drop in and out of the mix.

Amar Jyoti is an early outcome of a major technological development that had a profound impact on Indian film music. In the year before its release, the recording of sound and visual image, which previously had taken place simultaneously on a single strip of optical film, became two different processes. Sound and image were recorded separately on two strips and then mechanically synchronized onto a single strip for the final release print. Thus, although Apte sings as well as acts in this film, the two performances did not happen simultaneously. The "playback" system, as it came to be called in India, allowed music to be recorded under slightly more suitable acoustic conditions, in sessions devoted solely to sound recording. Songs were recorded before their scenes were filmed; the recordings then became sound tracks to which the actors' mimed. Songs became more musically inventive and sophisticated as a result of this more flexible technological process.

Ironically, it was composers at New Theatres, a studio in Kolkata, who were initially the most important in developing the Bollywood sound after 1935. Following the Kolkata lead, the orchestras in Mumbai film studios gradually grew from roughly fifteen to thirty players during in the 1930s and early 1940s.

The notion and practice of background music also developed over this period, from the sparse, almost total silence of the background in *Amar Jyoti*, where piano and drums provide music for chase or other dramatic action scenes only. Playback technology effectively required a conceptual change in the notion of background music since (a) there were no musicians present during the shooting and (b) background music now could be recorded after the images were filmed, and more carefully arranged in response to those images and their durations. There may well have been technological difficulties as well; but, for whatever reason, background music was a phenomenon that took a number of years to develop after playback established itself. Most musicians involved in the production of background music note the importance of foreign films in the gradual development of background music along foreign lines.

Orchestral musicians and conductors often were salaried employees in this period, employed by Mumbai film studios such as Ranjit, Wadia, Bombay Talkies, and Kardar. On the other hand, by the latter 1930s, more and more composers, called music directors, appear to have been working as freelancers, contracting to compose a specific film or series of films with a specific studio, but not tied permanently to a single studio. The studio's salaried musicians worked with whichever composer had been contracted for the film in question. Studios rarely kept enough musicians on salary to actually make the recordings, however; consequently, studio orchestras were complemented by freelance musicians when necessary.

One of the most important groups of musicians in the late 1930s and early 1940s was referred to as "A-R-P," an industry acronym for the trio composed of cellist Alphonso Albuquerque, saxophone player Ram Singh, and violinist/guitarist Peter Sequiera. This group and their associates appear to have been highly sought after by music directors; they are featured on many films of this period.

In addition to salaried and freelance musicians, many music directors had a small group of musicians with whom they worked on an almost daily basis, and who sat ambiguously between the freelance and the salaried system. Arnold reports, for example, that composer Anil Biswas "brought four musicians to Bombay with him [in 1934]" (1991: 54). Between them, this quartet covered cello, mandolin, violin, piano, guitar, and Hawaiian guitar. Such men were technically freelancers; but their incomes were connected in part to the level of demand for "their" music director's services. Another specialist group of musical contributors began to play a crucial role in the music production process during the latter 1930s. What is more, these specialists were most commonly members of two distinctive Indian subcultures.

The notion of orchestration and arranging gradually worked its way into Indian film music during the late 1930s and early 1940s. Music notation appears to have played a role in film music production quite early on: Musicians reading Western staff notation, as well as those reading either Hindi or Bengali syllabic notation, routinely played with musicians who had learned their parts by heart. Initially, leading studio musicians, such as A-R-P composed their own solos and, together with the music director, worked out who would play what as part of the rehearsal or recording process. A-R-P saxophonist, Ram Singh, whose father had played in the ceremonial band of the governor of Mumbai, arranged the music for many of Anil Biswas's scores.

For the most part, arranging and orchestration are associated strongly with staff notation and with Western notions of harmony and ensemble playing. Among the early arrangers was the jazz bandleader Antonio Vaz—better known by his professional name, Chic Chocolate—who collaborated with music director C. Ramchandra. Ramchandra reportedly would come into the clubs where Vaz's band was playing in order to recruit musicians for that night's recording session, which Vaz would arrange.[3] This collaborative relationship appears to have been a crucial factor in the introduction of dance band instruments and styles into Bollywood's music culture. Johnny Gomes, another jazz musician, and the more classically oriented Anthony Gonsalves also provided notated scores, orchestration, harmonized arrangements, and sometimes musical interludes for the compositions of music directors during the latter 1930s.

The musical results of the freelance/studio musician collaboration, the presence of specialist arrangers, and improving sound technology and expertise can all be heard in Mehboob Productions' *Humayun* (1945). In the early 1940s, Mehboob Productions employed roughly fifteen musicians on salary, who were complemented in this film by the small group of freelance musicians who were associated regularly with the film's music director Ghulam Haider.[4] Six of Haider's musicians had come with him to Mumbai from Lahore and many, like Haider himself, did not read Western notation. The group that Haider used to record *Humayun* also included Mumbai-born Vistasp Balsara, however, who had joined Haider recently after working as a salaried musician for Filmistan studios. Balsara did read Western notation, and consequently arranged, orchestrated, and conducted the recordings of Haider's compositions for *Humayun* and other of Haider's films in these years.

Humayun's soundtrack illustrates how far music had progressed in the nine years since *Amar Jyoti*, both musically and technologically. The playback-singer system was now firmly in place; the voices of Shams Lucknavi and Shamshad Begum (whose name is mysteriously absent from the title credits) dominate the sound track. The title music displays all the features of contemporary dance band music: muted trumpets, clarinet trios, and sectional call and response arrangements. "Aey chaand bata de," the third music scene in *Humayun*, is considerably longer than those of *Amar Jyoti* (4 minutes, 30 seconds). A short solo on what appears to be an *úd*, musically and structurally part of the background score, precedes the song's own lengthy introduction (30 seconds) in a new key. The melody that follows has a much simpler and more repetitive structure than "Suno Suno." Much of the melodic interest clearly is shifted to the instrumental interludes, of which there are four, each roughly fifteen seconds in length, with fully developed melodic and harmonic content. The vocals are accompanied by unison playing as in *Amar Jyoti;* but the cello plays accompanimental arpeggios that provide harmonic and rhythmic underpinning. *Humayun* has an effective background music score that demonstrates increased range and flexibility and that continues under dialogue when appropriate, supporting the emotional content. In films such as *Humayun,* all the primary elements of the Bollywood sound fall into place; composers expanded and developed these elements in subsequent decades until, by the 1970s at the latest, they had become almost totally subject to conventional treatment.

The Haider-Balsara combination is but one instance of the increasingly common collaborative pattern of the 1940s. Composers, who often had little experience or training in European music, harmony, theory, or notation, employed assistants or arrangers who did. The former group was composed exclusively of Hindus or Muslims from a variety of cultural and geographic backgrounds; but the vast majority of the latter group were Christian (especially Goan) or in a few cases, Parsi. In the cultural environment of these latter communities, Western music of various kinds was valued; access to Western music education was often readily available. Goan and Parsi musicians were also the most active Indians in the subcontinental jazz and dance band scene and consequently had the greatest familiarity with Western popular styles, repertoire, and arranging practices.

The Bollywood Sound

In the 1940s, the results of a number of fundamentally disruptive events allowed or encouraged the transformation of the Indian film industry into what is today called Bollywood: (1) the Second World War; (2) Indian Independence and the creation of Pakistan in 1947; and (3) subsequent national government policies around taxation, alcohol, censorship, and import/export. In the film industry, the most obvious change was the collapse of the studio system. Harpreet Kaur (2004) specifically points to the falling value of the Indian rupee, the escalation in Mumbai land prices, and an escalation in star fees as immediate causal factors. Although some studios survived into the 1950s and beyond, almost all salaried positions for orchestral musicians, arrangers, or music directors disappeared.

The Indian government imposed tax rates on aspects of the film industry that sometimes cumulatively exceeded 200 percent; but despite such adverse conditions, the hegemonic importance of film culture grew substantially after 1947, aided, perhaps, by other regulations that made the import of foreign culture a financial and bureaucratic nightmare (c.f. Das 2001). In the ten years after Independence, the average yearly film output of the Mumbai industry increased by 16 percent in comparison to the average of the ten years leading to Independence.

At the same time that film culture was establishing its stranglehold on India's popular culture, the dance-band industry that had thrived on colonial-era nightlife was collapsing. Many musicians who had been making their livings in touring jazz bands found that a sedentary life in Mumbai, working in the film studios, where they could see their families on a regular basis, was a more viable (and enjoyable) life, especially in a market divided by newly created international borders and depleted of most of its British patrons. The newly created governments of India and Pakistan each had their own reasons for not encouraging foreign popular musical styles. It is perhaps ironic that many dance-band musicians chose to work in the Hindi film industry despite their preference for other musical styles. Many of these musicians were Goans, who spoke little Hindi and who rarely (if ever) watched for pleasure the films whose music they played for profit.

Whether they liked it or not, by the early 1950s an increasingly large pool of musicians—many with performing and arranging experience in Western popular music—was available to meet a growing demand. In the late 1940s and early 1950s, the forty- or fifty-piece film orchestra became the industry norm. Naushad Ali was a distinctive composer who experimented with larger orchestral forces in the 1940s. Nausahd Ali himself credits R. C. Boral and Kemchand Prakash, early composers working in Kolkata's New Theatres studios, with the initial development of an Indian orchestral sound.[5] O. P. Nayyar is also associated with the growth of the film orchestras; but the social and industrial institutionalization of the large film orchestra seems to be more properly attributable to the coincidental collaboration of four individuals.

Shankar Raguvanshi (1922–1987) and Jaikishan Panchal (1929–1971) began their careers working as theater musicians and may have been sensitized therefore to the special concerns of music in narrative. Known by their forenames, Shankar-Jaikishan, the pair joined the broader shift to films, working as musical assistants to various music directors. They assumed complete musical responsibility for actor/director Raj Kapoor's enormously popular second film, *Barsaat* (1949), considered an artistic breakthrough in part because of the success of the collaboration between Kapoor and his new music directors (Dissanayake and Sahai 1988). Kapoor's third film, *Aawara* (1951), featured an extended music scene ("Ghar aaya mere pardesi"), which included a long dance/dream sequence. Kapoor encouraged Shankar-Jaikishan to create an especially complex score for what turned into a ground-breaking, nine-minute sequence in which instrumentation, tonality, rhythm structure, text, and musical style all work together in the expression of the film's core narrative tensions. Changes of tonality and texture, referential musical sounds (church and temple bells especially),

Indian dance rhythms, and harmonized sectional playing are all employed here, with the song itself coming slightly more than halfway through the sequence. According to participants, roughly 120 musicians participated in a marathon recording session that lasted nearly twenty-four hours.[6]

A preoccupation with size on the part of India's most popular actor/director, therefore, coincided with an increasing availability of Western-trained musicians, and the growth of an increasingly dominant and internally imitative industry. "Ghar aaya mere pardesi" "was considered both original and imaginative, and it inspired a frenzy of imitations—elaborately staged song and dance sequences amidst enormous sets" (Dissanayake and Sahai 1988:45). The orchestra that Shankar-Jaikishan employed for this song was almost certainly not the first large orchestra recording in the Mumbai cinema. Nevertheless, the dramatic impact of "Ghar aaya mere pardesi" and the overall popularity of the film made it especially influential. Producers and directors who wanted their own "Ghar aaya mere pardesi," so to speak, naturally demanded similarly large orchestras.

Aawara's credits list pianist Sunny Castelino as Music Assistant, a role that normally involves arrangement as well as notation. According to some oral accounts, however, much of the arranging was undertaken by the fourth figure in my proposed quartet of innovators, arranger Sebastian D'Souza (1906–1996).[7] D'Souza had been playing and arranging for his uncle's jazz band in Lahore prior to Partition in 1947. Sometime in 1950 or early 1951, he joined Shankar-Jaikishan as arranger, formally replacing Castelino half-way through *Nagina* (1951) and working on every subsequent Shankar-Jaikishan film. He became the industry's most highly regarded arranger.

There are musical and industrial aspects to the importance of the Shankar-Jaikishan-Kapoor-D'Souza interaction. It appears that D'Souza, with his dance-band experience, pursued the syncretic patterns established by the Vaz-Ramchandra collaborations, integrating Western styles and orchestral practices with the fundamentally Indian aesthetic and content of most film songs of the period. D'Souza's professionalism (oral accounts emphasize the speed at which he could work, together with his flexibility) and the commercial success of the Kapoor-Shankar-Jaikishan films established a musical, professional, and economic framework that effectively normalized the use of a larger and more diverse film orchestra in the productions of scores in which harmony, sectional playing, and counterpoint figured prominently. In Shankar-Jaikishan songs, instrumental interludes have an expanded presence and are often tightly integrated with action on the screen; there is regular use of what some in the industry call obbligato (that is, the use of contrapuntal melodies as accompaniment to the song melody). D'Souza developed a standard division of labor within the increasingly large violin sections. The violins came to be divided into rows of eight to ten musicians each; the first row would play the melody of the song; the second and third rows would play harmony and counter-melody.[8] Some suggest that D'Souza more successfully integrated Indian and European instruments and produced a more satisfactory harmonic approach to the modal structures for which Indian classical music was famous.[9]

Shankar-Jaikishan cannot be viewed as the sole innovators of this period. Other high-demand music directors (especially O. P. Nayyar and Naushad Ali, but also S. D. Burman and Madan Mohan) made their own significant stylistic contributions. Each had their own distinctive style; but Nayyar and Burman also employed D'Souza as their arranger at least occasionally. What is more, the freelance orchestral musicians of the period who played with Shankar-Jaikishan frequently played for these other composers as well. Finally, all of Mumbai's music directors were using the same very small pool of engineers, recording studios, and playback singers, in a tightly knit industry where musical ideas were shared and copied as a matter of course. Indeed, the importance of the Shankar-Jaikishan group may lie in the longevity of this duo's career, their early entry and association with India's most popular filmmaker, and the success (to which they contributed in many cases) of so many of the films with which they were associated. Their importance also arises from the extent to which they effectively institutionalized professional practice in a period almost totally devoid of industrial institutions.

Shankar-Jaikishan composed songs, sometimes separately and sometimes together, and rehearsed them in their large music room at Famous Studios in the Mahalaxmi area of Mumbai.[10] When composing, they were accompanied by one or two musicians (called sitting musicians): their assistant and rhythm arranger, tabla/dholak-player Dattaram Waadkar, and usually a guitarist as well. The duo also instituted the practice of morning rehearsals—held outside the context of the recording studio—for imminent recordings, which were attended by what was, in effect, a fairly regular twenty- to thirty-piece orchestra. In addition to Shankar-Jaikishan themselves, these rehearsals were overseen and usually conducted by D'Souza. Final rehearsals with the full orchestra were conducted with singers in the recording studios (usually Famous Studios, Tardeo). It was not unusual for days to be spent rehearsing a song for recording. This had to do with technological constraints that I describe below. When the song was ready to be recorded, a number of complete takes were made, after which everyone moved on to their next rehearsal or recording. It sometimes took as many as fifteen days for a Shankar-Jaikishan song to be composed, arranged, rehearsed, and recorded.

This pattern of composition-arrangement-rehearsal-full rehearsal-recording went on consistently in Mumbai, in the workshops of all the major music directors; but those musicians who were active in the 1950s tend to associate notions of regularity and longevity, as well as a distinctive social, professional, or collegial solidarity, specifically with Shankar-Jaikishan. They, more than their colleagues, appear to have enabled or embodied the musical and socio-professional characteristics of Bollywood's music culture at a time when the economics of the profession were undergoing considerable change. In contrast to changing economics, however, the technological and industrial patterns of the 1940s were gradually becoming set in stone, for what, in some cases, would turn out to be a very long time. Economics and technology in Old Bollywood thus both require further discussion.

TECHNOLOGY IN OLD BOLLYWOOD

From 1931 through the mid-1950s, film music was recorded directly onto optical film. Aside from its acoustic limitations, the technological limitations of optical film meant that (a) the film had to be sent for developing before it could be played back and (b) post-recording editing was difficult, limited to major breaks in the musical structure. What is more, all analogue sound recording and editing in India was vulnerable to changes in pitch due to voltage fluctuations in the power supply. In consequence, the orchestra, singers, and soloists recorded songs as if they were live performances: all together in the same space, playing from beginning to end. The pressure for error-free musical consistency and the social and musical pleasure that came from playing in a large ensemble are some of the most consistent comments made by Bollywood's studio musicians.

One of the most distinctive features of the Bollywood music industry—its dual identity as the production center for film soundtracks and for a nation's popular music—had a profound impact on its technological infrastructure and practices. Although it is beyond the scope of this article, that dual identity also radically affected the ideological capabilities of film music in any sense. It restricted the ability of composers to define musically or ideologically distinct genres and identities and directed the music industry itself toward an inevitably cinematic notion of genre construction.

Initially, there were always two different recordings sessions: one on optical film to be used as the soundtrack, and one made on a disc cutter that would produce the HMV discs. The two recordings were not always exactly the same; usually the HMV version would be shorter than the film version (the disc version of "Ghar aaya mera pardesi," for example does not contain all the orchestral music).

The sound recording format gradually shifted to monaural, single-track 35-millimeter magnetic tape. Some participants state that this transition was not complete until the late 1960s, although it appears to have begun in the latter 1950s in some studios.[11] This tape format remained the final audio medium for the majority of films until the ready accessibility of digital technology in the 1990s. Even after the change to magnetic tape, the "live" recording practice for most film songs remained largely unchanged. Vocal dubbing began in the latter 1970s, followed by some solo instrument dubbing in the following decade; but because of the cultural and industrial integration of music and film, sound recording continued to be conceptualized in terms of film production. Until the 1990s, "non-film studios," as they were known (those that used the more sophisticated ½-inch, 1-inch, etc., formats that were being used for popular music in the rest of the world) remained discrete and somewhat isolated features of the sound-recording landscape in Mumbai. These popular music tape formats did not have the all-important capability to synchronize sound and image. Indeed, an innovative attempt to record the songs for *Silsila* (1981) on a brand new 1-inch, 8-track magnetic recorder, owned by the HMV/EMI studios, severely threatened the film's viability. The synchronization of sound and image proved almost impossible without drastic editing of the latter. It was consequential issues of this nature that kept the majority of recordings for film monaural and the majority of orchestral recordings "live" throughout the Old Bollywood period.

THE ECONOMICS OF THE BOLLYWOOD SOUND

The technological conditions of recording effectively determined many of the professional and musical patterns established by Shankar-Jaikishan and their colleagues. The socio-professional structures and processes, in which sitting musicians worked with music directors to develop songs, arrangers arranged those songs, and finally a larger ensemble rehearsed and recorded those songs, developed in the early 1950s and continued through the 1980s at least. Perhaps as many as three hundred musicians worked between forty and sixty hours per week throughout most of the Old Bollywood period, playing in the rehearsals and recording sessions of Shankar-Jaikishan, S. D. Burman, O. P. Nayyar, Chitragupt, Roshan, and others, as called for. The same number of additional musicians may have worked on a part-time basis. In a socio-professional environment that had every appearance of stability, musicians bought or rented apartments or houses, raised families, and retired over the thirty to forty years of Old Bollywood.

This industry, however, was actually a complex workshop system based on informal and extremely short-term financial arrangements. The music directors, assistants, arrangers, sitting musicians, and recording musicians who produced the industry's music constantly were being reconfigured by contracts between film producers and music directors into film- or even song-specific music production teams. Although musical styles changed at the superficial level (for example, the appearance of rock 'n' roll in the 1960s or the engagement with disco in the 1980s), the arrangers and orchestras remained largely unchanged.

Music directors were effectively master artisans who maintained workshops for the production of specialized goods that were produced on commission. These were sometimes physical spaces (as in Shankar-Jaikishan's room at Famous Studios) and sometimes "virtual," as in the case of another prolific music director, Ravi, who composed at home and rehearsed in whatever studio had been hired by the producer of the film of the day. The economic structures of Old Bollywood, however, were similar to the technological structures in that the identity of film songs as the products (in one sense or another) of two different media industries (popular music and popular film) interacted to produce specific behaviors and outcomes. One veteran of the music business historicizes this interaction in terms of the major source of profit: "before, this was a film industry, now it is a music industry."[12] This interaction was, responsible, in part, for the sound of Bollywood.

THE PRODUCTION OF POPULAR (FILM) SONGS

For an agreed-upon fee, usually negotiated as a set price per song, Old Bollywood's music directors undertook the composition of the agreed-upon number of songs and the oversight of their development, arranging, rehearsal, and recording. If the music director was expected to compose the background music as well, this was negotiated separately. Some music directors routinely composed background music, while others just as routinely did not. The amount paid to a music director naturally varied at different periods in time and in response to his or her status. Shortly after 1947, some music directors were being paid between two and four thousand rupees per song. Forty years later, this was the lower end of the range; a handful of highly successful music directors were being paid as much as ten times those amounts.

Most arrangers also had a fixed fee that they charged per song or per film. These were relatively consistent across arrangers and eventually were set at agreed-upon rates by the musicians' union. Arrangers' fees were so much lower than those of the music directors' that negotiation was hardly necessary: No one apparently bothered to talk about them.

Orchestral musicians were paid hourly wages. Wages were uncertain in the 1940s; freelancers (those not on salary to a studio) were often paid as much as a month after the session, sometimes less than the agreed-upon wage, and sometimes not at all. In 1952, however, the demand for orchestral film music was strong enough to lead to the creation of the Cine Musicians' Association (hereafter CMA). In a series of negotiations over the entire history of the industry, the leaders of CMA negotiated with all concerned to regularize the length of recording sessions and establish rates of pay according to a graded scale based on a combination of musical proficiency and seniority. Four-hour "song sessions," and later, ten-hour "background sessions" became the norm. Overtime rates were applied to sessions that went on for longer. In rupees, the CMA hourly rates for musicians were 62.50 to 120 in the 1950s (depending on the grade assigned by the union to each musician) and 150 to 660 in the late 1980s. Musicians received what were effectively token payments, between 10 and 200 rupees, for their participation in rehearsals and sittings. Rehearsals and sittings were one pathway to recording work, but naturally, those musicians who could get away with it often avoided rehearsals or sittings if they had better-paying work elsewhere.

In theory, music directors controlled access to all the musical work on their projects, from daily sittings in their music rooms to the rehearsals and recordings in the studios. But by the 1950s, music directors were using intermediaries (called messengers, coordinators, or informers) to organize their orchestra of the day. The music director normally would specify some of the musicians needed for the song in question—soloists, friends, especially well-known section players, and so on—and then say to their messenger, "plus so many violins, cellos, trumpets, etc." Messengers were paid fees; but at times they are reported to have charged each musician a percentage of their daily earnings in return for the musician's inclusion in that recording session. Musicians, especially those of low standing, had to maintain good relations with messengers if they hoped to be called regularly for work.

A film's producer was normally the owner of the songs once they were recorded. These would then be sold to HMV, which had a near-monopoly on the music-recording business, in practical terms, until the advent of local cassette companies in the 1980s. HMV bought songs on royalty agreements (usually 10 to 12 percent of sales), never for cash. Most film producers had to share between 1 and 2 percent of their royalties with the music director. This system had many opportunities for manipulation. HMV appear to have underreported sales from time to time. Later, producers who had good reputations—and who perhaps had a very popular music director's songs in their pocket—might demand an advance on their royalties. Some popular music directors (such as Naushad Ali) could demand that the film's producer pay them a larger share of the royalties. Once a song was recorded and sold, however, a whole new set of interactions took place that affected how profits were derived from it.

Songs often were released a month or two before their films reached the theaters. Initially, the theory was that if the songs were well received, the audience would flock to see the film when it came out because they liked the music and were anxious to see the songs' picturizations. In other words, songs were seen as advertisements for the films. Of course, if the picturizations, or the film itself were extremely popular this might (re)energize music sales. In practice, market interactions between songs as popular music and as components of popular films were extremely difficult to predict and changed on an almost case-by-case basis. Nevertheless, a success in either recording sales or box office returns boosted the consumption of both the song and the film. This interaction, and the assumption that a film would have songs, kept Mumbai's musicians working.

In the early 1970s, T-Series and other indigenous cassette companies (such as Venus, Time-Life, MagnaSound) appeared and significantly increased the competition for profits from the film-music industry. Among other innovative practices, T-Series often bought songs outright, with cash advances. Later, cassette companies began investing in the production of films themselves, giving credence to the proposed transformation of a film industry into a music industry. At the same time, however, once magnetic tape cassettes became the standard consumer format, the entire industry became much more vulnerable to piracy. By this time, however, the film-music interaction and the nature of film funding structures began to have a further impact on the sound of Bollywood.

MUSIC DIRECTORS AS STARS

The collapse of the studio system in the 1950s saw an enormous change in the ratio between the number of producers responsible for a given year's output to the number produced in that year, from 56 percent in 1947 to a remarkable 99 percent in 1977.[13] Working as independents, most producers could only manage to focus on one film at a time; at best producers had funding in hand for that one film (if that).

Virmani points to the consequent lack of financial predictability, not to say profit, that characterized the film-making process in Old Bollywood. "In the old days and until as recently as 2002, the producer was traditionally far removed from the shooting of a film . . . Films were financed under the debt model of shoot-now, pay-later" (2004:27). Those paying for films were increasingly outsiders, who had business profits (legally and illegally generated) to invest; but who had little (if any) experience in the world of films and popular media culture. For such investors, the rewards of film investment did come in part from the possibility of high financial returns on their investment. The 1949 Indian Film Enquiry Committee (IFEC), for example, found that "such is the glamour of quick and substantial returns . . . that the industry has shown no signs of suffering from lack of new entrepreneurs who are prepared to gamble for high stakes" (reported in Raina 1983:12). The opportunity to transform illegally generated investments into legal business profit was another significant motive for some investors. As the IFEC noted, however, the film industry was an increasing source of cultural prestige as well as economic gain. For some investors, the chance to meet the stars and be associated with their social world was a factor that actually could outweigh financial considerations. Madhava Prasad has described this as the "subordination of the production process to a moment of the self-valorization of merchant capital" (-Prasad, 2000:31).

Prasad also has noted the increasing diversification in film production in Old Bollywood. In contrast, there was a consolidation of music production during that same period. With the hindsight of historical analysis, this thirty-year span divides rather neatly in the first half of the 1960s.

Figure 1 shows that, measured at five-year increments, three music directors were active throughout the fifteen years from 1947 to 1962; this table also shows, however, that six additional music directors dominated the final ten years and that collectively, these nine composers dominated an increasing proportion of the industry's film output from 1947 to 1957. The list shown here includes composers who worked on very low-budget and extremely high-budget films. Musical styles changed on the surface, but the relatively small group of the same composers, orchestras, and arrangers worked steadily through the period. Although more than ten years of such systemic and personnel consistency is remarkable, it is equally remarkable that the trend was exacerbated in the subsequent fifteen years, as I will show.

When a music director's songs generated high record or cassette sales, were perceived to help sell a film, or were associated consistently with successful films, that music director's prestige increased. Eventually he (or she, in the sole female instance of Usha Khanna) could demand a higher rate per song from producers who sought music for their films. In 1960, for example, an agreement to participate in a film project by Shankar-Jaikishan would have been a saleable commodity for a would-be producer. It might attract investors who would support the film, distributors who would pay him for distribution rights, or investments in the film's songs by a record

	1932	1937	1942	1947	1952	1957	1962	1967	1972	1977	1982	1987	1992	1997
RC Boral	3	3	1											
Madhulal Damodar Sharma	2	5	3											
Nagardas Nayak	2	2												
Rafiq Ghaznavi	2	0	3											
Kemchand Prakash			6	5										
C Ramchandra			2	8	6	5	0	1						
Bulo C Rani				5	3	2	2							
Chitragupt				3	3	6	8							
Husanlal-Bhagatram				3	2	3								
Naushad Ali			2	3	2	0	0	2						
Roshan					5	4	4	2						
Madan Mohan					4	6	2	4	3	1				
Avinash Vyas					3	5	2							
SD Burman				3	3	4	4	2						
Salil Chaudhuri						5	3	0	5					
SN Tripathi			2	0	1	4	7	1						
OP Nayyar					2	8	2	2						
Shankar-Jaikishan					3	2	6	9	8	2				
Ravi						2	7	4	3	2	2	3		
N Dutta						3	4	2						
Laxmikant-Pyarelal								11	17	23	22	18	11	4
Usha Khanna								9	4	0	9	7	4	2
Kalyanji-Anandji							2	6	12	14	5	3		
RD Burman								2	18	10	16	9	6	
Sonik-Omi									8	8	3	10	2	
Satyam									6	2				
Rajesh Roshan										10	7	5	5	7
Ravinder Jain									1	10	6	7		
Bappi Lahiri										5	10	16	13	8
Nadeem-Shravan											3	0	13	4
Annu Malik											1	7	7	10
Anand-Milind												1	26	13
Dilip Sen-Sameer Sen													8	6
Jaitin-Lalit													3	5
Anand Raj Anand														3
AR Rehman														3
Total Films	9	10	19	30	37	59	53	57	85	87	84	86	98	65
Year's Total Film Output	177	177	177	177	104	112	91	83	129	128	152	147	188	121
Percentage of Total Film Output	5.1	5.6	10.7	16.9	35.6	52.7	58.2	68.7	65.9	67.97	55.26	58.5	52.1	53.7

Figure 1. Music directors who appear among the top ten (as measured by yearly output) in at least two of years measured.

company. Since producers often took their own profits directly from the investors' input rather than from the film's revenues, this was a significant matter. For the dynamics of the music industry, however, this situation had other important consequences. Because investor response to a film project was improved if that project included known, successful music directors, this aspect of film and music funding gradually changed the status and dominance of key music directors, along with the dynamics and structure of the music industry. Figure 1 shows the beginnings of this process, while Figure 2 makes clear its development in subsequent years.

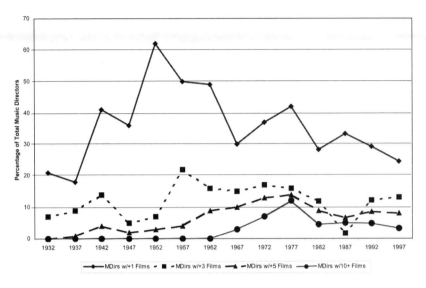

Figure 2. Music Director Dominance as a Percentage of Total Music Directors per Year

The consolidation of control of music production takes place across almost the entire history of the Mumbai film industry in Old Bollywood and is reflected in the gradual but almost constant decrease in the percentage of music directors relative to yearly film releases, from 66 percent in 1937 to 34 percent in 1977. The more important aspect of this phenomenon is shown in the lower three lines of Figure 2, which indicate music directors in five-year increments as a percentage of the total number of contributing music directors in a given year. There is a considerable post-Independence "spike" in 1952: 62 percent of music directors with releases in 1952 did more than one film score that year. Given this relatively egalitarian demand for all (any) music directors, few music directors could be offered more than three films over the course of the year. In 1957, however, many music directors who had contributed two or three scores in 1952 were edged out by those doing as many as five films. This increase in output among an increasingly small group of music directors was repeated in 1962, when the most successful music directors increased their output to more than five film scores (9 percent of all music directors). After 1962, the extremes of success increasingly meant producing ten or more film scores per year. In 1977, music directors who contributed more than three scores represented close to half (42 percent) of all the music directors in that year. In 1982, there was a sudden growth in the number of music directors relative to the number of films.

In effect, Figure 2 illustrates the development of a "star-system" as applied to music directors as well as to actors and playback singers, in which a small handful of the most successful composers, came to dominate more and more of India's film music output. Numerically defined "star" music directors are shown in Table 1.

It is relevant to note here that part of the importance of Shankar-Jaikishan in the institutionalization of the Bollywood music industry arises from the fact that theirs was the only workshop consistently to produce more than one film score per year in each of the years counted over the entire 1952 to 1977 period. While this phenomenon is significant in its own right, by the 1970s and into the 1980s, star music directors were having a direct impact on the size and quality of Bollywood orchestras and the sound of the resultant film scores.

In Old Bollywood, the fees that a producer negotiated with a music director covered only the costs of composition and production oversight. Other costs of music production—fees for the arrangers and the playback singers, the wages for all the musicians, the rental of studio time, and so on—were all additional to the music director's fee. Music directors were in charge of, but not financially liable for, song recording. As the orchestras got bigger, the increased costs of music production were passed directly onto the film's producer. What is more, many of these costs had to be paid "on the spot," as CMA described it. At the end of every recording session, the producer (or more accurately, his accountant and cashier) appeared with the cash to pay all the musicians, whether they had been there for a single four-hour session or for twelve hours straight. The messengers could help keep track of who had played and what their hourly wage was, but hours required for a song recording were always subject to change without notice. In this system, production fees took on a degree of unpredictability that could add up over the cost of six or eight songs and a background track.

As the star system took hold amongst the most successful music directors, some began to incur higher and higher costs for their producers by hiring more musicians or spending more time in the recording studio. Ravi, a music director whose output peaked relatively early (in the 1960s), notes that he normally did not concern himself with music production costs. Demand for his scores was such that he could make musical decisions without consulting the film's producer even though his decisions had financial implications for the producer.[14]

The importance of "star" music directors, such as Ravi, Shankar-Jaikishan, and others, increased in the 1970s and 1980s, as did their apparent freedom to create with little concern for production costs. The immensely successful duo Laxmikant-Pyarelal epitomized the height of the large-orchestra Bollywood sound in this period. Expanding on the practices of

Table I.

Music Directors Producing Five or More Film Scores, 1962–1977

1962 Music Directors	Number of Films	1967 Music Directors	Number of Films	1972 Music Directors	Number of Films	1977 Music Directors	Number of Films
Chitragupt	8	Laxmikant-Pyarelal	11	R. D. Burman	18	Laxmikant-Pyarelal	23
Ravi	7	Shankar-Jaikishan	9	Laxmikant-Pyarelal	17	Kalyanji-Anandji	14
S. N. Tripathi	7	Usha Khanna	9	Kalyanji-Anandji	12	Rajesh Roshan	10
Shankar-Jaikishan	6	Kalyanji-Anandji	6	Shankar-Jaikishan	8	R. D. Burman	10
Sonik-Omi	8	Sonik-Omi	8				
Satyam	6	Bappi Lahiri	5				
Usha Khanna	5						

Shankar-Jaikishan and other predecessors, and taking advantage of the demand for their work, the pair habitually arranged songs and composed background music with the orchestra assembled in the recording studio. This allowed them to try out various instrumentations, harmonizations, melodies, and so forth, but naturally involved a great deal of waiting on the part of the musicians and engineers while the music was composed and parts were written out. Music production costs under such a scenario went up markedly.

The Laxmikant-Pyarelal duet "Chup gaye sari," from the 1969 film *Do Raaste*, features Lata Mangeshkar and Muhammad Rafi, the defining voices of the mature Bollywood sound. Characteristically, the voices and some instruments are reinforced by electronic reverberation. The music itself is both more harmonic and more contrapuntal than earlier examples. Rhythmic accompaniment is provided by not one, but probably four barrel-drums (dholaks) playing in unison (a practice the pair developed), with harmonic reinforcement from guitar and mandolin. The virtuosic drumming is full of rhythmic flourishes both ornamental and structural. Solo instruments include vibraphone (another defining element of the Bollywood sound of this period), santur, and flute. Soloists and a large string section are all featured in three instrumental interludes, each with different combinations of melody and instrumentation. These include typically elaborate unison phrases by the strings, which also provide harmonic accompaniment throughout the song. The song is not heavily orchestrated; but it is instructive to imagine the entire string section assembled and waiting patiently through the arranging of the solo parts, rehearsals by dholak players, and the copying of parts, all to play the relatively small amounts of music for which they were used in this song. In fact, musicians report precisely these kinds of scenarios in the Mehboob studios where Laxmikant-Pyarelal worked and recorded.[15]

"Chup gaye sari" is one song from one of the seventeen Laxmikant-Pyarelal film scores that were released in 1969. In the 1970s and 1980s, many producers were paying as much as 100,000 to 200,000 rupees in production costs for each song this duo recorded.[16] Producers were paying somewhat less for songs of the other top music directors, such as Kalyanji-Anandji or R. D. Burman; but the costs were still extremely high. Naturally, lesser-known music directors, often involved in what might be called "B-grade" films, were producing songs for considerably less than Laxmikant-Pyarelal. In low-budget films, music directors often did discuss music budgets with their producers.

Star music directors could experiment, hire additional musicians, do another take, and so on, in pursuit of quality and innovation; without having to pay the costs (directly or indirectly) of what sometimes appears to have been a rather extravagant process. Although hiring Laxmikant-Pyarelal or R. D. Burman for a film meant a significant increase in costs for a producer, their record of hits and consequent appeal to investors made it more likely that a film with one of these names signed actually would be completed and that it would be well received.

I should note that music production was only a very small part of the larger financial investment required for a film's production; traditionally a film score was understood to represent less than 10 percent of the total budget. The amounts were very important to the music directors, arrangers, and musicians whose livelihoods they represented, but film producers were usually much more worried about demands from their stars. It is also important to remember that in the context of a film's overall production, songs were recorded very early on. Producers often felt more optimistic about their budgets and could view investments in a film's songs as investments in the film's chances of success. Significantly, some musicians responsible for musical tasks that came toward the end of a project, such as post-production and background music, report that funds were often very short at this point.[17]

The demand for star music directors continued to narrow the field to the point that two competing music production "camps," one belonging to Laxmikant-Pyarelal and the other to R. D. Burman, gradually came to dominate the music industry. The contributions of these two composers collectively represented 12 percent of yearly Hindi film output in 1966; but through the 1970s and mid-1980s, their film scores represented 22 percent, on average, of the total film-score output. There was considerable exchange of musical ideas and personnel between the two groups, and a remarkable level of mutual respect; but these two production teams completely dominated the Bollywood sound of the 1970s and 1980s. What it more, although musicians would, in theory, work for anyone, the increased activity of these two music directors meant that musicians who gave regular commitments to one composer found it increasingly difficult to give commitments to others. Musicians could and did describe themselves as belonging to one "camp" or the other.

By the middle of the 1990s, R. D. Burman and Laxmikant had passed away, effectively putting an end to the dominance of both groups. A final late group of Old Bollywood–style music directors (e.g., Anu Malik, Rajesh Roshan, Anand-Milind, Ram-Laxman, Nadeem-Shravan, Jaitin-Lalit, Uttam Singh) appeared during the 1980s; they initially replicated the processes and sounds of their elders; but the conditions of production that supported those processes and sounds distortions were beginning to disintegrate. New Indian cassette companies such as T-Series, Venus, and others began investing directly in film production in the 1980s, transforming films into advertisements for cassettes rather than the reverse. By the mid-1990s, the economic and technological conditions that had supported those large orchestras had changed irrevocably. Within the music industry, there was a growing awareness that "the Bollywood sound" and the livelihood it represented was also changing.

"New" Bollywood

A combination of technological constraints and a free-wheeling economic structure helped create and sustain the Bollywood sound; those factors also led to its collapse and the beginnings of what can only be called "New" Bollywood. In the second half of the 1980s, Prime Minister Rajiv Gandhi led a limited liberalization of India's restrictive import and economic policies, greatly increasing the flow of foreign information, technology, and cultural products. Satellite television brought access to MTV and soon to the Asian/Indian versions of that phenomenon. Among other things, the surge in transnational influences altered audience expectations with regard to musical content and production quality. In the early 1990s, especially after the introduction of DVD technology, a new distribution territory, overseas, became established formally. Bollywood's syncretic approach continued; but now existed in a transnational cultural context where a larger segment of the Indian audience than previously had direct access to the foreign models that were being adapted or (in some cases as always) copied and in which the global Indian diaspora represented a major market for Bollywood films.

New sound studios began to appear, whose crystal motor tape and digital hard disc recorders were impervious to voltage fluctuations. In the mid-1990s, Dolby Sound's digital 5.1 sound system began appearing in Indian theatres, helping to revitalize theatre attendance that had suffered from the widespread advent of videocassettes for home viewing. Digital technology also allowed the much easier addition of subtitles (especially in English) to films, making Hindi films accessible to foreigners and Indians living abroad. Bollywood formally recognized the implications of this by adding a new distribution territory, "Overseas," to its list. By the later 1990s, computer-based sound recording and editing systems replaced magnetic tape with hard-drives. Thus, the early 1990s marks the first time that Mumbai recording studios could obtain and rely on recording systems in which multi-track recordings, stereo recording, track editing, looping, and dubbing were matters of course. Sampling software also achieved a professional level of sophistication. With these developments, the need for large orchestras, long rehearsals, and "live" one-take recording all vanished. As the collective "live" recordings ceased, large recording studios were dismantled or divided into smaller spaces.

Maachis, directed by Gulzar and released in 1993, appears to have been the first digital stereo sound track to take advantage of these changes. The sound track by Vishal, however, demonstrates tendencies toward the deconstruction of the orchestral sound that were played out in the scores of a more popular new music director, A. R. Rahman. Like Shankar-Jaikishan in the late 1940s, Rahman is significant not only for the popularity of his songs, but also for the way in which he successfully worked out the musical and industrial implications of the new conditions of production. Rahman combined synthesized sounds, soloists, and small acoustic and electric ensembles as needed, reconstituting the Bollywood sound on a non-orchestral basis. In a style that might be considered truly postmodern as well as transnational, Rahman's ensembles feature many traditional Indian instruments (probably more than many of the scores of R. D. Burman), but combine them in new, more global musical textures. Sitars and sarangis are not limited to the specific kinds of music scenes and emotions of the conventional cinema but appear on a more equal footing with the synthesizers and instruments of contemporary Western pop. Working in collaboration with Director Mani Ratnam and then others, Rahman also responded to the global influences of MTV. Resultant music scenes had a faster editing-style, camera angles, and shorter shots reminiscent of Western music videos.

Rahman's score for the 1999 release, *Taal,* includes the song "Dil bechain ve," which occupies an early place in that film similar to those of the other songs discussed here; but at 4 minutes and 50 seconds, it is the longest song of the five considered in this study. The song's sound track fades in gradually under the previous scene and includes an extensive (50 second) introduction dominated by atmospheric synthesizers leading to traditional Indian percussion and rhythmic recitation. The songs uses a small violin section (fifteen players) along with a short flute solo and longer sarangi solo, together with a female chorus and the tabla/dholak, these are the only acoustic voices employed. Musicians who were working with Rahman at this time state that he meant this song to be his "Laxmikant-Pyarelal" style song.[18] Nevertheless, unlike earlier songs (including "Chup gaye sari"), the instrumental interludes are asymmetrical and more importantly, there is no assumption that a forty-piece string section is part of the equation. The musical content is extremely harmonic, but the harmonies are supplied by electronic sources, with none of the highly elaborated melodic lines, stereotyped passagework, or contrapuntal textures of Old Bollywood. I would further suggest that in the scores of New Bollywood, the electric bass, for the first time, regularly provides the rhythmic and harmonic foundation in ways familiar to Western popular-music listeners (e.g., the song, "Ishq bina," also heard in *Taal*). Rahman's later scores (as well of those of other new music directors) include the range of contemporary African-American popular music influences and styles. The borrowing of such styles is by no means a new exercise for Bollywood musicians or composers, as I have noted. What was perceptibly new in the context of the late 1990s and after, however, was the immediacy of the transfer and the fact that Bollywood studios could compete on an equal technological footing with those in the West.

Technology and politics, however, have not been alone in changing the face of the Bollywood music industry. Following the engagement of cassette companies in the finances of film production, a new group of financially sophisticated film producers appeared whose motivations were more purely economic than had been the case in the past. These new producers were prepared to treat film culture as business and a source for economic rather than cultural capital. Music became simply one more piece of the final package.

The demise of the star music director workshops of the 1970s and 1980s was thus not followed by a new generation of star music directors who could create without financial constraint. Music became a more negotiable component of the film package (as films with fewer songs or even no songs in some cases began to achieve commercial success). Instead of paying the music directors fees and covering other production costs themselves, the new producers offered music directors fixed amounts to compose, produce, and record their songs. In these circumstances, and unlike the past, modern music directors confirm that hiring more musicians or using studio time lavishly directly affects their own income.[19] With this kind of economic incentive, with a reduced demand for film music generally, and with technological alternatives that were professionally acceptable, the complex socio-professional structure of Old Bollywood's music culture simply collapsed.

Studio musicians who had begun the 1990s working the same forty- to sixty-hour weeks that their fathers or uncles had worked, ended the decade working forty-hour months. Many took up teaching, or simply left Mumbai altogether, for Goa or other places where they hoped a live-performance career would be possible. It would now not be possible to assemble in Mumbai the large, well-rehearsed orchestras that provided song and background music for Hindi films in the past.

Finally, arranging as a key intermediary skill between composition and performance was replaced largely by computer programming. Computer-generated versions of songs were recorded track by track, one musician after another in a process that was the antithesis of the large group social process of Old Bollywood.

Conclusions

One of the remarkable things about the Bollywood sound is the longevity of its dominance in Indian popular culture, and its ongoing importance to that culture even after the actual and specific processes of production have changed completely. I have argued here that the sound itself, characterized by large orchestras, eclectic and sometimes distinctive instrumentation, stereotypical use of electronic effects, and so on, was the result of the specific industrial and cultural context in which this music was created; an industry with enormous cultural prestige and in which there was considerable money collectively, but in which that money was continually "up for grabs" by whoever had the most attractive-sounding project.

Would-be producers needed to convince investors that their film project would be successful. The presence of film songs was one more factor in that negotiation. Once the project was underway, the actual songs themselves were sometimes used to encourage additional investment from these non-professional but very important individuals. Composers and musicians worked with this reality very much "in their faces" and sometimes created music with these issues in mind. Investors' insistence on the conventional six to eight music scenes per film forced film producers to invest in the most successful and therefore most expensive music directors they thought they could afford, since it was assumed that the music director's reputation would make the film more attractive to investors and audience alike. Film producers were caught between a music production system that was often at least partly beyond their control and a popular music industry that was content to let them take all the risks in a financial system that did not or could not count the costs until well after the event, if at all.

This matter of dual identity is, from an industrial perspective, one of the most fascinating aspects of the Bollywood sound. I get the sense that some music directors, intentionally or otherwise, took advantage of the difficulties that producers encountered in managing this dual system to exceed the financial and technological limits of what should have been possible. The most successful music directors, Shankar-Jaikishan, Laxmikant-Pyarelal, the younger and elder Burmans, and Kalyanji-Anandji to identify some of the obvious choices, exceed these boundaries for long periods over the course of their careers. In the dual-industry structure of Old Bollywood, it was hard to separate out costs across the different areas of music and film production, especially when budgets were ad hoc and there was sometimes little consistency from film to film in matters of accounting. Because of music's perceived importance to a film's success, producers kept on investing in pursuit of the proverbial hit, and the music directors and the musicians had steady work and incomes. When a new breed of film producer and their accountants actually started counting, and when technology offered alternatives, the process of music production in Old Bollywood collapsed. I have only hinted at the depth and complexity of the relationship between Mumbai's popular film industry and its popular music industry. Although musicians often had to fight to get their wages, it appears that music directors and musicians all benefited in some ways from the sometimes loose financial practices associated with film production in Old Bollywood. Despite complaints about pay scales, many musicians lived remarkably comfortably. Despite difficult technological conditions, the composers and arrangers of Old Bollywood created the rich orchestral popular music of the period. The ambiguous identity of film songs as popular music and as components of popular films, together with the interrelationships between the music and film industries made this music possible. This story, however, requires considerable further research.

Finally, the oral accounts of the musicians involved in the production of the Bollywood sound, upon which I have relied extensively in this chapter, reveal the relatively complex and labor-intensive process required for these songs to reach the screen. One of the most frustrating aspects of research in this area is the lack of any documentation about the actual life of music in the Mumbai studios and about the process of music making on a day-to-day basis. The popular response to the sixty or seventy thousand songs that were the outcomes of that process, however, was sufficiently profitable to ensure that the music at least, remains available.

Notes

1. The early films of Prabhat Studios are being released on DVD in India. The website, www.prabhatfilms.com, may offer access to these products.

2. See Booth 2000 for an explanation of the term "musical scene" and its usage.

3. Kersi Lord and Cawas Lord, personal communication, 2004.

4. Detailed information on Mehboob Productions and Ghulam Haider provided by Vistasp Balsara, personal communication, 2004.

5. Naushad Ali, personal communication, 2004.

6. Dutta Ram Waadkar, personal communication, 2004.

7. Dutta Ram Waadkar and Victor D'Souza, personnal communication, 2004.

8. Anil Mohile, personal communication, 2004.

9. Dutta Ram Waadkar, personal communication, 2004.

10. Famous and the other "studios" referred to from this point forward were not producing studios, merely industrial spaces for hire.

11. Suresh Kathuria, personal communication, 2004.

12. Abbas Ali, personal communication, 2004.

13. Statistical information is developed from Singh 1980, 1984, and 1986; Chatterjee, 1991; and Rajadhyaksha and Willemen, 1995.

14. Ravi Shankar Sharma, personal communication, 2004.

15. E.g., Bosco Menezies, Joe Pinto, Mario Fernandes and others, personal communication, 2004.

16. Pyarelal Sharma, personal communication, 2004.

17. Kersi Lord and Avinash Oak, personal communication, 2004.

18. Shankar Indorkar, personal communication, 2006.

19. Louiz Banks, personal communication, 2004.

Works Cited

Arnold, Alison. 1988. "Popular Film Song in India: A Case of Mass Market Musical Eclecticism." *Popular Music* 7:177–88.

——. 1991. "Hindi Film Git: On the History of Commercial Indian Popular Music." Ph.D. diss., University of Michigan.

Barnouw, Erik, and S. Krishnaswamy. 1980. *Indian Film.* New York: Columbia University Press.

Booth, Gregory D. 2000. "Religion, Gossip, Narrative Conventions and the Construction of Meaning in Hindi Film Songs." *Popular Music* 19, no. 2:125–46.

Chatterjee, Bishwanath. 1991. *Hindi Film Geet Khosh, Volume 5, 1971–1980.* Kanpur: Mrs Satinder Kaur.

Das, Gurcharan. 2001. *India Unbound.* New York: Alfred A. Knopf.

Dayla, John. 1983. "The Role of the Government: Story of an Uneasy Truce." In *Indian Cinema Superbazaar,* ed. A. Vasudev and P. Lenglet, 53–61. New Delhi: Vikas Publishing House.

Dissanayake, Wimal, and Malti Sahai. 1988. *Raj Kapoor's Films: Harmony of Discourses.* New Delhi: Vikas Publishing House.

Kaur, Harpreet. 2004. "Churning Out Classics." *Jetwings* (March):166–69.

Prasad, M. Madhava. 2000. *Ideology of the Hindi Film: A Historical Construction.* New Delhi: Oxford University Press.

Raina, Raghunath. 1983. "The Context: A Socio-Cultural Anatomy." In *Indian Cinema Superbazaar,* ed. A. Vasudev and P. Lenglet, 2–18. New Delhi: Vikas Publishing House.

Rajadhyaksha, Ashish, and Paul Willemen. 1995. *Encyclopaedia of Indian Cinema.* New Delhi: Oxford University Press.

Singh, Harmandir. 1980. *Hindi Film Geet Kosh 1951–1960, Vol 3.* Kanpur, India: Sumer Singh Sachdev.

——. 1984. *Hindi Film Geet Kosh 1941–1950, Vol 2.* Kanpur, India: Sumer Singh Sachdev.

——. 1986. *Hindi Film Geet Kosh 1961–1970, Vol 4.* Kanpur, India: Sumer Singh Sachdev.

Virmani, Ashish. 2004. The Prodooser Is Dead! Long Live the Producer!" *Man's World* (February): 77–79.

Filmography

Amar Jyoti. 1936. Director: V. Shantaram. Prabaht Films, Pune.
Awara. 1951. Director: Raj Kapoor. R.K. Films, Mumbai.
Barsaat. 1949. Director: Raj Kapoor. R.K. Films, Mumbai.
Do Raaste. 1969. Director: Raj Khosla. Raj Khosla Films, Mumbai.
Humayun. 1945. Director: Mehboob. Mehboob Productions, Mumbai.
Maachis. 1993. Director: Gulzar. Pan Pictures, Mumbai.
Nagina. 1951. Director: Ravindra Dev. Pancholi Productions, Mumbai.
Taal. 1999. Director: Subash Ghai. Mukta Arts Productions, Mumbai.

JOSEPH GETTER AND B. BALASUBRAHMANIYAN

Tamil Film Music
Sound and Significance

·◉·

Chennai, the great metropolis on the coast of South India by the Indian Ocean, is vibrantly full of music. In its public and private spaces, visitors and residents alike can hear recordings and live performances of many different musics: religious songs, classical Indian *rāga*, songs of work and daily life, domestic and foreign pop, and film music (to hear examples of many South Asian musical genres, visit a website such as http://www.music indiaonline.com, or others listed at the end of this chapter). Among these different yet interconnected musical expressions, it is perhaps the songs of the Tamil language cinema that are most audible in Chennai and Tamil Nadu, the state containing the city. Film songs are an ever-present reflection of Tamil culture and sentiments.

The history of cinema in India begins in the first days of film itself. In 1895 and 1896, Louis Lumière and Thomas Edison developed motion picture technology and presented it to audiences. In India, films were first exhibited in Bombay (now renamed with the post-colonial appellation Mumbai) in 1896, and the following year in Madras (now Chennai) and Calcutta (Kolkata). Beginning in 1898, Hiralal Sen and other Indian filmmakers produced short films on subjects such as sporting events, train arrivals, and public ceremonies (Rajadhyaksha and Willemen 1999:17). Films soon began to tell stories and lengthened into feature presentations. Filmmakers adapted elements borrowed from European theater and South Asian proscenium stage plays, as well as local traditions of folk theater and storytelling. The first Indian feature is thought to be *Puṇḍalik* (of 1912; see Rajadhyaksha and Willemen 1999:243), the biography of an ancient saint. Most early films were saint bio-pics or "mythologicals," portraying ancient religious epics and stories.

From the very inception of sound technology, music has always been an indispensable ingredient of movies made in India. Sound was introduced to Indian films in 1931, four years after it transformed commercial cinema in the United States. Early Indian sound films followed conventions for musical accompaniment from local theater forms, and thus a movie might have as many as seventy distinct musical pieces, ranging from background scoring, to song fragments sung by a single actor, to elaborate production numbers set in exotic locales with grand sets, elaborate costumes, and dozens of dancers. In some early sound films, each actor might use his or her own language, so that a single film would be in Hindi-Urdu, Tamil, and Telugu. The first Tamil talkie (sound film) was *Kālidās* (1931), the story of the great Sanskrit poet (c. 4th–5th century C.E.). Produced in Bombay and directed by H. M. Reddy, it contained over fifty pieces of music (Rajadhyaksha and Willemen 1999:254).

Filmmaking philosophies in India usually are categorized into two schools: the art/parallel cinema, and the commercial/popular cinema. However, some films are hard to fit into this dichotomy, and any filmmaker must consider budgetary limits and the whims of the audience. The fact that India has a hegemonic mainstream commercial cinema inevitably means that alternative films are produced. Noncommercial films are possible due to the availability of equipment, skilled crews, and occasional government funding, along with some filmmakers' desire to deviate from established commercial genres, to critique popular culture, or to examine the problems of the society. Aside from the bio-pic and mythological, Indian film genres include social, patriotic, action, family, and romance films, often all combined with songs into what is often known as the *masālā* film (named for a mixture of spices). Usually a single movie has several interrelated plot lines that unfold simultaneously, reaching a resolution at the climax near the end.

The commercial cinema industry of India long has been one of the world's largest, producing around seven hundred to a thousand feature films annually in recent decades. The industries of Mumbai—the internationally famous Bollywood—and Chennai are the major centers of film production, followed by Kolkata (in the state of West Bengal, home of Satyajit Ray), and other smaller centers, including Hyderabad (in Andhra Pradesh), Salem and Coimbatore (Tamil Nadu), and Tiruvanathapuram (Kerala). Reflecting a broad division of the nation's cultures into North and South India, Southern films exist in the four major languages of the region, Tamil, Telugu, Kannada, and Malayalam, each corresponding roughly to a state territory (as has been the case since India was reorganized in 1956 along linguistic lines). The many film studios of Chennai produce films not only in these languages, but also in Hindi (a North Indian language promoted as a national link language, and therefore quite useful while often vehemently opposed), English (the language of the former colonial power), and other languages.

Film songs are essential to the creation and reception of movies in India, and they play a key role in the expressive nature of the cinema. Commercial films from about the mid-twentieth century onwards generally adhere to the convention of including about a half-dozen or more songs, in addition to background musical scoring. In Tamil, the term for a song is *pāṭṭu*. Some common song types in Tamil films are "melodious" songs performed by two lovers at a slower tempo, "pep numbers" for fast-paced group dances, songs based on Indian classical or folk music, Western music influenced songs, *gānā* songs (music of Chennai's slums, sung by laborers and fisher folk), and *ḍappāṅguttu* songs (catchy dance songs in fast *tiśra naḍai* or 12/8 time, with four beats subdivided into triplets). Films always use background scoring as well, to support the action and dialog between the songs. Movies are often about 160 minutes in duration, with two to three songs in the first half and another two to three after the "interval"—most Indian films contain an intermission. Outside of the cinema hall, one may hear film music in settings such as homes, transportation vehicles, tea stalls, shops, restaurants, car back-up warning sounds, mobile (cell) phone ringtones, temple festivals, marriage functions, light music concert programs, university events, and more.

Tamil film songs have a distinctive relationship with the musical, social, cultural, and political lives of Tamil people. The songs are a source of joy and nostalgic memories, a background to daily life, and a force in the formation of identity. The fact that movies contain many well-loved songs goes a long way toward explaining why the activity of attending the cinema is so immensely popular in India. Indeed, repeated viewing by audiences keen on hearing the songs again is a well-known phenomenon. For much of the twentieth century, and at the outset of the twenty-first, going to the movies has been arguably one of the top forms of entertainment in India, and is certainly a very widespread and accessible means of experiencing mass media. However, it is also true that many people express ambivalence or even condemnation toward this music, saying perhaps that it is a simple, impersonal product catering to the masses, or that it is an unorthodox, culturally debased phenomenon. Moreover, the expansion of television during the past two decades has made an impact on cinema hall attendance habits, although many theaters have managed to survive and some have even remained full. A significant amount of television content consists of movies, and—increasingly as the economics of cinema become more difficult to sustain—television shows produced with the human and studio resources of the film industry. Nonetheless, Tamil film songs are a popular and dynamic aspects of India's culture today.

Of all the music genres in India, film songs of any language possess the largest audience and are the most geographically and culturally widespread. In Tamil Nadu, the same may be said of Tamil film songs, which are seemingly ubiquitous in the soundscape (by which we mean all the sounds heard by people in a given place). In this chapter, we focus on Tamil film songs and background music, first reviewing sources on Indian cinema and describing the context of Chennai. We examine musical resources, discussing the individual people who create this music, and then give an overview of the production process. Finally, we provide the reader with a roadmap for understanding how musical strategies are utilized in a sample film.

Sources on Indian Film Music

Sources on Indian film music take a variety of forms. For decades, journalists have chronicled the nation's film industries, in English language magazine such as *Filmfare* and *Screen,* and in newspapers like *The Hindu, Indian Express,* and *The Times of India.* These and many more such national publications reach audiences of millions with reviews of the latest films, gossip about stars' personal lives, and stories on films in production, the cinema industry, and the impact of governmental policies. Published writing by stars and film directors, such as the 1977 book by K. A. Abbas, can provide very good insider accounts of the industry. The essay and fiction author R. K. Narayan wrote a short yet evocative piece on watching films (1990).

The past few years have seen a tremendous growth of cable and satellite television in India, with a great deal of content dedicated to Indian cinema. On various television channels, one may view programs such as interviews of singers and music directors, amateur singing contests, complete movies new and old, and shows of songs excerpted from films. Satellite television brings the broadcast of Tamil channels such as STAR's Vijay TV and Sun Network's SunTV to India, the United States, and many other countries. Shortwave, AM, and FM radio broadcasts in India also include film music in their broadcasts.

The internet abounds with content on Indian films. Access to the web has increased substantially in India during the past few years as well. On the web, one can visit sites created by fans about stars and musicians, download audio (for example, see http://www.raaga.com), read and contribute to online forums and discussion (http://www.tfmpage.com), and view pages created from within the film industry (such as top singer S. P. Balasubrahmanyam's official website, http://www.spbala.com). In addition, video and audio recordings of films and film music are available widely from shops both in India and abroad, as well as online (see "Web Resources" at the end of this chapter for more). The reach of these print, recording, broadcast, and online media is thus truly global.

In the past decade, Indian film studies has become established as a legitimate field of academic discourse. Perhaps the book that best signals this arrival is Ashish Rajadhyaksha and Paul Willemen's *Encyclopaedia of Indian Cinema* (first published in 1994; revised ed., 1999), a massive, detailed, and insightful compilation of data, plot summaries, actor and producer profiles, and interpretations of films. An influential monograph in Indian film studies is Sumita Chakravarty's *National Identity in Indian Popular Cinema, 1947–1987* (1993), which offers an insightful analysis of Hindi films. Chakravarty shows how the cinema can articulate a sense of identity within the postcolonial Indian state. Her metaphor of "imperso-nation" includes

the notions of changeability and metamorphosis, tension and contradiction, recognition and alienation, surface and depth. . . . [Imperso-nation] also encompasses . . . the piling up of identities, the transgression of social codes and boundaries. (A mundane example might be the Hindi film heroine changing sarees in different shots of a single romantic song sequence to signify affluence, freedom, fantasy). (1993:4–5)

Chakravarty's example of the visual and narrative elements of a song sequence is apt, since these can easily express a mutable identity. Moreover, a film song is a special moment within a film, and can express emotions and identities in ways unlike the balance of a movie (Getter 2000, 1999). There are now many works of Indian cinema studies; see for example Pendakur (2003), Gopalan (2002), Mishra (2002), Vasudevan (2001), Gokulsing and Dissanayake (1998), Prasad (1998), Nandy (1998), and Guy (1997). For the most part, these do not address music except in passing, but rather focus upon characters, narrative, visual elements, governmental policies, or industrial histories.

Tamil language writers also publish accounts of the Tamil film industry. Two such are PRO (Public Relations Officer) and film ephemeralia collector "Filmnews" Anandan, who has published a detailed compendium of film dates and information (2004), and the writer Vamanan, who has written many profiles of music directors (2003). Little academic literature has been published specifically on film music in India. Some works include Alison Arnold on mid-twentieth-century Hindi film song (1991, 1988), Peter Manuel's influential *Cassette Culture* (1993) on the rise of user-recordable audiocassette technology in India, and Paul Greene on the playing of audio recordings in rural Tamil Nadu (2000a, 2000b, 1999, 1995). Scholarship that is specifically concerned with Tamil cinema includes Hughes (2000), Guy (1997), Baskaran (1996, 1981), and Pandian (1992). Sara Dickey's ethnographic account (1993) of audiences and cinema reception in Madurai, Tamil Nadu, is the best work available on the meaning of film in South Indian social life. Preminda Jacob (1994) studied the spectacle of film advertisements in South India—known as hoardings, these ubiquitous film ads and icons of the stars often tower fifty feet or more over the streets of cities such as Chennai. These artifacts are now in flux: As of 2005, almost all such hoardings in Chennai are no longer hand-painted, but rather are printed mechanically on plastic, thereby displacing artisan painters with computer-based designers and printers.

Chennai and the Tamil People

Metropolitan Chennai has an estimated population of over four million (Chennai District 2007), and commonly is ranked as India's fourth-largest metro. The area was once fishing villages, some important Hindu centers such as the Kapaleeswarar Temple of Mylapore, and a port of the Pallava kingdom (2nd–9th century). There is a legend that Thomas, an apostle of Jesus, came to India and was killed in 78 C.E. on a hill now within Chennai. The Portugese and Dutch were the first Europeans to arrive, and soon thereafter the British established one of their earliest Indian trading posts in 1639. Madras was incorporated as a city by the British in 1688; soon it became the capital of British-ruled South India and their most important colonial city until Calcutta was developed later.

Chennai has undergone tremendous change in the last few decades, as has all of India and South Asia. There was the achievement of national independence in 1947, increasing urbanization, governmental policies of economic liberalization in the 1990s, and now globalization. Many say that Chennai is a culturally elevated city, with a culture and lifestyle that is more traditional and conservative than that of other Indian cities. Tamil is the main language; English is also widely spoken, often mixed into Tamil in a usage known informally as "Thanglish." Other languages in Chennai such as Telugu, Malayalam, and Kannada reflect the movement of these speakers to the city. Many people are multilingual, and may have a mother tongue (for example, Urdu or Telugu for home and community), a place language (Tamil for use in the city), one or two link languages learned in school (commonly Hindi and English), and perhaps a religious language (Sanskrit or Arabic).

Most residents of Chennai are Tamil people, an ethnic group defined principally by their mother tongue, the Tamil language, and origins in the area now known as the state of Tamil Nadu. Tamil literature extends back two millennia, and today this written heritage and the beauty of the spoken language are highly prized. Tamils also make up a significant portion of the population of Sri Lanka. There is a large Tamil diaspora, with people emigrating as laborers during the colonial era to Southeast Asia, South Africa, Fiji, and the Caribbean; in the last several decades as laborers or professionals to Europe, North America, the Persian Gulf, and Australia; and as war refugees: in the last twenty years many Sri Lankan Tamils have fled their island nation for Canada and elsewhere. Thus many residents of Chennai have strong connections to friends and family who have traveled or settled abroad.

Chennai today is a national center for education, industry, technology, and the arts, and is a major producer of films and film music. The city's film industry is often called "Kollywood," referencing Hollywood but with a "K" representing Kodambakkam, a locale with many studios. The output of these studios is around 100 to 150 feature films per year, rivaling the more well-known Hindi-language Bollywood industry of Mumbai. There are many cinema theaters in Chennai, such as the old, single-screen, monaural sound Kamadhenu; the Hindi language Ega; and the modern digital multiplex-cum-shopping plaza Abirami. Chennai is also the most important center in the world for the South Indian classical performing-arts traditions of Karnāṭak music and Bharata Natyam dance. The city is home to many writers, visual artists, actors, filmmakers, craft artisans, folk performers, dancers, and musicians.

Many genres of music are produced in Chennai, including background music for television, title songs for television shows (often composed by top music directors, featuring leading film singers), film music, nonfilm Tamil pop music, advertisement jingles for television and radio, brass band music at weddings and festivals, stage show concerts by light music troupes, rock, jazz, fusion, Indian and Western choral groups, Western classical guitar and orchestral ensembles, music for theater and drama productions, and background music for television programs (for more on music in Chennai, see Booth 1996 and 1990; and L'Armand and L'Armand 1983). Film and light music troupes are busy performing, particularly in the Tamil month of Adi, when many temples arrange such bands for the festival of Mariamman (mother goddess). The Lakshman Sruthi 100% Manual Orchestra is aptly named for the fact that no sequencers or pre-recorded sounds are utilized in their live stage show. The Tamil pop genre has the potential for individual expression, while film songs must adhere to the film's narrative and thus are not intended to convey the singer or composer's personal point of view. For example, a review of the pop album *Mugangal* noted that it "is an effort to portray some of [the] emotions encountered in our daily lives" (Ram 2002: paragraph 3).

Rock music thrives in Chennai as well, with many bands playing covers of songs by U.S. and British rock groups or originals influenced by genres such as metal, funk, classic rock, and Indian classical music. The rock scene has not yet achieved a level of commercial success comparable to film music, despite enthusiastic fans and a rock music circuit of colleges and music festivals that extends across India. The band Moksha states on its website that rock in India has not fared well, due to a lack of support from recording labels and broadcasters, and because of the failure of bands to develop their unique identity and repertoire of original songs. (Moksha 2004: paragraph 1). In Chennai, rock, pop, and film music shows are put on by many college such as the Indian Institute of Technology or Loyola College, and by event management companies like Boardwalkers. An article about this company noted that the past decade has seen so much growth in nonfilm popular music scene that some people now proclaim Chennai as "happening," replacing its previous image as the "sleepy city" (Kumar 2000: paragraph 1).

Resources and Personnel

Tamil film music springs from many sources of the past and present. One important influence is the classical music of South India, Karnāṭak music (also spelled Karnatic or Carnatic). A great introduction to this music is *Music in South India* by Viswanathan and Allen (2004); see also websites such as http://www.sangeetham.com and http://www.carnatica .net. Film music also borrows from Hindustani (North Indian classical music), Bharata Natyam dance music, the bands and orchestras of colonial-era British rulers and Indian Maharajas, foreign popular music, Western classical music, Hindi *filmi gīt* (film song), urban Indipop, and many genres of religious, popular, and folk music from all over the India. Music from neighboring South Asian nations has had an impact, such as *qawwāli* from Pakistan. Western influences are often quite prominent, especially orchestral music, rap, rock, disco, Latin sounds, and MTV-style music-video visual aesthetics and dancing; top film dancer Prabhudeva has been dubbed the Indian Michael Jackson.

The palette of sounds, instruments, voices, ensembles, and recording techniques available to film musicians comprises what we may call the "resources" of Tamil film music. The use of certain instruments can help create a setting in time and place, a pace for the action, and an emotional feeling. Instrumental timbre (tone quality) is significant, often signaling important ideas to the audience: a particular *rāga* (melodic mode) can quickly set a certain mood, a folk rhythm can establish a rural scene, or a techno beat can evoke a modern character or milieu. Instruments from North or South India can lend a regional "flavor" to the movie (as described by A. R. Rahman in an interview on SunTV on August 15, 2004). A fast-tempo film song featuring a large group of dancers can generate great excitement in the cinema hall; whistles and shouts are heard, and the so-called "front-benchers"—not the leading members of British Parliament, but rather folks in the cheap seats down front—may get up and dance a bit.

A typical ensemble for film music is difficult to define, but most often will include some combination of Indian and Western sounds created by both acoustic and synthesized instruments. The arrangement of songs and background music usually calls for a solo instrument playing the melody, keyboards or strings providing harmony, and percussion supplying rhythms and beats. A composer may draw from a vast array of sounds and instruments: synthesizer, sampled sound, violin, string ensemble, trumpet, saxophone, clarinet, acoustic, electric and bass guitars, drum set, vibraphone, Indian percussion such as *mridaṅgam* and *tavil* (double-headed barrel drums), *urumi* (folk friction drum), *tabla* (North Indian pair of drums), *dhōlak* (Northern folk drum), *ghaṭam* (clay pot), Northern and Southern styles of bamboo flute, *nāgaswaram* (double-reed horn), *shehnāi* (North Indian double-reed horn), *vīna* (Southern stringed lute), *sitār* (Northern lute), Caribbean steel pan, and much more. Sounds may be pre-recorded as samples, then later placed into the film's soundtrack. During a studio session in Chennai, for example, music director Dhina scrolled through many percussion ensemble loops on his computer, listening to snippets while searching for the desired texture to fit a film scene (interview of Dhina by Getter, January 11, 2005). Sounds can also be generated from performances by live musicians in the recording studio. Many performers trained in various instruments and music genres reside in Chennai and are available for recording sessions and live stage-show performances of film songs.

In the early era of Tamil cinema, film music more closely resembled South Indian classical Karnāṭak music. This similarity was due to the fact that the same musicians were active in both fields. For example, Papanasam Sivan was a major composer of both Karnāṭak music and Tamil film music. Randor Guy, an authority on Indian films, writes that Papanasam Sivan "truly laid the firm foundation for film songs to become popular during the 1930–1940's almost single-handedly. Besides he made Carnatic music popular among the common folks with his scintillatingly melodious film songs" (Guy 2000: paragraph 1).

Tamil film songs expanded the audience for Karnāṭak music by making it accessible and easy to digest. In Sivan's times, the lyrics were often a mix of Sanskrit and Tamil languages. He wrote lyrics as well as composed tunes, activities that are more often divided between two specialists. Sivan also acted in films. In those years, the Tamil film industry included many famous Karnāṭak musicians, such as Musiri Subramania Iyer, Maharajapuram Viswanatha Iyer, Dandapani Desigar, G. N. Balasubramaniam, and M. S. Subbulakshmi. Since they were accomplished classical singers, they sang film songs composed in a Karnāṭak vocal style, using *rāga*s such as Kāmbhōji, Śaṅkarābharaṇam, Pantuvarāḷi, Kalyāṇi, or Ṣaṇmukhapriyā. In the 1930s and 1940s, the essential requirement for securing employment as an actor in films was that one must be a good singer, with a melodious and strong voice suited to the limitations of early sound technology. Many successful film actors also achieved fame as great singers, including K. B. Sundarambal, P. U. Chinnappa, M. K. Tyagaraja Bhagavatar, T. R. Mahalingam, P. Bhanumathy, and others.

Composers of film songs are known as "music directors," or simply MDs, and when successful their fame can rival and surpass that of star actors. The duo M. S. Viswanathan and T. K. Ramamoorthy were the leading MDs of the 1960s and 1970s, while Ilayaraja dominated the 1980s and A. R. Rahman the 1990s. Viswanathan and Ramamoorthy created many hit songs with beautiful vocal melodies; Viswanathan (known as MSV) is an excellent singer and player of the harmonium (bellows keyboard), and is able to compose and arrange music very quickly. His songs take Karnāṭak music's heavy classicism and sweeten it, producing a "light" variety of songs; he is called *mellisai mannar* (the king of light music). MSV has continued to sing, compose, and perform well into the first decade of the twenty-first century. Music directors are often people who can appreciate and enjoy a huge variety of music. MSV was known to frequent a place where he could listen to the latest arrivals in foreign and Indian records (interview of R. Gurumurthy, son of painter and musician S. Rajam, by Getter, December 30, 2000). A. R. Rahman noted that his favorites include the Hindustani vocalist Ustad Bade Ghulam Ali Khan as well as Western music composers Verdi and Janacek (interview of A. R. Rahman on SunTV, August 15, 2004).

In the late 1970s, music director Ilayaraja broke into the Tamil film-music industry, establishing himself as an innovative, clever composer. He is widely respected as a brilliant musician, and remained the dominant MD until the early 1990s. He was born in 1943 to a poor Christian family in a small rural village in the Madurai district of Tamil Nadu. In 1958, he began to perform throughout the state as a harmonium player with his brother's troupe. Ilayaraja (sometimes spelled Ilaiyaraja, also known as Raja, or IR) moved to Madras in 1968, and there began formal music education in Karnāṭak music under the guidance of T. V. Gopalakrishnan and in Western classical music with well-known private teacher Master Dhanraj. Ilayaraja also learned Western classical guitar through lessons at the Musee Musical Center in Chennai, in which students learn from local teachers according to a syllabus from London's Trinity College of Music, and then take annual musical examinations administered by visitors from London. IR's debut film score was the hit *Annakkili* (1976), and since then he has composed music for over eight hundred films.

Ilayaraja introduced the instruments, melodies, and feelings of Tamil folk music to film songs. He is noted for his intricate, surprising, and suddenly shifting arrangements for a mixed Indian and Western ensemble. He is skilled in handling Karnāṭak music *rāga*s such as Kēdāram, Rītigauḷai, Malayamārutam, Hamsanādam, Chandrajyōti, Sāramati, Naḷinakānti, Gauḷai, and so on; for example, he used *rāga* Māyāmālavagauḷa (from the beginning lessons of Karnāṭak music) in several films. After Ilayaraja's entrance into the Tamil film industry, the importance of film songs reached new heights in Tamil society, and some say he managed to shift the listening habits—of audiences and music directors alike—away from the Hindi songs that had dominated music in Tamil Nadu. At the same time, Ilayaraja benefited from the circumstances of his era: the emergence at the outset of his career of user-recordable audiocassettes facilitated his reach to people across the socio-economic spectrum and throughout Tamil Nadu.

Ilayaraja's music is distinctive for its complex instrumental arrangements and unique blend of Tamil folk, Indian classical, and Western classical and pop music genres. Film scholar Theodore Baskaran described Ilayaraja's music as both "innovative" and "authentically folk" (Baskaran 2002), in that it is fresh, challenging, and interesting, while remaining tied to local styles and traditions. Raja is known to have a deep understanding of Western classical music and has released nonfilm music albums of his compositions that are a fusion of Indian classical and Western classical music systems. *How to Name It?* (1987) features violinist V. S. Narasimhan (who himself was trained in both Western and India music), and *Nothing But Wind* (1992) features a track entitled "Mozart I Love You" and the North Indian flutist Hariprasad Chaurasia. In 2004, Ilayaraja undertook the "Thiruvasakam in Symphony" project, composing a piece for Western orchestra inspired by an ancient Tamil philosophical poem. His goal was to use performances, recordings, and Western notation to make available to the entire world an Indian "musical masterpiece in an universally accepted format which others can read and play" ("Thiruvasakam in Symphony"

2004). He toured the world visiting associations of Tamil people to raise funds for this work and for an envisioned music education center that he will direct in Chennai.

The top Tamil film music director of the past dozen years is A. R. Rahman (also spelled Rehman, sometimes abbreviated as ARR). Born in 1966 in Madras as a Hindu named Dileep Kumar, his father was R. K. Sekhar, a Malayalam filmmusic director who tragically passed away just as his first film as MD was to be released. At the time Rahman was only nine years old; just two years later, he joined Ilayaraja's filmmusic orchestra as a keyboardist. Like Ilayaraja, ARR also learned Western music from Master Dhanraj and studied through the Trinity College of Music program. Before coming to film music, he performed in rock bands and composed music for some three hundred television advertisements, many remembered to this day. He converted to Islam after a Muslim saint saved the life of his sister, and is known to be very devout, having completed a *hajj* (pilgrimage) to Mecca, and is inclined towards mysticism. His debut filmscore, *Roja* (1992), was very popular and won many awards, including the Government of India's National Film Award for best music director. Today, Rahman is the one of the most sought-after and highly paid music directors of the entire Indian film industry; he is active in the Hindi industry of Bollywood, scoring such hits as *Lagaan*. Rahman's songs formed the basis of the Andrew Lloyd Webber musical *Bombay Dreams,* produced in London and New York in 2002 to 2004.

Rahman is a pioneer in musical sounds, instrument technology, and recording techniques. He constructed a sophisticated home studio, the famous Panchathan Record Inn in Chennai, and maintains it as one of the best-equipped studios in the nation. Rather than working from large rented studios on film lots, as his predecessors had done, Rahman composes and records in his own space. He is known to work alone, very late at night, and often records single performers rather than capturing the sound of an entire ensemble at once. After performing and recording basic rhythm and harmony tracks from his keyboards, he will call in a soloist. Guitarist R. Visweswaran described being allowed to play freely as Rahman recorded sounds that later would be cut and pasted on his Apple computer digital recording workstation (interview of R. Visweswaran by Getter, January 3, 2001). Rahman is himself quite capable of operating his recording gear and MIDI sequencers, though he has assistants, including two highly regarded sound engineers, H. Sridhar and Sivakumar.

Regarding his musical style, many say that Rahman has created a new sound for the present-day younger generation. In the analysis of Gregory Booth (in this volume), Rahman's music has "a style that might be considered truly postmodern as well as transnational," in his reconfiguration of the old sounds of Bollywood via new technologies. Hallmarks of ARR's style include very modern rock and funk grooves, arrangements that are at times economical or sparse, lush string orchestrations that mix live and sampled sounds, extensive use of synthesizers, and inclusion of rap, English words, and unusual voices. At the beginning of his film career, he was noteworthy for being an early adopter of sampling technology, and his style was quite distinct from the field; but his success has shifted musical tastes and production strategies so much that now all of Tamil film music seems to bear a resemblance to his sounds and methods.

Many film musicians are involved in performing or composing several genres of music. Rahman has written scores for both Tamil and Hindi films, released albums of pop and patriotic songs, such as his revival of the national anthem *Vandē Mātaram* (1997), and is reported to be working on a symphonic piece. Recently, he collaborated with Britain's Yusuf Islam (formerly Cat Stevens), helping to record vocal tracks in India for Islam's tsunami benefit song "Indian Ocean," his first pop song in decades (Islam 2005). Though ARR had met with him previously, Islam was not present in Chennai for the session; tracks were exchanged between their studios via the internet, a technological advance now also used to score films in India (interviews of Rahman and sound engineer Sivakumar by Getter, January 15, 2005).

There are many other Tamil music directors of past and present. It is difficult to generalize about their backgrounds since they are so varied, but it would be safe to say that all have skills in more than one genre of music (such as knowledge of both Western and Karnāṭak music), the ability to create music quickly, and leadership and organizational skills. A keen understanding of the history of Tamil film music is also essential, to facilitate innovation and novelty, as well as imitation and mimicry; wholesale borrowing of previously released music is not unknown. Music directors come from a variety of family backgrounds, including some with origins outside of Tamil Nadu; it is the case that all but a small handful of MDs have been men. This is likely the result of limited training and work opportunities at music studios for women, as well as more general societal constraints on women's behavior and mobility. Some women music directors are Saraswati Devi (1912–1980) and Usha Khanna from the Hindi industry, P. Bhanumathi and Hamsalekha from the Telugu industry, and Srishaila from Kannada films; from the Tamil industry, presently Bhavatharani (the daughter of Ilayaraja) has sung and scored for films. Some other significant composers of Tamil film music of past and present

Figure 1. Music director Bharadwaj (tallest person, at center) in the A.V.M. re-recording studio. Photo by J. Getter, January 4, 2005.

include Bharadwaj, Deva, Dhina, G. Ramanathan, Harris Jayaraj, K. V. Mahadevan, Karthik Raja, S. A. Rajkumar, S. M. Subbaiah Naidu, Vidyasagar, and Yuvan Shankar Raja.

Lyrics and the human voice are essential not only for film music but for all genres of Indian music; vocal melodies and the poetics of language are the heart of Tamil film songs. Some observe that the past few years have seen the rise of "fast" or "beat" music, and many object to its overshadowing of melody by rhythm. For example, singer P. Unnikrishnan said "melody has taken a back seat" in a television interview (Vijay TV New Year's Eve program, December 31, 2004). Conversely, some audiences enjoy and may even prefer other elements of a song, such as its "picturization" (the filmed song sequences), beats, rhythms, instrumental timbres, textures, or arrangements. Opinions about the merits of various films, composers, singers, lyricists, and music directors are great topics for casual conversation or heated debate (for examples, read the discussion forums at http://www.tfmpage.com).

Singers are deeply loved by their fans, and may achieve more popularity than film stars and music directors. Some popular vocalists include Anupama Deshpande, Anuradha Sriram, Chitra, Febi, Harini, Hariharan, K. B. Sundarambal, K. J. Yesudas, Kavita Krishnamurthy, L. R. Eswari,

M. K. Thyagaraja Bhagavatar, M. S. Rajeswari, Malaysia Vasudevan, Min-
mini, Neol James, P. Leela, P. Susheela, P. Unnikrishnan, P. B. Srinivasa, S.
Janaki, S. P. Balasubramanyam, Sadhana Sargam, Shahul Hameed, Shankar Mahadevan, Sujatha, Suresh Peters, T. M. Soundarajan, Udit Narayan,
Vasundara Das, and others. Particular singers often are associated with certain music directors. For example, MSV's songs frequently made use of the
distinctive voices of T. M. Soundarajan and P. Susheela; Ilayaraja had many
hits with S. P. Balasubramanyam (known as SPB) and S. Janaki; while Rahman is noted for occasionally introducing new and different voices. Some
singers such as Nityashree Mahadevan and P. Unnikrishnan are active
Karnāṭak classical singers as well as film singers, and are able to concert-
ize in both genres in India and abroad. Anuradha Sriram has sung on
pop music albums in the Hindi, Tamil (Sriram 1997), and Malayalam
languages, for Hindi and Tamil film scores, for Tamil language Hindu
devotional music, and for children's music, and is a classically trained
singer in both Hindustani and Karnāṭak systems; she is unique in the
film world in that she holds a graduate degree in ethnomusicology (see
Mohan 1994).

Lyric writers, instrumentalists, music copyists, arrangers, conductors,
computer operators, and assistants make up the remainder of the production team. A small number of performers create the large corpus of film
music. Instrumental musicians generally work on daily contracts with specific music directors. For instruments used in larger number such as violin,
there may be more qualified players available, while for certain instruments
there are fewer. For example, the two flutists Naveen and Natraj are heard
on many recordings by various music directors (interview of Natraj by
Getter, January 3, 2005). Lyric writers are perhaps fewest in number, and
over the years have included Gangai Amaran, Kalidasan, Kannadasan,
Madhurakavi Bhaskaradas, Papanasam Sivan, Pattukottai Kalyanasunda-
ram, Pulamai Pithan, Vairamuthu, and Vali. In the 1960s and 1970s, Kannadasan and Vali wrote beautiful Tamil lyrics that were very popular. Since
the 1980s, Vairamuthu has penned many lyrics for hit films, and fans say he
has taken Tamil film music into a new dimension. The expression of romantic love, ranging from tender to vulgar, is overwhelmingly the most
common subject of film lyrics. After the entry of A. R. Rahman, song lyrics
have begun to include more English words. Lyrics are of particular interest
to audiences. Booklets of lyrics are available in shops and near cinema halls;
nowadays lyrics are posted online. Fans use such resources to sing film
songs, and they may share their renditions as karaoke or in games that test
one's knowledge of the repertoire.

In this section, we will describe how film songs and background score are created in the Tamil industry, processes that may be thought of as "strategies" for composing and recording; see Gregory Booth's article in this volume for an account of the Bollywood industry. The process of composing a film song is a team effort that must meet the requirements of the movie's situation as well as the standards of song form and style. This workflow was observed in sessions with music director M. S. Viswanathan and singer P. Unnikrishnan, and is common to many other MDs. The process demands the cooperation of many people; M. S. Viswanathan keeps a Successories "Teamwork" motivational poster in his home reception area to remind people to work together. Typically, the film's producer, director, and music director begin with a discussion of the film's story and overall style. The music director, alone or with assistants, develops appropriate songs that are then shared with the film's producers in a "composing session." At this session, a lyrics writer may be present, crafting lyrics on the spot. Next, instrumental tracks are recorded in a studio, and then temporary vocal tracks are added (interview of M. S. Viswanathan by Getter, January 2, 2001). The music director may also personally adjust the lyrics to suit previously recorded songs and instrumental tracks (interview of A. R. Rahman on SunTv, August 15, 2004).

Star singers are brought in later to re-record the vocal tracks, and then the song is ready for release to the public, perhaps ahead of the film itself as a promotion. There are many modern digital audio recording studios throughout Chennai, such as Prasad, Audio Media, A.V.M., Karthik Garden, and Pallavi Digital Audio. The singer will listen to the temporary vocals, read the lyrics, and practice the song. Recording is a nonlinear process that starts and stops a great deal. Early takes attempt to record as much music as possible, while later takes use punching-in to capture better performances of single lines, or as little as a word or two. The music director may not be present for the singer's recording, but will have representatives in the recording booth. The lyricist or an assistant will check the singer's pronunciation carefully for accuracy; each and every syllable must be perfect (interview of P. Unnikrishnan by Getter, December 18, 2000). Each MD has his or her own working style: MSV sings parts to his musicians, IR is known to notate everything, while ARR often works alone at a computer.

Songs are then "picturized," a process in which scenes are filmed to fit a song. As the prerecorded song plays on the filming location or set, actors mouth the lyrics while dancing to the song. Hence the term "playback" describes film singers and their singing. Often, a number of choreographed dancers will be used in the scene. Dance in Indian commercial films is a unique blend of influences, in a similar fashion as film music. The finished song sequence then becomes part of the film, but also may circulate independently outside of movie theaters. Audio tracks of film songs are released on audiocassette and compact disc, frequently ahead of the film's release as a promotional tool, and eventually songs may be compiled into packages of hits by a particular singer, music director, or actor. Video compact discs and DVDs are marketed similarly, sold online and in music recording shops ranging in size from tiny stalls on the street to megastores in malls. Television became very widely available near the close of the twentieth century in Chennai, and nowadays many satellite and cable channels broadcast entire films and programs of songs. There are many avid readers of film and music reviews published in magazines and newspapers. Chennai's film-music culture also encompasses the major public holidays commemorating deceased actors, and the past and present famous actors who became prominent politicians.

The typical form of a Tamil film song has sections similar to verses, choruses, and instrumental breaks. The "background music" (or "BGM") is an instrumental interlude, and may open the song or be interspersed through the song (its term is not to be confused with the "background score" accompanying non-song scenes). The use of BGM is likely a holdover from the first decades of sound film, when poor conditions dictated that actors had to stand still while singing in order to get a good audio recording; BGM gave them a chance to dance a bit during the song. The next section of a typical song is the *pallavi,* the equivalent of a refrain or chorus. This repeated main part always has the same lyrics, and usually supplies the song title with its first line. The third part is the *caraṇam,* or verse, which will have a different melody from the *pallavi.* When the *caraṇam* repeats, its lyrics will change. A model form would be: 1st BGM, *pallavi,* 2nd BGM, 1st *caraṇam, pallavi,* 3rd BGM, 2nd *caraṇam, pallavi.*

A few filmmakers have made a movie without songs (while retaining the background score), although very few attempt this since none have achieved commercial success with a songless film. Famous and versatile actor Kamal Hassan once wished to make a film without songs, and so acted in *Kurudhippunal* ("River of Blood," 1995). Despite its high-quality production and good reviews, the film did not perform particularly well at the box office because it lacked songs. One user comment submitted to the website IMDb.com remarked that the film "was well appreciated in urban circles" (The Internet Movie Database [n.d.]: paragraph 3), alluding not so much to differences in urban versus rural audience tastes, but rather to how issues of class and education can contribute to opinions about film among the Tamil audience.

After songs are recorded and the scenes are shot and edited, the last stage of film-music production is the creation of the background score. This process is known in the Tamil industry as "re-recording," a Hollywood term from the dawn of the sound film era, meaning that sound is recorded later after shooting (Davis 1999:27). Music directors and film directors feel that this score can have a predictable yet powerful effect upon the audience, and describe it as "storytelling" (interview of A. R. Rahman on SunTV, August 15, 2004). This music is designed to support the "situation" of the action, scene, or narrative. In a general sense, this music works in a similar way to any film music from the Hollywood superculture, with devices such as leitmotifs to identify characters. To understand Tamil re-recording music more fully, the Tamil cultural context must be recognized. One aspect of this is the identity of the characters, who may be differentiated by their gender, age, social status, occupation, religion, caste (which includes the broad divisions of *varṇa* and the clan-like groupings of *jāti*), urban or rural setting, and other distinctions. It is important for background scoring to articulate these differences so that audiences may perceive the characters. Re-recording music is occasionally a topic for discussion among fans and filmgoers, but it usually does not circulate outside of the film itself as do the songs.

The background score can accent specific points in the flow of the film's narrative and action. For example, to give emphasis to moments of tension in a scene for the film *Iyer IPS* (2005), music director Dhina used a device commonly heard in Tamil film: a loud, resonant, low-pitched drum hit that he called a "stroke." Working with just his assistant Kingsley in a small personal studio, Dhina also asked him to stretch the sound in time for an extended effect (interview of Dhina by Getter, January 11, 2005). Re-recording also can be used to signal the entrance of a character. This use of music is thought to derive from principles codified in the *Nāṭya Śastra*, the first or second century C.E. Sanskrit treatise on drama. In this work, *dhruva* compositions are described as musical pieces employed for each character, so that audiences may identify a particular character by hearing a composition. In film, music director Ilayaraja made very effective and innovative use of this type of background music. For instance, in the film *Mouna Ragam* ("Silent Music," 1986), particular music was added to the soundtrack when characters appear.

Emotions of the scene's situation are accented through the music of re-recording, in combination with the film's dialog, sound effects, and visual elements. The Sanskrit language word *bhāva* may best capture a sense of the meaning of emotion as it relates to Tamil film. Some emotions commonly found in films are pathos, joy, anger, tension, humor, and *bhakti* (devotion). Methods for expressing emotions in Tamil film are very loosely based upon *rasā*, a key concept in Indian aesthetics that can be translated as the essence of an emotion. Musicians, actors, and directors may have studied the nature of these qualities and learned how to express them, particularly if they learned Indian classical music and dance, since these art forms are permeated with *rasā*. Audiences may feel these emotions even if they do not associate a film's feelings explicitly with the details of aesthetic theory. The *Nāṭya Śastra* delineated eight *rasās*, to which a later commentator added a ninth. These are: *śringāra* (erotic), *hāsya* (humor), *karunā* (pathos), *raudra* (anger), *vīra* (valour), *bhayānaka* (fear), *bībhatsa* (disgust), *adbhuta* (wonder), and *śānta* (peace). An Indian classical dancer learns how to portray these qualities through particular facial expressions, and a classical musician learns how to express what is known as *rāga bhāva*, the feeling of a melodic mode. Tamil film musicians, on the other hand, need not adhere to these stricter idioms, but nonetheless may make use of them as devices to create emotions.

Many types of cultural activities can be expressed in the background score, by drawing upon musical expressions from daily life. In films there are songs for many different occasions: *tālāṭṭu*, a lullaby; *saḍuguḍu* and *kabaḍi* game songs; paddy field songs such as *naḍavu pāṭṭu;* puberty and marriage time songs *naluṅgu, ūñjal, mālai māṟṟu;* music of Hindu temple rituals, such as *karagāṭṭam, oyilāṭṭam, mayilāṭṭam, kummi, kolāṭṭam, silambāṭṭam,* and *urumi mēḷam;* the musical bow *villuppāṭṭu,* and so on. In the film *Iyer IPS,* a character sang *oppāri,* a traditional weeping song of grief, to lament the death of a relative (interview of Dhina by Getter, January 3, 2005).

Re-recording must adhere to a certain work flow. In a typical re-recording session, the music director works on scenes from a single entire reel (about 11 minutes) for which the film director has completed the editing. In the past, the reels would arrive in the re-recording studio as actual reels of film (usually thirteen to fifteen reels for a feature film), but today the film's images are converted to DVD and then loaded into computers with nonlinear audio-editing software such as Logic, Nuendo, or Soundscape R.Ed. Dialog and sound effects will be in place and finished at this time, meaning music is the final element of the sound track to be added. Once edited reels of film are ready for re-recording to be added, the music director and assistants go through the scenes and mark points that require music; in the past, a worker known as the "marker" would mark the film physically, but now this is done on a computer. Meanwhile, the MD, in

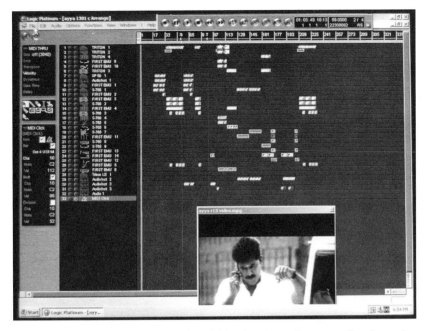

Figure 2. Screen of a computer workstation with Logic software, for re-recording the music of *Ayyā* at A.V.M. Studios. Photo by J. Getter, January 4, 2005.

consultation with the film director, takes notes on the musical requirements of each scene and shot of the film.

Later, the musicians gather in a re-recording studio. The music director may play and record his or her own keyboard performances to accompany the scenes, or may delegate this task to assistants. This description is based upon observations of music director Bharadwaj as he worked on *Ayyā* (2005) in the re-recording sound studio of A.V.M. studios in Chennai (interview of Bharadwaj by Getter, January 3–4, 2005). These sessions differed from those of Dhina mentioned above, in that while Dhina worked with just one assistant in his personal studio, while Bharadwaj's team included about two dozen musicians, plus a few sound engineers in a rented re-recording theater. Bharadwaj oversaw the entire process from the main mixing board, listening to ensure his stylistic "stamp" was executed and that the film's needs were met. As three assistants at their own keyboard-computer workstations each worked on various sections of the film, a violin section was recorded simultaneously in the main booth. A good assistant can grasp the needs of the film completely, and is also able to create music in the style of the music director. After basic tracks are recorded, more layers of keyboard-based synthesized drums, melody, and harmony are added, as well as accents and other short musical sounds that support the action. Finally, acoustic instruments are recorded to add the beauty and quality of realistic sounds. This procedure is common for many larger budget productions; smaller films might use only synthesizers, employ a smaller staff, and try to get the job done as fast as possible. Re-recording may take from a day or two up to a week or more, depending on the score's complexity, the film's budget, and everyone's availability. A. R. Rahman worked over a period of two months on *Bombay*, due to its complexity and the minimal amount of dialog in many scenes (interview of A. R. Rahman on SunTV, August 15, 2004).

The final stage in the creation of a Tamil film soundtrack is audio mixing. This account is based upon observations at the A.V.M. and Prasad studios and talks with their sound engineers. To begin, dialog, sound effects, and music are each recorded separately. It is a common practice in Tamil films that all dialog is recorded later in an audio studio and then dubbed in, primarily due to uncontrollable set noise. Dubbing is also done in order to release a film in another language, or perhaps to substitute an actor's voice with that of a voice actor who is more suitable for a character. Thus the screen actor's voice may or may not supply the sound the audience will hear. Next, the elements of dialog, effects, and music are each mixed as separate entities, and then these three are combined into a final mix that will accompany the film to theaters. Sound may be either monaural optical (sound printed on the film), or digital 6-channel DTS mixes (in which the sound is played from compact discs specially formatted for DTS; one CD accompanies each film reel). Mono is for older theaters, while DTS (which is similar to Dolby) is for newer cinema halls.

To create a good DTS audio mix for a film song or background score, the engineer must grasp the film's narrative, genre, and feeling. Sound engineers often work separately from the music director, although the film director will give final approval for the audio mix. Usually the songs are mixed with vocals in the front center channel, vocal effects such as reverb in front left and right, melody instruments in front left and right plus rear left and right, and finally, bass sounds such as kick drum in the bass channel. Equalization and effects may or may not have been added by the music director, so mixing engineers must adjust these as needed. Sound engineers and others in the industry believe that the volume level of a film in the cinema hall should be quite loud, particularly for songs, since that is what audiences have come to expect (interviews by Getter of A.V.M. engineer Ayyappan, January 3, 2005; and Prasad engineer S. Chandra Kumar, January 18, 2005).

Listening to the Film Kandukondain Kandukondain

The music for a Tamil film is perceived by a Tamil audience in certain ways. Scholar of Indian films Rajadhyaksha writes that "any encounter with a film is always pre-structured, given that people are never utterly empty-headed when watching it. Reliance on the film alone is as misguided as an overestimation of the secondary discourses. As always, we have to see one in terms of the other" (Rajadhyaksha and Willemen 1999:11). In the following section, we analyze one film in detail in order to reveal its internal musical workings, references, and logic. Some of this may not be readily apparent to non-Tamil or non-Indian audiences, while this is not to say that any Tamil person would comprehend this music precisely as we have outlined here.

For our sample film, we have selected Rajiv Menon's critically acclaimed *Kandukondain Kandukondain* (2000), also known as *Kaṇḍukoṇḍēn Kaṇḍukoṇḍēn* ("I have found it! I have found it!"). Menon is based in Chennai, and has family roots in the neighboring state of Kerala. He is well known for his television advertisement films, but has produced only one other feature film, *Minsara Kanavu* (1997, dubbed in Hindi as *Sapnay*). He pioneered the use of the Steadicam in India, and worked as a cinematographer for other directors' film, such as Mani Ratnam's controversial *Bombay* (1995).

This Tamil language film features top actors Mammooty (who plays the character Major Bala), Ajith (Manohar), Tabu (Sowmya), and Aishwarya Rai (who plays Meenakshi). Rai was Miss World in 1994; in 2005, talk-show host David Letterman called her "the most beautiful woman in the world." The story is about the romances of the two sisters and their family's struggles. The film has very strong, independent female characters who achieve success in the modern world. Ajith plays an aspiring film director, giving the film reason to include many behind-the-scenes views of film shootings and also film-music recording. The music director is A. R. Rahman, with lyrics by Vairamuthu.

In the following section, we list the sound and musical elements as they occur in the opening hour of the film, including analysis of three songs. Music that is described as "diegetic" emanates from sources that are known to the audience to be part of the scene or story, while "non-deigetic" music issues from a source that is not a part of the scene. (Note: in the United States this film is available for rent from South Asian grocery and video stores, and may be purchased from sources listed at the end of this chapter as well as from Amazon.com. If you don't have access to the film, then this section should remain useful for understanding some aspects of a Tamil film score).

Transcription of Music in the Film Kandukondain Kandukondain:

Time	Notes on Scene/Section of Song	Notes on Sounds and Music or Visuals
0:00	Censor's certificate and acknowledgements	no sound or music
0:36	waterfall scene; helicopter enters and army commandos jump out	keyboard pads (a type of synthesizer timbre that is light and sustained, with a soft attack) in a minor key; music is foreboding, with quiet yet driving percussion rhythms for suspense
1:29	small school in a jungle	children's recitation of the poem "Ātticcūḍi" by the ancient Tamil poet Avvaiyar; the lines begin in alphabetical order
1:53	tension builds as a militant sneaks away	an orchestral "stroke" emphasizes the tension
2:00	militants and army clash by the school	gunfire sounds, drum beats (toms and high-hat cymbals) create suspense and support the action's faster pace; the scene ends with an explosion as a wounded man sails through the air
2:38	main title sequence	"Kaṇḍukoṇḍēn Kaṇḍukoṇḍēn" song performed as a melodious free-rhythm instrumental; Indian bamboo flute alternating with soprano saxophone play the melody, supported by synths, pads, bass, piano
4:01	scene of a film crew shooting a scene outdoors; for the film audience, the Tamil pop song is diegetic music (emanating from the shooting scene), while from the point of view of the dancer and crew filming her lip-sync singing, the music's role is non-diegetic (the musical source is not meant to be present)	tambura (stringed drone), female chorus (group of vocalists), synth pop beat; song text meaning, "lips, eyelashes, shiver [of excitement on the skin]"; the music begins at a higher volume and fades so the dialog may be heard

Time	Scene	Music
4:16	song stops at a cut in shooting; director begins it again by yelling (in English) "start sound"	
5:50	rural landscape	*rural theme* music: folk melody on high-pitched flute, with *tappu* folk drum (in *tisra nadai* or 12/8 time, four beats subdivided into triplets), pads, bass
6:07	outside a Hindu temple	the particular Sanskrit chant heard indicates the act of *āratti* (offering of a flame) at a Śaivite Hindu temple; reverberation effect on voice mimics the acoustics of a large stone temple's interior
6:19		bells are rung by devotees; *rural theme* continues
7:07	Chettinad area, exterior of a Chettiar mansion (a distinctive architectural style)	double-reed *nāgaswaram* plays a folk-style tune, evoking the rural setting, accompanied by bass guitar, tambourine, and synths
7:21	interior of the family's home	music from outside continues, now played by *vīna* (a lute), conveying a sense of home, as well as sophistication since it is usually a classical Karnāṭak music instrument; music fades for dialog
7:54	Grandpa cannot speak to communicate regarding his will	keyboard chords and *nāgaswaram* express pathos with slow, minor key music; reverb and low volume makes it seem that the music comes from far in the distance
8:28	two sisters in their bathing pool, exterior scene	*two sisters' theme* is used throughout the film to identify these characters, with music expressing a happy mood; instruments include a bell-tree, synths, bass, percussion, and an electric violin; the music begins loud then fades under dialog
9:44	rice paddy field scene	1st song "Koñjum Mainākkaḷē" (meaning "little bird"), sung by Sadhana Sargam, featuring the character Meenakshi (played by Aishwarya Rai)

Transcription of Music in the Film Kandukondain Kandukondain *(continued)*:

Time	Notes on Scene/Section of Song	Notes on Sounds and Music or Visuals
1st Song		
9:44	1st BGM	humming and nontextual singing; at first, only a high-hat cymbal accompanies, then synths, bass, percussion; melody is related to the Karnāṭak classical *rāga* Brindāvana Sāranga
10:09	*pallavi*	group of male dancers, with black and white make-up vertically splitting their faces and torsos; Meenakshi dances with dance harvest, and uses Bharata Natyam *mudras* (hand gestures) that portray the maina bird of the song's title
11:05	2nd BGM	Kathakali (Indian theater from Kerala) masks; male chorus, plucked guitar-like sounds, strings, funk music feel; then a solo by a high-pitched flute
11:39	1st *caraṇam*	masks of Ganesha (elephant-headed god who removes obstacles), as Meenakshi rides on a large tree swing, symbolizing her carefree nature and attractiveness; then masks of Bharathi (famous early twentieth-century Tamil poet)
12:24	*pallavi*	a portion of the pallavi is used; voice is overdubbed in multiple parts for a special effect
12:33	3rd BGM	tiger make-up from Puliyāṭṭam folk art of South India; high flute, small drums, lower drums with variable pitch (like left hand of *tabla* drums), synth friction drum (like *urumi*), and frame drums
13:04	2nd *caraṇam*	in second part, voice is doubled with the same melody
13:43	*pallavi*	vocals are again layered with several parts

14:18	(end of song)	no music
14:20	interior, Sowmya's office	
14:35	interior of home	*two sisters' theme*
15:12	interior, a prospective groom for an arranged marriage with Sowmya visits	background diegetic music is a recording of Tevaram devotional song by an *ōduvār* singer; as the electricity fails, the pitch of the recording falls off as though the gramophone has lost power
15:49	exterior of home	*love theme* music: slow, free-rhythm, with keyboards, Rhodes electric piano synth timbre
16:09	power is restored	a bell-tree sounds
16:21	interior	*love theme* repeats after a pause
16:47	Grandpa struggles to speak	strings are added for feeling of pathos
17:23	argument between the sisters' mother and her father (Grandpa)	no music
17:47	argument ends	*love theme* sounds
18:20	comedy scene	clay-pot *ghaṭam* drum plays a rhythm; this instrument often accompanies comedy scenes; a separate click sound defines the beat
19:02	a cassette player is shown playing a recording of *keṭṭimēḷam* (just its beginning, for about 3 seconds)	this *nāgaswaram* and *tavil* (drum) music accompanies the specific moment in a Hindu marriage ritual when the sacred thread is tied around the bride's neck, after which the couple is considered to be married

Transcription of Music in the Film Kandukondain Kandukondain (*continued*):

Time	Notes on Scene/Section of Song	Notes on Sounds and Music or Visuals
19:24	comedy	*ghaṭam* accompanies; plucked mandolin-like strings play a fragment from the melody of the song "Kaṇḍukoṇḍēn"
19:42	two cats are brought together in a mock marriage, as a joke to appease the mother who wishes for someone to get married	*keṭṭimēḷam* plays on cassette (more complete, for about 8 seconds)
20:04	interior of home, sisters with mother	*two sisters' theme*
20:49	at the door of the home, Manohar arrives to ask permission for film shooting	doorbell
21:04	Sowmya answers the door thinking he is a prospective groom; they meet and are immediately interested in one another	*Manohar's theme* music (taken from 1st BGM of "Enna Sollap Pōgirāi" from this film): plucked strings, tambourine, and Rhodes keyboard
21:52	music stops as couple speak	a cow is heard, indicating the rural setting
22:06	couple talk	*Manohar's theme* stops and starts a few times; pads and synths add tension with dissonant harmonies
22:58	Manohar realizes the family is speaking of marriage, and they realize he is speaking about film shooting	the music stops with a falling pitch in the synth sounds
23:31	Manohar is thrown out	*love theme*
24:00	exterior of home, Manohar and Sowmya look at one another	Western-style violin adds pathos

24:12	exterior	*rural theme* of folk music, percussion, flute
24:28	they speak of love	the percussion fades out but the flute continues
25:40	at Bala's flower nursery	a worker walks along singing a famous film song from the 1960s, "Kēļvi pirandadu anṛu" ("a question came a long time back, the answer came today"), composed by M. S. Viswanathan
26:14		synth with a plucked string sounds plays "Kaṇḍukoṇḍēn" melody fragment, with *ghaṭam*
26:45	exterior of a hall with a festival in progress; Nataraj icon is given offerings; an auspicious occasion	two *nāgasvarams* and a *tavil* play the kriti (Karnāṭak music composition) "Māmava sadā varadē" by Swati Tirunal (*rāga* Natakurinji, rupaka *tāla*, a three-beat time cycle); we cannot see the musicians, but hear a rendition compressed in the manner of old 78-rpm records—all three sections (*pallavi, anupallavi,* and *caranam*) are played quickly in succession, allowing the entire composition to fit onto a three minute record side; the music does not change when Sowmya and Manohar see one another
28:15	interior of the festival hall	2nd song "Kaṇṇāmūcci ēnaḍā" ("why this hide and seek, Krishna?"), sung by Chitra, featuring the character Meenakshi (played by Aishwarya Rai)
2nd Song		
28:15	*pallavi*	Meenakshi and many female dancers; musical introduction begins with voice, synth playing harmonies, tuned percussion play off-beats; then funk electric bass enters; at a change of melody, more tabla-like tuned percussion added
29:34	1st BGM	first the music is quieter as a dialog occurs; then an acoustic violin in Karnāṭak classical style plays during a Bharata Natyam–influenced dance sequence

Transcription of Music in the Film Kandukondain Kandukondain (*continued*):

Time	Notes on Scene/Section of Song	Notes on Sounds and Music or Visuals
30:07	*caraṇam*	the location shifts to the world of fantasy: a studio set with a minimalist design, featuring giant peacock feathers attached to giant swings
31:23	*pallavi*	(same set and music)
31:34	2nd BGM	new studio set, with very abstract cloth pieces and an animal shape; music features solos by *sarōd* (North India fretless lute) and violin
32:06	2nd *caraṇam*	song returns to the festival hall; changes in the keyboard harmony
33:04	*pallavi*	(same music)
33:14	(end of song)	abrupt ending as Major Bala falls down drunk
33:22	Bala yells at a bystander	pads, strokes lend emphasis
33:31		*pathos theme*: synth clarinet with reverb and string sounds express pathos
34:28		dissonance creates a dark, angry sound
34:34	Meenakshi criticizes Bala	no music
35:04	Bala criticizes Meenakshi because her song shifted from Natakurinji to Śahānā *rāga* (which happened in the song)	*pathos theme* heard again
35:24	rural exterior, then inside a van on the road, with Manohar taking an inebriated Bala home	clarinet sounds *pathos theme*, and continues during a flashback to the jungle fight from the film's first scene

36:40	flower nursery at night	no music, cricket noises are prominent
37:56	next day, Sowmya's car	no music
38:47	stopped at a railroad crossing; a passenger train goes by as Manohar expresses his love	train sounds are dramatic
38:49	at rail crossing	3rd song "Enna Solla Pōgirāī" ("what will your answer be?"), featuring the characters Manohar and Sowmya, sung by Shankar Mahadevan
3rd Song		
38:49	introduction	vocal, free rhythm, synths and strings
39:12	1st BGM	location shifts to an exotic desert; accordion solo, plucked strings (same music as *Manohar's theme*), finger snaps, bass
39:24	*pallavi*	rail tracks in the desert; Manohar and Sowmya are separated, moving closer together along the tracks, each with a group of dancers of the same gender
41:05	2nd BGM	clearly non–South Asian locale in shots of the landscape; flute, with pitch-shifter effect adding a flute harmony line and an ethereal quality; then an acoustic bamboo flute plays in Karṇāṭak classical style; bass, plucked strings, frame drums
41:40	1st *caraṇam*	stone temple scene; acoustic classical guitar accompanies
42:14	*pallavi*	in second scene of this *pallavi*, Egyptian pyramids finally revealed as the location
42:52	3rd BGM	Egyptian musicians and dancers in the scene; a large orchestra with strings and winds plays in a style influenced by Egyptian nightclub orchestral sounds
43:28	2nd *caraṇam*	*dumbek*, a Middle-Eastern drum

Transcription of Music in the Film Kandukondain Kandukondain:

Time	Notes on Scene/Section of Song	Notes on Sounds and Music or Visuals
44:03	4th BGM	mandolin-like plucked strings, bowed violin section
44:12	*pallavi*	at the base of a pyramid, she is separated from him by her family
44:47	(end of song)	
44:47	sisters' home, interior, Sowmya talks to Grandpa	no music
45:03	Sowmya thinks of Manohar	*Manohar's theme* is heard
45:23	different room, a *tambura* is presented to Meenakshi by Bala, as he asks her to practice her music; exterior, she asks him not to drink	
46:08	music lesson scene; the teacher is portrayed by director Rajiv Menon's mother Kalyani Menon, who also does her own playback singing for this scene; the student is Meenakshi (Rai), with playback singing by Nityashree Mahadevan	phrases in *rāga* Nalinakānti (with a similarity to the beginning the title song's melody); *tambura* and two vocalists
46:48	Bala's nursery; comedy scene	*ghatam* clay pot
48:18	(end of transcription)	

Figure 3. Meenakshi (Aishwarya Rai) and dancers with Bharathi masks. Still from the DVD of the film *Kandukondain Kandukondain*.

Summary of Strategies

pads   synthesizer timbre that is light, sustained, with a soft attack

stroke   single accented note, percussive or orchestral, for a suspenseful moment

melodious   song with a beautiful melody

diegetic   music emanates from the scene

non-diegetic   musical source is not meant to be present in the scene

pop   modern electronic music, for youth, modernity, urban life

tambura   stringed drone instrument, for Indian ethos or to signify refined culture

folk music   often played by a high-pitched flute and drums, for a rural setting

vīna   the South Indian lute, conveys a sense of home, as well as sophistication

pathos   sad feeling with minor key music, may be slow

rāga   melodic mode concept from classical Karnāṭak music

BGM   background music, instrumental interludes in a song

pallavi   the refrain or chorus of a song

caraṇam   the verses of a song

devotional   religious songs, such as an *ōduvār* singer's Tevaram song

ghaṭam   clay-pot drum that is often used for comedy scenes

keṭṭimēḷam   music played by *nāgaswaram* (double-reed horn) and *tavil* (drum), for the specific moment when a couple is considered to be married in a Hindu wedding

Conclusion

In many ways, the film *Kandukondain Kandukondain* described above represents a typical contemporary commercial Tamil film and its musical score. The film blends romance, comedy, family drama, song sequences, and star actors. In some critical aspects, however, this film differs somewhat from the average output of the Tamil film industry: *Kandukondain* has an unusually high standard of technical production, the story is realistic, and there is great restraint in the acting. In an average Tamil movie, the actors' emotions are often exaggerated, played at 110 percent, but they are much more realistic here. At the box office, the film was not a huge hit, but neither was it a flop. It is regarded as having been more successful in urban theaters than in rural markets, perhaps in part because the film's realism appealed more to well-educated city-dwellers. Many critics praised the film, and its successes lifted the careers of those involved in the production. The film also continues to be one of a small number of newer movies to be shown periodically on the Tamil-language television station SunTV, further indicating the film's significance and appeal.

The story of *Kandukondain Kandukondain* is a family-based drama, like many Tamil films. But as with the naturalism of the acting, the film's story is also much more realistic than usual. An average Tamil film will exaggerate aspects of life, such as creating superhero characters and fantastic fight scenes, in order to give the audience the experience of something beyond what is possible in their usual daily life. In this film, the scenes, situations, and action are closer to real-life experiences. Director Rajiv Menon wrote the descriptions of the scenes for *Kandukondain Kandukondain* in the English language, but wrote the actors' dialogs in his mother tongue Malayalam. Subsequently, a scriptwriter rewrote the dialogs in the Tamil language, and then later this Tamil script was translated to English and published (Menon 2000: preface). The film is based upon Jane Austen's novel *Sense and Sensibility,* and the foreign origin of the story caused some to criticize Menon. However, he stated that the film has a "totally Tamil ethos . . . It is full of [Tamil poet] Bharathiyar, Karaikudi [district of Tamil Nadu], Carnatic music, etc." (Tamil Movie Cafe 2001: paragraph 11).

Compared to many other Tamil films, *Kandukondain Kandukondain* shows that great care and attention was devoted to the crafting of musical details throughout the background score of the film. This is likely due to the fact that director Rajiv Menon hails from a strongly musical family; his mother is singer Kalyani Menon, who makes a cameo appearance in the film as a vocal music teacher giving a lesson. Menon has a direct understanding of *rāga* and the power of music to a degree that is uncommon for a film director (for example, during our conversation, he sang many classical music phrases; interview of Menon by Getter, January 4, 2001). Overall, the film's music has a soft sound that suits the realism of the characters and story.

Aspects of Tamil and Indian traditions and modernity are all blended together in the film *Kandukondain Kandukondain.* The characters are metaphors for this combination of new and old. They are tied to family, traditions, and place, but they also have traveled abroad, work in modern fields such as the cinema industry, and include female characters striving for economic self-sufficiency. Similarly, the music performs the task of encoding the blending of cultures and ideals. The section above, "Summary of Strategies," lists a wide variety of musical sounds and sources, from electronic washes of sustained and short synthesizer tones, to folk music, ritual sounds, classical music, and modern pop, used as components of the background score. These join seamlessly into a whole that expresses a contemporary Tamil and Indian experience.

In this essay, we have presented some ways of understanding Tamil film music in its social and musical contexts. The settings, musical resources, people, and processes described here all contribute to the meaning and significance of this music. India's National Film Development Corporation published a "Brief History of Indian Cinema" on their internet website, expressing the range and importance of films in Indian society:

The film industry has . . . [a] . . . unique blend of commerce, art, craft, star glamour, social communication, literary adjuncts, artistic expression, performing arts, folk forms and above all a wide-ranging and abiding appeal to the heart, the mind and the conscience. (2000: paragraph 8)

Similarly, film music provides all types of musical variety under one roof, and thus appeals to a broad range of fans. Film melodies are generally simple to sing, in comparison with, for example, Karnāṭak classical music. These factors, together with the far reach of various media, have allowed Tamil film songs to spread into every corner of Tamil Nadu and beyond to many places around India and the world.

Despite the diversity of resources and strategies employed by music directors in creating background scores and songs, there are nonetheless several factors that lend unity to Tamil film music. Films often project a strong sense of Tamil regional identity by portraying aspects of daily life and culture that are often quite distinct from the broader national scene of India. Film scores and songs likewise often make references to particular local musical traditions, instruments, and melodic materials. Tamil films exhibit the filmmaker's and music director's consciousness of the history of South Indian film music.

Does Tamil film music have rules to which musicians must adhere? The answer is definitely yes, when considering such aspects as how rerecording music that accompanies a scene must function as a support for the situation, or how songs make use of familiar *rāga*s and forms. Conversely, the answer may be no, particularly with regard to the celebration of change, innovation, and creativity in this music. The liner notes of an audiocassette release contain this quote from music director Ilayaraja: "I have no parameters to restrict myself. Whatever comes to my mind, I have no hesitation in doing . . . I have no bounds" (Ilaiyaraja 1992: paragraph 7). There are no strict rules, but nonetheless the music must be intelligible and enjoyable. Should Tamil film music be considered as traditional or modern? Perhaps it is both at once. The cinema in India is seen by some as a very modern form, with its technological borrowings from Hollywood, while others think of it as "neo-traditional," such as in its use of indigenous forms of theater, acting and expression, narrative, and musical accompaniment (see Rajadhyaksha and Willemen 1999:10). One can say that unreal film-story situations often appeal to film audiences, because they desire to see that which is impossible in real life. Tamil film music is a genre of music that draws connections to daily life, yet transcends it with beautiful melodies, danceable rhythms, and all manner of things that sound familiar yet are all new.

Joseph Getter wishes to acknowledge the support of the Jon B. Higgins Memorial Fund of Wesleyan University, and faculty research grants from Southern Connecticut State University, which facilitated his fieldwork in Chennai during 2000–2001 and 2004–2005.

Bibliographic and Internet References

Abbas, K. A. 1977. *Mad, Mad, Mad World of Indian Films.* Delhi: Hind Pocket Books.
Anandan, Filmnews. 2004. *Sadhanaigal Padaitha Thamizhthiraipada Varalaru.* Chennai: Sivagami Publications.
Arnold, Alison E. 1988. "Popular Film Song in India: A Case of Mass Market Musical Eclecticism." *Popular Music* 7, no. 2 (May):177–88.
———. 1991. "Hindi Filmi Git: On the History of Commercial Indian Popular Music." Ph.D. dissertation. Urbana-Champaign: University of Illinois.
Baskaran, S. Theodore. 1981. *The Message Bearers: The Nationalist Politics and the Entertainment Media in South India, 1880–1945.* Madras: Cre-A.
———. 1996. *The Eye of the Serpent: An Introduction to Tamil Cinema.* Madras, India: East-West Books.
———. 2002. "Music for the People." *The Hindu,* online edition, January 6, 2002. http://www.hindu.com/thehindu/mag/2002/01/06/stories/2002010600150500 .htm (May 20, 2004).
Booth, Gregory D. 1990. "Brass Bands: Tradition, Change, and the Mass Media in Indian Wedding Music." *Ethnomusicology* 34, no. 2:245–62.
———. 1996. "The Madras Corporation Band: A Story of Social Change and Indigenization." *Asian Music* 28, no. 1 (Fall/Winter):61–86.
Chakravarty, Sumita. 1993. *National Identity in Indian Popular Cinema, 1947–1987.* Austin: University of Texas Press.

Chennai District. 2007. "Census 2001 Data." Online edition; follow links to Profile and then to Population. http://www.chennai.tn.nic.in/ (April 29, 2007).

Davis, Richard. 1999. *Complete Guide to Film Scoring.* Boston: Berkelee Press.

Dickey, Sara. 1993. *Cinema and the Urban Poor in South India.* Cambridge: Cambridge University Press.

Getter, Joseph M. 1999. "Imagining the Image of India: Symbols of the Nation in Two Films." Paper presented at the meeting of the Society for Ethnomusicology, Northeast Chapter, Eastern Connecticut State University.

——. 2000. "A New Sound for a Globalizing India? National Identity in A. R. Rahman's Music." Paper presented at the annual meeting of the Society for Ethnomusicology, Musical Intersections Conference, Toronto.

Gokulsing, K. Moti, and Wimal Dissanayake. 1998. *Indian Popular Cinema, a Narrative of Cultural Change.* Staffordshire, England: Trentham Books.

Gopalan, Lalitha. 2002. *Cinema of Interruptions: Action Genres in Contemporary Indian Cinema.* New Delhi: Oxford University Press.

Greene, Paul. 1995. "Cassettes in Culture: Emotion, Politics, and Performance in Rural Tamil Nadu." Ph.D. dissertation. Philadelphia: University of Pennsylvania.

——. 1999. "Sound Engineering in a Tamil Village: Playing Audio Cassettes as Devotional Performance." *Ethnomusicology* 43, no. 3:459–89.

——. 2000a. "Pop Music and Audio-Cassette Technology: Southern Area." In *The Garland Encyclopedia of World Music. Volume 5, South Asia, The Indian Subcontinent,* ed. Alison Arnold, 554–59. New York: Garland.

——. 2000b. "Film Music: Southern Area." In *The Garland Encyclopedia of World Music. Volume 5, South Asia, The Indian Subcontinent,* ed. Alison Arnold, 542–46. New York: Garland.

Guy, Randor, ed. 1997. *Starlight, Starbright: The Early Tamil Cinema.* Chennai: Amra Publishers.

——. 2000. "Papanasam Siva: Cinematic Perspective." *Sangeetham.com.* http://www.sangeetham.com/others/archive.php3?combo_title=&combo_date+2000-05-15&butt_archive=Ok&percent24combo_title=&percent24combo_date=&idval=Movies +and+Musicians&fea=Movies+and+Musicians (June 27, 2005).

Hughes, Stephen. 2000. "Policing Silent Film Exhibition in Colonial South India." In *Making Meaning in Indian Cinema,* ed. Ravi Vasudevan, 39–64. New Delhi: Oxford University Press.

Internet Movie Database, The. [n.d.]. "Kuruthipunal: User Comments." *IMDb.com.* http://www.imdb.com/title/tt0285665 (August 16, 2005).

Jacob, Preminda Susana. 1994. "Film and Political Advertisements of South India: Urban Spectacle, Popular Culture, Third World Industry." Ph.D. dissertation. Los Angeles: University of California.

Kumar, Rajat. 2000. "From Staid to Swing—with the Boardwalkers." *Chennaionline.com.* http://www.chennaionline.com/bandstand/boardwalkers.asp (May 31, 2004).

L'Armand, Kathleen, and Adrian L'Armand. 1983. "One Hundred Years of Music in Madras: A Case Study in Secondary Urbanization." *Ethnomusicology* 27, no. 3:411–38.

Manuel, Peter. 1993. *Cassette Culture.* Chicago: University of Chicago Press.

Menon, Rajiv. 2000. *The Script of Kandukondain Kandukondain.* Chennai: Westland Books.

Mishra, Vijay. 2002. *Bollywood Cinema: Temples of Desire.* New York and London: Routledge.

Mohan, Anuradha. 1994. *Ilaiyaraja: Composer as Phenomenon in Tamil Film Culture.* Master's thesis. Wesleyan University, Middletown, Connecticut.

Moksha. [2004]. "Rock in India." *Mokshaonline.com.* http://www.mokshaon line.com/rock.htm (February 1, 2004).

Nandy, Ashish, ed. 1998. *The Secret Politics of Our Desires: Innocence, Culpability and Indian Popular Cinema.* Delhi: Oxford University Press.

Narayan, R. K. 1990. "On Films." In *A Story-Teller's World.* New Delhi: Penguin Books, 110–12.

National Film Development Corporation of India. 2000. "A Brief History of Indian Cinema." *nfdcindia.com.* http://www.nfdcindia.com/cinema-history.html (Feb. 19, 2000).

Pandian, M. S. S. 1992. *The Image Trap: M. G. Ramachandran in Film and Politics.* Delhi: Sage.

Pendakur, Manjunath. 2003. *Indian Popular Cinema: Industry, Ideology, and Consciousness.* Cresskill, N.J.: Hampton Press.

Prasad, M. Madhava. 1998. *Ideology of the Hindi Film: A Historical Construction.* Delhi: Oxford University Press.

Rajadhyaksha, Ashish, and Paul Willemen. 1999. *Encyclopaedia of Indian Cinema.* New Revised Edition. London: British Film Institute, and New Delhi: University Press.

Ram, Vignesh. 2002. "*Mugangal:* Music Review." *Nilacharal.com.* http://www .nilacharal.com/enter/review/mugangal.html (May 29, 2004).

Tamil Movie Cafe. 2001. "The Making of Kandukondain Kandukondain." *Tamil Movie Cafe.* http://web.archive.org/web/20010702191010/tmcafe.com/interview /rajiv/rajiv_interview.htm (June 5, 2001).

"Thiruvasakam in Symphony." [2004]. "The Project Plan." http://www.thiruvasakamin symphony.com/v_eng.htm#8a (May 8, 2004).

Vamanan. 2003. *Tirai Isai Alaikal.* Chennai: Manivacakar Patippakam.

Vasudevan, Ravi, ed. 2001. *Making Meaning in Indian Cinema.* New Delhi: Oxford University Press.

Viswanathan, T., and Matthew Harp Allen. 2004. *Music in South India.* New York: Oxford University Press.

Discographic References

Ilaiyaraja. 1992. *Nothing But Wind.* Echo Recording, FCR 5020.

Ilaiyaraaja. 1987. *How to Name It?* Oriental Records, ORI CD 115.

Islam, Yusuf. 2005. "Indian Ocean." Song downloadable from http://www.yusuf islam.org.uk/indexindianoceansplash.shtml (July 1, 2005).

Rahman, A. R. 1997. *Vande Mataram.* Columbia Records/Sony Music Entertainment India, CK 68525.

Shankar, Mahesh and Anita Chandrasekaran. 2002. *Mugangal.* Dreams Audio.

Sriram, Anoorada. 1997. *Chennai Girl.* Magnasound, C6-P2417.

Filmographic References

Annakkili. 1976, dir. Devaraj-Mohan.

Ayya. 2005, dir. Hari.

Bombay. 1995, dir. Mani Ratnam.

Iyer IPS. 2005, dir. Harirajan.

Kalidas. 1931, dir. H. M. Reddy.

Kandukondain Kandukondain. 2000, dir. Rajiv Menon.

Kurudhippunal. 1995, dir. P. C. Sriram.

Minsara Kanavu. 1997, dir. Rajiv Menon.
Mouna Ragam. 1986, dir. Maniratnam.
Pundalik. 1912, dir. P. R. Tipnis and N. G. Chitre.
Roja. 1993, dir. Mani Ratnam.

Web Resources for Tamil Movies and Songs

http://www.indiaplaza.com (general shopping)
http://www.nehaflix.com (movie shopping)
http://www.vistaindia.com (music and movie shopping)
http://www.dhool.com (online audio files, Tamil film music)
http://www.raaga.com (online audio files, film music)
http://www.musicindiaonline.com (online audio files, many genres)
http://www.tfmpage.com (forums, articles, lyrics)
http://www.spbala.com (singer S. P. Balasubrahmanyam's official website)
http://www.raaja.com (music director Ilayaraja's official website)
http://www.rahmania.com (fan site dedicated to music director A. R. Rahman)
http://www.museemusical.com (music store and school in Chennai)
http://www.lakshmansruthi.com (music store and music troupe in Chennai)
http://www.sangeetham.com (information about Karnatak music)
http://ww.carnatica.net (information about Karnatak music)

ABDALLA UBA ADAMU

The Influence of Hindi Film Music on Hausa Videofilm Soundtrack Music

·◈·

Introduction

This chapter analyzes the emergence of Hausa film music in terms of both its technology and its sociology. It pays homage to the structural character-istics of Hausa traditional music in order to provide a template for under-standing how radically different the Hausa videofilm soundtrack is from the Hausa entertainment mindset. The chapter hopes to provide insights into the emergence of altered Hausa entertainment identities, which was caused by media influences, as distinct from traditional entertainment.

As Blakely (2001) points out, academic responses to various facets of global entertainment have changed drastically over the last forty years, re-flecting for the most part huge changes in technology, media infrastruc-ture, and entertainment content. This naturally led to the development of theories of imitation—with the view that availability of new communica-tion technologies would enable developing countries to imitate the West in a process of modernization.

Additionally, Curran (2000) argues that two contrasting attitudes to-ward globalization can be found. The first is expressed by cultural theorists who welcome globalization as a means for reinforcing international di-alogue. It enables minorities to gain attention beyond national borders. An opposing point of view stresses the threat that globalization poses to de-mocracies and international politics, aiming at limiting the influence of worldwide capitalism. Both these views agree upon a certain degree of weakness in adopting systems as a result of the transnational flow of influ-ences. What needs to be determined is the extent to which the recipient systems are transformed.

Indeed Media and Cultural Studies' theories of globalization tend to focus attention on the role of mass media in the society (e.g., Beck,

Sznaider, and Rainer 2003, Appadurai 1996), how they are communicated and preserved in transnational context. Another focus is on how people appropriate media, and which identities they create with the newly transformed media (see particularly Sreberny-Mohammadi 1996, Schiller 1976, and Boyd-Barrett 1977).

Thus as Patterson (1994) argues, industrialization and modernization both entail the spread of common sets of behaviors and attitudes within the context of economic change. However, the globalization of culture also takes place independent of whatever economic changes are occurring in a particular region or society. Traditionally, the transmission of culture across societies was facilitated by two main media: migration and literacy. People learned about other cultures either through traveling themselves or from travelers, or by reading about other cultures and adopting or adapting what they learned. These traditional media could be effective in the transmission of cultures across the globe, under certain circumstances.

An additional source of learning is media bombardment, which, in the case of northern Nigeria, created spaces for the continuous broadcast of foreign media cultures, especially from India—introduced by local Lebanese merchants—in the form of Hindi films. This deluge often comes in the way of cross-border free flow of packaged media products that enable communities to absorb (but not export) media re-enactment of popular cultural forms of other societies. In this way, Hindi film-music culture found its way into Hausa popular-musical culture and eventually supplanted it.

An essential tension exists between Muslim Hausa public culture and popular culture. Public culture reflects the quintessential Hausa social makeup with its agreed boundaries defined by cultural specificity such as dress code, language, and rules of social discourse. Popular culture, on the other hand, is seen as the realm of the unsophisticated working class. Music, in all its forms, belong to this class.

Hausa society, being structured on specific occupational hierarchies, often considers music a low-art commercial form. Musical appreciation, however, can be both low or high. For instance, the existence of complete orchestras in palaces of Hausa emirs from Zaria to Damagaram indicates the acceptance of music as an entertainment genre within the conventional establishment. However, it is not acceptable for the ruling class to engage in the same music—thus a prince cannot be a musician.

But perhaps the biggest ripple in the Hausa concept of a highbrow musical genre was the media intrusion of Hindi film soundtracks from popular Hindi films. These soundtracks, introduced via radio and cinema houses from 1960 when Nigeria became independent from Britain, leapt from the screen to the street, first via children's playground songs patterned on the most popular Hindi film music tracks. This was taken up almost immediately by "low-brow" bar and club circuit musicians such as Abdu Yaron Goge, who picked up "Raati Suhani" from the film *Rani Rupmati* (1957), and Ali Makaho, with his rendition of "Kahbie Khabie" from *Khabie* (1975), who popularized not just the soundtracks, but also the adaptive process they introduced.

However, the most pervasive influence of Hindi film soundtrack on the Hausa musical genre was the emergence of Hausa videofilms from 1990 on. These are video dramas shot with a VHS camera (although filmmakers are increasingly using digital camcorders) to record a three-hour drama (often split into two parts). It is an invariable article of faith of the Hausa video dramatists to include a series of song-and-dance routines in their video dramas. As much 80 percent of the Hausa video dramas are appropriated directly from Hindi films in one form or another, including the music soundtrack, which is Hausanized.

The Genre of Hausa Music

The Hausa are a predominantly Muslim group in northern Nigeria and form the largest ethnic group in the country. The Hausa language itself is spread widely from northern Nigeria to the Niger Republic and all the way to other parts of sub-Saharan Africa, stretching to Ghana, Cote d'Ivoire, Gambia, and Senegal. Due to their contact with Islam as early as 1320, the Hausa have acquired a considerable Arabic vocabulary in their language, such that at least one-fifth of Hausa words, from 1750 to 1960, are directly Arabic in origin (Abubakar 1972). Despite this linguistic affinity, however, Arab popular culture, in the form of classical or contemporary music, theater, and literature has never had wide appeal among the Muslim Hausa. Consequently, Arab sources generally were not seen as a basis for inspirational adaptation for Hausa popular culture. An exception to this was the adaptation of various Middle Eastern folklore into the Hausa language under the tutelage of the British colonial authorities in the early 1930s, which saw the emergence of what has remained the most quintessential Hausa literary reference point, *Magana Jari Ce,* published in 1938. This was actually the beginning of a process that saw Hausa literati preference for Arab and Middle Eastern entertainment templates over "African," a preference strongly encouraged by the British colonial administration.[1]

According to Michael Smith (1959:249), the Hausa system of social status has three or four "classes." Sometimes the higher officials and chiefs are regarded as constituting upper "class" by themselves, sometimes they are grouped with the Mallams and wealthier merchants into a larger upper class. The lowest "class "generally distinguished includes the musicians, butchers, house-servants and menial clients, potters, and the poorer farmers who mostly live in rural hamlets. The great majority of the farmers, traders and other craftsmen would, therefore, belong to the Hausa "middle-class."

This categorization, as imperfect as Smith himself identified it to be, nevertheless serves as a rough guide to the position of a musician in Hausa society. The main reason for including musicians in the lower status level is the client-focused nature of Hausa music. With its main preoccupation of appeasing specific clients, it thus becomes a non-art form—art for art's sake—but tailored toward a specific paying client. A song composed for one client, for instance, will not be performed for another client. What further entrenches the lower status of musicians is the *maroki* (praise-singer) status of most Hausa traditional musicians—praising their clients for money or other material goods. A mean client gets the short end of the musician's stick, often with sarcastic barbs thrown in for good measure. Naturally, a very generous patron gets the full-blown poetic powers of the musician.[2]

Mainstream popular traditional Hausa music is divided into two distinct categories: the instrumental accompaniment and the vocals. This division might seem trite; but it should be pointed out that vocals form the main component of the music. It is very common for Hausa musical groups to play on one type of instrument—predominantly a percussion instrument such as the *kalangu* or "African" drum, maintaining more or less the same beat throughout the song. The skills of the lead "musician" are essentially in the philosophy and poetry of his songs.

Thus, about three distinct structures typify Hausa music. In the first instance, even if it has no specific instruments, but relies on the voice, it is still called *music*. Secondly, it is predominantly a single-instrument process in which a single type of instrument, mainly a drum, is used in a variety of combinations, with the lyricist providing the focal point of the music. The words, as with some musicians such as Muhammad Dahiru Daura, a blind beggar minstrel poet, can be in the form of opera. Third is the gender dimension of Hausa music, which sees a strict separation of the sexes, in effect a reflection of the Hausa traditional society that segregates the sexes. Hausa traditional music, like most musical forms around the world, is based on a single gender voice: either male or female, but rarely a combination of the two in the same composition, even in a duet form. This is essentially because the female voice in Islam has a diminished aural presence, especially in a mixed gender setting.

When Hausa societies became more cosmopolitan, and began to absorb influences from other cultures, limited mixed-mode instrumental "groups" started to appear, combining the percussion instruments with predominantly stringed instruments such as *goge,* or *kukuma* (fiddles) leading the orchestra, or as in the case of *koroso* music, a combination of flute, drums, and *lalaje*— calabash discs pierced by a stick to form a rattle. Rarely are there musical combos with string, percussion, and wind instruments in the same band. Indeed, wind instruments, such as *kakaki* (trumpet) are mainly royal palace instruments, while *sarewa* (flute), which is predominantly used in Fulani music genres, is often a solo instrument used on its own, or accompanied by voice. *Sarewa* often was used in TV drama-series soundtracks. However, all this changed with the appearance on the popular culture scene of Hausa videofilms.

The Genre of Hausa Videofilm

The main cinematic interest of the Muslim Hausa of northern Nigeria before the advent of home video was the Hindi cinema that was brought to northern Nigeria by Lebanese distributors after independence from Britain in 1960. From 1937, when the first cinema was opened in Kano, to 1960, film distribution was controlled exclusively by a cabal of Lebanese merchants who sought to entertain the few British colonials and other imported non-Muslim workers in northern Nigeria by showing principally American and British films.

Despite strict spatial segregation (from 1903 when the British conquered the territory to 1960), the British did acknowledge that the locals (that is, Muslim Hausa) might be interested in the new entertainment medium, and as such special days were kept aside for the Hausa audience in the three theaters then available. The British, however, were not keen to see films from either the Arab world, particularly Egypt with its radical cinema, or any other Muslim country that might give the natives some revolutionary ideas. Indeed, no attempt was made to develop any local film industry, or even to provide African-themed entertainment for the locals (Adamu 2004).

After the 1960s, there were a few attempts to show cinema from the Arab world, as well as Pakistan, due to what the distributors believed to be a common religious culture between the peoples of the Middle East and Muslim northern Nigeria.[3] However, these were not popular with the Hausa audience, since they were not religious dramas, but reflected the culture of the Arabs. And although the Hausa share quite a lot with the Arabs (especially in terms of dress, food, and language—see Adamu 1968, 1998; Abubakar 1972), nevertheless they had different entertainment mindsets, so these Arab films did not go down well.

The experimental Hindi films shown from November 1960 on proved massively popular, and the Lebanese thus found a perfect formula for entertaining the Hausa audience. Subsequently, throughout urban clusters of northern Nigeria, in Kano, Jos, Kaduna, Bauchi, Azare, Maiduguri, and Sokoto, Lebanese film distribution of Hindi films in principally Lebanese-controlled theaters ensured a massive influence of Hindi film genre and storyline, and most especially song-and-dance routines, on the urban Hausa audience.

However, the biggest boom for Hindi cinema in Northern Nigeria came in the 1970s, when state television houses began operating and became the outlet for readily available Hindi films on videotapes targeted at home viewers. The NTA Kano alone screened 1,176 Hindi films on its television network from October 2, 1977, when the first Hindi film (*Aan Bann*) was shown, to June 6, 2003.[4] At the time that Hindi film appeared in Hausa television houses, young schoolboys and girls aged seven and under became avid watchers of the films and gradually absorbed templates of behavior from screen heroes who they thought shared similar patterns of behavior as themselves.

The entire commercial Hausa videofilm industry started in Kano, in northern Nigeria, in 1990 with a videofilm titled *Turmin Danya,* a traditional boy-meets-girl drama. By 2004, the industry had grown and spawned more than 1,500 videofilms, with most production and distribution facilities located in Kano, an ancient Islamic and commercial entrepot in the north of Nigeria, whose videofilm industry came to be referred to as *Kanywood.*[5] This is to distinguish it from *Nollywood,* the Nigerian video-film industry, dominated by Christian southern Nigerian filmmakers. Besides religion, the two "woods" differ radically to the extent that they are mutually exclusive culturally and aesthetically, and could conveniently be thought of as representing two totally different countries. The main focus of Nigerian Nollywood films is on tribal rituals, political corruption in the polity, Christianity, social problems such as armed robbery, and political issues such as resource control.[6]

Basic Characteristics of the Hausa Videofilm

Over the last sixteen years (1990–2006), Hausa videofilms evolved three main characteristics, all borrowed heavily from and inspired by Hindi cinema.[7]

The first motif in Hausa videofilm is *auren dole,* or forced marriage. In these scenarios—reflecting outdated customs in a contemporary society, but nevertheless providing a tapestry for a good story—a girl (or in a few of the films, a boy) is forced to marry a partner other than her choice.

The second characteristic of Hausa videofilms is the love triangle, with or without the forced marriage motif. It is inevitable that a narrative conflict indicating rivalry between two suitors (whether two boys after the same girl, or two girls after the same boy) be created in which antagonists are given the opportunity to wax lyrical about their undying love for each other and the extent they are willing to go to cross the Rubicon—whether cultural (parental, religious), economic (rich-poor divide), political (parents belonging to different political ideologies), or even geographical (separated by different countries) that separates their love.

Thus the third characteristic of the Hausa videofilm is the song-and-dance routine—again echoing Hindi cinema style—which is buried within the matrix of the love triangle. The fierce rivalry between suitors is best expressed through long song-and-dance routines, which indeed often tell the story more completely than the dialogue. These are used to embellish the story and provide what the filmmakers insist is "entertainment." This entertainment is also a marketing strategy aimed at capturing an audience and masking weak storylines in a creative process that sees repetitions of the same narrative in almost all the films. Indeed, in some of the videofilms, the songs themselves become subplots of the main story in which poetic barbs are thrown at each other by the antagonists.

The song-and-dance sequences do not necessarily have a cohesive relationship to the storylines, as they often are pasted directly on the story and not tied to the narrative. This does not bother either the producers or the audience; what matters is the lyrical power of the song, its tunes, and the costumes the singers (especially the girls) wear. Further, in Hausa videos, as in Hindi films, songs are

part of an elaborate system of allusions to, rather than explicit portrayals of, sexuality and physical intimacy in Hindi films as filmmakers navigate the perceived moral conservatism of their audiences, as well as the representational boundaries set by the Indian state through its censorship codes. Songs are the primary vehicles for representing fantasy, desire, and passion, so any form of sexual activity in a Hollywood film would most likely be transformed into a song sequence in Hindi film. (Ganti 2002: 294)

Indeed, the most commercially successful Hausa videofilms of all time (*Sangaya, Taskar Rayuwa, Salsala, Kansakali, Ibro Awilo, Mujadala*) succeeded precisely because of their song-and-dance routines, rather than because of the strength of their storylines or their messages.

The predominance of song-and-dance routines in Hausa videofilms is shown in Figure 1, which indicates the numbers of officially registered Hausa videofilms from 1997 to 2001 with song-and-dance routines as a

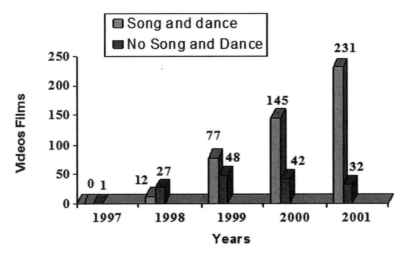

Figure 1: Song and dance occurrences in Hausa videofilms.

main element. There was a general decline in the number of videos without song and dance. The figures rose from 1998 (27) to 1999, but peaked at 48 in 1999, and declined to 42 in 2000, before going down further to 32 in 2001. The number of video titles with song-and-dance routines, however, showed ascendancy right from the beginning, with 12 titles in 1998 moving to 77 in 1999, 145 in 2000, and 231 in 2001 (figures provided by NFVCB 2002, 2003).

Overriding these structural elements, a typical Hausa videofilm also directly appropriates Hindi film in style (as in above characteristics) or in text, which is translated. The reasons for doing this, as Brian Larkin observes, is that

Hausa fans of Indian movies argue that Indian culture is "just like" Hausa culture. Instead of focusing on the differences between the two societies, when they watch Indian movies what they see are similarities, especially when compared with American or English movies. Men in Hindi films, for instance, are often dressed in long kaftans, similar to the Hausa *doguwar riga,* over which they wear long waistcoats, much like the Hausa *falmaran.* The wearing of turbans; the presence of animals in markets; porters carrying large bundles on their heads, chewing sugar cane; youths riding Bajaj motor scooters; wedding celebrations and so on: in these and a thousand other ways the visual subjects of Indian movies reflect back to Hausa viewers aspects of everyday life. (Larkin 1997b; see also Larkin 1997a)

As a result of this perceived similarity, the most commercially successful Hausa filmmakers prefer simply to convert a Hindi film into Hausa, or to borrow elements from various Hindi films, rather than go to the trouble of acquiring or completely writing a script. The route followed in this conversion differs remarkably from that followed by creative remakes of other films by producers in other film settings. As Leonardo Quaresima points out:

In the case of the remake, we might adopt the definition that Umberto Eco proposes in his "Tipologia della Ripetizione" whereby the remake is seen as a variant of the tracing "to reformulate a popular story without the consumer being made aware of it." The tracing, together with the revival, the series, the saga and the phenomena around dialogism, make up a part of the system of seriality. The remake, in this view, is seen as an "explicit and declared tracing." (Quaresima 2002:76–77)

A typical film remake often pays homage to the creative qualities of the original, and indeed can be seen as an artistic commentary on the original. However, this is different for Hausa videofilms. As explained by Abubakar "Baballe" Hayatu, the main script writer for FKD Studios based in Kano in an interview with *Fim* in November 2002:

if you notice, our culture (Muslim Hausa) is similar to Indian culture, the difference being in fashion and make-up only. I am not the only one who watches the Indian films (during screenplay adaptation). We used to watch the films with Ali Nuhu and note the things we should change such that a typical Hausa person can relate to it as his culture, rather than shunning it. Thus we adapt what we can to suit our culture and religion. If any scene is neutral on these two issues, we leave it as it is. (Hayatu 2000:47)

Thus Hausa videofilm remakes deliberately set out to draw attention to the original and indeed were passed as more socially acceptable versions of the originals that might contain elements inimical to the religious and social culture of the Muslim Hausa. They were thus substitutes, rather than remakes. This is further evidenced by the fact that in some cases female artistes with faint resemblance to Indian actresses, in appearance as well as in costume are preferred in commercial Hausa videofilms.

Even poster artwork is often designed to replicate the Hindi film being appropriated, as shown in Figure 2. The producers' argument for the appropriation was that even if they do create a story, it is likely to have a Hindi cinema motif, so it is easier simply to copy a popular Hindi film directly into Hausa. As further advanced by a leading proponent of this practice, Ali Nuhu, the Hausa videofilm megastar (nicknamed Shah Ruh Khan since high school days in the 1980s):

people are accusing our company, FKD, of solely relying on copying Hindi films, and not being original. This is rubbish! We did many original films, but they were not commercially successful. For instance, *Kudira* and *Sabani* were all original stories, yet they were not as commercially successful as *Mujadala, So* and *Zubaida* (which were all based on Hindi films) . . . We are sticking to our methods and will continue copying Hindi films into Hausa!" (Nuhu 2003:24)

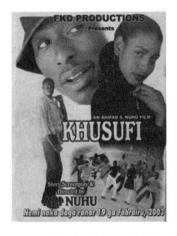

Figure 2: Hindi-to-Hausa videofilms: Khusufi as Taal.

The first Hausa videofilm to copy a Hindi film was *Akasi* (2000), based
on the Hindi film *Sanam Bewafa* (1991). When the Hindi film *Dillagi* was
released in 1999, it immediately was appropriated and converted into one
of the most appealing Hausa videofilms, *Mujadala,* in 2000 and this con-
ferred commercial legitimacy on the Hindi film-conversion strategy among
the more commercially oriented Hausa filmmakers. It was at this point that
the Indian cinema influence came to the fore in full force and the new crop
of Hausa videofilm producers introduced *Bollywoodanci*—appropriating
Hindi films into Hausa—as a creative norm among the vast majority of
Hausa videofilms film producers from 2000 to 2004.

Screen to Street: Hausa Adaptations of Popular Hindi Film Music

As indicated earlier, Hindi films became popular simply because of what
urbanized young Muslim Hausa saw as cultural similarities between Hausa social behavior and mores (e.g., coyness, forced marriage, gender stratification,
obedience to parents and authority) and those depicted in Hindi films. Further, with heroes and heroines sharing almost the same dress code as Hausa
(flowing saris, turbans, head covers), especially in the earlier historical Hindi
films that were the ones predominantly shown in cinemas throughout northern Nigeria in the 1960s), young Hausa saw reflections of themselves and their
lifestyles in Hindi films, far more than in American films. Added to this is the
appeal of the soundtrack music and the song-and-dance routines, which do
not have ready equivalents in the Hausa traditional entertainment ethos. Soon
enough, moviegoers started to mimic the Hindi film songs they saw.

The first audience for this entertainment to make the cultural leap from screen to street were predominantly young boys who, incapable of understanding Hindi film language but captivated by the songs in the films they saw, started to use the meter of the playback songs, but substituted Hausa prose for the "gibberish" Hindi words. Four of the most popular Hindi films in northern Nigeria in the 1960s that provided the model for adaptation of the tunes and lyrics to Hausa street and popular music were *Chori Chori* (1956), *Rani Rupmati* (1957), *Amar Deep* (1958), and *Khabie Khabie* (1975).

The second leap from screen to street was mediated by popular folk musicians in the late 1960s and early 1970s, led by Abdu Yaron Goge, a resident *goge* (fiddle) player in Jos. His greatest contribution to Hausa popular culture was in picking up Hindi film playback songs and reproducing them with his *goge*, vocals, and *kalangu* (often made to sound like the Indian drum, *tabla*) as indicated in his Hausa adaptation of "Raati Suhani" from the film *Rani Rupmati.*

Even cultured Hausa poets were not averse to borrowing a Hindi film meter to compose Hausa songs to make them more palatable to their audience. An example is an adaptation of "Panchi Banu" from the Hindi film *Chori Chori,* by a noted and well-respected Hausa political poet, Akilu Aliyu.

Transition from Big Screen to Small Screen: The Hausa Videofilm Soundtrack

The first Hausa videofilms from 1990 to 1994 relied on traditional music ensembles to compose the soundtracks, with *koroso* music predominating. The soundtracks were just that—incidental background music to accompany the film, and not integral to the story. There was often singing, but it was itself embedded in the music, for instance during the ceremonies that seem to feature in every drama film. The Hausa videofilm to pioneer a change over to electronic music (in the sense of Yamaha keyboard melodies) was *In Da So Da Kauna* in 1994. The video was an adaptation of a best-selling Hausa novel of the same title.

The initial soundtrack for the video was composed with Hausa traditional musical instruments by the Koroso Entertainment ensemble housed at the Kano State History and Culture Bureau (HCB). It featured the Fulani *sarewa*, accompanied by drumming and a *lalaje*. It was this music that was featured in the film when it was shown throughout cinema houses in northern Nigeria, as was the practice then.

However, when the video was screened at the Dawud Cinema in Maiduguri, Borno State, it was pirated, and soon enough a bootleg of the tape was making the rounds in various markets in northern Nigeria. Ado

Ahmed Gidan Dabino, the producer (and also director) was upset, but since there was little he could do, he decided to release his own official version of the home video in 1995, and also decided to include deleted scenes and other changes, as well as compose a different soundtrack, in order to make the second version as different from the bootleg version as possible. It was in the process of seeking a new sound for the home video that he came across Nasir Usman Ishaq Gwale, an artist with a residency at the Kano State History and Culture Bureau.

Nasir earlier had been given a toy, but fairly functional, Casio keyboard in 1985—when he was still in high school—by his brother, Bello Usman Ishaq, a resident graphic artist with the HCB. In the same year, an African-American researcher, Richard Donald Smith, a flutist and then a lecturer at the United Nations International School in New York, visited the HCB and was captivated by the enthusiasm with which Nasir used his Casio keyboard. The following year, in 1986, he brought a gift of a Casiotone MT-140 to the bureau.

Nasir immediately started playing around with it and soon enough perfected it to further enrich his informal musical repertoire. When Nasir finished high school in 1986, he honed his skills in music by forming a smallish ensemble that revolved around the Casio organ, providing an alternative form of "modern" (as opposed to traditional) entertainment for youth in and around the Kano metropolis, mainly at functions, ceremonies, and other social events. In 1988, he was employed as a resident artist at the HCB's Performing Arts division and became resident musician and artist for the HCB. He attracted other young members of the HCB, such as Alee Baba Yakasai, Shu'aibu "Lilisco" Idris (a former champion disco dancer), and Muktar Kwanzuma.

The HCB also played host to other ensembles, particularly one formed by a school teacher who was trained in Sudan and formed a band based on Sudanese music styles, with a strong emphasis on the accordion. One of their greatest hits was *Halimatu Sadiya*—an ode to a girl of the same name—which in the late 1980s changed the pattern of popular entertainment in Kano and made it clear that the future lay with organs and synthesizers, rather than traditional Hausa instruments, especially among the youth. All these contributed to enrich Nasir's musical set pieces. Under the tutelage of his teacher at the Bureau, Musa Ahmed, and with help from his friends Muktar Kwanzuma and Shu'aibu "Lilisco" Idris, also of the performing arts division, a more or less official ensemble was formed by 1993.

By the time Ado Ahmad Gidan Dabino was looking for a new sound to accompany the video release of *In Da So Da Kauna*, Nasir Usman Ishaq Gwale had become a sought-after keyboardist. He was commissioned to compose the soundtrack. It was this soundtrack that was used in the "official" video release of *In Da So Da Kauna* in 1995. It was the first Hausa videofilm with a modern music soundtrack. Clearly seeing the future in keyboard music, Hamisu Lamido Iyan-Tama, an entrepreneur who was to become an actor and producer, decided to invest in a music studio, and in 1996 a music and videofilm studio, Iyan-Tama Multimedia, was formed in Kano. Its first purchase was the Yamaha soft synthesizer series, starting with a PSR-220. The studio then employed Nasir as a consultant resident musician in the studio.

The Yamaha PSR-220 provided an instant appeal to a Hausa musician seeking ways to explore combinations of sounds without being hampered by the inability to play real traditional Hausa music instruments. It also made it possible to do the impossible in Hausa music: Produce a perfect blend of various instruments, thus breaking the monopoly of the single-instrument characteristic of traditional Hausa music. In so doing, it gave Hausa videofilm composers the opportunity to approximate the creative space of Hindi film music, which they copied avidly. This was made possible because Yamaha took actual instruments and digitally recorded them, giving the keyboard everything from the standard piano, to a jazz organ, to a distorted guitar, and even a full orchestra voice section. In addition, it features ninety-nine voices to choose from (plus a drum kit).

In the same year, 1996, Dan Azumi Baba, a novelist and also a *bandiri* musician and singer, wrote a love song for two girls. The song was called *Badakala*. Dan Azumi Baba said he was inspired not by Hindi films (to which he admitted being an avid fan), but by Middle Eastern folklore heroes such as Antar who, it seemed, also sang love serenades. In an innovative move, he decided to create a soundtrack for the song "Badakala" with handclaps, hands beating a wooden bench, and eventually empty plastic storage jars ("jerrycans"). When he heard Ado Ahmad Gidan Dabino's modernized soundtrack for *In Da So Da Kauna,* he immediately got the musician, Nasir, to set music to the words of "Badakala." The resultant audiotape was meant to be sold in the markets as an independent new music production, and it signaled the emergence of a new youth Hausa pop music (as contrasted to the traditional "classical" music). The tape, however, was rejected by marketers in Kano. The main reasons were two. First, it contained *kidan fiyano* (or piano music), an instrument associated with the church in northern Nigeria, and therefore avoided by Muslims. Secondly, Allah was mentioned in the lyrics to the song. To the marketers, this was akin to blasphemy—to utter the name of the creator with piano music! Afraid of the possible backlash from society, which could even lead to a full-scale religious riot, they rejected the tape. In the Hausa society of northern Nigeria in the 1980s to 1990s, even the use of widespread *bandiri* in religious poetry by Sufi adherents, especially the Qadiriyyah, was frowned upon and often considered controversial, with opposing camps of Muslim scholars constantly debating the issue. A "piano" sound in an almost-religious context simply muddled the issue further. This was because the sound of the piano is normally associated with Christian religious music in Muslim northern Nigeria. Combining what seemed to be a Christian sound with Islamic lyrics was perceived by the marketers as asking for trouble. In order to cut his losses, the producer of "Badakala" took the further innovative and historic move of converting the song into a screenplay for a videofilm of the same name. It marked the first time a song formed the basis of a videofilm and was to become a common pattern by 2004.

By 2004, the main selling points for Hausa videofilms were the songs, not the storylines. While the song-and-dance routines are separate elements—and often not even related to the narrative—nevertheless they constitute what the Hausa videofilmmakers consider a "film soundtrack." This is recorded separately on compact cassette tapes and CDs and sold alongside the videotape releases. The music between the scenes—in effect, the actual soundtrack—is relegated to the background, often in the form of a single tune repeated throughout the film (such as in *Awarwaro*).

The Hausa videofilm had metamorphosed into a musical film, with song taking the most prominent position throughout. A videofilm without song-and-dance sequences may sell, depending on the reputation of the stars and the director, but one with production numbers sells more. The more sexually suggestive the dances performed, especially by the girls, the higher the sales potential of the videofilm (examples include *Numfashi, Bakar Ashana, Rukuni,* and *Guda*). In a sense, the videofilmmakers use the medium to fantasize the sexuality of essentially urban Hausa youth closeted by the values of a traditional society that enforces the segregation of sexes due to adherence to Islamic social values.

The expectation of the entertainment value of the song and dance over the storyline is reflected in, for instance, the trailer for *Buki Buduri* (2004), which generated a lot of audience excitement and anticipation precisely because of a routine featuring old Hausa actresses seriously getting down during a wedding ceremony party. However, that particular sequence was cut off by the Kano State Censorship Board for the commercially available tape. This created a lot of angry feedback to the producer from clients who bought the tape expecting to see the dance sequence. Reactions included returning the tape to the shops and phone calls to the producer to curse him for "cheating." Word-of-mouth criticism of the film brought down sales dramatically.

Similarly, *Bakar Ashana* (2004) generated a lot of controversy and anticipation over a song-and-dance sequence performed by a troupe composed of normal actresses and female commercial sex workers drafted specifically for the scene. The producer, learning from the lessons of *Buki Buduri,* took the bold step of refusing to submit the video for censorship in Kano, after it had been censored by the National Film and Video Censors Board in Abuja. The videofilm was a massive underground cult hit, at the same time drawing sharp criticism over the lewd dance scenes (which, if anything, boosted sales). The Kano State Censorship Board banned the tape, seized all copies from the shops, and ordered the arrest of the producer. Although convicted and ordered to pay a fine of N20,000 (about $143), he was happy because he sold at least 20,000 copies of the tape at N40 (29 cents) to the dealers (who sell it at N250 to buyers), earning him about N800,000 ($5,417) plus CD rights, which he sold for additional N300,000 ($2,142). The total of over one million naira in sales was an enormous amount in just two weeks of the film's release before it was banned.[8]

The Process of Composing a Hausa Videofilm Soundtrack

The process of composing a song-and-dance routine for a Hausa videofilm, which is considered the "soundtrack" by the videofilm industry, includes two stages. In the first stage, an independent lyricist composes a song (or series of songs) and takes it to a studio session musician. The latter would ask the lyricist to sing the words. From the style of the singing, the musician constructs an accompanying melody, usually using a Yamaha PSR synthesizer.[9] Music scores are not written; every note is picked up from a database of stored musical samples of many different instruments. The lyricist often has no specific input into the type of music to be composed, leaving all such creative decisions to the studio session keyboardist.

The second stage involves taking the finished product to a producer who then incorporates it at any stage in a film. There does not have to be any link between the videofilm and the particular song. Indeed, the titles of some of the films are based on the fact that a song has been created first with that title (e.g., *Rukuni, Guguwa*).

A frequent source of inspiration for the composition of the lyrics is most commonly a Hindi film source, but increasingly, other sources are used, such as African-American rap music, as in *Kallabi,* which adapts various rap songs. Whatever the creative source of the song, it *must* be a duet, with a boy/man and a girl/woman singing, either to each other, or accompanied by a chorus, and all dressed in pretty costumes that, for the girls,

Figure 3: Hausanized and Globalized Hausa female videofilm stars: *Gidauniya* (2004) [left] and *Yari* (2004).

must reveal their shapes. Examples include *Gidauniya* and *Yari,* as stills from the two videofilms show in Figure 3.

The singing and dancing is done not only by teens (as in *Mujadala, Rawani,* and *Awarwaro*), but also by married couples (such as in *Dami A Kala, Nagari, Hakuri, Makamashi, Guda,* and *Dabi'a*) to appeal to a mature audience, although such people, for the most part, consider singing and dance among adults ridiculous.

Noticing the demand for soundtrack music for Hausa videofilms, many studio session musicians started developing a repertoire of songs that they have set to catchy music and marketing them to executive producers. If a deal is struck, the song is used in a film, whether or not its words are related to the theme of the film. Its main selling point is not the meanings of the words, but the resonance between the lyrics and the music. A very important element in this process is the close imitation of the usually soprano voices of Hindi film soundtrack female playback singers by their Hausa equivalents. Since the idea is to imitate Hindi cinema as much as possible, the male playback singers also attempt to adopt the voice patterns of popular Hindi film.

Nollywood videofilms (from southern Nigeria) also use synthesizers and computer programs to generate soundtrack music; however, they are remarkable in the professionalism of their soundtracks. Music generally has been accepted as an art form in Christian southern Nigeria, and over the years, world-class musicians such as Victor Uwaifo, King Sunny Ade, Lagbaja, and the late Afrobeat founder Fela Anikulapo-Kuti indicate the excellence and quality of what conveniently can be termed "Nigerian" music, despite representing an extremely tiny proportion of the country's musical heritage. Southern Nigerian film makers have a seriously professional musical pool to draw from, and this is reflected in the quality of the soundtracks of films such as *The World Is Mine, Love Boat, Evas River, Real Love,*

Missing Angel, My Love, and *Christ in Me.* Further, the use of the Fruity Loops software program ensures the professionalization of Nollywood soundtrack music and enhances its international appeal.

The flexibility given by the PSR-220 synthesizer thus enabled Hausa studio session musicians to create complex scores that would not have been possible with Hausa traditional orchestras. Significantly, the PSR-220 enabled a combination of sound samples whose outcomes clearly departed from the traditional definitions of Hausa sounds, even if retaining a digital sound-alike of Hausa instruments such as *bandiri* (tambourine), *sarewa* (flute), *ganga* (drum), *goge* (fiddle), and others. It is interesting to note that the actual purpose of the synthesizer—to generate artificial sounds—is not utilized fully in the Hausa soundtrack music. Synthesized music often is limited to small sketches that are used to provide aural accompaniment between scenes, or during actual scenes, which often makes it difficult to hear the actors' voices (e.g. in *Aliyu*). Hausa videofilm soundtrack musicians focus their creative energy on using the synthesizer's digital samples to imitate real-life instruments since they cannot play these instruments.

Another turning point for the Hausa videofilm soundtrack came in 1999, when Iyan-Tama studios bought a Yamaha PSR-730 keyboard. With a vastly expanded range of country, jazz, dance, Latin, rock, soul, and waltz sounds, the PSR-730 opened the doors to revolutionizing Hausa videofilm music. The first playback song to benefit from its superior range of sound samples was *Sangaya,* from a video of the same title. The song was composed in October 1999 and attached to a trailer of the videofilm, which was released in 2000. Trailers of the home video, with the lead song, "Sangaya," being performed in the background—complete with choreography—immediately captured the imagination of the Hausa urban audience, helped along by the inclusion of a whole array of instrument sound samples such as flute, tambourine, and African drums. The music, and most especially the choreography, from the soundtrack catapulted the video into the charts of "big league" Hausa videofilms, and it became one of the most successful Hausa films of all time.[10] Four years after its release, it still remained the definitive reference point for the emergence of Hausa videofilm music. The synthesizer business in Kano blossomed. Iyan-Tama Multimedia studios purchased an even higher level Yamaha, a PSR 740, in 2001. By then, other music studios had been established in Kano. These included Muazzat, Sulpher Studios, and in Jos, Lenscope Media. Sulpher Studios, in addition to a Yamaha PSR-2100, also use Cakewalk Pro music software to compose Hausa videofilm soundtrack music.

The availability of these modern studios opened up a whole new range of services for individuals interested in music—not just videofilm producers. Islamiyya school pupils, who hitherto had remained in vocal groups, joined in the act, and started using the Yamaha sound for their recordings, which are sold in the markets, generating a modest revenue. In a fascinating cross-fertilization of influences, the Islamiyya school ensembles stopped using meters from Hindi film songs and started using the meters of Hausa videofilm soundtracks. Soundtracks from popular Hausa films such as *Sangaya, Wasila, Nagari,* and *Khusufi* were adapted by Islamiyya pupils, often with Arabic lyrics.

It is significant that in almost all Hausa videofilm soundtracks, the songs are duets, with a boy and a girl singing. Yet the "Islamized" versions use only one voice, either a male or a female voice. The Islamic etiquette of not allowing mixed-gender formations effectively prevents a reproduction of the Hindi film soundtrack format in the Islamized versions.

The success of *Sangaya* sent a strong commercial message that singing and dancing can sell massively, especially if done with what the practitioners call a "piano." It was at this point that the Hindi cinema influence came to the fore in full force and a new crop of Hausa videofilms producers, intent on repeating the success of *Sangaya,* took over with Hindi film cinema storylines. In their desire to replicate Hindi films as closely as possible, Hausa video producers had to rely on the synthesizer to enable them to create the complex polyphony of sounds generated by the superior musical instruments of Hindi film music. While many of the songs in the Hausa videofilms were original to the films, quite a sizeable number are direct copies of the Hindi film soundtracks, even if the Hausa main film is not based on a Hindi film. This, in effect, means that a Hausa videofilm can have two sources of Hindi film "creative inspiration": a film for the storyline (and fight sequences), and songs from a different film. The song-and-dance routines in Hausa videofilms, by and large, are appropriated directly from the songs (although due to obvious acrobatic and choreographic limitations, not the dances) of major Hindi films.

Besides providing templates for storylines, Hindi films provide Hausa videofilmmakers with similar models for the songs that they use in their videos. The technique often involves picking up the thematic elements of the main Hindi film song and then substituting Hausa lyrics. Consequently, anyone familiar with the Hindi film song element will easily discern the film from the Hausa equivalent. Although this process of adaptation is extremely successful because the producers make more from films with song and dances than without, there are often dissenting voices about

the intrusion of the new media technology into the film process, as reflected in this letter from a correspondent:

I want to advise northern Nigerian Hausa film producers that using European music
in Hausa films is contrary to portrayal of Hausa culture in films (videos). I am appealing to them (producers) to change their style. It is annoying to see a Hausa film
with a European music soundtrack. Don't the Hausa have their own (music)? . . .
The Hausa have more musical instruments than any ethnic group in this country, so
why can't films be produced using Hausa traditional music? (Asarani 1999:10)

Interestingly, other musical sources, borrowed from a totally different
source, often are used as templates. *Ibro Dan Indiya,* which had an adaptation of a song from *Mohabbat,* also appropriates "Ah Ndiya," a composition by Oumou Sangare, the Malian *wassolou* diva, which was redone as
"Malama Dumbaru" in the Hausa videofilm.

Conclusions

In this essay, I have looked at the structural transformation of Hausa
videofilm soundtrack music, and in the process I have traced how such
transformation leads to what I prefer to call "opportunistic transformation" of a music genre. As we have seen, the direct inspiration for Hausa
videofilm soundtrack music is the Hindi film. Sound in Hausa videofilms
differs remarkably from its classic use in film genres. Filmmakers have always understood the power that sound and music have to enhance storytelling. However, in the Hausa videofilms, the "soundtrack," as it were, is
basically a song-and-dance sketch lasting anything from five to ten minutes
in which an operetta is enacted, often in total contrast to the actual plot of
the videofilm. Hausa videofilms also have what the producers refer to as
"background music," but such incidental music rarely has any direct artistic
connection to the actual film. The choice of the incidental music to be used
as more or less background "muzak" is made randomly by the producer
and tacked onto the film.

In Hausa popular culture, the most significant effect of media flow of
influences—whether from the West or from the East—is the radical transformation of Hausa music. A push and pull factor is at play in the process.
Hausa traditional music seemed to have outlived its client focus in a de-
pressed economy where the patrons cannot afford the praise singing that
kept the traditional musicians working. Further, quite a few of the musicians have declared that they do not wish their progeny to succeed them in
the business. A typical example is this answer by Alhaji Sani Dan-Indo, a
kuntigi musician who responded to the question of whether he wants his
children to succeed him:

Unless it is absolutely necessary. I definitely don't want my son to become a (Hausa) musician. I have seen enough as a musician to determine that my son will really suffer if he becomes a praise-singer. You only do praise-singing music to a level-headed client, and it is only those who know the value of praise-singing that will patronize you. Those times have passed. I certainly would not want my own son to inherit this business. I would prefer he goes to school and get a good education, so that even after I die, he can sustain himself, but I don't want him to follow my footsteps, because I really suffered in this business. Therefore I am praying to Allah to enable all my children to get education, because I don't want them to become musicians like me. (Dan-Indo 2001:48)

With the reluctance of the traditional musicians to pass on their skills to their own children, or even to open music "schools" to train others, and with the legendary ones dying (such as Mamman Shata, Haruna Oje, and Musa Dankwairo), the Hausa traditional musical genre has become wide open to influences that follow the path of least resistance.[11] Hindi film culture provided this roadmap, and the Yamaha soft synthesizer enabled younger Hausa "musicians" to follow that path to a transnational flow of influences. In effect, what the Hausa videofilm soundtrack musicians are doing is to fill the teen entertainment vacuum created by the departure of the traditional Hausa musicians. In so doing, they have altered radically the landscape of Hausa music and its status in the Hausa society, in addition to creating a specific unique Hausa videofilm soundtrack genre.

First, they have introduced the multi-instrumental mode to Hausa music. Besides the film soundtrack, the new technique is now used widely in radio jingles to advertise products and services. Advertisers became aware of the strong pull of soundtrack music and quickly adapted its structure to selling their products and services, constantly reinforcing the social relevance of the new form of music. It has become legitimized in the Hausa public sphere, in contrast to its position in 1996, when dealers refused to stock the tape of *Badakala* because it contained *kidan fiyano* (piano music). Even Hausa traditional musicians now often go to the studios (such as Sulpher Studios in Kano) and ask for drum synthesizers to be played for them until they get the closest approximation to their natural drum sounds, and they overlay the sample with their voice. A perfect example is Abdu Boda Mai Asharalle from Katsina, who plays *duma* and *tandu* drums for his *Asharalle* music form, and who has abandoned these traditional percussion instruments and gone over to Yamaha. Incidentally, Abdu Boda also became a filmmaker, producing *Tauraron Bisa Hanya*, *Nasir,* and *Sarauniya,* in which he composed his own soundtrack music (not using traditional drums but the Yamaha sound). He became the first traditional Hausa musician to cross over to the film soundtrack medium using the new technology. He was also the "star" in all three videofilms!

Perhaps surprisingly, one finds almost total acceptance of the Yamaha synthesizer sound by the *bandiri* musicians who use the instrument in Sufi religious poetry. Many, such as Rabi'u Usman Baba and Bashir Dandago, have abandoned the *bandiri* and have gone for the synthesized version in the Yamaha. The best-selling Muslim evangelical pop hit of 2004 in northern Nigeria was a poem composed for Fatima, the Prophet Muhammad's daughter, titled "Fadimatu." It was accompanied by the Yamaha sound in a religious community that has now accepted the instrument as a symbol of modernity, essentially to attract a younger audience to religious poetry. Another appeal of the song is that it has a backing chorus of girls, answering the refrain in the standard female Hindi high-pitched voice.

Secondly, the new technology and its purveyors have created what I call "mixed-space" interfaces in Hausa music by providing templates for male and female interaction. Hausa music evolved as a single-sex, single-voice process. The Hindi film cinema created a dialogic state that overlaps male and female spaces, during which terms of endearment are intensified with a background symphony of sounds. Religious groups who accepted the new technology (e.g., *bandiri* musicians and Islamiyya school choirs) have retained the single-sex voice due to the strict separation of the sexes in a Muslim polity, especially on religious occasions. The realm of public culture, however, has accepted this new gender configuration and as such the playback singers and musicians have created a new avenue for advertising music, which in almost every case is a reflection of the Hausa videofilm soundtrack.

Thirdly and finally, the Hausa film soundtrack genre has led to a redefinition of the musician, at least in the youth culture of Hausa society. The keyboardists and playback singers of the Hausa videofilm soundtrack genre have become megastars, attracting hordes of gawping young boys. By 2004 the image of the musician as a praise-singer has been altered by a new social reclassification made possible by the popularity of using the new media to express music, even in an artificially traditional form. Traditional Hausa music, which still appeals to the thirtysomethings and above, did not actually die; it just ceased to be relevant to the teen brigade, which is the main target audience for the Hausa videofilms. With MP3 players virtually glued to Snoop Dogg, Eminem, 50 Cents, Coldplay, and Beyoncé, the "international sound" of the Hausa film soundtrack thus finds a nice niche among this category of users. And with the traditionalist migrating to the synthesizer, a new voice for Hausa traditional music is certainly in the offing.

What is eclipsed in this opportunistic transformation is the Hausa traditional music genre. Very few traditional musicians are willing to sustain the process of acquiring new traditional musical instruments, especially when all the sounds they generate are reproduced easily by the Yamaha synthesizer. Since the Yamaha synthesizer became available to the Hausa videofilm industry, only one Hausa film director, Shu'aibu "Lilisco" Idris, has experimented with creating a videofilm soundtrack using traditional instruments, abandoning the synthesizer. This was done in his 2004 videofilm, *Gamji*, which used *sarewa, duman girke, kuntigi, lalaje,* and *duma*. It was the first and only Hausa videofilm to be shown on an overseas cable channel (South Africa's M-Net).

As this narrative indicates, the very concept of global entertainment seems to be changing due to the increasing availability of the infrastructure of media technologies. In traditional societies such as northern Nigeria, opening up to media globalization often comes in the form of pirated American music and films from Asia, such that the audience in Kano often see American blockbusters even before they are shown in Europe. Internet access merely accelerates the process by providing download sites for pirated music and film in almost all cities of northern Nigeria. For youth in Kano and other cities of northern Nigeria, American rap artists and their often-pirated clothing merchandizing—50 Cent, Eminem, Jay Z, DMX, Kanye West, The Game, D12, and Snoop Dogg—are the standard musical fare. African artists, even those sharing the same cultural and often linguistic space as Muslim Hausa northern Nigerians, such as Ali Farka Toure, Yusuf N'Dour, Baaba Maal, Saadou Bori, Oumou Sangare, Pope Skinnie, Lakal Kaney, and Aichata Sidibe are barely known, although their music is available in the local markets.

Of greater significance, however, is the availability of NileSat and ArabSat cable facilities that see the continuous piping of Arab and Middle Eastern entertainers to the audience in northern Nigeria. These Arab alternatives were tolerated by the local hardcore religious establishment as preferable alternatives to the influences of American or American-inspired (for instance, southern Nigerian rap music) popular culture, particularly post-9/11, when the American political response to the terrorist incident created an image in northern Nigeria that anything American is evil. These cable companies are often cited as examples of barely acceptable entertainment within a religious setting, despite the explicit attempts by the Arab entertainers to clone as much of MTV and other American music ethos as possible, including dressing and the sexuality of body language.[12]

Arab pop musicians such as Khaled, Nancy, Ruby Arjam, Ragheb Alama, Hussain El Jasmi, and Jad Choueiri increasingly are providing alternative models for young Hausa listeners and soundtrack musicians, if only to sidetrack the constant criticisms of the religious establishment about the links between their art and "decadent" American music. What needs to be addressed further is the issue of whether the end product can be exportable, that is, if it would have an appeal beyond its immediate audience. The media barrage suggests that this is merely a matter of time and market. It seems that the battle lines for "globalization" of the Hausa videofilm soundtrack have been drawn.

Notes

1. For a historical development of the Middle Eastern antecedents to Hausa popular culture, especially literature, see Adamu 2003.

2. For detailed studies of Hausa *maroka* (griots), see Smith 1957; Besmer 1971; and Podstavsky 1992.

3. In Kano, the first "Indian" film screened was *Ghenghis Khan,* shown in the Palace cinema in Kano City in December 1960. It is interesting to note that the film was not "Indian," but was seen as such. Before independence, films shown in northern Nigerian cinemas were American cowboy, war, and feature films.

4. Figures were obtained from the daily program listings of NTA Kano library, June 2003.

5. Data from National Film and Video Censors Board (NFVCB), 2002, 2003.

6. For details of the Nigerian home video themes, see Owens-Ibie 1998 and Servant 2001.

7. Prior to the commercialization of Hausa videofilms, there were extremely popular television dramas. Indeed the home videofilm industry was initiated by television soap opera stars. For a detailed analysis of Hausa television dramas, see Bourgault 1995, 1996.

8. Information about *Bakar Ashana* obtained from an interview and discussions with the producer, Amin "Mugu" Bala, in Kano, February 2005.

9. The Yamaha series of soft synthesizers is the only range used by Hausa videofilm soundtrack musicians. To non-musicians in the Hausa society, the Yamaha is simply a "fiyano" (piano).

10. The Hausa videofilm tape was sold for N250 ($1.80). *Sangaya* then sold for about $107,914 (at N139 to USD in 2000). The sales figures were revealed by Alhaji Auwal Mohammed Sabo, the producer of the videofilm (Kano, July 2003).

11. The son of the late *kukuma* player, Garba Supa, picked up his father's plectrum, as it were, and sustained his repertoire.

12. The appeal of Arab musicians to Muslim Hausa listeners is not based on religion—for many of the Arab entertainers are not even Muslim—but language. The Arabic language, being the language of the Qur'an, is held in high esteem, and many Hausa youth latch on to Arab popular music to learn the language. Interestingly, such educational functions of media and popular music are not extended to Western music, especially rap, whose English lyrics often are considered obscene ("batsa") and therefore not "copyable" English for learning purposes.

Works Cited

Abubakar, Aliyu. 1972. *Al-Thakafatul Arabiyyati Fi Nigeriya, 1750–1960* [Arabic Literature in Nigeria, 1750–1960]. Ph.D. dissertation, Ahmadu Bello University, Zaria, 1972.

Adamu, Muhammadu Uba. 1968. "Some Notes on the Influence of North African Traders in Kano." *Kano Studies* 1, no. 4: 43–49.

———. 1998. "Further Notes on the Influence of North African Traders in Kano." Paper presented at the International Conference on Cultural Interaction and Integration between North and Sub-Saharan Africa, Bayero University Kano, 4–6 March 1998.

———. 2003. "Istanci, Imamanci and Bollywoodanci: Evolutionary Trends in Hausa Use of Media Technologies in Cultural Transformation," in Adamu, A. U. et al., eds., *Hausa Videofilms: Society, Technology and Economy.* Proceedings of the First International Conference on Hausa Films, August 2003. Kano, Nigeria, Center for Hausa Cultural Studies.

———. 2004. "Oddities: Urban Space, Racism and Entertainment in Northern Nigeria, 1930–1968." An unpublished seminar/discussion paper, Department of Education, Bayero University, Kano, Nigeria.

Appadurai, Arjun. 1996. *Modernity at Large: Cultural Dimensions of Globalization.* Minneapolis: University of Minneapolis Press.

Asarani, Umar Faruk. 1999. Letter in *Fim* 4, December 1999, 10.

Beck, Ulrich, Natan Sznaider, and Winter Rainer, eds. 2003. *Global America? The Cultural Consequences of Globalization.* Liverpool: Liverpool University Press.

Besmer, Fremont Edward. 1971. *Hausa Court Music in Kano, Nigeria.* PhD thesis, Columbia University.

Blakely, Johanna. 2001. *Entertainment Goes Global: Mass Culture in a Transforming World.* Lear Center Entertainment Goes Global Project, Norman Lear Center, January 2001.

Bourgault, Louise M. 1995, *Mass Media in Sub-Saharan Africa.* Bloomington: Indiana University Press.

———. 1996. "Television Drama in Hausaland: The Search for a New Ethic and a New Aesthetic." *Critical Arts* 10, no. 1: 61–84.

Boyd-Barrett, Oliver. 1977. "Media Imperialism: Towards an International Framework for the Analysis of Media Systems." In *Mass Communication and Society,* ed. James Curran, Michael Gurevitch, and Janet Woollacott, 116–35. London: The Open University/Edward Arnold Publishers Ltd.

Curran, James. 2000. Introduction to Curran and Park 2000.

Curran, James, and Myung-Jin Park, eds. 2000. *De-Westernizing Media Studies.* London and New York: Routledge.

Dan-Indo, Sani. 2001. Interview in *Annur* (Zaria, Nigeria) 1 (August), 48.

Ganti, Tejaswini. 2002. "And Yet My Heart Is Still Indian": The Bombay Film Industry and the Indianization of Hollywood, in *Media Worlds—Anthropology on a New Terrain,* ed. Faye D. Ginsburg, Lila Abu-Lughod, and Brian Larkin, 281–300. Berkeley: University of California Press.

Hayatu, Abubakar. 2002. Interview in *Fim* (Kaduna, Nigeria) (November): 47.

Larkin, Brian. 1997a. "Indian Films and Nigerian Lovers: Media and the Creation of Parallel Modernities," *Africa: Journal of the International African Institute,* 67, no. 3: 406–40.

———. 1997b. "Bollywood Comes to Nigeria." *Samar* 8. Accessed online on January 28, 2007 at www.samarmagazine.org/archive/article.php?id=21.

National Film and Video Censorship Board (NFVCB). 2002. *Film and Video Directory in Nigeria, Vol. 1.* Abuja: National Film and Video Censors Board.

———. 2003. *Film and Video Directory in Nigeria, Vol. 2.* Abuja: National Film and Video Censors Board.

Nuhu, Ali. 2003. Interview in *Fim* (Kaduna, Nigeria) (February): 24.

Owens-Ibie, Nosa. 1998. "How Videofilms Developed in Nigeria." *Media Development* 1.

Patterson, Orlando. 1994. *Global Culture and the American Cosmos*. Paper No. 2 in the Series. The Andy Warhol Foundation for the Visual Arts Paper Series on the Arts, Culture, and Society. Washington, D.C.: Center for Arts and Culture.

Podstavsky, Sviatoslav. 1992. *Hausa "Roko" and "Maroka": Social Dimensions of Professional Entertainment in Argungu, Northern Nigeria*. PhD thesis, Columbia University.

Quaresima, Leonardo. 2002, "Loving Texts Two at a Time: The Film Remake." *Cinémas Cinélekta* 4 12, no. 3 (Spring): 76–77.

Schiller, Herbert. *Communication and Cultural Domination*, New York: International Arts and Sciences Press.

Servant, Jean-Christophe. 2001. "Nigeria's Flourishing Home-Video Industry." *Le Monde Diplomatique* (February). Accessed online on January 12, 2007, at http://mondediplo.com/2001/02/15nigeria.

Smith, Michael G. 1957. "The Social Functions and Meanings of Hausas Praise-Singing," *Africa: Journal of the International African Institute*. 27, no. 1 (January): 26–45.

———. 1959. "The Hausa System of Social Status." *Africa: Journal of the International African Institute* 29, no. 3 (July): 239–52.

Sreberny-Mohammadi, Annabelle. 1996. "The Global and the Local in International Communications." In *Mass Media and Society,* 2nd edition, ed. James Curran, Michael Gurevitch, and Janet Woollacott, 177–203. London: The Open University/Edward Arnold Publishers Ltd.

Filmography

The Hausa videofilms referred to in this chapter can be obtained only in northern Nigeria. Even then, videofilms more than six months after release are assumed to have "expired" by the marketers (who do the distribution) and new releases often are recorded on the unsold tapes. The taped and often CD soundtrack music for the films, however, have longer shelf-lives. Further, Hausa videofilm producers do not have an international outlet for their videofilms, in contrast to southern Nigerian filmmakers, who have websites and outlets in major American and European cities.

SUE M. C. TUOHY

Reflexive Cinema

Reflecting on and Representing the Worlds of Chinese Film and Music

·◉·

It's 1902 in Beijing, and a crowd has gathered at the Fengtai Photography Studio to watch Master Ren and his assistant Liu photograph the Peking Opera star Lord Tan.[1] The crowd cries out "sing us a song!" and a small ensemble of musicians begins to play as Lord Tan sings and moves. Just then Raymond Wallace arrives, babbling in a mix of English and Chinese: "My pictures *nengdong*; they can move! *Genghao* [better]! It's a worldwide phenomenon!" Master Ren drops a few coins in Wallace's hat before tossing him out of the studio. Undeterred, Wallace sets up a theatre to show "moving pictures" (*huodeng zhaopian*); his sign reads "Paris Shadow Theatre" (*Bali yingxi*).[2] Intrigued by new technologies, Assistant Liu wants to learn about moving pictures. Impressed with his technical skills and ability to attract a paying audience, Wallace hires Liu as his assistant.

But Liu faces some dilemmas. Although excited by film's potential, Liu loves Lord Tan's daughter and fears this new medium, if successful, will threaten her father's opera theater business. Theatergoers also debate their choices: "Let's go see the foreign shadow theater. What about Lord Tan's new opera? Foreign moving pictures—wonders from a thousand miles away! That's foreign mischief; we should be loyal to Lord Tan." Liu decides to continue working with the foreigner to screen foreign films and to film Chinese scenes, while explaining his visions to Master Ren. "I want to record life before it changes forever . . . Let's make our own films and present them to the world!" Liu's enthusiasm wins over Master Ren. Three years later, another crowd has gathered at the Fengtai Photography Studio, this time to watch Master Ren and Assistant Liu take moving pictures of Lord Tan as he sings and moves to the accompaniment of a small ensemble. They are making the Peking-Opera film *Dingjun Mountain*. It is a silent film.

Some version of these events was enacted in the early twentieth century, but this rendition comes from *Shadow Magic* (2001), a feature film that tells a story of the introduction of filmmaking to China. Acting out new career options and entertainment genres available to their real-life counterparts, *Shadow Magic's* fictional characters discuss the potential impact of film on their lives. By the end of the film, they realize they do not have to choose between Chinese opera and foreign films; they can film opera. But they can only guess the paths down which their choices will lead. The makers of *Shadow Magic,* however, are in a different position as they look back one hundred years later. They know that Liu and Master Ren made *Dingjun Mountain* (1905), a film with scenes from a Chinese opera starring Lord Tan, Tan Xinpei (1847–1917). They not only have seen still photographs from this film but have inserted them into their film.[3] They know that Chinese filmmakers will continue to film opera but that the popularity of live Peking Opera will decline and new choices will emerge. They know that Raymond Wallace is right when he says to Liu, "The future belongs to the motion picture. We might even go down in history." Indeed, *Shadow Magic* has inscribed the fictional Wallace into the history of Chinese filmic discourse.

Introduction: A Tradition of Chinese Reflexive Film

Shadow Magic is a Chinese film about Chinese film, and it is not the first one by a long shot. I argue that it is one film in a long tradition of reflexive films that take the materials and processes of filmmaking as part of both their stories and their techniques of construction as they reflect upon and represent the Chinese film industry, its products, personnel, and contexts. Reflexive films such as *Shadow Magic* portray fictional filmmakers in action watching films (those made by themselves or others), debating their views on filmmaking, and enacting their thoughts as scenes. And many extend their scope to reflect on the effects of film and film music on Chinese society. These films are shaped by and represent the social-political upheavals and economic changes of twentieth-century China. The meanings that reflexive films explore often are tied to the political commitments of their filmmakers and musicians as well as to the social roles they chose to adopt as members of a community of artists and entertainers. Their choices frequently have been constrained by the political and societal conditions of China's revolutionary century. As Mark Slobin explains in the introduction to this volume, we can view filmmakers as a type of ethnomusicologist, but in this case they analyze their own worlds with the goal of presenting their audiences with a logical and integrated view and soundscape of society as it exists or as it can be imagined to exist. Through such films, we can approach the cultural understanding of film through a filmic understanding of culture.

I draw upon the "the thick tangle of terms" that cluster around the term "reflexive" to discuss these films (Myerhoff and Ruby 1982:1). Building upon Barbara Babcock's seminal work on reflexivity (1980), Myerhoff and Ruby explain that, among its primary meanings, "reflexive" describes "the capacity of any system of signification to turn back upon itself, to make itself its own object by referring to itself." The processes and products of reflexivity—including films about filmmaking—demonstrate "the human capacity to generate second-order symbols or metalevels—significations about signification" (Myerhoff and Ruby 1982:2). As metadiscursive communicative forms, a portion of these films go beyond self-reflexive thinking about thinking to put the very processes of reflexivity on display by showing what it looks and sounds like to be reflexive as well as to be the objects of their own reflection. Some films are more explicitly self-reflexive, revealing and reveling in their own processes, producers, and products (Ruby 1980). Other films, such as *Shadow Magic,* are second-order reflections that portray the processes, producers, products, and reflexivity of fictional others rather than their own. Such films reflect less on their own techniques of construction than on the broader tradition of Chinese film that they simultaneously work within, represent, and create.

The circulation of musical styles, musicians, and songs contributes to the construction of this reflexive tradition, particularly through a subset of reflexive films that focus on the intersection of the film and music worlds. Rather than using music as an accompaniment or enhancer of dramatic action, these films feature music as a central plot element and musicians as main characters. In depicting the social-occupational worlds of musicians working within the film industry, filmic narratives often explore the effects of the film industry on the music world more generally or portray the power of film music to transform society. Their musician-characters reflect on music and discuss their choices amidst the changing conditions of the industry and China as characterized in the films. As they discuss the role of film and music in society, characters comment on artistic and social values—issues that also are discussed off-screen in film criticism. While sometimes pulling discursive forms from elsewhere onto the screen, these films enact the discourse, providing it with sounds and images within a narrative context. Rather than emphasizing the off-screen commentary on film, here I attend to the ways that cinematic discourse constitutes its own form of cultural critique as it represents itself and its worlds.

While I draw from scholarship on reflexive films produced in other parts of the world, my inspiration for analyzing this corpus of Chinese films as a tradition comes from Philip Bohlman's work on the intellectual history of ethnomusicology (Bohlman 1988 and 1992) and Richard Bauman and Charles Briggs's analysis of the dialectic between performance, as a "reflexive arena," and "its wider sociocultural and political-economic context" (1990:60, 61).[4] Bohlman identified a common set of topics and persistent practices used to represent music and culture to illustrate a coherent tradition of ethnomusicological writing. Extending Bohlman's methods, I aim to identify the work done to construct the tradition of Chinese reflexive cinema, while identifying the set of practices it uses to represent film and music. Because this richly complex tradition has been constructed through the reworking of both materials and representational techniques of film, it is open to the type of analysis of the forms, meanings, and metacommunicative functions of performance and discourse proposed by Briggs and Bauman. Their discussion of the processes of extextualization, decontextualization, and recontextualization is particularly relevant here. As the authors explain, the process of extextualization makes "a stretch of linguistic production into a unit—a *text*—that can be lifted out of its interactional setting." When recontextualized into another context, "the resultant text carries elements of its history of use within it" (73). Through such transformative processes, "texts both shape and are shaped by the situational contexts in which they are produced," and their performance in one context connects them to their prior contexts as well as future ones. Thus, it becomes possible to construct "histories of performance" with the goal of "illuminating the larger systemic structures in which performances play a constitutive role . . . in the production and reproduction of social life" (76, 80). As Bauman and Briggs convincingly argue, these transformations contribute to a process of traditionalization and to "the symbolic construction of discursive continuity with a meaningful past" (78). As will be illustrated below, in the case of these Chinese films, it is not only linguistic utterances that are extracted from one context (from a film or real life) and recontextualized in other filmic contexts. Musical figures and topoi, songs, scenes, plots, and characters repeatedly find their way into films through quotation and other forms of reference. These types of intertextual moves constitute the process of traditionalization that creates a coherent tradition of Chinese reflexive film. It has become intertwined through the repetition of narrative themes, overlaps between filmmakers and characters, and layers of intertextuality as one film references another. Together these techniques have woven together a tradition, one made up of reflections of reflections and representations of representations.

This chapter offers directions for beginning to navigate Chinese reflexive filmmaking by laying out the basic parameters of the tradition and by outlining some of its paradigmatic modes of representation and reflexive techniques. The analysis aims to delineate dimensions of the film tradition and to illustrate how they are exemplified within specific films. Within the confines of a short chapter, I focus on a subset of films that deal with the intersection of the worlds of filmmaking and music. Much of this discussion centers on the filmic discourse and on diegetic music and musical activities (rather than on background music)—music that is part of a film's narrative universe, comes from a source within the story, or is discussed by its characters. These films are set and produced, at least partially, within the official borders of the People's Republic of China (PRC) today, with the reminder that it includes films produced before the PRC was established in 1949 and during a period when Hong Kong was a British colony on loan from the Chinese empire.[5] Even within these limits, there is room for an examination of only a few films in any detail, with brief references to other films to which they are connected. After brief sections on Chinese film and scholarship and on conceptual and historical issues, the chapter moves to the description and analysis of individual films that illustrate dominant themes in the Chinese reflexive film tradition. These sections highlight three musical topoi: the Chinese opera world, the role of the film music composer, and the role of the actress-songstress. As one of the major pre-cinematic performance forms, Chinese opera became a popular topic for film, and film personnel often were drawn from the opera world. But the newly emerging film industry simultaneously opened up new professional opportunities for urban-based composers and women. Thus, movies reflecting on cinematic history may be cast more broadly as examinations of the intersection of the film, opera, and urban entertainment worlds.

The Changing Landscape of Chinese Film and Scholarship

The ongoing movement of people, materials, and ideas across borders of many types continues to transform our access to and understanding of Chinese films. In the last two decades particularly, Chinese film scholarship has burgeoned, and new and newly accessible materials have yielded a broader picture of the diverse contexts of Chinese film production. The study of Chinese film music has been slower to develop, remaining at the peripheries of several disciplines.[6] Scholars in Chinese film studies have written little about film music; and musicologists and film-studies scholars, who produce much of the film-music scholarship, have tended to focus on Western film (Neumeyer 2000). Earlier ethnomusicologists, who have studied non-Western music, gravitated toward the study of live performance and what often are called "traditional" musical forms that many (including some characters in *Shadow Magic*) feared were threatened by the very processes through which film flourishes: mass-mediated electronic technologies, commercialization, and global flows. But these too have become central topics of ethnomusicology, and we can anticipate the continued expansion of the topics of film-music studies.

The border crossings within scholarship, nations, and the film industry also complicate the discussion of Chinese film. Some characters in *Shadow Magic* speak of "Chinese" and "foreign" as oppositional categories as do some of their real-life counterparts (Semsel et al. 1990). The notion of "Chinese film" becomes more complex, however, as we take into account the changing and contested concepts of what is included within "China" and as categories of regional and dialect cinemas are thrown into the typological mix. Recent scholarship reflects these complexities as it renegotiates the position of Chinese film within other typologies, often using the plural form of "cinema" to talk about Chinese-language and transnational Chinese cinemas.[7]

Choices for Chinese filmmaking extend beyond national film studios and centers of production in Taiwan, Hong Kong, and mainland China to include independent films and multinational productions that defy territorial classifications. Feature films such as *Beijing Bastards* (1993; about Beijing's independent rock scene) and *Platform* (2000; about new musical and career choices for former members of a PRC state theater troupe) are made by production teams without explicit geographical mooring. Chinese filmmakers work within American-based film studios to produce global blockbusters. These too have become topics for reflection in films such as *Big Shot's Funeral* (2001), a comedy that tells a complex story of the American director Tyler, who becomes (seemingly) critically ill while in Beijing to do a remake of Bertolucci's *The Last Emperor;* a Chinese cinematographer making a documentary about Tyler's work; and the production of a grand-scale and commercialized funeral (with prime advertising space on the hearse) for the not-yet-dead Tyler. It features American star Donald Sutherland, Hong Kong star Rosamund Kwan, and the mainland Chinese comic actor Ge You. Such films aptly illustrate Slobin's earlier point about the fluid interactions of world cinema systems.

The growing availability of older materials also is changing our assessment of the past, as we come to understand the entanglement of influences and interchange of personnel between film production centers. The range of materials now available is impressive, with the republication of early writings, such as anthologies of Chinese film criticism of the 1930s

(Dianyingju 1993) and of twentieth-century Chinese film theory (Luo 2003); books such as *Old Shanghai Films* (Huang 1998) and *Old Movie Stars, Old Movies* (Guo 1998); and CD compilations of original music, particularly of famous actress-songstresses. Film archives have published encyclopedic filmographies that give us a sense of the tremendous number and variety of films produced. The first volume of *Classic Chinese Films* lists over seven hundred feature and opera films produced in mainland China between 1905 and 1930 (ZGDYYS 1996), and *The Chinese Filmography* contains information on nearly twenty-five hundred films produced in the PRC between 1949 and 1995 (Marion 1997). They also remind us of what we do not know. The Hong Kong Film Archive was able to compile information on nearly four hundred films produced in Hong Kong from 1942 to 1949, but researchers had access to only ten of the actual films (Hong Kong Film Archive 1997:xiii).[8] It is the existence of such materials, along with increased access to old and new films, that makes feasible this approach to analyzing patterns within a one-hundred-year tradition.

Reflexive Film Techniques: Intextuality and Metacommunicative Forms

Intertextual practices and metacommunicative forms are at the center of reflexive filmmaking. Because many reflexive films refer to or rework prior filmic material through processes of extextualization and recontextualization, they necessarily create intertextual relations among films. The processes of commenting upon or quoting prior film material lead to a recycling of themes and of the vocabulary, images, and sounds used to enact them on screen. A film about film is by its very nature a metacommunicative form and provides metacommunicative signals that serve as instructions for interpreting the techniques by which the film is constructed (as it switches between scenes imagined or remembered by its characters) and for distinguishing its own filmic material from the insertion of scenes from other films (whether they be original or restaged footage or scenes shot by its characters). Most of *Shadow Magic*, for instance, consists of the newly filmed scenes, including those of the fictional Wallace-Liu duo shooting and editing footage (doing "new tricks" such as splicing in scenes from preexisting footage available to them) and of the films they made. The fictional audiences also listen to foreign music and watch films that Wallace brought with him to China, some of which are original audio recordings and clips from real films made a century ago.[9]

Similar techniques apply to treatments of music. The simplest method is to film stage performance, what the fictional filmmakers did when they made the nonreflexive film *Dingjun Mountain.* The makers of *Shadow Magic,* however, restaged the staging and the filming of *Dingjun Mountain,* treating both diegetically. Other films add reflexive layers by portraying a song being composed by a character within the film, who discusses it with colleagues and then rehearses it in a film studio. A film's narrative context also directs the interpretation of music. These techniques may be combined as a film inserts a recording of popular song from real life as diegetic music, then, through dramatic action and dialogue, interprets its meaning within the narrative universe in which the filmic characters live.

Later films may have more technology and prior filmic material from which to draw, but layers of reflection are not new. As early as the 1920s, Chinese filmmakers were experimenting with the capacities of film to record sounds and images from real life and to record staged life. In *The King of Comedy Visits China* (1922), the first feature film made by the real Mingxing Studio, Charlie Chaplin (played by a British actor) is taken to the fictional Mingxing Studio to watch Chinese filmmakers make *The Ox Herder.* Characters in *Memories of the Old Capital* (1930) listen to and watch Mei Lanfang (1895–1961) perform the concubine's sword dance from the Peking Opera *Farewell My Concubine.*[10] In *The Case of the Jealous Actor* (1939), based on a real-life murder case (in both real and filmic life, the actress had an affair with one of the actor's students, whom he then shot), two Chinese opera stars play themselves; inserted in the film are scenes from one of the couple's real-life performances that they now watch as characters. These are only a few of the metacommunicative devices by which reflexive films generate intertextual relations as they move between films, between real and filmic life, and between different genres of film and music.

Self-Referential and Contextualizing Themes

The film business is a popular topic of cinema, and many of the themes of Chinese films are similar to those from other parts of the world. Filmmakers and musicians reflect on what is on their minds, including their occupations. Film characters discuss problems in the film world, from affairs and jealousies to film criticism and censorship.[11] *The Mad Director* (1937) dramatizes the process by which a famous director is driven mad after his unsuccessful attempts to make a new actress into a star. In *Shadow Magic,* when the Wallace-Liu duo screens a film for the Empress Dowager in the Imperial Palace, the projector catches fire.[12] Reflexive films depict the changes in the industry and in society with which their characters often must struggle.

Films use specific techniques to represent their characters and their choices, with the most common being to limit characters to two or three clearly delineated types that often are posed as oppositional categories. Structurally, the films resolve the opposition through an either/or choice, a transformation (by which the bad is converted to good, for instance), or mediation. These techniques are applied to the characters and roles for people as well as to genres of film and music. Pre-existing social categories and ideologies available in society off the screen also shape the way themes are depicted.

Many of the films deal with choices about the type of film or music to make and its potential benefits and harms, for instance. Looking at the corpus as a whole, nearly any type of music is possible. But again, individual films usually delineate only two or three musical choices, such as whether to compose revolutionary music to strengthen the nation or decadent "yellow" music that will weaken it. Characters debate whether they should make films to educate or pander to the "base desires" of their audiences, to make didactic political films or commercially successful entertainment films. The vocabulary for film choices includes "serious" or "blockbuster," "progressive" or "regressive"/"feudal." The fictional director in *Phantom in the Limelight* (1951), for instance, uses a dancing girl to seduce investors; he tells another actress (who wants to make "serious" films) that "because the audience is inferior . . . there is no need to be serious; instead, we can make money."[13]

The Chinese films exhibit many of the characteristics of the classic "backstage musicals" of Hollywood identified by Jane Feuer. As films about themselves and their place in the world of entertainment, they show what it is like to be in the business. Like Hollywood musicals, the Chinese films portray the worlds backstage and behind and in front of the camera; they show the preparations and rehearsals for performances as well as the "internal audience" of spectators within the film watching the final performances (Feuer 1993:42–47, 11, 25–34). Some films—such as those set in the cosmopolitan context of 1930s Shanghai—even showcase some of the same performance genres as Hollywood musicals, such as those of night clubs and vaudeville shows (ix). But here the musical activities are represented as aspects of the realities of Chinese urban life and through the particular ideologies of the Chinese filmmakers.

Some entertainment films may be considered culturally conservative as they promote and reproduce urban commercial music forms. Other films—such as those produced by leftist "progressive" Shanghai filmmakers in the 1930s—are aimed at transforming the society they represent, a goal discussed on-screen by the protagonists within the films. Other differences relate to the genres of musical performance popular within China. A large portion of Chinese movies about the entertainment world centers on Chinese national and regional operatic forms and narrative storytelling traditions. Many explore issues related to the low social-economic status of their performers; and even those portraying opera "stars" often show them as suffering with the changing whims of audiences and changing conditions of Chinese life more generally. Film occurs within, reflects, and represents its contexts and, thus, common themes are refracted through the particular circumstances of Chinese history and society.

Contextualizing the Chinese Film Industry; Filming Its Contexts

Shadow Magic is a useful example for introducing reflexive techniques and themes, but its narrative stops at 1905, just as the Chinese film industry begins. It developed within contexts that included the fall of the last Chinese empire, foreign imperialism, the construction of the nation, and wars and revolutions through much of the first half of the twentieth century, followed by the Cultural Revolution (1966-1976) in the PRC. An extended discussion of this complex historical environment is beyond the scope of this paper, but certain aspects of the Chinese film industry's development that made possible and constrained filmic choices are especially salient for understanding films discussed below.[14] This section briefly introduces four issues reflected in many films: foreign influences and choices, the urban setting of the film industry and of reflexive films, the introduction of sound film, and war.

FOREIGN INFLUENCES AND CHOICES

The earliest film technologies, filmmakers, and films came to China from Western Europe and the United States. Films and filmmakers from the Soviet Union were influential particularly on 1930s and 1940s leftist filmmakers and PRC filmmakers from 1949 to 1960. Japan exerted a strong influence on film during its occupation of parts of Chinese territory in the 1930s—when it set up studios and film schools but also tried to recruit or censor Chinese filmmakers—and beyond. During the first few decades of the century, when foreign films dominated commercially, Chinese responses varied from learning from and working with the foreign, to banning at least some foreign films.[15] Reflexive films, however, seldom show their characters viewing foreign films. Instead, their filmmaker characters visit the sets of other Chinese filmmakers to learn filmic techniques, and their internal audiences usually watch Chinese films.

Filmic discourse takes on foreign/native distinctions in diverse ways. Multiple interpretations about sounds, images, and entire plots are given within and about one film, as illustrated in *Shadow Magic*. When Liu shows his own Chinese-made film (with scenes of China) in a Chinese theatre, two signs advertise it: "Chinese shadow theatre" (*Zhongguo yingxi*) and "Foreign Images" (*xiyangjing*). When listening to a recording of piano and violin music, the character Lord Tan calls it foreign music and makes clear his position by saying "I admit, these things of foreigners have some merit, but on the whole, I find their music lacking the refinement of our tradition." The character of the film composer in the film *Nie Er* (discussed below) takes a different stance in relation to both Chinese and foreign musics. Whether to mark something as "foreign" and, if so marked, to represent it in opposition to "Chinese" or as desirable or harmful are among the choices available to filmmakers (Tuohy 1999a).

URBAN SETTINGS

People and institutions associated with early Chinese film were located primarily in coastal urban centers where concentrations of people, technology, and commerce made possible the industry's development. Thus, the narratives of reflexive films tend to be set in places such as Beijing, Shanghai, and Hong Kong. Although different in many respects, the Hong Kong and Shanghai film industries were connected to each other in concrete ways as film personnel moved between the two cities (depicted in *Centre Stage* [1992], for instance). Reflexive films represent the film world in relation to urban environments. Some films portray country bumpkins going to the big city, intrigued by the neon lights, action, and theaters; others represent city life more generally as decadent—a dangerous site of prostitution, debauchery, and social-economic inequality.

The number of films on Shanghai alone is overwhelming, with many associating it with the modern.[16] For example, the film *Three Modern Women* (1932) links its focus on modernity to its Shanghai setting as well as to ideas of possible roles for women and of the individual's responsibility to the nation. It contrasts three types of modern women, each attached in some way to Zhang, the lead male character who leaves his fiancée in Northeast China when the Japanese invade. In Shanghai, he becomes a movie star tainted by the glamour of the movie industry until the Japanese invasion of the city arouses his patriotism and he joins the Red Cross to care for wounded soldiers. There he meets his ex-fiancée, a college student who also fled from the Northeast; she is an exemplary woman who cares about the nation. Mr. Zhang's girlfriend, however, cares more for the good life and leaves Shanghai to marry a Hong Kong businessman. The third type of modern woman is one of Zhang's adoring fans. After Zhang tells her he loves another but she still can star with him in a movie, she is desolate and commits suicide in the middle of filming. The film itself becomes a reflexive object of later films. For instance, scenes in *Centre Stage* (discussed below), portray the director and cast of *Three Modern Women* discussing the three characters and shooting the film. And *Centre Stage's* own cast members reflect upon the world of 1930s Shanghai and its film stars.

The commercial musical industries also were concentrated in urban centers, with their opera theaters, stage hall musicals, and record companies. Thus, the diegetic use of music in these films was predisposed toward urban entertainment forms. Set in 1930s Shanghai, *New Year's Coin* (1937) devotes several scenes to the popular music theater, with on-stage performances (one featuring a Chinese Shirley Temple) and back-stage discussions of the hard life of the female stage musician. The film includes the music heard in the dance halls and street scenes that it depicts as part of its narrative, which deals with issues of foreign imperialism and economic, social, and gender inequality (Tuohy 1999a:217–19). These themes also mark *Street Angel* (1937). Actor Zhao Dan plays a poor trumpet player who helps a young female singer (played by the actress-songstress Zhou Xuan) avoid being sold into prostitution, a fate of many real-life and filmic "singsong girls."

The urban concentration of people within the music, drama, and film industries also facilitated fluid relationships and movements among members of those professional communities. The crossover between the opera stars (*ling*) and film stars (*xing*) in Hong Kong is the theme of films such as *Silver World of Fantasy* (1951), "made to mark the nineteenth anniversary of the publication" of *The Opera and Movie Stars Daily* (*Lingxing;* Hong Kong Film Archive 2000: 234). It tells the story of two sisters who are opera actresses desiring to become film stars. One is duped by a man who pretends to be a film star; the other substitutes for a film actress-songstress who could not participate in a benefit concert and is discovered by a film director. Such films brought Hong Kong–based musicians and musical forms into Chinese cinema. Likewise, film music crossed into real life, to be performed live and released on record—activities made possible with the beginning of sound film.

THE INTRODUCTION OF SOUND IN FILM

Outside of Raymond Wallace's theater in 1902, one of *Shadow Magic's* characters asks Assistant Liu (who is playing the "Blue Danube Waltz" on a phonograph to attract customers) if music will be part of the show. The answer is yes, as Liu brings the phonograph inside the theater. In real life, early Chinese films were accompanied by recorded or live music, but only three years after the first sound film, *The Jazz Singer*, was produced in 1927, Shanghai theaters were showing foreign sound films and Chinese filmmakers were experimenting with their own sound films.[17] With the possibility for music and dialogue in film came new career options for musicians and new choices to be made concerning language and musical genres.

Those making sound films in the early 1930s often chose Chinese opera music or opera topics as the subjects for at least portions of their films. *Wild Flower* (1930; partial nonsynchronized sound film) was written and directed by Sun Yu, who was among the first to experiment with music in film (Wang 1995:7–10). The flower-seller Lilian is saved by a musician who teaches her music, and together they stage a successful opera. But his family disapproves of Lilian's profession, and he then must choose between his love for her and his family; she has no other choice but to work in the dance hall scene. Including excerpts from operas as part of the narrative, *Singsong Girl Red Peony* (1930, nonsynchronized sound film), is about a sing-song girl (played by Hu Die) with an abusive husband who tries to sell their daughter to a brothel to make money. The film sets out themes that will continue, with different endings, for actress-songstresses in film and in real life.

The increasing production of sound films necessitated a steady supply of musicians. By the early 1930s, studios began to establish their own music divisions and troupes, such as the Lianhua Studio Song and Dance Troupe (*Lianhua gewuban*). In *Two Stars in the Milky Way* (1931, among the first synchronized sound films), the producers of the fictional Yinhan Studio, in the midst of shooting a film, hear singing in the background. The director discovers the singer and puts her in a new musical he is filming. The composers Xiao Youmei and Li Jinhui were responsible for the music in the real film, some of which is heard in the fictional film within it, including Li Jinhui's "Work Hard" (Nuli).[18] Starring in the film were Li Lili and Wang Renmei, members of Li Jinhui's real-life song-and-dance troupe and of the Lianhua Studio troupe. The Tianyi Film Studio also produced films about opera and urban entertainment forms with music by Li Jinhui, such as *A Singer's Story* (1930) and *Entertainment* (1932).

The introduction of sound also raised the problem of spoken language, since many dialects of Chinese are mutually unintelligible and different dialects are favored by different groups of people. In Shanghai films, stars who spoke Mandarin had the advantage, a topic dramatized in *Centre Stage* (1992; see also HKIFF 1993). The scene is set in the 1930s at a dinner party for film workers. The head of the Lianhua Film Studio tells the group, "I'm going to the United States to see them shoot sound films; they also haven't been doing it for long and often make mistakes too." They thank (in English, then translated into Chinese) the American Mr. Skinner for helping them set up the studio's sound-synchronizing department. As they discuss the possibilities for sound film, actress Ruan Lingyü—a native Cantonese speaker—says in Mandarin "the next time I talk on the screen, I will speak Mandarin"; she has been studying it with the actress Li Lili.[19]

WAR AND REVOLUTION

Films about the 1930s are filled with stories of musicians participating in the Anti-Japanese War effort and of scenarists writing patriotic movie scripts. Delineating the types of choices available for music and film (and for responses to the war more generally), many films articulate a relation between women and the nation. *Three Women* (1949), another film depicting three contrasting types, is set in Shanghai when the Japanese partially occupied the city (1937–1941). It begins with subtitles that explain the aims of its real-life filmmakers: "Mr. Tian Han [the screenwriter] portrays three modern women. They live in different social worlds and normally their paths would not cross; but they live in the same times. They suffer as Chinese women and bear the fate of the nation" (*minzu*).

The first type of woman, a poor worker, is raped by Japanese soldiers and becomes a prostitute to support her family after her husband is blinded with limestone dust by government thugs. The second is defined through her marriages; she is weak and refuses to join her first husband in the Japanese resistance forces. In a scene that makes use of the referential qualities of music and language, the film introduces her as she sits with her second husband and dog listening to the radio: "Four hundred million Chinese people are happy under the [Japanese] imperial army's protection" (in Japanese). She turns off the radio, her husband turns it back on, and the dog howls. Her husband tunes it to popular music; she switches it to a station run by Chinese forces in exile. Nervous because that station is banned in Shanghai, he tunes it to the Nationalist government station. "If you don't want to listen to this, what then?" She tunes it to Chinese opera. The third woman is a strong, patriotic activist and headmistress of a girls' school who helps both women "raise their consciousness" even after they both try to commit suicide. The film ends with her lecturing: "We must know we have only one enemy, the imperialists and feudal exploiters. Sisters, let us struggle!" The film's message is reinforced through a reflexive framing device, as subtitles of the lyrics of "Song of the New Women"—the theme song of *New Women* (1934) composed by Nie Er—scroll across the screen.

Creating opportunities for filmic discourse about the "proper" aim of filmmaking, filmmakers present their characters with choices such as whether to perform for or against the Japanese and whether to write decadent entertainment or "progressive" scripts.[20] In *Lovers of the Silver Screen*

(1939) an actress and actor star in "inconsequential melodramas because producers feel they cannot make money with national defense movies." Although the actress does not care either way, her husband wants to serve the country; his career declines while hers rises. Finally she has a change of heart and, at a ceremony to honor her as the "Movie Queen," she makes a speech denouncing the film industry (Hong Kong Film Archive 1997:348).

Another film focusing on the entertainment world during the war years and upon the position of female performers in Chinese society is *Stage Sisters* (1965). Set from 1935 to 1950, the film follows the paths of two Yueju (Shaoxing) Opera actresses. Fleeing their home because of problems caused by the Japanese invasion, they arrive in Shanghai in 1941 to encounter other enemies: theater managers, corrupt Nationalist officials, thugs (who temporarily blind the "good" actress by throwing limestone dust in her eyes), and decadent city life. One actress, feeling that "lowly entertainers" (*xizi*) have no other choice, succumbs. The other actress pursues a noble path, encouraged by a female activist-reporter. When the actress forms a collectively run female troupe, its members "study" the progressive films recommended by the reporter. A subplot, about the suicide of an older Yueju Opera actress, allows the film's characters to discuss newspaper articles, with headlines such as "A Tragic Life and a Lavish Funeral," that reveal the "inside story" about the plight of female entertainers.

By the time the film's subtitle appears, indicating that it is 1950, a number of transformations have been accomplished. The "workers-peasants-soldiers" have created their own theater and, by the end of the film, the opera troupe is performing revolutionary operas such as *The White-Haired Woman* (in real life made into a film in 1950; a filmed stage performance of it was shown repeatedly during the Cultural Revolution). Within the dialogue and lyrics of a song performed by a background chorus are numerous references to depraved and correct paths. The film concludes when the decadent and weak actress reforms, saying, "I won't forget that I took the incorrect path," and her stage sister enthusiastically responds "let's reform ourselves and sing a generation of revolutionary operas!"

After the 1950s, the connections between the Hong Kong and PRC films worlds decreased for several decades. Hong Kong, a British colony and capitalist center, looked more toward Hollywood. In the PRC, state-run film studios had closer ties to the Soviet Union for a time. Film was to educate and serve the people, and the industry was explicitly and officially anti-commercial. Movies about the urban-based film and music industries declined in favor of those set in the countryside and border regions, with plots about socialist construction and featuring the "common people" (the folk, peasants, minorities, and so on). During the Cultural Revolution

(1966–1976), filmmaking of all sorts was severely curtailed. Subsequent political and economic reforms in the PRC both stimulated the film industry and became the topics of films. Filmmakers returned to making reflexive movies about the film and music industries, portraying the historical changes and the new choices available.

The Chinese Opera World as a Filmic Trope: Cinematic Reflections of Change

As portrayed in *Shadow Magic*, Chinese opera was the subject of the first Chinese-made movie, and it remained popular for the next one hundred years, with filmed stage performances and films about the opera business and actors' lives. Opera also proved a useful lens through which to explore the theme of political, economic, and artistic change in China. As with reflexive cinema generally, the reworking of materials in this subset of films creates a web of intertwined themes, with common phrases and musical works that are varied in particular films. Here I will discuss three recurring themes in the cinematic portrayal of the opera world: the arduous training and low status of the opera performer; responses to change; and scenes from the Peking Opera *Farewell My Concubine*, more recently also made famous through the movie *Farewell My Concubine* (1993), which illustrates these three themes but without explicit diegetic connections to film.

Many films about the opera world characterize the training of performers as long and difficult, showing groups of young novices practicing their singing, spending hours perfecting physical moves, and enduring beatings by the opera masters. Their characters discuss the dedication needed to withstand difficult circumstances, such as their low social status. As the master of the opera school in the film *Farewell My Concubine* says, "Prostitutes and actors are looked down upon equally." Films usually contrast opera training with training in another type of art or profession. In *Shadow Magic*, for instance, the contrast is with film as Lord Tan says, "Our opera has a long tradition. It takes years to turn a student into an artist. Why should we compare ourselves to this shadow magic?"

Individual films delineate and characterize the types of change occurring that impacted the entertainment world, but each film lays out several choices available for responding to it. Many portray a decline in the economic viability of opera in relation to new art forms and media such as film. In *Opera Stars and Song Girls* (1935), real-life Cantonese Opera singers play characters strategizing to attract paying audiences by including dancing girls and popular songs in their shows. The financial problems of the fictional troupe in *Stage Lights* (1938) lead it to perform on radio while searching for rich investors. The fictional actress in *Stage Door* (1996) hires a Broadway-style director to help her revitalize Cantonese Opera.

Although the varied use of the opera *Farewell My Concubine* throughout the film tradition is complex, it functions repeatedly as a reflexive device. Briefly, Peking Opera star Mei Lanfang rewrote the opera in the 1920s, adapting it from an older one (*The Hegemon King Bids Farewell to His Queen* is set circa 200 BCE and recounts the military defeat of the King of Chu). By the time of the parting scene between the King of Chu and his concubine (both roles usually played by male actors), it is clear that all is lost; his kingdom will fall to the surrounding Han armies attacking on all sides. The king reflects on his life, his power, and the loyalty of his horse as he worries about the fate of his beloved concubine. He begs her to escape, but she remains loyal. As she dances for the king, she grabs his sword and kills herself. Various films over the last eighty years have used scenes from the opera diegetically (such as the previously mentioned *Memories of the Old Capital,* 1930). *Farewell My Concubine* takes the opera's plot and lines to advance the film's narrative and its representation of social-political change in twentieth-century China. The film's two lead male roles are opera actors who play the roles of the king and the concubine. In their final stage performance, the character playing the concubine grabs a real sword and takes his (the actor)/her (the concubine) life during the sword dance.[21]

Made five years before *Farewell My Concubine, Painted Faces* (1988) is an example of a film that reflects upon the intertwined histories of Chinese opera and film. Its narrative begins in Hong Kong in 1962 when a poor mother turns over her son to Master Yu's Peking Opera school.[22] While discussing the rapid changes in Hong Kong society, the film directly addresses the three themes outlined above. It follows the lives of young opera students as they mature, with scenes of their arduous training and opera performances in an amusement park. The film portrays Peking Opera as on its last legs, its popularity declining in relation to the rise of popular music and film. The diegetic recontextualization of lines and scenes from the opera *Farewell My Concubine* allows its older characters to reflect on their own lives as opera performers and on the changing conditions of their art form.

The character Master Yu often refers to the arduous training and low status of Peking Opera actors. His neighbor—angry because Master Yu's pupils taunted his son, a public school student—says "actors are low class people, the worst type." After quoting the proverbial expression "A prostitute has no true love; an actor has no real feelings," he says "my son will have a steady life, unlike your baldies who are always doing somersaults and never standing on solid ground." Master Yu responds: "We have high aspirations" and quotes another proverbial expression: "It takes three years to train a scholar; ten years to become an actor." Later, he compares Peking Opera with Cantonese Opera: "No one can compare with the skills of a Peking Opera troupe; we have the toughest vocal and physical training of all." He exhorts his students not to look down on themselves, even if others do.

Painted Faces lays out its characters' choices for responding to opera's decline. When Uncle Wah—Master Yu's friend and classmate in opera school in the 1920s—is unable to get opera parts, he becomes a stuntman in Hong Kong action films. At first, Master Yu's choice for his pupils is to continue performing opera to smaller and smaller audiences. But Master Yu later must reconsider this choice when the amusement park decides to replace the troupe's opera show with a "girlie" dance show and the government plans to demolish the building housing his opera school. In a scene set in the wax museum (which has a historical exhibit of Chinese opera), Master Yu discusses his plans to dissolve his troupe. "I'll let the children try other trades or go back to school. Hong Kong is too westernized. Who cares for traditional opera anymore? It's a dying art." Master Yu's pupils—who are ill-prepared to attend public school—decide to work in a film studio.

Painted Faces is reflexive on many levels. It is loosely based on the lives of the Seven Little Fortunes—real-life stars such as Yuen Biao, Jackie Chan, and Sammo Hung—all former opera pupils who moved into the film industry. The real-life Sammo Hung plays Master Yu, and a child actor plays the character of young Sammo. The film's fictional pupils get their first jobs in the Shaw Brothers Studio (which produced *Painted Faces*). As they look around at the studio sets, they reflect on the films made there. "Isn't that the fortress in *The One-Armed Swordsman*? And that's the valley in *Fourteen Amazon Women*! The Movie Queen Lilly Ho flew over it beautifully; Uncle Wah was her stuntman. I hope I can be the Movie Queen's stand-in some day." The character of Uncle Wah is played by Lam Ching-Ying, another former opera singer turned stuntman in real life. *Painted Faces* also uses scenes and lines from operas reflexively, with some moving on and off the stages on which its characters perform. One of the pupils arrives on stage late but says his lines (from *Farewell My Concubine*): "Your majesty. We're surrounded by enemies on all sides! This time we're doomed!" From the audience, Master Yu responds "You're doomed for sure. The enemies [referring to audience members] have returned home to listen to the radio show."

One of *Painted Faces'* most poignant scenes is accomplished through reflexive layers, quoting the lines of the King of Chu in *Farewell My Concubine* as a metacommunicative signal of reflection. Master Yu is at the film studio watching Uncle Wah rehearse a scene that he has bungled several times (he's in danger of losing his job). The fictional movie being rehearsed is a historical action film set in the courtyard of a wealthy family's mansion, where its characters are watching shadow puppet theater (not only a traditional Chinese theater form but also a referent for early concepts of Chinese film as "shadow theater"). As stuntman Wah flies through the air to kidnap the family's baby, the line holding him breaks and he falls. His shadow appears behind—and his blood is streaked on—the shadow puppet theater screen.

Obviously hurt and confused, he screams "I want to act" (Peking Opera music begins in *Painted Faces'* background score) and "With blood I'll imprint eternally my name" (lines from an opera). He jumps around wildly, finally making his way to the beams holding the klieg lights high up in the studio. When Master Yu climbs up to save him, he realizes that logic won't prevail. Standing on the lighting beams, Yu takes the stance of an opera actor playing the King of Chu and sings out his lines: "Alas! Looking back at my life." When Wah hears this, he imagines he once again is performing on the opera stage and assumes the submissive stance of the concubine. Master Yu (as the king) continues: "With strength to move mountains, and power to rule the world. My time has come to a halt, my light shines no more." When Wah nearly falls, he slips out of his role and thinks he is a pupil in the opera troupe forty years ago: "I fell off the stage again; this time Master will kill me." Master Yu saves him and says, "Let's finish the song together." He resumes as the king: "Nothing is left my dear queen, nothing but you and me."

The "performance" ends without Wah completing the concubine's sword dance. When he asks if his performance was good, Master Yu tells him it was brilliant and points to the huge audience (the film crew and cast, looking up aghast from 50 feet below them on the studio floor). When he returns to the floor, Wah thanks them for coming to his show, and the ambulance takes him away, ending Wah's career as both opera and film actor. After another parting scene—this between Master Yu and his pupils—we hear the sound of opera pupils rehearsing lines from an opera: "Or has the best season gone altogether?" Subtitles explain that the pupils remained in Hong Kong and became superstars, and Master Yu moved to Los Angeles to teach Peking Opera and "hold onto his art," a theme of yet another set of interconnected films on opera.

The Film Music Composer as Film Subject: Nie Er *and* The National Anthem

Few films have as their lead character the film-music composer, but two films that do are about Nie Er and Tian Han, a composer and a lyricist (and screen writer) who are connected to dozens of other films as real-life film personnel, as characters in films, and through the songs they compose for movies. Both *Nie Er* (1959) and *National Anthem* (1998) culminate in the depiction of the composition of "The March of the Volunteers," the theme song of another film on which the two collaborated in real life, *Children of Troubled Times* (1935). As *National Anthem*'s subtitles explain, this song also "was chosen as the temporary national anthem and played at the founding ceremony of the PRC in 1949, then chosen as the official anthem in 1982." Thus, not only are their songs repeated and discussed within the films, but Nie and Tian themselves become the objects of entextualization and recontextualization.

Both *Nie Er* and *National Anthem* are set in 1930s Shanghai during the war years. Portrayed as ardent patriots committed to using the arts to encourage Chinese to save their nation, their characters work in progressive-leftist arts organizations. These concerns are highlighted throughout both films as their characters undergo transformative processes through which they become aware of the potential of film and music as tools for the mass dissemination of ideas and for the arousal of emotions. Their success in "awakening" the masses to their own conditions is obvious through scenes of packed movie theaters and throngs of Chinese citizens singing their songs in the midst of battle.

The central character of *Nie Er* is the musician Nie (1912–1935; played by Zhao Dan [1915–1980], an actor who worked with Nie and Tian in real life during the 1930s). A composer and conductor of 1930s Shanghai film music, Nie has been one the most consistently praised film composers in the PRC through the mid 1980s.[23] The playwright and film scenarist Tian Han (1898–1968; played by He Zhengjun, who became well known in post-1980s films) is the central character in *National Anthem,* usually with Nie at his side.[24] *Nie Er* was made by cast and crew members who worked in leftist arts circles in Shanghai during the 1930s.[25] All of its scenes, including those depicting earlier films, are newly filmed. *National Anthem,* on the other hand, uses original clips from and restages earlier films, but makes far less diegetic use of Nie's songs, and its background orchestral score seldom references his music. Both films are based on real events and people, although *Nie Er* primarily features fictional characters modeled on the historical figures, while *National Anthem* names names.

Nie Er portrays Nie as reflexive and open to transformation. He is passionate about music, arriving in Shanghai with his *yueqin* (four-stringed plucked lute), then quickly mastering the violin by practicing day and night. He becomes even more passionate about the idea of going to the Soviet Union to study music, and he breaks down in joyful tears when the Chinese Communist Party (CCP) underground organizer Su Ping (based on the real-life figure Xia Yan) tells him he has been approved for CCP membership. His talent is recognized in many circles. He auditions at the Mingxing Film Studio; although his audition is successful, the job requires insurance that Nie cannot afford. His audition for the Five Flowers Song and Dance Troupe also is a success, and he lands the job. But when his patriotic female friend sees one of the troupe's shows, she cries "You're working in *this* kind of place, wasting your talents and your fate?! Chinese youth need passion! Put forth your musical voice." Nie goes home to reflect, playing her words in his head and writing in his journal (throughout the film, these actions signal Nie's internal reflection and his process of transformation). "Can I really be satisfied in this kind of musical life? No! I want to be a real musician; I must rigorously study, study, study!"

Scenes throughout the film allow for filmic discourse on the potential role of music in film and in stimulating social-political change as well as on the type of music to be used. Nie auditions at the Conservatory, impressing the music professors with his musical talent but not his views. Nie says "music is a product and reflection of society, the voice of the people" (*dazhong*), to which the professor responds by referencing a common figure: "Do the people understand Beethoven!" Nie also has problems with the song-and-dance troupe because it performs popular music-hall songs such as "Misty Rain" and "Peach Blossom River," which this film (and others) portrays as decadent and harmful to society.[26] After learning that Nie has published criticisms of the troupe in *The Silver Screen and the Stage* magazine, the troupe leader is upset. "I've been leading this difficult life for decades, devoting myself to the advancement of the art of Chinese song!" Nie responds, "It's not art, it's poison!" This type of music is pitted against the progressive and uplifting type of music Nie will come to write after he is transformed through further reflection and learning.

The characterization of Chinese and foreign music is complex. Some "Chinese" music is marked as "bad" through dialogue and image. Other music that is marked as both "foreign" and "good" also tends simultaneously to be contextualized—in the film and in real-life leftist circles of the time—as socialist and revolutionary. For instance, in one scene, Nie looks with delight on the scores of Glinka brought to him by a reporter from a Soviet Union arts magazine. At a Red Cross Station, members of the song troupe become uncomfortable when they see the disgusted looks on the faces of wounded soldiers as they listen to the troupe's performance of the "decadent" urban popular Chinese song "Peach Blossom River." Nie steps in to counter the song with a rousing and well-received Chinese-language rendition of the French song "The Marseillaise." As they listen, bleeding soldiers rise from their cots. The singing increases in volume as Nie is joined by others, such as the revolutionary playwright and arts activist Kuang Wentao. When the song is finished, Kuang declares that "singing the 'Marseillaise' is fine, but we must have a Chinese 'Marseillaise'" (*Zhongguode Masaiqu*).[27] This scene effectively sets up Nie's later transformation to a revolutionary songwriter and film-music composer. Later in the film, Kuang states that "film is an effective weapon for struggle; we want to take it from the hands of the capitalists and use it to serve the revolution." At home at night, Nie reflects on all of this, telling himself, "I want to become a revolutionary musician!" Scenes of Nie composing what would later become revolutionary classics in real life—such as "The Graduation Song" (*Biyege*) for *The Plunder of Peach and Plum* (1934)—are followed by those of Nie conducting the song as it is being filmed in a studio. People in a theater watch the film, and the song is sung off-screen by groups of workers in factories and students in schools. Scenes of Nie feverishly composing are overlaid with images of published scores and records of songs such as "The Pioneers" (*Kailu xianfeng*), "The Song of New Woman" (*Xinnüxing ge*), and "The Song of the Big Road" (*Dalu ge*).[28] Portrayals of the enthusiastic reception by the "masses" to Nie's music are followed by scenes of thugs (hired by corrupt Kuomintang [KMT] officials) smashing leftist movie studios and the record stores that sell those songs, while a loudspeaker mounted on a telephone pole blares out Nie's film song "The Pioneers" (accompanied by people singing it live from their balconies) and a man yells "you're not allowed to sing that song!"

Toward the end of the film, Su Ping visits Nie (now in hiding from the government) and asks him to set to music the lyrics of "The March of the Volunteers," written by Tian Han (who has been arrested by the government). "I'll compose it tonight!" At home alone—with a thunderstorm roaring outside—musical motifs play in his imagination. As he composes, he envisions scenes of his friends being executed and of his song being sung by revolutionaries in future battles. Like Nie's other songs, this "Chinese 'Marseillaise'" is based on tonal harmonies and is performed in four-part choral form, accompanied by a large orchestra (musical materials that are not marked in the filmic discourse as "foreign"). The next day, Nie boards a ship headed for the Soviet Union (without mention of a stop in Japan made by the real-life Nie). The last scene is of the first National Day in Tian'anmen Square in 1950, with the "The March of the Volunteers" now in the background score; the film ends with the lyrics, "Advance, advance, advance!"

The 1998 film *National Anthem* portrays the world of progressive art circles as vibrant and volatile. The underground CCP arts organizers Xia Yan and Yang Hansheng stop by a rehearsal of Tian Han's play to tell him that plans for the next day's performance have changed. They instead are now to perform his opera *Death of a Famous Actor* (*Mingyou zhisi,* itself a reflexive opera about the opera business). Their dialogue and the scene portraying the performance both focus on the role of stage arts and performers in social-political transformation. "The benefit performance is aimed at all sectors of society. *Death of a Famous Actor* is mature art, and the participation of film stars will give it more influence inside and outside of China," says Xia Yan. The actress Mei Ning, based in Malaysia, has come to Shanghai to study with Tian, bringing with her donations for the resistance effort. They—and nearly every other important person in Shanghai—all go to the theater to watch the Shanghai Arts World benefit performance, emceed by actress-songstress Wang Renmei. The list of people on stage reads like a Who's Who list of famous people in real-life Shanghai music and film worlds, including Zhao Dan; director Yuan Muzhi; and actress-songstresses Hu Die, Li Lili, and Ruan Lingyü.

Based on the first three quarters of *National Anthem,* however, it would seem that few people sang songs in Chinese social-political movements or in Shanghai, apart from the Japanese soldiers dancing on a ship while singing "The March of Manchuria" (*Manzhou jinxingqu.* Tian yells at them in Japanese, "This is China" and they respond, "Soon you'll be singing our Japanese national anthem."). The composer Nie barely talks about music until after the Japanese attack Shanghai. In the next scene, the composer and lyricist come to realize—and then articulate—the qualities of film and music that make them effective tools for social transformation. Looking around at the ruined buildings and dead bodies, Nie says to Tian, "I left Yunnan to study music in Shanghai, but since the 9-1-8 incident [the September 18 incident marking the Japanese occupation of Northeast China in 1931], I've almost given it up. Instead, I go to plays, work as a handyman, and so on in order to resist the Japanese . . . We've done so many plays." "Drama isn't enough," responds Tian. They look at each other and, in unison, shout, "We need songs!!" Tian tells Nie, "You're good at music. Songs can be sung anywhere, any time; they spread quickly and rouse feelings of indignation as a high tide!" Nie agrees. "You write the lyrics, I'll write the tunes!"

A bit earlier, Xia Yan had a similar epiphany about film as he gazed at the battle being fought around him: "Drama and the stage can't portray such a heroic scene; we need to use film to record this stirring battle." A team makes a short documentary that, when screened to other arts workers, brings them to tears. Tian stands up in front of the screen, saying to Xia Yan, "We're going to make movies!" And they begin to learn by observing other Chinese filmmakers in action. On the set of *Children of Our Time*

(1933, with actress Ai Xia), the actors are having trouble with their parts, so the director asks screenwriter Xia Yan to explain the characters' motivations. "Your performance must reflect the firmness and spirit of the Chinese people (*Zhonghua minzu*) when encountering hardship."

A scene in the Diantong Film Studio office provides the characters with another opportunity to discuss their efforts and their success. Talking with Tian and Xia Yan, Manager Zhang says, "You've made the Diantong Studio rich. The audiences love the scripts you left-wing writers write" (a line also in *Nie Er*). Xia explains, "That's because film follows the trends of the times, so the masses welcome us." He turns the conversation to *Children of Troubled Times* (1935), saying to Tian, "You really must write a good theme song for this movie. They're singing our songs not only in Shanghai but all over China."

Toward the end of the film, Xia visits Nie, who is in the midst of composing the music to Tian's lyrics for "The March of the Volunteers." "You've come at a good time; the lyrics are so exciting and tonight's thunderstorm makes it a great time to compose." Xia informs Nie that the CCP is sending him to Europe to avoid KMT persecution. Tian already is in jail and "his greatest wish is to have the song disseminated; now it's not just *Children of Troubled Times* that needs the song; the whole nation needs it!" Nie goes off to Europe (subtitles explain he "unfortunately drowned in Japan"). Standing within the prison walls, Tian hears his song. His friends—who are outside the prison in a boat on the river, with a phonograph on board—play a recording of the Diantong Film Studio Chorus singing "The March of the Volunteers." Tian tells his fellow inmates "I wrote the lyrics for the Chinese people," as the phonograph blares out "advance, advance, advance!"

The Actress-Songstress: Centre Stage

Nearly all the film and music industry characters in *National Anthem* (and many other 1930s Shanghai films) are recontextualized as characters in *Centre Stage* (1992) and as characters in quoted and restaged films within the film. Some also appear as themselves in filmed interviews with *Centre Stage*'s director Stanley Kwan. Using virtually all forms of reflexive technique, *Centre Stage* portrays the entertainment worlds of 1930s Shanghai along with the connections between the Shanghai and Hong Kong film industries, while telling stories about the actress Ruan Lingyü (1910–1935).

The actress-songstress is as common a topic of Chinese film as opera. Prior to the twentieth century, female Peking opera characters were played by men; in the twentieth century, more roles for women opened up in

Peking and other opera forms, including females playing male roles (as portrayed in *Stage Sisters* above) and in film. These films share many traits with Hollywood musicals. Their plots deal with themes such as the women's entrance into the film world and their rise to stardom; they show the backstage and off-screen lives of actresses and their performances on stages and in film. But they also comment upon and represent the position of women in the particular circumstances of Chinese society.

Many films featuring "musical" women show them as having a limited range of real-life and film roles. They may play roles of the songstress, dance-hall girl, and prostitute/courtesan (the fortunate ones succeed in business or become happily married with children); or they may be music teachers and activists (always a good choice when one can make it). A string of movies portrays these two professional categories in relation to two categories of music: (1) the oppressed, low-status female entertainer who may sing one of two Chinese popular songs mentioned above— "Misty Rain" or "Peach Blossom River"; and (2) the music teacher–activist who teaches children and/or women to sing strong, patriotic songs, often those composed by Nie Er and made famous through prior films. Some films give multiple choices to one woman, then show her moving through a series of transformations. The actress in *Fallen Angel* (1939) "transforms herself from a country girl to a famous star . . . becomes a rich man's wife, a social butterfly, a famous dance hall girl and a big star; [then] . . . falls to the gutter, becoming a criminal, a beggar, a drifter and a prostitute." After being redeemed, she "returns to the countryside where she marries a cow-herd, advocating conservation and agricultural production" (Hong Kong Film Archive 1997:287).[29] Other films provide another choice: suicide.

Centre Stage explores all these issues. In at least three different restaged scenes, *Centre Stage* portrays the 1930s male film directors and studio heads discussing the types of female characters and female actresses in their films in terms of types. *Centre Stage* quotes from or restages original films, including *Three Modern Women* (1932, discussed above) and *The Goddess* (1934), that portray those types. In one scene, the character of Ruan (played by Maggie Cheung) arrives at the Lianhua Film Studio. She has heard rumors that film star Ai Xia has committed suicide. Director Cai Chusheng tells her "Ai Xia was killed by society. Damn those tabloid reporters! I feel Wei Ming's pain is a reflection of Ai Xia's." Cai's mention of Wei Ming references a character in a new film Chu will direct, *New Woman*, which is to be based loosely on the life of Ai Xia and on a film script she wrote; Ruan is to play the lead. *New Women*, released in 1934, is a real-life film that tells the story of music teacher Wei Ming, who falls on bad times, reluctantly turning to prostitution to pay for her daughter's hospital care.

Another educator-activist, who composes and teaches patriotic songs, tries to help her, but to no avail. After her daughter dies, Wei commits suicide, although she has a change of heart as she lies dying. *Centre Stage* restages the original hospital scene, with the fictionalized Ruan playing the part of Wei Ming and screaming "I want to live!" just before she dies. The camera pans back to show Kwan and the *Centre Stage* crew filming Maggie Cheung playing Ruan. With *Centre Stage*'s background score continuing, the scene shifts to a 1930s film studio screening theater filled with angry "tabloid reporters" watching the original 1934 film (with the original Ruan screaming "I want to live" in subtitles; it was a silent film); the music shifts to source sounds of Nie Er's "Song of the New Woman."

Centre Stage sets several scenes that include the character of Nie Er and his songs in the Lianhua Film Studio. The sound of Nie's violin can be heard in Ruan's dressing room as she talks with Lianhua actress Chen Yan-yan (also appearing in *Centre Stage* as her real-life older self in a 1991 interview). Downstairs, in the studio's courtyard, Nie introduces Wu Yonggang and other Lianhua personnel to students from Fudan University. They discuss the Japanese Occupation of Northeast China and turn to Li Minwei (Lai Man-wai [1893–1953], the "father" of Hong Kong cinema; here portrayed as a young man). "Mr. Li, you're a revolutionary; you lead us." Li, who also made documentaries, responds: "When I followed Dr. Sun (Sun Yatsen), I carried a camera rather than a gun."

Later, fictional Ruan walks into the studio as personnel are discussing a song Nie is composing. Director Sun Yu says, "It's a great start; I must film this song!" It is the "Song of the Big Road," which the real-life Sun Yu will make as the theme song of a future movie, *The Big Road*. Ruan tells Nie that she's sorry she did not take part in his movement (she left for Hong Kong when the Japanese attacked). "Don't worry, there will many more chances in the future. The Japanese won't leave. Then it will no longer be a matter of singing for the army or nursing wounded soldiers in the hospital." In the end, neither the character of Ruan nor the real Ruan will join that struggle. Early in the morning of the day she is to speak to students of her teacher-activist friend for Women's Day, she commits suicide.

Ruan's real life parallels themes in films about Chinese actress-songstresses. Her father died when she was six. Her first lover and scoundrel husband was a son in the house in which her mother worked as servant. His brother, a film actor, helped Ruan get into the industry. She became famous when she began playing "serious" roles. Her picture was on the covers of all the film magazines, and tabloid newspapers carried articles about her "scandalous life" after she became the mistress of a film investor. Her funeral (portrayed in *Centre Stage*) was a big media event, covered as far away as the *New York Times*. She became the subject of future films, including *Who's to Blame?* (1937), featuring her ex-husband playing himself. Kwan includes in *Centre Stage* a film clip from a 1991 interview with old Shanghai film scenarist Hong Shen. When asked if the "progressive roles" played by Ruan influenced her life, Hong reflects back and explains that "circumstances were beyond her control."

Like *Shadow Magic*, *Centre Stage* is a reflexive film about a short period of Chinese film history. But unlike *Shadow Magic*, it reveals not only the products, processes, and producers of its fictionalized filmmakers but also its own. The actors playing the characters of fictionalized actors are shown discussing the real-life figures upon which their roles are based. They compare their own lives as stars of music and film in contemporary Hong Kong to those of their counterparts in 1930s China. Together they sit with director Stanley Kwan, watching videos of interviews he conducted with film personnel now in their golden years. The shifts between these multiple narrative universes are marked by metacommunicative signals ranging from the use of black-and-white still photographs and film clips and songs from the original films to the use of subtitles. Subtitles perform another important function of making the dialogue intelligible to viewers as the spoken language moves between Cantonese, Mandarin, Shanghainese, and English. In many ways, *Centre Stage* comes full circle as it simultaneously looks back to portray the fluid contexts of early Chinese film and portrays the fluid contexts of its own production.

Conclusions

As I wrote the draft of this chapter, the new film *Electric Shadows* was showing in theaters and international film festivals. Already labeled by multiple reviewers as a Chinese *Cinema Paradiso*, it is one of the newest additions to the Chinese reflexive cinema tradition. The filmic discourse spans over seven decades as it discusses actresses from 1930s Shanghai, quotes Chinese and foreign films from the 1940s through 1970s, and depicts scenes in which its characters watch films outdoors in the village, inside theaters, and in their imaginations. The film begins in today's Beijing, where delivery boy Mao Dabing runs into the agitated female character Lingling when riding his bicycle. While she is in the hospital undergoing psychiatric evaluation, he goes to her apartment and discovers her collection of film memorabilia (film prints, books, and projectors) and her passion for 1930s actress-songstress Zhou Xuan. As he reads Lingling's diary, he also begins to discover that she was his childhood friend twenty-five years ago.

The scene shifts to a village in Ningxia province in the early 1970s. Lingling's mother admires Zhou Xuan and aspires to be like her, but her dream of becoming a famous actress-songstress is ruined when her boyfriend leaves her after she becomes pregnant. Like film actresses and characters before her, alone and the topic of gossip, she considers suicide. This time, however, the female characters in the films screened in the village's outdoor theater give her courage. She watches every film available to her, whether revolutionary operas or patriotic socialist films. Lingling's life is intertwined with films at every step. She is born during the screening of an Albanian film and later becomes friends with Mao Dabing, who often imagines himself as a soldier portrayed in his favorite film, *Tunnel Warfare*. Lingling's mother has an affair with the village's film projectionist, so mother and daughter spend much time with him is his office where he previews films. Lingling goes on to adopt her mother's dream of becoming an actress, having grown up watching films (scenes from which are shown throughout *Electric Shadows*). As time goes on, post-Cultural Revolution economic reform and change signal the decline of these rural outdoor film shows as they lose their government subsidies (a topic of the documentary *Carriers of Electric Shadows* [1993]). But the expanding commercial film industry supplies more than enough material for film buffs such as Mao Dabing, played by Xia Yu—who also plays the character of Assistant Liu in *Shadow Magic*.

As portrayed in *Shadow Magic,* film technologies and films were imported to China over a century ago, but they were at least partially assimilated within the already metropolitan urban centers of China. And within a few short years, Chinese filmmakers made use of the filmic medium to do just as the fictional Assistant Liu envisioned—they made Chinese films about Chinese life. At different periods, Chinese filmmakers and musicians continued to incorporate foreign themes and techniques, either directly from foreign films or as these materials were mediated within Chinese society. Thus, the foreign is embedded within the tradition of Chinese reflexive film.

Produced in and reflecting upon turbulent changes over the course of the last one hundred years in China, the films are remarkably similar in their basic thematic materials and paradigmatic modes of representation. As they return to quote, comment upon, and represent the familiar in varied ways, films add to the layers of representation and to the connections between themselves that create the tradition of reflexive film. This reflexive film tradition turns back on itself to reflect upon and to produce its own images of itself. In the process, it creates the shadows and echoes that constitute the traces between films that weave together the tradition.

Notes

1. I am grateful to Robert J. Eno, Cornelia Fales, and Mark Slobin for their insightful comments on earlier drafts of this chapter. I also wish to thank Zhang Yingjin, who not only has taught me much about Chinese film but also, over a decade ago, encouraged me to pursue research on Chinese film music.

2. *Ying* can mean shadow, image, reflection, or photograph; *xi* refers to staged and narrative performance forms. *Dianying,* "electric shadow," is the term for film used most often today. Other early terms for foreign film were *xiyang yingxi* (Western-foreign shadow play) and *xiyangjing,* the Chinese title of the movie *Shadow Magic.* For the beginnings of film and shadowplays, see Du Wenwei 2000; Chen Xihe 1990; Li and Hu 1996.

3. Most sources cite *Dingjun Mountain* as the first Chinese-made narrative film. Chinese-language filmographies list the cinematographer as Liu Zhonglun; at least two names are given for Master Ren (1850–1932), Ren Qingtai and Ren Jingfeng. In this article, Chinese names will be given with surname first, followed by given name, using the *pinyin* system except in cases where other spellings (such as Cantonese spellings and English names) have become well known and accepted. I use "fictional" to refer to filmic portrayals and "real" or "real life" to refer to people and things off the screen; I do not use the terms to arbitrate matters of "truth," but simply as a shorthand method to distinguish between filmic and nonfilmic discourse.

4. Popular film criticism takes a particular interest in self-reflexive film and in ferreting out connections between real life and cinematic portrayals. A portion of the scholarly writing on reflexive films centers on documentaries; ethno-musicological and anthropological scholarship offers useful perspectives on reflexivity (sometimes in relation to film); see, for instance, Babcock 1980; Plantinga 1997; Ruby 1980 and 2000; and Barz and Cooley 1997.

5. Documentaries are among some of the most reflexive films, but present a different set of analytic issues. Among the relevant documentaries on Chinese film are: *HHH: A Portrait of Hou Hsiao-hsien* (1996), *Lai Man-wai: Father of Hong Kong Cinema* (2001), *My Camera Doesn't Lie* (2003), and *Swing in Beijing* (2000).

6. This is true even within Chinese applied film theory and fan sites. Apart from those cited elsewhere in this chapter, among the English-language writings on Chinese film music (which draw upon and include references for the Chinese-language scholarship) are HKIFF 1987 and 1993; Jones 2001; Tuohy 1999a and 1999b; Yeh Yueh-yu 1995, 2000, and 2002.

7. Zhang Yingjin discusses the problem of "Chinese national cinema" in relation to Stephen Crofts' typology of national cinemas, for instance (2004:1–12). See also Fu 2003, Lu 1997, Lu and Yeh 2005 (on Chinese-language film). Other scholars focus on Chinese films in relation to particular places and times, such as Pang 2002, which includes the chapter "Shanghai or Chinese Cinema," covering the 1930s debates about national, local, and dialect film.

8. See also Pang 2002 (244). The filmographies of the Hong Kong Film Archive as well as similar materials published by the Kong Hong International Film Festival (HKIFF 1986, 1987, 1993, 1995) are published in Chinese and English; Zhang and Xiao 1998 is an excellent English-language source. Although variant names (in both Chinese and English) and spellings complicate the process of searching for Chinese films, an increasing amount of information is available through specialized internet sites such as Liberty House Company, *Chinese Movies, DVDs,* 2007, www.echinese movie.com; Lü Pin, *Chinese Movie Database* (in Chinese and English), 2007, www.dianying.com; Laurent Henry, ed., *Hong Kong Cinemagic,* 2007, www.hkcine

magic.com; *Hong Kong Movie Database,* 2005, http://hkmdb.com; Zhang Yingjin, *UCSD Chinese Cinema Web-based Learning Center,* University of California, San Diego, 2006, http://chinesecinema.ucds.edu/; Beijing Film Academy, *Beijing Film Archives* (in Chinese), 2007, www.bfa.edu/cn.

9. Some are from films made by the French diplomat Auguste Francois in China from 1896 to 1905. With a camera borrowed from the Lumiere brothers, he filmed music performances and scenes of daily life and war. These can be seen in the documentary *Through the Consul's Eye* (1999). *Shadow Magic* also inserts stills from the original *Dingjun Mountain* film. These original materials are not the topic of the filmic narrative in that *Shadow Magic's* characters do not discuss them as such (for the characters, these are new materials).

10. Since this was not a synchronized sound film, however, real-life film audiences saw only the images of Mei as they listened to a phonograph playing music of the *qin,* a zither (Wang 1995, 9).

11. See also Zhang Zhen (2005). While completing pre-publication revisions to this article, I became aware of Zhang's *An Amorous History of the Silver Screen,* titled after the Mingxing Studio film *Yinmu yanshi,* a reflexive film (as Zhang states, a "back stage drama . . . [and] a self-portrait of Mingxing and a synecdoche of the broad film world in the 1930s" [xiv]) released in 1931, at a time when "the Chinese film industry . . . was suddenly seized by an urgency to reflect upon its own history on the screen" (xiii). With detailed descriptions and analysis of a wide range of films from the early decades of the twentieth century, the book is a "cultural history of Chinese modernity through the lens of the Shanghai cosmopolitan film culture of the prewar period" (xxvii). Apart from noting that a number of Zhang's interests and observations parallel my own, I have added references to materials that Zhang discusses that are relevant to issues raised here. It is clear that this article, as well as my earlier article, "Metropolitan Sound: Chinese Film Music of the 1930s" (Tuohy 1999a), are in dialogue with her discussion.

12. See Zhang Zhen (2005) for discussion of such themes in several Shanghai films of the 1920s and 1930s. Other more recent films dealing with film industry problems include *Behind the Screen* (1984; about problems encountered by a film academy graduating class making a film); *Filmmakers* (1988); and *Quitting* (2001; a bio-pic about Jia Hongsheng, who plays himself, and his problems with fame, depression, and drugs).

13. Off-screen, the real-life director of *Phantom in the Limelight* wrote of his hope that "the audience will gain a behind-the-scene understanding of how softcore fantasy pictures are made, and be revulsed . . . We intend to draw them out of the dark side . . . and tell them how to look at a good picture" (Hong Kong Film Archive 2000:264). See also Zhang Zhen's discussion of such debates as well as of film criticism in 1930s Shanghai (2005, 244–54).

14. The opening sections of Zhang and Xiao (1998) provide an excellent, concise, English-language introduction to Chinese film history, with sections on mainland, Hong Kong, Taiwanese, and Chinese transnational cinemas as well as on foreign films in China and Chinese films in the West.

15. A portion of Chinese film personnel studied abroad. But by the mid 1920s, at least fifteen film schools were established, several run by Chinese studios. Several students returning from abroad set up a correspondence school in 1924, and universities offered film classes by 1930s (Zhang and Xiao 1998:165–66; Zhang Yingjin 2004:50–51; Zhang Zhen 2005:130–36).

16. Among the many publications on Shanghai film and images of Shanghai are Zhang Yingjin 1994 and 1999, Zhang Zhen 2005, Pang 2002, Cao and Wu 1987.

17. As the Chinese film industry made the transition to sound films from 1930 to 1940 — dealing with problems such as securing the capital and equipment needed

for filmmaking and playback in theaters, as well as with foreign patents—they produced a combination of silent, partial sound, and synchronized sound-on-film films (Wang 1995; Li and Hu 1996); for English-language overviews, see Zhang and Xiao (1998:16–17) and Zhang Zhen (2005:302–19).

18. Commenting on this piece, a 1931 reviewer in *Film and Theatre Magazine* said Li's music "strengthened our fighting spirit," an opinion that will contrast starkly with those expressed in films discussed below (*Yingxi zazhi* 2, no. 3 [January 1931]; quoted in Wang 1995:13). In 1927, Xiao Youmei established the National Music Academy (*Guoli yinyueyuan;* changed to *Guoli yinyue zhuanke xuexiao;* Wang 1995:12), the model for the fictional school portrayed in *Nie Er*. A well-known musician, Li Jinhui established schools and performance troupes, such as the Chinese Music Troupe (which also toured Southeast Asia); his Bright Moon Troupe (*Mingyue gewushe*), of which Nie Er was a member for a short time, is the model for the troupe portrayed in the film *Nie Er*. In 1931, Li and Luo Mingyou (manager of the Lianhua Film Studio) negotiated a deal through which the film studio troupe was formed (Chang 1999:146). See Tuohy 1999a and Jones 2001 for discussions of Li Jinhui and Nie Er.

19. Zhang Zhen (2005:xxiv) cites a similar real-life example from the 1930s, this of the Shanghainese actress Xuan Jinglin (1907–1992).

20. The real-life choices are portrayed in the documentary *The Worlds of Mei Lanfang* (2000). Mei (who played female roles) grew a beard and intentionally made himself ill through an injection of typhus vaccine to avoid performing for the Japanese; the documentary shows clips of his troupe performing Japanese-resistance operas. Film actress-songstress Hu Die ("Butterfly Wu") refused to perform in the proposed propaganda movie *Butterfly Touring Tokyo*. The two did go together on tours in the Soviet Union and United States.

21. For articles on the film *Farewell My Concubine,* see Du 2000 (with an insightful analysis of the film's use of *Farewell My Concubine* and other operas; the article also discusses opera films generally, focusing on the mutual influences among Chinese theatrical forms and film and television) and Beaster 2003; see also Berry and Farquhar 2001. Mei Lanfang also played roles in films such as *Eternal Regret* (1948; China's first full-color film) and *Dreaming after a Spring Outing* (1960).

22. *Farewell My Concubine* includes a similar, albeit more dramatic scene; the mother, a prostitute, chops off the sixth finger of her son's hand so the opera school will accept him.

23. Nie Er escaped most criticism during the Cultural Revolution, perhaps because he died in 1935 when he was twenty-three and at a career high point but before doing too much that later might be labeled as counterrevolutionary or worse. *Beginning of Life* (1992) is a children's feature film about Nie Er.

24. By far the senior of the two, Tian was labeled a counterrevolutionary-revisionist and died during the Cultural Revolution; his name was omitted from song books published in the PRC from 1964 through at least the late 1970s, when he was posthumously "rehabilitated" and again became a candidate for the filmic representation of a hero. His name is mentioned in *Nie Er* but he does not appear as a character. Tian also wrote the lyrics of Nie Er's first film song, "The Miner's Song" (*Kaiguangge*) for the *Light of Motherhood* (1933). According to Wang Wenhe and other PRC reference works, Tian discovered Nie Er performing in the Bright Moon Troupe in 1931 and introduced him to the Lianhua Film Studio, the Friends of the Soviet Union (Nie Er and Zhang Shu were members of its Music Group) in 1932, and the CCP (Wenhe 1995). These same sources say Nie was on his way to the Soviet Union to study when he died in Japan.

25. *Nie Er*'s director Zheng Junli (1911–1969) and cinematographer Huang Shaofen (b. 1911) worked in the Lianhua Film Studio at the same time as Nie. *Nie*

Er crew members contributed to a book that reflects on the process of writing the screenplay and music; it contains quotations from his diaries and articles (ZGDYCBS 1963).

26. In an article on the scoring of this film, Ge Yan labels these songs as "yellow music" (1963:382).

27. For those familiar with films such as *The Marseillaise* (1938) and *Casablanca* (1942), it may be tempting to see this scene as a remake of one or more scenes from these prior films; but I have yet to locate a reference from the makers of *Nie Er* indicating this to be the case. The scene may be a filmic restaging of one of the real-life situations in which Chinese revolutionaries in the early decades of the twentieth century sang the song. It was among the songs included in the Chinese publication *Songs of the Revolution* in 1929, for instance (Jones 2001:120), and was generally popular in leftist circles. Another rousing scene in *Nie Er* shows the musician leading a theater audience in the singing of "The Internationale" (*Guojige*) after government troupes enter the theater and close down the performance.

28. These are among the songs used most often in other films. For instance, *Lianhua Symphony* (1937), comprised of a series of eight short feature films, begins and ends with a scene of Lianhua Film Studio personnel singing "Song of the Big Road," the theme song of another Lianhua film, *The Big Road* (1934); as they sing, the movie studio and its technology are revealed as the camera pans back.

29. The portrayal of women in film is the topic of much scholarly writing; see, for instance, Chang 1999, Cui 2003, Field 1999, Harris 1997 and 2003, Ho 1993, Shen 2000, Zhang Yingjin 1999, Zhang and Xiao 1998 (268–69).

Works Cited

Babcock, Barbara A. 1980. "Reflexivity: Definitions and Discriminations." *Semiotica* 30:1–14.

Barz, Gregory F., and Timothy J. Cooley, eds. 1997. *Shadows in the Field: New Perspectives for Fieldwork in Ethnomusicology*. New York and Oxford: Oxford University Press.

Bauman, Richard, and Charles L. Briggs. 1990. "Poetics and Performance as Critical Perspectives on Language and Social Life." *Annual Review of Anthropology* 19:59–88.

Beaster, Yomi. 2003. "*Farewell My Concubine:* National Myth and City Memories." In Berry 2003, 89–96.

Berry, Chris, ed. 2003. *Chinese Films in Focus: Twenty-five New Takes*. London: British Film Institute.

Berry, Chris, and Mary Farquhar. 2001. "Shadow Opera: Towards a New Archaeology of the Chinese Cinema." *Essays in Film and the Humanities* 20, nos. 2–3:25–42.

Bohlman, Philip V. 1988. "Missionaries, Magical Muses, and Magnificent Menageries: Image and Imagination in the Early History of Ethnomusicology." *The World of Music* 33:5–27.

———. 1992. "Representation and Cultural Critique in the History of Ethnomusicology" and "Epilogue." In *Comparative Musicology and Anthropology of Music*, ed. Bruno Nettl and Philip V. Bohlman, 131–51 and 356–60. Chicago: University of Chicago Press.

Cao Maotang and Wu Lun. 1987. *Shanghai yingtan huaji* [Reminiscences of the Shanghai Film World]. Shanghai: Shanghai wenyi chubanshe.

Chang, Michael G. 1999. "The Good, the Bad, and the Beautiful: Movie Actresses and Public Discourse in Shanghai, 1920s–1930s." In Zhang Yingjin 1999, 128–59.

Chen Xihe. 1990. "Shadowplay: Chinese Film Aesthetics and Their Philosophical and Cultural Fundamentals." In Semsel et al. 1990, 198–204.

Crofts, Stephen. 1993. "Reconceptualizing National Cinema/s." *The Quarterly Review of Film and Video* 14, no. 3: 49–67.

Cui Shuqin. 2003. *Women through the Lens: Gender and Nation in a Century of Chinese Cinema.* Honolulu: University of Hawaii Press.

Dianyingju, Dangshi ziliao zhengji gongzuo lingdao xiaozu [Film bureau, working group on materials related to the history of the Chinese Communist Party], ed. 1993. *Sanshi niandai Zhongguo dianying pinglun wenxuan* [An anthology of Chinese film criticism of the 1930s]. Beijing: Zhongguo dianying chubanshe.

Du Wenwei. 2000. "*Xi* and *Yingxi:* The Interaction between Traditional Theatre and Chinese Cinema." *Screening the Past* 11 (www. screeningthepast.media.latrobe .edu.au; uploaded 1 November 2000).

Feuer, Jane. 1993. *The Hollywood Musical.* 2nd ed. Houndmills and London: Macmillan Press.

Field, Andrew D. 1999. "Selling Souls in Sin City: Shanghai Singing and Dancing Hostesses in Print, Film, and Politics, 1920–1949." In Zhang Yingjin 1999, 99–127.

Fu, Poshek. 2003. *Between Shanghai and Hong Kong: The Politics of Chinese Cinemas.* Stanford: Stanford University Press.

Ge Yan. 1963. "Yingpian *Nie Er* yinyue chuangzuo suigan" [Notes on the composition of the music for *Nie Er*]. In ZGDYCBS 1963, 381–89.

Guangdianbu dianyingju, Xinhua chubanshe, Zhongguo dianying ziliaoguan, eds. 1995. *Zhonghua yingxing: 1905–1995* [Chinese film stars: 1905-1995]. Beijing: Xinhua chubanshe.

Guo Hua, ed. 1998. *Lao yingxing, lao yingpian* [Old movie stars, old movies]. 2 vols. Beijing: Zhongguo dianying chubanshe.

Harris, Kristine. 1997. "*The New Woman* Incident: Cinema, Scandal, and Spectacle in 1935 Shanghai." In Lu 1997, 277–302.

———.2003. "*The Goddess:* Fallen Woman of Shanghai." In Berry 2003, 111–19.

HKIFF (Hong Kong International Film Festival), ed. 1986. *Cantonese Melodrama: 1950–1969.* Tenth Hong Kong International Film Festival. In Chinese and English. Hong Kong: The Urban Council.

———, ed. 1987. *Cantonese Opera Film Retrospective.* Eleventh Hong Kong International Film Festival. In Chinese and English. Hong Kong: Urban Council.

———, ed. 1993. *Mandarin Films and Popular Songs: 40s-60s.* Seventeenth Hong Kong International Film Festival. In Chinese and English. Hong Kong: Urban Council.

———, ed. 1995. *Early Images of Hong Kong and China.* Nineteenth Hong Kong International Film Festival. In Chinese and English. Hong Kong: Urban Council.

Ho, Sam. 1993. "The Songstress, the Farmer's Daughter, the Mambo Girl, and the Songstress Again." In HKIFF 1993, 55–58.

Hong Kong Film Archive. 1997, 1998, 2000, 2003. *Hong Kong Filmography,* vol. 1 (1913-1941), vol. 2 (1942-1949), vol. 3 (1950-1952), vol. 4 (1953-1959). In Chinese and English. Hong Kong: Urban Council.

Huang Zhiwei, ed. 1998. *Lao Shanghai dianying* [Old Shanghai film]. Shanghai: Wenhui chubanshe.

Jones, Andrew. 2001. *Yellow Music: Media Culture and Colonial Modernity in the Chinese Jazz Age.* Durham, N.C.: Duke University Press.

Lai, Linda. 2000. "Hong Kong Cinema in the 1930s: Docility, Social Hygiene, Pleasure-Seeking and the Consolidation of the Film Industry." *Screening the Past* 11 (www. screeningthepast.media.latrobe.edu.au; uploaded 1 November 2000).

Li Suyuan and Hu Jubin. 1996. *Zhongguo wusheng dianyingshi* [A history of Chinese silent film] (*Chinese Silent Film History*), trans.Wang Rui, Huang Wei, Hu

Jubin, Wang Jingjing, Zhen Zhong, Shan Wanli, and Li Xun, 1997). Beijing: Zhongguo dianying chubanshe.

Lu, Sheldon H., ed. 1997. *Transnational Chinese Cinemas: Identity, Nationhood, Gender*. Honolulu: University of Hawaii Press.

Lu, Sheldon H., and Emilie Yueh-yu Yeh, eds. 2005. *Chinese-Language Film: Historiography, Poetics, Politics*. Honolulu: University of Hawaii Press.

Luo Yijun. 2003. *Ershi shiji Zhongguo dianying lilun wenxuan* [Anthology of twentieth-century Chinese film theory]. Beijing: Zhongguo dianying chubanshe; Zhongguo dianying jijinhui. Expanded edition of *Zhongguo dianying lilun wenxuan, 1920–1989* [Anthology of articles on Chinese film theory, 1920-1989, 2 vols., ed. Luo Yijun, Li Jinshen, and Xu Hong. Beijing: Zhongguo wenlian chubanshe, 1989.

Marchetti, Gina. 1989. "The Blossoming of Revolutionary Aesthetics: Xie Jin's *Two Stage Sisters*." *Jump Cut* 34:95-116.

Marion, Donald J. 1997. *The Chinese Filmography: The 2444 Feature Films Produced by Studios in the People's Republic of China from 1949 through 1995*. Jefferson, N.C.: McFarland & Co.

Myerhoff, Barbara, and Jay Ruby. 1982. "Introduction." In *A Crack in the Mirror: Reflexive Perspectives in Anthropology*, ed. Jay Ruby, 1-35. Philadelphia: University of Pennsylvania Press.

Neumeyer, David (with Caryl Flinn and James Buhler). 2000. "Introduction." In *Music and Cinema*, ed. James Buhler, Caryl Flinn, and David Neumeyer. Hanover, N.H. and London: Wesleyan University Press.

Pang Laikwan. 2002. *Building a New China in Cinema: The Chinese Left-Wing Cinema Movement, 1932–1937*. Lanham: Rowman & Littlefield.

Plantinga, Carl. 1997. *Rhetoric and Representation in Nonfiction Film*. New York: Cambridge University Press.

Reynaud, Berenice. 2003. "*Centre Stage*: A Shadow in Reverse." In Berry 2003, 31-38.

Ruby, Jay. 1980. "Exposing Yourself: Reflexivity, Anthropology, and Film." *Semiotica* 30, nos. 1/2:153-79.

———. 2000. *Picturing Culture: Explorations of Film and Anthropology*. Chicago and London: University of Chicago Press.

Semsel, George S., Xia Hong, and Hou Jianping, eds. 1990. *Chinese Film Theory: A Guide to the New Era*. New York: Praeger.

Shen, Vivian. 2000. "From "*Xin nüxing* to *Liren xing*: Changing Conceptions of the 'New Woman' in Republic Era Chinese Films." *Asian Cinema* 11, no. 1:114-30.

Tuohy, Sue. 1999a. "Metropolitan Sound: Chinese Film Music of the 1930s." In Zhang Yingjin 1999, 200-21.

———. 1999b. "The Social Life of Genre: The Dynamics of Folksong in China." *Asian Music* 30, no. 2:39-86.

Wang Wenhe. 1995. *Zhongguo dianying yinyue xunzong* [Following the traces of Chinese film music]. Beijing: Zhongguo guangbo dianshi chubanshe.

Yeh Yueh-yu. 1995. "A National Score: Popular Music and Taiwanese Cinema." Ph.D. dissertation, University of Southern California.

———. 2000. *Gesheng meiying: Gequ xushi yu Zhongwen dianying* [Phantom of the music: Song narration and Chinese-language cinema]. Taibei: Yuanliu chubanshe.

———. 2002. "Historiography and Sinification: Music in Chinese Cinema of the 1930s." *Cinema Journal* 41, no. 3:78-97.

ZGDYCBS. (Zhongguo dianying chubanshe; Chinese film press), ed. 1963. "*Nie Er*": *Cong juben dao yingpian* [Nie Er: From script to film]. Beijing: Zhongguo dianying chubanshe.

ZGDYYS. (Zhongguo dianying yishu yanjiu zhongxin; Chinese film arts research center) and Zhongguo dianying ziliaoguan (China film archive), eds. 1996 and 2001. *Zhongguo yingpian dadian* (Chinese classic films): *Gushipian, Xiqupian, 1905–1930* (Feature films and opera films, vol. 1) and *Gushipian, Wutai yishupian,* 1949-1976 (Feature films and performing arts films, vol. 4). Beijing: Zhongguo dianying chubanshe.

Zhang Yingjin. 1994. "Engendering Chinese Filmic Discourse of the 1930s: Configurations of Modern Women in Shanghai in Three Silent Films." *Positions* 2:603–28.

———, ed. 1999a. *Cinema and Urban Culture in Shanghai, 1922–1943.* Stanford: Stanford University Press.

———. 1999b. "Prostitution and Urban Imagination: An Aspect of Chinese Film in the 1930s." In Zhang Yingjin 1999a, 160–80.

———. 2004. *Chinese National Cinema.* New York and London: Routledge.

Zhang Yingjin and Xiao Zhiwei, eds. 1998. *Encyclopedia of Chinese Films.* London and New York: Routledge.

Zhang Zhen. 2005. *An Amorous History of the Silver Screen: Shanghai Cinema, 1896–1937.* Chicago: University of Chicago Press.

Filmography

Beginning of Life (aka *Le Debut de la Vie;* Ren Zhichu, 1992). Dir. Zheng Dongtian; sc.: Gu Ying. Children's Film Studio.

Behind the Screen (*Yingmu houmian,* 1984). Dir. Pan Xianghe and Chen Lu; sc. Kong Du and Yang Tao; music by Tan Dun.

Beijing Bastards (*Beijing Zazong,* 1993). Dir./sc. Zhang Yuan. Beijing: *Beijing Bastards* Film Team.

Big Road (*Dalu,* 1934). Dir./sc. Sun Yu; music by Nie Er; with Jin Yan, Zheng Junli, Li Lili, Chen Yanyan. Shanghai: Lianhua Film Studio.

Big Shot's Funeral (*Dawan,* 2001). Dir. Feng Xiaogang; sc. Li Xiaoming. China Film Group (Beijing), Hauyi Brothers Taihe (Hong Kong), and Columbia Asia.

Carriers of Electric Shadows (*Porteurs d'Ombres Electriques,* documentary, 1993). Prod. Herve and Renaud Cohen. First Run/Icarus films.

Casablanca (1942). Dir. Michael Curtiz; sc. Howard Koch. U.S.: Warner Brothers.

The Case of the Jealous Actor (*Luo Jiaquan sha Hu an,* 1939). Dir. Hong Zhonghao. Hong Kong: Wode Film Studio.

Centre Stage (aka *The Actress;* Ruan Lingyü, 1992). Dir. Stanley Kwan (Guan Jinpeng); sc. Ch'iu Tai An-p'ing (Qiudai Anping), based on the story by Chiao Hsiüng-p'ing (Jiao Xiongping). Hong Kong: A Leonard Ho–Jackie Chan film, Golden Harvest/Golden Way Films.

Children of Our Time (*Shidai de ernü,* 1933). Dir. Li Pingqian; sc. Xia Yan, Ah Ying, and Zheng Boqi; with Ai Xia, Zhao Dan. Shanghai: Mingxing Film Studio.

Children of Troubled Times (aka *Sons and Daughters of Troubled Times; Fengyun ernü,*1935). Dir. Xu Xingzhi; sc. Tian Han and Xia Yan; with Yuan Muzhi, Wang Renmei, Gu Menghe. Shanghai: Diantong Film Studio.

Dingjun Mountain (aka *The Battle of Dingjunshan; Dingjunshan,* 1905). Dir. Ren Qingtai; cinematographer Liu Zhonglun. Beijing: Fengtai Photography Studio.

Dreaming after a Spring Outing (*Youyuan jingmeng,* 1960). Dir. Xu Ke; with Mei Lanfang.

Electric Shadows (aka *A Childhood Dreaming of Movies; Mengying Tongnian,* 2004). Dir./sc. Xiao Jiang; music by Lei Qin. Beijing Dadi Century, Happy

Pictures Culture Communication Co. production. (Fortissimo Film Sales, Amsterdam and Hong Kong)

Entertainment (*Youyi dahui,* 1932). Dir. Shao Zuiweng; music by Li Jinhui. Shanghai: Tianyi Film Studio.

Eternal Regret (*Sheng sihen,* 1948). Dir. Fei Mu; with Mei Lanfang.

Fallen Angel (*Liu Manlin,* 1939). Dir./sc. Hou Yao. Hong Kong: Nanyang Film Studio.

Farewell My Concubine (*Bewang Bieji,* 1993). Dir. Chen Kaige; sc. Lilian Lee and Lu Wei; with Leslie Chueng, Zhang Fengyi, Gong Li. Hong Kong: Tomson Film.

Filmmakers (*Dianyingren,* 1988). Dir. Ding Yinnan; sc. Diang Yingnan and Miao Yue; music by Dai Dawei. Pearl River Films.

The Goddess (*Shennü,* 1934). Dir./sc. Wu Yonggang; with Ruan Lingyü. Shanghai: Lianhua Film Studio.

HHH: A Portrait of Hou Hsiao-hsien (documentary, 1996). Cineastes de Notre Temps. First Run/Icarus.

The Jazz Singer (1927). Dir. Alan Crossland; sc. Al Cohn. U.S.: Warner Brothers.

The King of Comedy Visits China (*Huaji dawang you Hua ji,* 1922). Dir. Zhang Shichuan; sc. Zheng Zhengqiu. Shanghai: Mingxing Film Studio.

Lai Man-wai: Father of Hong Kong Cinema (*Xianggang dianying zhifu Li Minwei;* documentary, 2001). Dir. Choi Kai-kwong. Hong Kong: Dragon Ray Motion Pictures.

Lianhua Symphony (*Lianhua jiaoxiangqu,* 1937). Series of short films with multiple directors. Shanghai: Lianhua Film Studio.

Light of Motherhood (aka *Motherly Love; Muxing zhiguang,* 1933). Dir. Bu Wancang; sc. Tian Han; music by Nie Er; with Chen Yanyan, Jin Yan. Lianhua Film Studio.

Lovers of the Silver Screen (*Yinhai yuanyang,* 1939). Dir./sc. Su Yi and Li Zhiqing. Hong Kong: Wannian Film Studio.

The Mad Director (*Kuang daoyan,* 1937). Dir./sc. Kwan Man-ching (Guan Wenqing). Hong Kong: Daguan Film Studio.

La Marseillaise (1938). Dir. Jean Renoir; sc. Jean Renoir and Carol Koch. France: RAC.

Memories of the Old Capital (aka *Reminiscence of Old Peking; Gudu chunmeng,* 1930). Dir. Sun Yun; sc. Zhu Shilin; with Ruan Lingyü. Shanghai: Lianhua Film Studio.

My Camera Doesn't Lie (*Meine kamera Lugt Nicht; Wode sheying jibu sahuang;* documentary, 2003). Prod. Solveig Klassen and Katharina Scheneider-Roos.

National Anthem (*Guoge,* 1998). Dir. Wu Ziniu; sc. Fan Zhengming, Su Shuyang, and Zhang Jiping. Changsha: Xiaoxiang Film Studio.

New Woman (*Xinnüxing,* 1934). Dir. Cai Chusheng; sc. Sun Shiyi; music by Nie Er; with Ruan Lingyü, Zheng Junli, Gu Menghe. Shanghai: Lianhua Film Studio.

New Year's Coin (*Yasuiqian,* 1937). Dir. Zhang Shichuan; sc. Xia Yan (originally listed Hong Shen to avoid censorship); with Hu Rongrong (Chinese Shirley Temple). Shanghai: Mingxing Film Studio.

Nie Er (1959). Dir. Zheng Junli, assisted by Qian Qianli; sc. Yu Ling, Meng Bo, and Zheng Junli; cinematographers, Huang Shaofang and Luo Congzhou; songs by Nie; music consultant, Meng Bo; Arrangers, Ge Yan, Li Yinghai and Liu Fu'an. Shanghai: Shanghai Haiyan Film Studio. Available through Nanhai films (nan hai.com).

Opera Stars and Song Girls (*Hongling genu,* 1935). Dir./sc. Kwan Ting-yam; with Tse Sing-nung, Tam Yuklan. Hong Kong: Yuanqiu Film Studio.

Painted Faces (*Qi xiaofu,* 1988). Dir. Alex Law; sc. Alex Law and Mabel Cheung. Hong Kong: Shaw Brothers Films.

Phantom in the Limelight (*Yindeng moying*, 1951). Dir. Chiu Shu-sun; sc. Cheng Shu-lin; Hong Kong: Daguan Film Studio.

Platform (*Zhantai*, 2000). Dir./sc. Jia Zhangke; music by Yoshihiro Hanno. Hu Tong Communication (Hong Kong) & T-Mark (Japan).

Plunder of Peach and Plum (*Taolijie*, 1934). Dir./sc. Ying Yunwei; music by Zhao Yuanren and Huang Zi; with Yuan Muzhi. Shanghai: Diantong Film Studio.

Quitting (2001). Dir. Zhang Yang.

Shadow Magic (*Xiyangjing*, 2001). Dir. Ann Hu; sc. Huang Dan, Tang Louyi, Kate Raisz, Bob McAndrew, Ann Hu; music by Zhang Lida. C&A Productions in association with Beijing Film Studio, China Film Co-Production Corporation, and the Taiwan Central Motion Picture Corporation. Distributed by Sony Classics.

Silver World of Fantasy (*Yinhai chunguang*, 1951). Dir. Yu Leung; sc. Mok Hong-si. Hong Kong: Dali Film Studio.

A Singer's Story (aka *Spring Arrives in the Singing World*; *Gechang chunse*, 1930). Prod. Shao Zuiweng (the elder of the Shaw Brothers; music by Li Jinhui. Tianyi Film Studio.

Singsong Girl Red Peony (*Genü hongmudan*, 1930). Dir. Zhang Shichuan, assisted by Cheng Buga; sc. Hong Shen. With Hu Die. Shanghai: Mingxing Film Studio.

Stage Door (*Hudumen*, 1996). Dir. Shu Kei. Hong Kong.

Stage Lights (*Wutai chunse*, 1938). Dir. Tang Xiaodan; sc. Hui Siu-kuk. Hong Kong: Daguan Film Studio.

Stage Sisters (aka *Two Actresses*; *Wutai jiemei*, 1965). Dir. Xie Jin; sc. Lin Gu, Xu Jin, and Xie Jin; composer (songs): Huang Zhun. Shanghai: Tianma Film Studio. Available, under *Two Actresses*, through Nanhai films (nanhai.com).

Street Angel (*Malu tianshi*, 1937). Dir. Yuan Muzhi; music by He Luting; lyrics by Tian Han; with Zhao Dan, Zhou Xuan. Shanghai: Mingxing Film Studio.

Swing in Beijing (documentary, 2000). Prod. Wang Shuibo.

Three Modern Women (*Sange modeng nüxing*, 1932). Dir. Bu Wancang; sc. Tian Han (under name Chen Yu); with Ruan Lingyü, Jin Yan, Chen Yanyan, Li Zhuozhuo. Shanghai: Lianhua Film Studio.

Three Women (aka *Female Fighters*; *Liren xing*, 1949). Dir. Chen Liting; sc. Tian Han and Chen Liting; with Zhao Dan, Huang Zongying, Xia Tian. Shanghai: Kunlun Film Studio.

Through the Consul's Eye (documentary, 1999). Prod. Jorge Amat. Tanguera Film. First Run/Icarus Film.

Two Stars in the Milky Way (*Yinhan shuangxing*, synchronized sound film, 1931). Dir. Shi Donghan; sc. Zhu Shilin. Shanghai: Lianhua Film Studio.

Wild Flower (aka *Wayside Flower*; *Yecao xianhua*, 1930). Dir./sc. Sun Yu; with Ruan Lingyü, Jin Yan. Shanghai: Lianhua Film Studio.

Who's to Blame? (*Shui zhi guo*, 1937). Dir. Shum Kat-sin (Shen Jicheng). Hong Kong: Huasheng Film Studio.

Worlds of Mei Lanfang (documentary, 2000). Prod. Chen Mei-Juin. Lotus Film Productions.

Cinema Moments

SUMARSAM

Music in Indonesian "Historical" Films
Reading *Nopember 1828*

·◉·

A number of studies have been conducted on Indonesian cinema, none of which deal with film music. This chapter marks a starting point, focusing just on historical films. This allows the discussion to center on the use of traditional music and the meanings and reception of film music in a national cinema. It will be helpful to begin with a survey of the historical and cultural background of Indonesian cinema, linked to the history of the nation itself.[1] Film production entered Indonesia in the early twentieth century during the long war of independence against the Dutch. This was also the period of Chinese domination in the economy of colonial Indonesia. Thus, it is not by accident that the Chinese (only a few Europeans) owned most of the means of production and distribution, as well as making up the majority of moviegoers. Naturally, early Indonesian film was connected to Chinese cinema, so much so that in one instance, the star of the film was imported from Shanghai (Said 1991:19). Whereas the early films employed a mostly Chinese cast, by 1930, the newly founded Dutch film company, Algemeen Nederlandsch-Indisch Film (ANIF) produced films with an all-Indonesian cast, marking a turning point in the history of Indonesia cinema. ANIF produced not only successful movies such as *Terang Bulan* (Full Moon, the first sound movie, which plagiarized Hollywood's *Jungle Princess*, starring Dorothy Lamour), but also documentary and propaganda films.

The outbreak of the Second World War in Europe disrupted the flow of Western movies to Indonesia, helping to increase the production of domestic film. These conditions quickly changed during the Japanese occupation of Indonesia in the early 1940s, as the Japanese banned film production and took over ANIF. More than anything else, the Japanese produced propaganda films. Interestingly, it was during the Japanese occupation that Indonesian moviegoers were given the opportunity to study and take part in film production, since the authorities created a Japanese monopoly that excluded the Chinese and Dutch from making films.

The Japanese surrendered to the Americans in 1945, and transferred the film company to the Indonesians. In turn, the Indonesians produced several documentary films. Meanwhile, Dutch film companies reappeared, employing Indonesian producers. During this sensitive period, they produced movies that avoided the war and political intrigue.[2] It was not until the 1950s, the early years of true independence, that historical films began to surface, as Indonesians were attracted to film production. In the meantime, Hollywood films were taking over the market, using very effective distribution techniques. Hundreds of films were shown in the early 1950s. As national fervor ran high, coupled with Islamic morality, the newly Indonesian-owned film companies voiced their opposition to the flood of American films. The objection to the coming of American movies was not so much the quantity of the films, but their unsuitable moral content, including explicit sexual content. Hollywood's portrayal of Asians as primitive people, such as in the film *Black Magic in Bali*, also caused offense. Hence, every year many American films were banned from circulation.

In this period, censorship became an important agenda of the Indonesian government and a relevant issue in the production of historical films. Besides celebrating the years of revolutionary experience, the movies from this period also highlight the moral ambiguities produced by the struggle for independence. In this context, censorship was extensive because of the sensitive nature of seeing the revolution in retrospect. The censors frowned on the depiction of the past physical and psychological conflicts of different segments of contemporary Indonesian society, including the traditional, Islamic, army, and Dutch/Indo (mixed-blood) communities, which they saw as detrimental to the present and future of Indonesian unity. Thus, the authorities favored contemporary political efficacy at the expense of historical accuracy.

In the 1970s "New Order," censorship began with the script, as well as affecting the completed production.[3] Film genres expanded. Heider (1991:39–49) identifies several: films based on local legend, films dealing with Dutch colonialism, films made during the Japanese occupation, films about the struggles of Indonesians against the Dutch after World War II, sentimental film, and horror film. There are other categories, including the comedy, the film about an expedition into the life of a "primitive tribe," the musical, and children's films. The most well-known musicals in the 1970s starred and were produced by Rhoma Irama, the well-known singer of *dangdut,* a hybrid, popular music that mixes Western rock and Indian film music.

The musical is not necessarily the only film to incorporate music and dance diegetically. From the earliest days of Indonesian cinema, indigenous music and dance are often an integral part of the film. They function as ethnographic markers of the narrative. Gamelan music appears in many legend-based films such as *Roro Mendut* (1983), in satirical films such as *Tamu Agung* (1955), and in historical films such as *Raden Ajeng Kartini* (1983).

This brief background of the development of Indonesian films gives us a clue to the richness of resources on film music waiting to be studied from historical or contemporary perspectives. Film scholars question the extent to which film is the creation of Western culture, and how local culture manifests itself. For Indonesian cinema, we also have to consider the nature of the Indonesian nation as multicultural and multilingual. I embarked on this present study as an Indonesian music scholar with a concentration in traditional music. After screening several dozents Indonesian films, I was struck by a particular historical film that uses predominantly Javanese gamelan and singing. Comparing the music of this film with other historical films became the basis of this paper.

Raden Ajeng Kartini

My screening of Indonesian movies has led me to conclude that these films use less music than do Western films. Perhaps a lack of resources has been the reason for this limitation. More importantly, according to the music critic Suka Hardjana (2004), producers place no high priority on music. He observes that most of the music in films are not original compositions; rather, they are selected from stock recordings or whatever resources are available to the music composer/arranger. Hardjana identifies only a handful of Indonesians who actually deserve to be called film composers. This condition prompts Hardjana to say that composing Indonesian film music is more like the arrangement of music for accompanying silent film. Be that as it may, there is a certain creativity in the making of Indonesian film music. As I will show below, not only does it have a tangible meaning, but it also supports the intangible meaning of the film.

Most Indonesian films employ Western music. When the films present local or historical narratives, the urge to use traditional or regional music becomes apparent, especially in historical films and films based on local legends. Composers either use Western instruments or ensembles to imitate the local music in question or they employ indigenous musicians from that region. The former is more common in providing music for all sorts of scenes, while the latter is apparent when the scene itself portrays local musical events. There are also in-between cases. Usually, the aim of introducing regional or traditional music is to establish the setting, but it often also is used to heighten the nuance of the scene. Sometimes, the local music becomes purely an ethnographic show inserted in the film.

The imitation of local music often alternates with Western music passages. For example, in *Raden Ajeng Kartini* (1983, see below) in the scene in the house of the *bupati*,[4] gamelan-like melodic passages played on harp punctuated by a Western chord mark the presence of the *bupati* (see Fig. 1). Similarly, in *Janur Kuning* (1979), a revolutionary films focusing on the 1948 attack on the Dutch in Yogyakarta by the Indonesian Armed Forces, *gambang*-like melodic passages mesh with Western music, setting the mood of a scene in the house of a Javanese Army general, Sudirman. Much of the music for *Tjoet Nya' Dhien*, featuring an Acehnese heroine who stands steadfastly against the Dutch and their Acehnese collaboraters, infuses a sense of Islamic modality—a reminder of a regional cultural space where Islam was embraced deeply.

The alternation from a local/regional Indonesian to a Western musical modality is in congruence with the film narrative. To discuss this point further, I would like to focus first on *Raden Ajeng Kartini*. It is a film based on the biography of a Javanese woman emancipationist in the early revolution period. Produced in 1983, the film was written and directed by Syuman Djaya, one of the most progressive and innovative Indonesian directors, from the 1970s until his death in 1985. Sudharnoto composed the music. He is known as the composer of several Indonesian patriotic songs.

Born in 1879, Kartini was the daughter of a *bupati* of Jepara on the north-central coast of Java. Her parents placed a high value on European education. Kartini, her brother, and two sisters were educated in the Dutch high school. Reading Dutch-language magazines and writing essays were among the main staples of the family. So was socializing with a Dutch family in their town. Other intellectual activities that Kartini engaged in included correspondence with the Dutch proponents of "ethical policy."[5] In fact, the history of Kartini is based largely on the collection of her letters with them.[6] Growing up in a Javanese cultural environment during the era of colonialism, Kartini also absorbed the Javanese social predicament and observed Javanese cultural practices, including Javanese language and music. In essence, the two worlds, Javanese and European, were embedded in her life. A scene in the film of Kartini studying the Dutch language, followed immediately by Kartini and her friends learning Javanese children's songs, makes this point very well.

Figure 1. A gamelan-like passage on harp, punctuated by a Western chord.

It was European education and experience that led Kartini and her sisters to their belief in women's equality, right to schooling, and monogamous marriage. More importantly, they felt that uplifting native women in general was their duty. However, Kartini's convictions went only so far, as she grew up in a strictly Javanese cultural tradition, at a time when female education, even for daughters of *priyayi* (Javanese elite), was unacceptable. *Alus* (refined behavior) was an important concept in the life of *priyayi*. The practice of *pingitan* (isolation) for a girl before she married was still common, and the tradition of high-ranking Javanese aristocrats having concubines was a feudalistic cultural norm.[7] As Kartini's European experience infused her soul, she rejected these traditional cultural practices, to no avail. These cultural and psychological conflicts are dramatized in several scenes in the films. A variant of Kartini's theme song (see below) and gamelan-like passages often accompany Kartini's state of anguish, punctuated by startling Western chords as the scene reaches a climax. As the Javanese cultural context informs the narrative, the occasional use of Javanese music is appropriate for setting certain Javanese modalities. In one of the beginning scenes, the *bupati*, his family, and his subjects are watching a dance performance of a battle between a princess and a demonic character.[8] In another scene, an excerpt of a Javanese *macapat* song sets the mood for two maids making batik cloth.[9]

On the basis of Kartini's courage and idealism, in 1964 the first president of Indonesia, Sukarno, elevated Kartini as a national heroine. An annual commemoration is held on her birthday, April 21. A patriotic song in the Western musical idiom was composed, entitled "Ibu Kita Kartini" (Our Mother Kartini). The song text follows:

> *Ibu kita Kartini, putri sejati*
> *Putri Indonesia, harum namanya*
> *Ibu kita Kartini, pendekar bangsa*
> *Pendekar kaumnya, untuk merdeka*
> *Wahai Ibu Kartini, putri yang mulia*
> *Sungguh besar cita-citanya, untuk Indonesia*
>
> [Our mother Kartini, a true heroine
> Lady of Indonesia, celebrated is her name
> Our mother Kartini, a champion of her nation

The champion of her community, for freedom
Oh mother Kartini, an illustrious lady
Very high is her aspiration, for Indonesia]

It is fitting, therefore, that melodic passages from the song (especially the opening passages) figure as the film's theme song. Toward the opening, this song punctuates an event when the *bupati* publicly announces the name of baby Kartini: "By the grace of God, and with the good wishes of you all, my citizens, my child is a girl, and I name her KAR—TI—NI." Immediately after the name "Kartini" is pronounced, the theme song epitomizes the event, and the title of the film appears on the screen (Raden Ajeng KARTINI), superimposed by the visual image of gentle waves on the ocean. The variant of the theme song provides background throughout the scenes of public celebration and a ceremonial initiation of the baby, as well as elsewhere in the film.

This fact tells us how strongly contextualized historic Indonesian films are. The music significantly reinforces the Indonesianess of the film. First, the switching from Javanese to Western music parallels the dualism in Kartini's psyche and behavior, and in colonial Indonesia generally. Second, the quotations from the "Kartini" song are acknowledged as such by moviegoers, who know the song. Film music "is itself not neutral. It embodies and disseminates meaning" (Gorbman 2000:234). Gorbman makes a very good point. She also speaks to the ways in which film music changes in response to social shifts, as she demonstrated well in her essay on the liberalizaton of Native American music in Hollywood film.[10] Technical factors also affect the shaping of film music, including the availability of resources, the interests of the director and music composer/arranger, and the story of the film, of which more below.

Let me reiterate one of the important points in our discussion on the music for *Kartini:* Music has tangible functions, such as narrative support, but it also conveys the intangible and cultural meanings of a film. To explore this point further, I would like to turn to another movie.

Nopember 1828

The scenes:

In a temporary fortress of the Dutch army, a dance troupe performs hobby-horse and mask dances with gamelan accompaniment. The sound of the Javanese oboe is particularly piercing. The Dutch forces, mostly Indos (a mixed group of Indonesian and European parentage) have a good time watching the performance. It ends as a female dancer takes off her mask and shoots the Dutch captain with a revolver; members of the dance troupe are actually the forces of the Javanese insurgent Sentot Prawirodirjo in disguise. Commotion ensues. The gamelan stops; the piercing sound of oboe continues to heighten the commotion.

The Dutch captain orders his men to detain members of the dance troupe and their leader. Later on, the Dutch captain delivers a fatal shot to the leader. Hearing a commotion in the vicinity—a mass of villagers move toward the gate of the fortress—the Dutch captain orders the gate to be closed. The villagers push and pound the gate with their hands. Finally, a few blows of a battering ram force the gate open. The villagers enter the fortress, launching an assault. A battle ensues. Dutch officers detain the villagers. The sound of rice-stamping in rapid rhythmic ostinatos accompanies this scene, including the scene of wonder and anguish of a young man and woman who are lovers). The sound of stamping rice creates a nuance of a village life, but also heightens the atmosphere of commotion.

Suddenly, Sentot Prawirodirdjo's forces arrive on horseback. With a sense of perfect timing to help the villagers to attack the Dutch forces, their arrival is marked by the sound of *Cara Balen,* a special court gamelan usually played to honor the arrival of guests at festive events such as weddings. Rhythmically similar to rice stamping, this gamelan features a rapid ostinato of four-pitch interlocking patterns. The battle continues. The two musics—stamping rice and *Cara Balen*—alternate, sometimes overlapping, throughout the battle. The battle ends with the Dutch captain surrounded by the Javanese forces. The electronically produced sound of repetitive patterns accompanies the death of the captain.

These scenes are from *Nopember 1828* (1979), an historical film depicting the reaction of the Javanese to the presence of the Dutch in their land. The story is set in a small village in central Java, in the vicinity of Diponegoro's headquarters. Diponegoro was a Javanese revolutionary figure whose movement triggered the five-year "Java war" in 1825–1830. Only his assistant, Sentot Prawirodirjo, appears in the film. Beside the general theme of Javanese reaction to the Dutch presence in Java, the story revolves around the Dutch imposition of tax collection on Java. The story is very dense, however. Besides the Dutch side, it involves different members of a village society: the corrupt village chief, an Islamic community, village combatants and insurgents, and a group of musicians and dancers. Moreover, the story also concerns betrayal, treachery, love, and psychological conflict on both sides.

As mentioned earlier, among the many Indonesian films that I have screened, one film caught my attention for its predominant use of Javanese gamelan and singing, *Nopember 1828.* The kind of gamelan, the choice of musical repertoire, and the creative use of music in the film provoke interesting questions about film music. Gamelan is used not only to signal geographic and ethnographic identity, but also to set and heighten the moods of the scenes; gamelan and Javanese singing are used in various ways, diegetically and non-diegetically.

Not unlike *Kartini, Nopember 1828* is about an episode of the history of colonial Java. Instead of presenting the theme of human emancipation as in *Kartini,* however, the latter focuses on physical and psychological conflict in the struggles of the Javanese against the Dutch. In the first place, the Javanese strongly opposed the presence of the Dutch in their lands. The Dutch and their Indo and Javanese allies had to confront the five-year "Java war" led by Diponegoro, a war that cost the Dutch dearly in money and lives. They wanted to exterminate Diponegoro's forces.[11] Concurrently, moral and philosophical issues revolving around the colonial treatment of the natives and Indos began to enter into the picture. In addition, the war also involved betrayal and spying among the individuals. Essentially, *Nopember 1828* is a film about family conflicts on both sides.

We might assume that, as in *Kartini,* a Java-Western musical combination would fit with *Nopember 1828*. But this is not the case. Instead, *Nopember 1828* employs predominantly Javanese gamelan and other genres of traditional Javanese music. The question is, why does gamelan dominate the music in this film? The answer lies in the composer-arranger's interest in gamelan. His name is Franki Notosudirdjo, but he is known familiarly as Franki Raden. He is a graduate of the Jakarta Institute of the Arts. He studied Western music with a German-trained Indonesian musicologist, the late Franz Haryadi, and with Slamet Abdul Syukur, a France-trained Indonesian composer, one of the last students of Olivier Messiaen; both were lecturers at the Jakarta Institute when Franki Raden was a student there in the 1970s. Additionally, he has trained himself as a music critic, writing for Indonesian newspapers, including the nationally known *Kompas.* Besides composing, his work experience includes organizing music festivals, mostly in Jakarta. He holds MA and Ph.D. degrees in ethnomusicology (1990 and 2001) from the University of Wisconsin-Madison. His interest in gamelan music began in 1975, after his exposure to gamelan classes at the Jakarta Institute. He was then composing new music for gamelan. As part of this experience, he spent three months at the Institute of the Arts in Surakarta (ASKI). His brief experimentation with the gamelan recurred when he was commissioned to compose music for *Nopember 1828*.

Gamelan is used predominantly in the film, and its efficacy became important for the film's reception by various ethnic groups. But before turning to this issue, it is useful to provide a brief background on Indonesian historical film, centering on *Nopember 1828*. Questions are often asked about the accuracy of a historical film. In his *Indonesian Cinema: National Culture on Screen,* Heider (1991) has dealt at length with this question. Unquestionably, historical film provides clues to the historical past, but from a contemporary view. The contemporary perspective is defined by public taste and often, in the case of Indonesian films, by a government censor. In this context, the director of *Nopember 1828,* Teguh Karya, is known for his position of viewing film as a parable that sets an example or offers a kind of metaphor (Heider 1991:100). He does not make historical accuracy a priority.[12] In other words, the historical context may be conceived of as a prop for the story. The film narrative is a fiction, featuring certain aspects of lives from the period in question, but meant to be constructed and construed from a contemporary angle. In the words of Sen (1988:59), referring to films made in the "New Order" period, historical film "is neither made nor read as a way of understanding or talking about the past. It needs to be understood in terms of the relationship between, on the one hand, those who have the power in the present socio-political structure to control the medium, and therefore the images on the screen, and, on the other, the audience."

One important aspect of colonial life in nineteenth-century Java is a hybrid or *mestizo* culture. It is a mixture of different influences, especially Indonesian and European. The culture of Indo-Europeans is the best example of the *mestizo* culture. Mixed-blood children of Indonesian-European parentage, the Indo (as the Javanese call them) grew up in European settlements in Indonesia. They knew Indonesian culture more intimately than European culture. The Indos rarely visited Europe; hence, most of their knowledge of European culture came from second-hand accounts, from their European parents and Dutch journals and newspapers. Unlike the Dutch figures in *Kartini,* those in *Nopember 1828* are not pure-blood Dutchmen (*totok*), but Indos. In a flashback scene, we learn that Captain de Borst and his lieutenant, van Aken, are the offspring of a Dutch father and Indonesian mother. In this scene, the little de Borst wants to become a Dutch general, while van Aken is asking his Javanese mother a touchy question: "Are the Javanese really evil?" The mother turns to his father to answer the question. He replies: "There are no evil people. There are only greedy persons, also amongst the Dutch" (Sen 1991).[13]

The producer chose Indonesian actors to represent Indos; in reality, the physical feature of an Indo person is often closer to European than to Indonesian. None of the Indo characters are made up like Dutchmen, except for their uniforms. In fact, their behavior is presented as closer to Indonesian than Dutch. The only one appearing like a Dutchman, that is, with tinted hair and beard, is Captain de Borst. Throughout the film, the Indos speak no Dutch; they all speak in unaccented Indonesian, except for the captain. In reality, the Indos spoke both Dutch and Malay, and even spoke regional languages such as the Javanese.[14]

It is worth noting that there are also two Indo corporals who are clown figures. The soldiers' facial features and behavior is Javanese. In most of their scene, they act funny and make slapstick jokes. It is most likely that this is inspired by the clown in the *wayang* shadow play or *kethoprak* folk drama. At the end of the film, in the midst of dead bodies everywhere and the detention of Dutch soldiers, one clown asks another: "How come we weren't taken prisoners? And we're not dead!" The other replies: "We're of no account. Dead or alive, . . . That's the way for people without a nation." It seems that this is to point out the position of Indos in the historical period in question—they were being marginalized.

How do these social realities play out in the film's music?

Western music is absent from the film (except for a fanfare), and gamelan and Javanese singing is used heavily in the film. I would like to suggest that the avoidance of Western music in the scenes of the Dutch forces arises not only from the specific geographic and cultural space within which the story is told (Javanese), but also from the in-between, *mestizo* character of the Dutch forces. Even the processional music used to accompany the marching army, part of the opening of the film, imitates a hybrid Java-European marching band called *musik prajuritan* (army music) in the courts of Surakarta and Yogyakarta. The ensemble consists of snare drums, European fifes, and a few Javanese gongs. The fife is playing a repetitive short passage in a gamelan-like scale.

As mentioned earlier, the selection of the type of gamelan and the musical repertoire used in the film pose interesting issues. In choosing Javanese singing, the music arranger, perhaps in consultation with musicians and dancers involved in the production (see below), made the "right" choice as to which song and song text would suit the mood of the scene. In watching the detention of Kromoludiro and the ways that the Dutch forces threatened his family, they present a young man singing passages modeled after a song of *dhalang* (puppeteer) for a sad scene, "Tlutur."

> Surem surem diwangkara kingkin
> Manguswa kang layon / Pindha ilang memanise
> Wada[na]nira kang landhung.

> [The sun is dim and subdued
> Embracing the departed one
> As if it has lost its charm
> Its face is long (pale)]

For the scene of the detained Kromoludiro, before he meets his daughter, they have him sing a few passages from a court poem of moral instruction. The song text resonates with the narrative line of the film, describing heroism and power.

> Ngrungkepi Ibu Pertiwi
> Beda lan kang watek lumuh
> Guna sekti setya ilang.

[To defend our mother of the earth
Unlike those who are not willing to struggle
Lost are his skill, power, and loyalty]

In other words, the music arranger paid careful attention to choosing music that conveys a mood originally intended to express that particular emotional state. This is also the case in the scene showing the *padhepokan* Islamic community, during which the Islamic students are having a good time, singing and dancing. The music is the *terbangan* ensemble, a Javanese version of an Islamic ensemble, using different sizes of frame drums for accompanying a male chorus. In the film, members of the chorus are singing and dancing in a circle. Commonly, the song contains moral instruction. The music is still heard when the scene changes to the encounter between the daughter of Kromoludiro and a young conspirator from the village, who is in love with her. The encounter is spotted by the son of the village chief (another one who is in love with her), who quietly follows the young instigator; the same music still provides the background. In this sense, the *terbangan* acts as a sound bridge, from the diegetic music of the *padhepokan* to musical background for a love intrigue.

The case of the use of *terbangan* differs from a common practice in Indonesian film production. Rather than setting the mood of that scene, the music sticks to an accurate representation. Usually, in a scene requiring indigenous music, the composer writes a piece for Western ensemble to imitate that music. In *Nopember 1828*, however, music in the *padhepokan* is not in simulated vernacular style, but actually reflects the common practice of the Islamic community. Evidence shows that *terbangan* music had existed in and before the nineteenth century, and was commonly an integral part of spiritual exercises or recreation in such Islamic communities (Sumarsam 1995).

It is true that in this case music represents the real practice of a musical tradition. However, composers also intensify the vernacular elements to heighten the story. In the scene involving hobby-horse dancing, the masks used by the dancers are not the original type used by this kind of hobby-horse troupe, notably the mask wore by the lead dancers. The masks were commissioned for this film (Endo, p.c. May 2005).[15] Another scene shows the nuances of this sort of extension of indigenous sound and context. Two young plotters are planning to bomb the headquarter of the Dutch army. They are entering a room, picking up the bombs. A commotion ensues when the son of the village's chief spots their activity, causing his detainment by the two conspirators. A slow ostinato on a two-note *kemanak* (a pair of bell-like instruments) provides the music throughout this activity and tumult. In Javanese music, the *kemanak* is used as part of small gamelan ensemble to accompany the most refined movement of a ceremonial court dance (*bedhaya* and *serimpi*). In this particular scene of *Nopember 1828*, the *kemanak* provides background to a night of stillness while the events unfold, from the two plotters' picking up the bombs to the commotion caused by the presence of the son of the village's chief.

It is true that to the Javanese, the sound of *kemanak* suggests solemnity, especially if one is familiar with its use in accompanying the refined and graceful movements of *bedhaya/serimpi* court ceremonial dances. The question is, will it have the same effect on non-Javanese Indonesians? This is in light of the fact that each of the three hundred ethnic groups in Indonesia has their distinctive music. This means that not all Indonesians are familiar with Javanese gamelan. Certainly, the same question applies to the use of gamelan music throughout the film. To the extent that *Nopember 1828* reenacts Javanese history, gamelan music is useful to remind the Indonesian spectator of the particular geographical location and cultural space. However, when music is meant to heighten the mood of a particular scene, the efficacy of gamelan becomes a moot question to a national audience. This is to say that non-Javanese could associate gamelan with the geographical and cultural space of Java and Bali, but can they relate specific gamelan music or repertoire to the particular modality of a certain event?

In the film itself, the use of music is not always unambiguous, such as in the scene of a party for the Dutch forces. The following is a case in point. The scene is a party, sponsored by Bondhan, the son of the village chief. The Dutch soldiers are having fun, taking a bath in the well. The clown-corporals are dancing and acting silly. The village young ladies are bringing and serving food, also giggling as they watch the soldiers' behavior. In the midst of this fun atmosphere, a young plotter pours poison in the food, resulting in the death of a soldier. Commotion breaks out. The captain orders Bondhan to be detained; he successfully slips out from the soldiers' blockade, running away from them. A soldier orders his men to shoot him, and the bullet fatally hits Bondhan. From the other direction, the Islamic leader runs toward Bondhan, intending to help him. A second shot is fired, killing the leader. It is striking that from the beginning of the party to the time when Bondhan is killed, the same gamelan piece, "Rondhon," provides musical background throughout. From the lively party to the commotion and the death of Bondhan, there is no musical change whatsoever.

"Rondhon" is a solemn and majestic gamelan piece, a favorite piece for experienced musicians for its elaborate treatment and length. For the Javanese who are familiar with gamelan, juxtaposing this piece with a rowdy party is a peculiar mixture. Hearing the same piece to heighten all the commotion is also unsettling. It is difficult to interpret the music arranger's intention in choosing this particular piece; it seems to diminish the atmosphere of the whole scene. It is not possible that the arranger chose the piece arbitrarily, since at the time of the making of the film, he had knowledge of Javanese gamelan tradition and was surrounded by musicians from the Institution of the Arts in Surakarta (see below). I suggest that the use of "Rondhon" follows the notion that music that acts to anchor the narrative can be expanded to provide counterpoint to the subsequent action. In the words of Slobin, "music inherently acts sometimes simultaneously, but certainly sequentially, to settle down and to unsettle the audiovisual experience of moviegoing."

For a similar example, let us consider the following scene. The gentle music of solo *gender* sets up the atmosphere of a conversation between the wife of the detained Javanese combatant leader Kromoludiro and her daughter; they are talking to each other about their grievances at a troubled time in their lives. Then the scene changes to a different location (although in the same complex), showing a conversation between the captain de Borst and a corporal-clown soldier; they are discussing the character of Javanese men. The scene returns to the mother and daughter, who are discussing two young men who are in love with the daughter. Throughout these three sequential scenes, the music of the solo *gender* does not change. Clearly, the music does not mark the change of locations and the difference of characters. It seems that the music diminishes a sense of the difference between the Javanese and the Dutch/Indo, but unites the emotional content of the scenes. In this sense, the music acts not only to heighten the scene, but also to corroborate the intangible meaning of the film's narrative.

The director, Teguh Karya, himself also sees the film as a story of family quarrels, perhaps a big family feud if we extend the family to include the Indo.[16] It is as if all the characters in the film are a large family who are either supporting or betraying each other. When Lieutenant van Aken confesses that actually it was he who told Diponegoro's forces about the anticipated attacks by the Dutch, de Borst immediately strips off his badges. All who are present (both Indo soldiers and Javanese) are stunned, confused, and show a feeling of sympathy. Similarly, when Kromoludiro is fatally shot by de Borst, everyone is shocked and sad, regardless of whether they are Javanese or Indo soldiers.

I have indicated above that repertoire from gamelan and singing is used in the film. There are a few exceptions. In providing an atmosphere of sorrow after the sound of the bullet that fatally hits Kromoludiro, the music is not from the traditional repertoire, although the structure is somewhat traditional. It is the sound of a *kethuk* (a small, horizontal gong) alternating with a combination of two *kenong* (large, horizontal gongs) of different pitch; this is one of a few new musical works in the cinema. The scene continues, showing Kromoludiro dying, while an Indo doctor closes the combatant's chest's wound with his hand. Then the clown-soldier takes away the revolver used to shoot the combatant. After a brief flashback scene of van Aken's childhood, a solo *rebab* accompanying a male chorus, singing the beginning passages of a song of the puppeteer in the Javanese shadow play ("Pathetan Pelog Lima"), provides music for the dying combatant, in a sequence with visual images of a river and agricultural fields (see fig. 2). The song texts is "*Mijilira sang hyang bagaskara, mancorong cahyane*" [the rise of sun, shine forth thy light]. The song fades when the dying Kromoludiro reappears, ending when his head sinks, a sign of his death.

I suggest that the showing of natural landscapes with the solo *rebab* and male chorus accompanying them (while the dying Kromoludiro disappears from the screen) is an aesthetic experience I would call the ornamentation of dramatic action. This is an aesthetic enjoyment commonly found in the *wayang* performance, in which the dramatic action is backgrounded, whereas other components of performance (music, dance, visual art, and literature) are fore-grounded.[17]

A few non-traditional musical passages are used in the film. But the majority of the musical sounds are traditional Javanese music, including the sound of rice stamping that establishes the village's cultural and spatial identity. As mentioned earlier, the sound of rice stamping is also used to mark the arrival of Sentot Prawirodirjo, alternating with Cara Balen gamelan (a musical icon of the Javanese elite). The conjoining of two musical sounds, rice stamping and Cara Balen, can be read as a metaphor of the unity between commoners (read villagers) and elite leaders. Toward the end of the film, an electronically generated sound, similar in structure to rice stamping and Cara Balen, provides the sound for the final battle, during which a young Javanese insurgent fires at de Borst, sending him to his death. The solo *gender,* playing nonmetrical melodic passages in a style of the accompaniment of *dhalang*'s song, provides music for a few scenes, including a conversation of the two corporal-clowns and the pronouncement by Sentot Prawirodirjo for the future hopes and aspirations of his nation. Subsequently, the solo *gender* is joined by *celempung* (a plucked-string instrument), playing a rather light piece, marking the departure of Sentot and his army. A Javanese motto, "Jer Basuki Mawa Bea" [To Achieve Prosperity Requires Sacrifices], in large letters, together with the slowing down and the end of the *gender-celempung* duet, marks the end of the film. Once again, the use of gamelan music and the showing of visual images of an un-translated Javanese maxim for the finale of the cinema reveals the extent to which Teguh Karya was fascinated by Javanese cultural tradition.

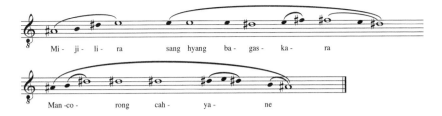

Figure 2. The beginning passage of a *dhalang*'s song ("Pathetan Pelog Livra"), accompanying the dying Kromoludiro and the visual images of natural landscapes.

This relates to the question I posed earlier, about the reception by Indonesian audiences of the predominant use of gamelan tunes and Javanese singing in the film: How do non-Javanese respond to this fact? To a certain extent, the question relates to the larger issue of whether Indonesian cinema can be seen as representative of a national culture.

Film Music and Nationalism

Indonesia is populated by more than two hundred million people made up of three hundred ethnic groups, speaking over three hundred regional languages and dialects, living across many thousand islands that made up the Indonesian archipelago, over a greater span than the United States. It would be difficult, therefore, to define what Indonesian culture is. Can Indonesian films be seen as depicting generalized Indonesian behavior, as well as the stripping of regional ethnic markers, as Heider suggests? (1991:10-13). He gives the following reasons for why Indonesian film creates a national cinema: Indonesian films almost exclusively use the Indonesian language, the national language since 1928, and the films are made in the capital, Jakarta, exported in fixed form all over the archipelago (ibid.). Heider insists that all members of the various regional cultures interpret Indonesian films the same way. He offers a practical suggestion for future research, that "it would be fascinating to follow one film across the archipelago, comparing the audience reactions in terms of local cultures" (ibid.).

Heider notes that there is "one area where Indonesian features films are almost ethnographic: in their depiction of domestic ceremonies like weddings, funerals, and even circumcision rites. The language is all Indonesian, of course, but the music for these sequences is right and elaborate costumes are authentically regional. And even though only a few moments of a ceremony are used in a film, those are generally the peak moments of symbolic significance" (ibid.:28). This explains well the gamelan and dance performance and the wedding ceremony in *Kartini*. It also explains the music of *Nopember 1828* for some scenes. However, as I mentioned earlier, gamelan and Javanese singing in the film do more than just portray an ethnographic scene. It is worth reiterating that in most cases gamelan repertoire and Javanese singing in the film were chosen with special attention to the original moods of the songs. Certainly this transformation is only possible if the music arranger has knowledge of the gamelan tradition. Above, I mentioned the composer Franki Raden's backgrounds and interest. This is how he remembers the thinking behind the score for *Nopember 1828:*

> Based on the *November* [sic] *1828* cultural contents, I came up with the idea of, again, employing gamelan as my compositional ingredients. This time I chose a different approach to implementing this idea, namely by collaborating with gamelan musicians. In the next six months I, along with Tony Prabowo, then my assistant, was working in Solo again with ASKI's students. Among them were AL Suwardi, Rahayu Supanggah, Pande Sukerta and Rustopo who have become prominent composers in their own right today. (Notosudirdgo 2001:342–43)

It is interesting to note that his statement, twemty-one years after the fact, about composing new music with gamelan ingredients, does not exactly reflect what we find in the film. *Nopember 1828* employs a mostly traditional repertoire of gamelan and Javanese singing. Only in a few instances did he compose new music: music for the dying Kromoludiro, sound to set the atmosphere when Kromoludiro's wife places an offering before the house pillar, and electronically generated music for the death of de Borst. Franki Raden elaborates at length his idea of composing new music, which seems to apply to composing new music in general, not necessarily for *Nopember 1828*.[18] What is important for our discussion is the fact that Franki took up a six-month residency at the Surakarta Institute of the Arts. There he had ample time to interact with members of the faculty. In so doing, besides spending his time working on experimental music using gamelan as sonic material, he was able to deepen his knowledge of gamelan; hence, his making the "right" choice of the pieces for *Nopember 1828*.

Conclusion

> We didn't want the film to be oriented towards the dramatic values of the west. There are various kinds of dramaturgy. There is a dramaturgy of the wayang, the randai, the ketoprak. A dramaturgy that is suitable for Indonesian films is something for which, up until now, we are still searching. (*Tempo* 19 Mei 1979: 46, in and translated by Hanan 1988:38)

The statement above is made by Teguh Karya, the director of *Nopember 1828*. It was his answer to a question about his being inspired by the play *Monserrat* in making the film (apparently, his Teater Popular group produced the play prior to the production of the film.)[19] He was rather surprised by the question. He goes on to say that he was influenced by Gandhi, Rizal, and by an Acehnese heroine Cut Nya Din. Basically, he downplays the question of the connection of the play with *Monserrat* and stresses the importance of searching for a film dramaturgy that could use the idioms of indigenous performing art. Particularly his mention of *wayang* and *kethoprak* folk drama explains the kind of dramaturgy embedded in his film. There is even one scene in the film that incorporates the idiom of a *wayang* performance. The scene is a debate between de Borst and his detained lieutenant, van Aken, who has confessed his role in siding with Sentot's forces. Van Aken's words and the accompanying sound punctuation, superimposed by the visual image of a series of paintings of a battle, are inspired by the performance style of *wayang beber*. This is a *wayang* performance in which a puppeteer unrolls a scene on a painted scroll as he narrates each scene.

> *van Aken:* You're in conflict with yourself . . . your private ambitions only add to more victims. You've seen it with your own eyes. Whereas in this killing, [*punctuated by the sound of* kepyak, *the visual image changes to painting of a battle between the Dutch and Javanese army, in the style of* wayang beber] you've seen both friend and enemy fall before you [*punctuated by* "ooh", *the voice of the* dhalang; *another painting of a battle appears*]. Arbitrary annihilations in Kembang Arum [kepyak *sounds, painting of close-ups of a Dutch captain, and a Javanese combatant, and then a scene of fierce battle*], Lengkong [kepyak *sounds, close-up of a Javanese combatant*], and Delanggu [*"ooh"*], they all are your victims, de Borst! Winning, all in the name of winning [*painting of an encounter between the Dutch and Javanese army; the sound of* kepyak, *overlapping with the sound and the visual image of de Borst slapping van Aken's face*].

This brief *wayang beber* style of episode is not ethnographic presentation; it is an "ornament" of the drama, the same notion as the showing of natural landscapes with the accompaniment of the solo *rebab* and male choral singing that I mentioned earlier.

Although I cannot find information about the collaboration between the producer and music arranger of the film, clearly Franki Raden's interest in gamelan matches Teguh Karya's fascination with traditional dramatic forms. I should mention that Sardono is listed as one of the music arrangers. I assume that he contributed to decisions about the kind of gamelan music and singing that would appear in the movie. Most likely he created the choreography of the hobby-horse dance drama in the movie, in which he acts as the lead dancer and the leader of the dance troupe.

The full support from the Surakarta Institute of the Arts, under the leadership of Humardani, cannot be understated in making the film. This included logistical support and the use of space and various gamelan ensembles for the filming (Supanggah, p.c. 2005). More importantly, as I have mentioned earlier, most of the dancers and musicians in the scene of the hobby-horse troupe are members of the faculty there, or artists who often worked for the Institute. Two of the musicians, Supanggah and Suwardi, not only have a deep knowledge of traditional music, but also began to rise as composers of contemporary music. Two of the dancers, Sardono and Soeprapto, were also interested in new work in dance. Later they became well-known contemporary dancers and choreographers. Sardono's works have even reached international audiences in a big way. By the time of the film, Sardono not only was one of the best dancers and choreographers of Javanese dance drama (including having deep knowledge of Javanese performing arts), but was also known for his experimental works. My assumption is that these individual artists have contributed to the shaping of the music and the scenes in the film that involve traditional performances.

In spite of the distinctiveness of *Nopember 1828*, with its potential for alienating non-Javanese audiences because of its predominant use of traditional Javanese music and dramaturgy, the film won the 1979 Citra award (an Indonesian version of the Oscar), including an award for the best film music. It is beyond the scope of this study to discuss the process of awarding the Citra to this film. But certain general issues about critically acclaimed films that receive the Citra will be useful here.

In the discussion of genre versus auteur, Heider (1991:5-6) points out the difficulty of explaining the precise definition of such categories. Genre or formulaic films are recognized as such, for they "are based strongly on traditional character types behaving according to traditional motivations in traditional plots." The auteur film, on the other hand, "is the conscious result of breaking the formula mold—to produce something different, "meaningful," something of a personal statement." In this sense, *Nopember 1828* is an auteur film because of Teguh Karya's vision of filmmaking. Heider also recognizes that the differences between genre and auteur are not great. In fact, these conventional categories tend to delimit the potential meanings of the film. In discussing transnational film, Naficy suggests that "films should be read and reread not only as individual texts produced by authorial vision and generic convention, but also as sites for inter-textual, cross-cultural, and translational struggles over meanings and identities" (2003:205). This not only will force us to reconcile different approaches to film studies, that is, generic, auteurist, and cultural studies, but also can lead us to blur the distinction between types of films, such as fictional, documentary, ethnographic, and avant-garde (ibid.). I would argue that these ways of reading *Nopember 1828* would allow us to understand the film's complex meanings. *Nopember 1828* is clearly an auteur film, "eschewing

the plots, the magic, and the sadistic sex of the Kompeni [genre] film."
(Heider 1991). Following Naficy, the film should be read intertextually
(that is, synchronically and diachronically) and as a crosscultural phenomenon, as fictional, and as documentary and ethnographic film.

These ways of reading *Nopember 1828* allow us to see the alignment of
the perspectives of the director, the music arranger, and the socio-political
climate of the "New Order" government. From the director's angle, as I
mentioned earlier, Teguh Karya is a filmmaker with idealistic visions. He is
especially interested to explore the Indonesian cultural practices embedded
in film dramaturgy. Contextualizing this interest with his national fervor,
he says, "To the extent that stress has to be laid on this cultural consciousness, we need to be aware of the fact that our country is a country of many
islands with many diverse cultural traditions. In the end, one cannot evade
the fact that the film is but a depiction of the nation. . . . To the man of arts,
film is also a medium for expressing his feelings inspired by the call of his
motherland and as such the national function of cinema becomes even
more important" (Karya 1988:38). Nationalistic fervor aside, Teguh Karya
is fully capable of creating a film with extended commentary on the contemporary political and social system.

For our purpose, we learn about Teguh Karya's interest in indigenous
Indonesian cultural forms as important ingredients in the development of
an Indonesian film. Franki Raden responded positively to Teguh Karya's
call. Raden sees the 1970s as a period of "revitalizing nationalism in the
contemporary political context and aesthetic expression" (Notosudirdjo
2001:342). In his view, the economic growth and political stability of the
New Order government have provided the working conditions for composers to produce their best works of new Indonesian art music (ibid.:430).
He himself was a very active composer at the time.

I pointed out earlier that Franki Raden's musical vision does not necessarily resonate in the film. But his feeling of musical nationalism is apparent
in his discussion of the gamelan in the new musical movement of the 1970s
onward. He says that in the context of Indonesian nationalism, the gamelan "can be viewed as no longer necessarily attached only with the Javanese
musical tradition. This ensemble has been de-java-nized and turned into a
'new' set of metallophone instruments that are potentially available for any
composer from other ethnic backgrounds to work with. In other words,
gamelan theoretically has been transformed from a regional into a national
musical property" (ibid.:357). By extension, the use of traditional gamelan
repertoire in *Nopember 1828* can be seen in this light.

Teguh Karya's and Franki Raden's statements are context dependent, of
course. Teguh Karya's statement was part of a paper presentation on the

history of the development of Indonesian cinema, which is also partly autobiographical; hence, it is a descriptive report.[20] Franki Raden's statement is from his dissertation, specifically the part that quantifies the development of new music in Indonesia. He is aware that his view is in disagreement with other scholarly views on the repressive policy of the "New Order" regime toward contemporary cultural expression. Raden's finding is intriguing, indeed. Does music convey a different kind of message than other forms of cultural expression, such as film or theater? If this is true, how do we reconcile the use of music in a film?

Order versus disorder has been used as a reference in discussing Indonesian cinema, especially films made during the New Order period. Heider (1991:38) thinks that "order" (not goodness), as the prime moral imperative throughout Indonesia, is the concern of most Indonesian films. Such a moral imperative also can be found in the *wayang* and gamelan tradition. In every all-night *wayang* performance, the disorder scene (usually combat) toward the end of each of the three divisions of a plot ends up with the planting of symmetrical tree figures in the middle of the screen; symbolically, order is restored. In gamelan music, gong punctuations at important structural points in the music underline the order of the piece. This structural order functions as a matrix for musical dynamics, which are created by the interactions among instrumentalist and vocalist in the ensemble. In any event, order has important symbolic significance, and no doubt it is a powerful aspiration. In this sense, searching for orderliness, symbolically and pragmatically, is an important goal.

In this context, and returning to our film reading, Sen suggests that the attention of the New Order regime to Indonesian cinema "can be seen as efforts to maintain cinema as an 'ordered' space and to expand the space in the mediascape overall" (1994:159). Sen rightly points out that cinema is more controllable, with less public resonance than any other form of cultural expression, such as theater, poetic readings, and rock concerts. The latter examples might "provide occasions where communally felt public pleasure, publicly expressed, can and do burst into disorderly, excessive, carnivalesque modes, breaching the 'order' that is the foundation myth of the new Order."

It has been observed that Indonesian film reaches its audience in great numbers, ranging from the middle class to the large section of the urban poor and to the village community. Producers deliberately make films with different audience segments in mind—the popular types of film for the underprivileged audience, and the sophisticated film for the middle class. It is the potential capability of cinema to reach a large audience of different classes that made censorship crucial to the Indonesian government. This also means that sending message through films is an issue in the mind of the power holder. This is done in order to support their nation-building project. In this context, as historical consciousness is important to success, historical film is the right medium for sending a message to all segments of the audience. Coincidentally, it is also historical film (commonly considered as "serious" film) that usually receives critical acclaim or the Citra award. Certainly *Nopember 1828* fit the criteria.

But this is not the only factor necessary for the film to receive the highest acclaim. One of the distinctive features of New Order cultural expression, as part of their nation-building project, was their robust project of representing or reinterpreting regional performing arts. It seems that the conspicuous presence of ethnographic scenes in *Nopember 1828*—from the hobby-horse dance to the practice of pounding rice (village arts), and by extension the sound of gamelan—are in line with the regime cultural project.

Cultural heterogeneity is a fact of life in colonial and contemporary Indonesia. Our reading of *Nopember 1828* points to this fact, in its narrative and music. Four different segments of society are represented in the film. It is revealing that direct or indirect musical association for each of the societal segments can be found in the film. The Java-European hybrid marching music (*musik prajuritan*) is associated indirectly with the Indo/Dutch armed forces. The sound of stamping rice and the performance of hobby-horse dance is the marker of the village community. The *terbangan* music marks the life of the Islamic *padhepokan*. And the aristocracy, represented by the marching of Javanese combatants led by Sentot Prawirodirjo, is marked by the Cara Balen gamelan.

It is worth reiterating here that, in spite of the predominant use of gamelan, the music for *Nopember 1828* signifies more than an ethnographic marker. The significance of film music should be seen in its larger cinematic context. It follows that the meaning of film is constructed on the basis of the interplay and relationship between dramatic action and other elements of the cinema. As an integral part of the film experience, music fleshes out cinematic meaning, either diegetically or nondiegetically; the former constructs a denotative representation, the latter a connotative meaning that addresses the senses.[21] The two meanings often overlap, however. On the basis of film as a product of culture, these meanings are culturally bounded. This is especially the case with the music of *Nopember 1828*. Whereas other Indonesian films use mostly Western music, this film employs Javanese gamelan, singing, and other Javanese cultural sounds. The Javanese time and cultural space of the film's narrative do make this musical and sound usage appropriate. But the interests of the music arranger and film director, in relation to the New Order cultural milieu, have shaped the creative approach to the sound usage and character of *Nopember 1828*.

I would like to thank Prof. Mark Slobin for inviting and guiding me to write this essay. Thanks to Chris Miller for sharing with me his interview with A. L. Suwardi and for his technical assistance.

Notes

1. This background section is drawn primarily from Sen (1994:13–26), but also Hanan 1997 and Said 1991.

2. It is true that the Indonesians declared their independence in 1945, after the surrender of the Japanese. But war with the Dutch continued until the late 1940s.

3. This is the period after the downfall of Sukarno's regime in 1965. Under President Suharto, the new government called themselves the "New Order" regime; the previous government was called the "Old Order."

4. *Bupati* are Javanese officials of the Dutch colonial government.

5. Declared in 1901, this is a policy that is concerned with elevating the life of the Indonesians. The policy was proposed by a new middle class of Dutchmen, including Dutch writers, lawyers, journalists, and government officials in Java.

6. The Indonesian translation of Kartini's letters was published by Balai Pustaka publisher (1951), with the title *Habis Gelap Terbitlah Terang* (After Darkness Comes the Light). See the English translation by Agnes Louise Symmers (1964).

7. *Pingitan* is a practice in which a girl of marriageable age is isolated from the world by being locked up in a room until she has been married to a husband of the parents' choice.

8. This dance itself has symbolic significance to the film narrative. It is a fight between Srikandhi, one of the female characters from the Mahabharata story in which the Javanese adore her as an aggressive heroine, and Burisrawa, a demonic character who is very insistent, and makes an unsuccessful attempt to marry her.

9. Actually, one of the maids is the biological mother of Kartini. As shown in the opening scene, Kartini was carried by the *bupati*'s concubine. Kartini was never told of this fact. The fact comes to light toward the end of the film, and Kartini forces her father to acknowledge the truth, asking the maid to have supper with the whole family.

10. This is also reflected in the modulation of the use of languages, that is, switching among Indonesian, Javanese, and Dutch, according to the scene and/or the speaker to whom she speaks. Kartini spoke all three languages.

11. Eventually, Diponegoro was tricked by the Dutch. While supposedly meeting for negotiations in the headquarters of the Dutch army, he was arrested and sent to exile in Makassar, where he died. A painting by Raden Saleh depicting this capture became a well-known work of visual art.

12. Endo Suanda (p.c. May 2005), one of the hobby-horse dancers in the films, mentioned to me that in making the film, Teguh Karya was very meticulous about the accuracy of the environment from the period in question. Certain plants that presumably had not yet been brought to Indonesia by the mid-nineteenth century had to be covered with other props.

13. In this flashback scene, the man cast as the Dutchman is a real Western person. He is an American, an MA music graduate from Wesleyan University.

14. This is before the Indonesian language was established as a national language, based on the Malay language.

15. I should mention that the hobby-horse dance troupe that appeared in the film is composed mostly of members of the faculty and staff of the Institute of the Arts in Surakarta, and a few dancers from outside of the Institute. They are not the "real" performers of this musical play.

16. For a different interpretation, see Hanan (1988). He suggests that the film's narrative shows cultural differences between the Javanese communality and Dutch individuality.

17. For the notion of ornamentation of dramatic action in Javanese *wayang* performance, see Sumarsam (1984).

18. Raden says: "My main idea was to deconstruct the aesthetic of gamelan in order to pursue the possibility of creating new gamelan compositions that were free of traditional constraints. With this in mind I introduced ASKI's students to the idea of exploring the pure sonic aspect of gamelan instruments. The first several months of our collaboration were spent developing new techniques in playing the instruments. My intention in this phase was to seek as much as possible the vocabulary of a new gamelan sound; timbre and articulation were thoroughly explored. In the next several months I focused my exploration on the idea of how to organize these new sonic materials in compositional forms and instrumentations. In this phase I recorded all the experimentations on the spot with a Nagra tape recorder. In other words, I did not use notation at all. In the final phase of my work, I remixed most of the materials in the recording studio to create new compositions in an electro-acoustic manner" (Raden 2001).

19. *Monserrat* is a play by Emmanuel Robes. Set in nineteenth-century Venezuela at the time of the rebellion led by Simon Bolivar, the play also has the theme of anticolonialism. In his Jakarta production, Teguh Karya set the play against the background of the Java war (Hanan 1988:38).

20. The occasion was the 1987 Winter Lectures Series at Monash University, Melbourne, Australia.

21. For a discussion of denotative and connotative meaning in film, see Monaco 2000:161–71.

Works Cited

Gorbman, Claudia. 2000. "Scoring the Indian: Music in the Liberal Western." In *Westen Music and Its Others: Difference, Representation, and Appropriation in Music,* ed. Deorgina Born and David Hesmondhalgh. Berkeley, Los Angeles and London: University of California Press.

Hanan, David. 1988. "Film and Cultural Difference: *November 1828.*" In *Histories and Stories: Cinema in the New Order Indonesia,* ed. Krishna Sen. Clayton: Center for Southeast Asian Studies, Monash University.

———. 1997. "Indonesian Cinema." In *The Oxford History of World Cinema,* ed. Geoffrey Nowell-Smith. New York and Oxford: Oxford University Press.

Hardjana, Suka. 2004. "Musik Film Belum Dianggap Penting" [Film Music Is Not Yet Considered Important]. In *Musik: Antara Kritik dan Apresiasi* [Musik: Between Critic and Appreciation]. Jakarta: Kompas.

Heider, Karl. 1991. *Indonesian Cinema: National Culture on Screen.* Honolulu: University of Hawaii Press.

Karya, Teguh. 1988. "In Search of Ways and Means for Making the Film an Instrument of Expression." In *Histories and Stories: Cinema in the New Order Indonesia,* ed. Krishna Sen. Clayton: Center for Southeast Asian Studies, Monash University.

Kartini, Raden Adjeng. 1951. *Habis Gelap Terbitlah Terang.* Jakarta: Balai Poestaka.

Monaco, James. 2000. *How to Read a Film: The World of Movies, Media, and Multimedia,* 3rd. edition. New York and Oxford: Oxford University Press.

Naficy, Hamid. 2003. "Phobic Spaces and Liminal Panics: Independent Transnational Film Genre." In *Multiculturalism, Postcoloniality, and Transnational Media,* ed. Ella Shohat and Robert Stam. New Brunswick, N.J. and London: Rutgers University Press.

Notosudirdjo, Franki. 2001. "Music, Politics, and the Problems of National Identity in Indonesia." Ph.D. dissertation, University of Wisconsin-Madison.

Said, Salim. 1991. *Shadow on the Silver Screen: A Social History of Indonesian Film.* Jakarta: Lontar.

Sen, Krishna. 1988. "Filming 'History' Under the New Order." In *Histories and Stories: Cinema in New Order Indonesia,* ed. Krishna Sen. Clayton: Center for Southeast Asian Studies, Monash University.

——. 1994. *Indonesian Cinema: Framing the New Order.* London and New Jersey: Zed Books Ltd.

Sumarsam. 1995. *Gamelan: Cultural Interaction and Musical Development in Central Java.* Chicago: University of Chicago Press.

——. 1984. "Gamelan Music and the Javanese Wayang Kulit." In *Aesthetic Tradition and Cultural Transition in Java and Bali,* ed. Laurie Jo Sears and Stephanie Morgan. Madison: University of Wisconsin, Center for Southeast Asian Studies.

Symmers, Agnes Louise (translator). 1964. *Letters of a Javanese Princess: Raden Adjeng Kartini.* New York: W. W. Norton & Company.

Filmography

Many Indonesian movies are available commercially in VCD format in Indonesia and Malaysia. Several Indonesian movies, with English subtitles, are distributed by Between Three Worlds Video (Monash Asia Institute, Building 11, Monash University, Victoria 3800, Australia). The movies listed below, except *Janur Kuning,* are available from them.

Terang Bulan, 1937. Directed by Albert Balink and Mannus Franken.
Janur Kuning [Young Palm Leaf], 1979. Directed by Alam Surawijaya.
Raden Ajeng Kartini, 1983. Directed by Syuman Djaya.
Nopember 1828, 1979. Directed by Teguh Karya.
Roro Mendut, 1983. Directed by Ami Priyono.
Tamu Agung [Exalted Guest], 1955. Directed by Usmar Ismail.
Tjoet Nya' Dhien, 1988. Directed by Eros Djarot.

MARILYN MILLER

"The Soul Has No Color"
But the Skin Does

Angelitos Negros and the Uses of Blackface
on the Mexican Silver Screen, ca. 1950

·◉·

The stereotype, because it prefers to work
with pastiche and caricature, always steals
something from black people. —Manthia Diawara 1999:14

In May of 2005, Mexican President Vicente Fox raised the ire of African-American leaders in the United States by claiming that undocumented Mexican workers living in the United States were doing work even Blacks didn't want to do. To make amends, Fox invited Jesse Jackson and other black leaders from the United States to his ranch in Mexico to iron things out. But a few weeks later, Mexico's attitudes toward Blacks and its historical representation of Blackness were again in the news as the country released a stamp commemorating Memín Pinguín, a beloved cartoon character that first appeared in the children's magazine *Pepín* in 1947. While critics from the United States claimed that the stamps celebrated and promoted a stereotypical figure with thick lips, bulbous eyes, and other exaggerated features, many Mexicans defended the well-known character, insisting Memín Pinguín was "not the popular icon of racism in Mexico." The two incidents propelled to the forefront of public debate the issue of Mexico's engagement with Blacks both inside and beyond its borders, and forced Mexicans to reconsider and re-evaluate the portrayal of Blacks in the popular press, the media, and the film industry.[1] As Joanne Hershfield has pointed out, the silver screen frequently has served as a battleground for displaying and defining such fraught notions of national identity:

Like most national cinemas, Mexican cinema has portrayed various contradictory relations among the country's history, Mexico as a national geographic and discursive space, and Mexican identity. And, as with other national cinemas, representations of the nation and national identity have been continually contested and transformed on the screens of Mexico, especially during moments of internal and external crises. (Hershfield 1999:81)

It is probably no coincidence that Memín Pinguín was "born" in 1947, when the editors of *Pepín* asked Yolanda Vargas Dulché to write a strip for children.[2] Having just returned from Havana, where she had worked as a radio singer, Vargas Dulché decided to include a Black child in the comic series. The character was so successful that within a year, Memín Pinguín was appearing on a daily basis. And just as Mexican children were becoming familiar with Black or Afro-Cuban identity through the antics of a seemingly inoffensive cartoon character, adults were consuming versions of that same identity in the form of film musicals that featured the performance of Afro-Cuban or other "Black" music, as well as the performance of Black identity, both by a handful of Black actors, and by non-Blacks in costume and/or blackface make-up. The middle of the twentieth century represents a high point in the collaboration of Mexican and Cuban filmmakers, as well as a crucial moment in the negotiation of Black identity in Latin America through the vehicle of the film musical.

In 1948, the Cuban singer and actress Rita Montaner traveled to Mexico to film *Angelitos negros* [Little Black Angels] with the Mexican film star Pedro Infante. Both Montaner and Infante were famous by that time, Montaner for her legendary stage and film performances in Cuba, Mexico, and elsewhere, and Infante for his role in a number of Mexican films with social themes directed by Ismael Rodríguez in the preceding years (García 1994:6–8). In what at least one critic has argued was the most insipid role of Infante's illustrious career (García Riera 1993:237), *Angelitos negros* casts Infante as the cabaret singer José Carlos Ruiz, who courts the platinum-blonde private-school administrator Ana Luisa de la Fuente, played by Emilia Guiú. The haughty Ana Luisa is at first cool to José Carlos' advances, openly repulsed by his portrayal of Black characters in his stage act, and disapproving of his friendship with fellow actors of a variety of darker skin tones. Despite these misgivings, the two eventually marry—without knowing that Mercé, the dark-skinned woman (played by Montaner in blackface) who was Ana Luisa's childhood nanny and still serves her as housekeeper, is in fact her biological mother. The secret's melodramatic qualities are enhanced by the fact that Ana Luisa is the "love child" of Mercé and her former *patrón,* the wealthy owner of a hacienda.

After a triumphant musical tour of Latin America that includes shows in Cuba, Puerto Rico, and Buenos Aires, José Carlos returns to Mexico with his new bride, who is now expecting a baby. When their visibly mulatta daughter is born soon after, Ana Luisa spurns the child and blames her husband for hiding his black heritage. Shocked into a "delicate" state of health by the birth of her dark daughter, Ana Luisa only learns the truth of her own and her child's genealogy at the end of the film, in a violent scene that leads to Mercé's death.

If such a plot demands much of the reader in terms of suspension of disbelief, its cinematic staging does little to bolster credibility. True to the prevailing standards of Latin-American melodrama, *Angelitos negros* is overtly sentimental and makes few concessions to verisimilitude. And yet, more than a half century since it was first screened, the film's loyal fans are legion, and in a *videoteca* located in Mount Pleasant, Washington, D.C.'s most densely Latino and Latin-American–populated neighborhood, the proprietor admits he rents the film maybe twenty times a week—and this in an establishment in which brown-skinned and Spanish-language pornography appears to get the most turnover. What is it that makes *Angelitos negros* such a beloved film for Latin Americans living inside and outside the region, despite dealing with issues of race that would seem to be more relevant to the first half of the twentieth century than to the early stages of the twenty-first? Is it the story or the form that still manages to move contemporary viewers to identify with a hyperbolic tale of hidden racial origins and the prejudices associated with them?[3] Clearly, both the tale and its melodramatic presentation remain relevant to contemporary issues of Latin-American national and regional identity as these are shot through with contentious questions of race.

Angelitos negros provides an outstanding example of how racial otherness and its exploitation could be staged, both on the stage itself, and on the stage-within-a-stage of the Latin American melodrama, in which cabarets and other performance venues were common backdrops. Rafael Aviña describes the classic melodrama as a genre that depended on exaggerated dramatic situations designed to affect and move audiences, a power *Angelitos negros* obviously still enjoys. By incorporating such characteristics as a highly sentimental plot such as a love story, action that is agitated or even violent, and conventional characters who ultimately triumph over sinister circumstances, melodramas call upon spectators to identify with innocence in danger of being lost or compromised (Aviña 2004:133). In a similar vein, Jesús Martín-Barbero has commented that melodrama often functions in Latin America as a "mediation" between existing and emergent cultures or between tradition and modernity. He notes:

In melodrama human existence becomes centered on the unravelling of secret fa-milial relationships—from the mysteries of paternity to people unaware that they are blood brothers or identical twins. Entailed in these revelations is the struggle against false appearances and malicious suppression of information. In this sort of plot is centred so much of the development of the drama: the movement from lack of recognition to rediscovery of long-veiled identities (Martín-Barbero 1993:118–19).

By explicitly foregrounding the denial of Black blood in one upper-middle-class Mexican family, *Angelitos negros* exposes the horror of Black-ness within the larger family of the nation and Latin-American region. Its filmic enactment, and particularly its dependence on the use of blackface musical performance, reveals, then, the deep ambivalence that character-ized sentiments toward the Black subject in the collective consciousness. Hence, a film produced more than half a century ago provides a venue for negotiating highly charged issues of family, race, and the performance of national and regional identity that are still very much alive in contemporary Latin-American cultural expression, as evidenced by the recent debate over Mexican attitudes toward its own and other countries' Blacks.

In her study of Latin-American melodrama, Ana López has emphasized the "hidden radical potential" of a genre typically associated with hyperbole and overdrawn sentimentality. She argues that this radical potential is often held in check by the fact that the films are projected from the perspective of the hegemony, that is, "radical" ideas are fomented from mainstream posi-tions. López notes that the melodrama is "particularly well suited to repre-sent the sociopolitical conditions of modern Latin America *from the position of the dominant classes*" (López 1991:597, my emphasis). As a result, when a melodrama takes up an issue such as racial prejudice, this dominant stance may elicit an intense reaction of identification, but it can also obscure the marginal experience the film purportedly aims to reveal.

As a spectacle, the melodrama fosters immediacy, recognition and identification; it leads the spectator to hang on every gesture and expression of an actor or actress, to adopt his or her aspirations and to suffer from the gap between these aspirations and their realization in the ordinary world. Rhetorically, it tends to obscure the so-cial complex by reducing it to a small number of simplified options that lure the viewer/reader into adopting pseudopolitical positions without full knowledge or even awareness of other information and possible positions. (ibid. 597)

Both López and Aviña point to the continued presence of many of these melodramatic qualities and narrative postures in the contemporary genre of the *telenovela,* a Latin-American limited-run serial television program sometimes compared to the soap opera in the United States, which also deals intensely with family dramas and social issues. One important con-nection between musical melodramas and *telenovelas* that has not been studied sufficiently is the foregrounding of a theme song, very often a *bo-lero* or ballad, composed and/or sung by a famous singer, that runs at the beginning of each *telenovela* episode. Frequently, these highly sentimental *telenovela* theme songs become popular hits throughout Latin America.

The soundtrack of *Angelitos negros* is a classic case of how the film melodrama could both create and exploit popular music success stories. As the opening credits of the film roll, an imposing, heavily orchestrated version of "Angelitos negros" sets the tone for the poignant story that follows. Then, in the first number that José Carlos performs on stage at the school where Ana Luisa is principal, he sings the syrupy "Mi primer amor" [My First Love] by Mexican composer Chucho Monge, complete with the plucking of harpstrings. But in his nighttime stage show, the singer portrays a broader range of characters. The first number we see begins with the throbbing of the bongo drums, as José Carlos and his female co-star appear in blackface to sing and dance to an Afro-Cuban number.[4] That piece segues into a second section even more insistently anchored to the rhythm of the drums, in which the Afro-Cuban deities Yemayá and Changó are invoked. "Que locura que fascina" [What fascinating madness], sings José Carlos.

It is in this fascination with Afro-Cuban or Afro-Caribbean music, dance, and cultural icons that *Angelitos negros* exhibits the allure of Blackness within the frame of popular music and dramatic performances, and the ways in which that Blackness was more easily *simulated* than *assimilated*. Despite its title and overt treatment of Blackness, *Angelitos negros* depends for the most part on a cast of *non-Black* Mexican actors. As García Riera wryly notes, the only "negro verdadero" (true Black) in the film is José Carlos' friend Chimi Monterrey, played by Cuban actor Fernando Valdés. Montaner in her role as Ana Luisa's maid Mercé, Chela Castro as José Carlos' stage companion Isabel, and Titina Romay as the mulatta offspring, all appear in varying shades of blackface. And as previously noted, Infante himself wears not only blackface, but in fact, *blackbody,* painted from the waist up (with a tell-tale band of light skin showing above his waistband) for his interpretation of the Afro-Cuban numbers in his cabaret act. García Riera comments, "all that cosmetic blackness obliges the wearers to constantly look at their hands, to see if they still have the right color, and even Chimi Monterrey does this, just in case" (1993:236).[5]

Though this constant self-inspection of course functions within the plot not to check whether the dye is still in place but to draw attention to the characters' color(s) and the difficulties they represent, García Riera is correct to suggest the instability and superficiality that underlie the film's assumptions of and about Blackness. Aviña demonstrates that despite the fact that racism is often the focus of the Mexican melodrama, "the curious thing is that Mexican cinema took great pains to 'denounce' the contempt for this or that skin color, as well as the injustices of the most needy, and at the same time, dedicated itself with equal fervor to showcasing blue-eyed actors and pretty blond actresses without a trace of Indian features" (1993:134). All *negrura cosmética* is not equal, and in the many versions of blackface in *Angelitos negros* and other film musicals from the era, we begin to discover some of the complexity of the "Black question" in mid-twentieth-century Mexico and Latin America, questions that clearly have bearing on the contemporary moment.

In his role as a singer and dancer who not only performs alongside Black and mulatto performers but who temporarily appropriates Blackness through the use of blackface, Infante made famous a number of songs included in the film soundtrack, arguably one of the best known of any twentieth-century moving picture in Latin America. As a result, *Angelitos negros* the movie inevitably is associated with "Angelitos negros" the song, a pitiable lament that set to music the lines of Venezuelan writer Andrés Eloy Blanco's poem of the same name. The lyrics of "Angelitos negros" are perhaps as compelling as its sad, plaintive melody, composed by the Mexican musician Manuel Alvarez Maciste in 1946:

> Painter, born on my land
> holding a foreign brush
> Painter, you follow the path
> of so many painters in the past.
>
> Even though the Virgin is white
> please paint little Black angels for me.
> For all the good Blacks
> also go to heaven.
>
> Painter, if you paint with love
> why do you reject their color?
> If you know that in heaven
> God also loves them?
>
> You, who paint saint figures
> if you have a soul
> why is it that in your paintings
> You forget the Black ones?
>
> Whenever you paint churches
> you paint beautiful angels
> but you never remembered
> to paint a Black angel.
> (cited in Aparicio 1998:176, 279)

In its broad appeal to pathos, "Angelitos negros" touches deeply resonant chords in the history of the inclusion or exclusion of Blacks in the cultural and political composition of the region. The poet-singer's questions to the painter of church saints seek to establish the full humanity and participation of the Black subject in that history. Black people, he points out, are also loved by God and go to heaven. Blanco's poem recalls the debates that periodically took place from the fifteenth to the nineteenth centuries in Latin America, in which scholars—including many clerics—vehemently denied or confirmed the full humanity of indigenous and/or Black persons, and consequently, their ability to participate fully in the spiritual and political life of the Latin-American colonies. Thinking about *Angelitos negros,* I find it ironic that the poet's appeal is directed to an artist or artisan who refuses to *paint* Black characters for the church alcoves, since the film is replete with actors *caracterizados* (characterized) with various degrees of blackface and body *paint.*

In her study of plastic art, literature, and film, Susan Gubar has adopted the term *racechange* to "suggest the traversing of race boundaries, racial imitation or impersonation, cross-racial mimicry or mutability, white posing as black or black passing as white, pan-racial mutuality" (Gubar 1997:5). Using a host of examples from different media, Gubar contends that the appropriation of racial otherness through blackface and similar practices not only or necessarily demolishes racial stereotypes or vindicates the full humanity of racial others, but also can function to reiterate racist paradigms. She notes that "representations of racechange test the boundaries between racially defined identities, functioning paradoxically to reinforce and to challenge the Manichean meanings Western societies give to color" (ibid.:5–6). By applying Gubar's analysis of blackface in the United States to Latin-American musical and filmic performance, we see that such enactments constitute an ambivalent treatment of race at best:

This liberal traffic across the color line makes us appreciate why and how throughout the twentieth century white impersonations of blackness functioned paradoxically both as a deeply conservative (even racist) as well as shockingly radical (sometimes anarchic) mode of cultural production, one that has played a complicated role in film, fiction, poetry, painting, and photography. (ibid.:12)

In *Angelitos negros,* this "traffic across the color line" is both visual and audible. The title song is played frequently throughout the film, and some critics have indeed wondered whether the film was intended as a vehicle to accompany the song, rather than the other way around. Certainly, the success of "Angelitos negros" was well established before the film was released, and became so popular, in fact, that it enjoyed a long career that spanned vast regions of Latin America, where it was sung by such luminaries as the Cuban Antonio Machín and the Mexican singer Toña la Negra, as well as in the United States, where it was covered in English by Eartha Kitt, Roberta Flack, and others.[6] In his "Letter to Antonio Machín," posted to the internet, Barcelona writer Ramón Fernández Larrea affirms the immense popularity of "Angelitos negros" in twentieth-century Spain as well, suggesting finally that if Dr. Martin Luther King had known the song and its poignant argument for racial justice, he might have included a gospel rendition of it in his "I Have a Dream" speech.

Within this broad diffusion of "Angelitos negros," the well-known interpretation by Toña la Negra, a singer from Veracruz, one of the regions in which the Afro-Mexican presence is most notable, is particularly important. In her seminal study *Listening to Salsa* (1998), Frances Aparicio asserts that Toña la Negra stands with other Latin-American female film and recording stars who emerged in the 1950s and 1960s, such as Celia Cruz in Cuba and Ruth Fernández in Puerto Rico, who together opened up Afro-Caribbean musical performance to the presence of female subjectivities and who "contested, by their racially marked presence, the predominance of whiteness in the media" (Aparicio 1998:75). According to Aparicio, the singer from Veracruz left one of her deepest imprints with her interpretation of "Angelitos negros," which "denounced the colonialist, Eurocentric, and whitened paradigms in the visual arts that have prevailed throughout Latin American high culture . . . Through Toña la Negra's voice, the urgency of examining the arts from the perspective of racial exclusion took on a strong personal tone" (ibid.:175–76).

Ironically, however, it is a "white" character, José Carlos, who intones "Angelitos negros" in the film version, singing it to his mixed-race daughter on the occasion of her fourth birthday. How did film viewers perceive his appeal and the film's argument in general? According to Montaner's biographers, *Angelitos negros* drew a passionate response from its audiences, signaled a new focus on race in Latin-American film, and was destined to revolutionize the Latin-American public (Fajardo Estrada 1997:305). The film grappled explicitly with the problem of family fragmentation or dysfunction in Latin America through the erasure or suppression of Black ancestors, but it also dealt implicitly with the failures of *mestizo* or mixed-race paradigms to seamlessly incorporate the Black element in Mexico and elsewhere. The non-Black father cooing over his "*chapopote*" (a term roughly equivalent to "tarbaby") and his "little cinnamon-flower" stands in stark contrast to the "Black" but (unknowingly) passing-for-white mother who insists the child be removed from her sight, and who refuses to acknowledge her maternal obligations to the little girl. As such, Ana Luisa is the polar opposite of another deeply embedded tradition in Mexican and Latin-American film, the maternal figure as a model of unfailing self-sacrifice and abnegation. This kind of binary character development is common in the melodrama, which demands "the systematic implementation of two operations—schematizing and polarization" (Martín-Barbero 1993:116).

These two features are very much in evidence in *Angelitos negros,* where behaviors are constantly juxtaposed and characters are relentlessly typecast to the point of caricature. For example, the *nana* Mercé tirelessly cares for and praises her daughter and granddaughter, even when Ana Luisa refuses to assume her maternal duties, and is told by her husband "Tú no tienes entrañas de madre!" (You don't have the guts of a mother!). In a different kind of polarization, the "white" mother is "protected" from the knowledge of her Black blood, while her child Belén grows up excessively aware of her color and its disadvantages, despite her father's attempts to mitigate the effects of maternal rejection, attempts that culminate with Infante's tear-jerker rendition of "Angelitos negros" sung to his young daughter. Though José Carlos is not Black, he sympathizes with the rejection his partially Black child experiences at the hands of her own mother. The film thus transfers "Angelitos negros" from the scene of the church interior in its earlier sung versions to the heart of domestic space, with all the allegorical possibilities that this domestic, familial space offers to the discussion of national identity in Mexico and elsewhere in Latin America. At the same time, it transfers the burden of Blackness to dominant whites who sympathize and empathize with racial injustice, and often show that sympathy in the performance of Black musical and dramatic numbers.

As the character in *Angelitos negros* who epitomizes repugnance toward Blacks, and thus, unconscious self-hate, Ana Luisa rejects Blackness in both its natural and staged representations. Early in the film, after watching José Carlos perform his Afro-Cuban numbers, she asks, "Why does an artist like you need to dance with a mulatta? Wouldn't it be better if you went on stage as you are?" José Carlos responds, "People like to see me in blackface. It goes with the number," emphasizing that if certain musical numbers are to be performed "authentically," they should be presented by someone with Black(ened) skin. And in a crucial scene that displays Ana Luisa's overwhelming shame at having a daughter who is a "negrita," she receives a visit from her old friend Manu, who brings along her blonde, blue-eyed baby girl. "Que linda!" "que mona!" "que chula!" gushes Ana Luisa over Manu's baby ("How pretty!" "how cute!" "how charming!"). "What blue eyes she has!" When her own daughter enters the room, and Manu innocently asks, "Who is this nice little darkie?" Ana Luisa is unable to claim the child as her own, and lies to Manu, telling her (correctly, as it turns out) that Belén is the granddaughter of her *nana* Mercé.

For his part, José Carlos calls attention to the physical characteristics of those around him time and again while simultaneously insisting that such differentiations don't matter. After he first kisses Ana Luisa, he calls her his "pelitos de oro" (little golden-haired one). He tells Mercé, "You are one of the fine darkies (negritos), those that are made from the carbon of diamonds." When Mercé, trying to convince him that the newborn baby he holds in his hands is in fact his own child, by revealing to him the secret that she is Ana Luisa's mother, José Carlos assures her that he can indeed love the child. "Don't I love you, my little piece of tar?" he asks Mercé. But the "Black" characters in *Angelitos negros* have a tougher time with Blackness than someone who can choose to be Black or not, depending on the stage numbers he has scheduled that night.

The two most important "Black" characters in *Angelitos Negros* are arguably the *nana* Mercé and her mulatta granddaughter. As noted, both Romay's portrayal of the young Belén and Montaner's interpretation of Mercé are authenticated and rendered more credible through the use of blackface. Herself a mulatta (actually *cuarterona* or quadroon), Montaner appears in the film in fairly dark face paint that recalls some of her earlier blackface performances in other parts of Latin America. In 1934, for example, she had appeared *caracterizada* or *maquillada de negra* (made up as a Black woman) in a production of *La Calle 125* staged in Argentina at the Teatro Buenos Aires. Adapted from a work developed earlier in Harlem, *La Calle 125* featured an entire cast of singers and dancers in blackface, and was an enormous success with Argentine audiences (Fajardo Estrada 1997:123). Despite the show's success, Montaner was clearly aware that such "characterizations" posed risks for her as a creative performer, and as an ambassador of Cuban identity to the rest of Latin America. In an interview with the Buenos Aires newspaper *La Nación* prior to her debut, Montaner had told a reporter,

True popular art from Cuba is unknown outside the country, where it is spoiled or denaturalized. I think the same thing happens with Argentines and their folklore. That's why my "debut" worries me a little bit, because maybe what the public wants from me is one of those rumbas with a lot of movement and a lot of noise from the *timbales,* danced by a black woman. And that would be tedious for me. . . . I can interpret popular genres, street music, music from the countryside, etc., and give each song the accent and touch it requires, without needing to wear blackface, or continually change my costumes. I perform a new style and I can truly say that I've created it, because the Cuban authors have written the songs for me, so that I can interpret them, following some of my own indications as well. All of this is what I'll present to the Argentine public, and I hope they like it. (ibid. 121)[7]

Given her insistence that such costuming or facial masking was not necessary to the authentic interpretation of an Afro-Cuban song or sketch, it is somewhat surprising how often Montaner appeared *caracterizada* in subsequent stage and film performances. She was darkened, though not nearly as radically as in *Angelitos negros,* to play the *santera* or Afro-Cuban priest-ess Caridad in another 1948 film, *María la O,* this one produced through joint Mexican and Cuban efforts. In that film, Montaner provides *santería*-inspired advice and invocations to her mulatta friend María, played by Issa Morante, who also appears in blackface (though significantly lighter).[8] As Laura Podalsky has pointed out, *María la O* is one of several Cuban-Mexican co-productions that "characterized the struggle between blacks/mulattoes and whites as paradigmatic of Cuban culture, associating African culture with untamed sexuality and Spanish/criollo (Creole) cul-ture with social repression" (Podalsky 1994:64). Podalsky does not reflect at length, however, on the strategic employment of blackface or Afro-Cuban musical soundtracks in these films. While they perform Blackness in specific ways, the Black overlay and soundtrack in each is a significant clue to the complex negotiation and management of that Blackness, as ex-pressed in cinematic and musical languages.

Students of the film-musical tradition in Mexico and elsewhere in Latin America should also carefully consider its antecedents in stage productions from a variety of venues that ranged from backstreet brothels and cabarets to the elaborate theaters of Havana, Mexico City, Buenos Aires, and other major metropolitan centers. A genre particularly relevant to Mexican "ra-cial melodrama" was the *teatro bufo,* a nineteenth-century Cuban tradi-tion, similar in some respects to the minstrel show in the United States, in which stock characters such as the *negrito,* the *mulata,* and the *gallego* (Galician) were portrayed. What is interesting to our discussion of film melodrama is the *teatro bufo's* tendency to parody serious theatrical melo-drama from the same period and its penchant for exposing racial tensions and doing so through the artifice of blackface. Arrizón maintains that the actors who appeared in *teatro bufo* were most often whites, performing the Black body (2000:147).[9]

The subsequent employment of blackface for Black and mulatto charac-ters in so many Mexican or Cuban-Mexican films from the so-called Golden Age of cinema prompts us to ask several key questions.[10] Why were so few Black actors and/or musicians cast in these productions? When Cuban actors were enlisted in such projects, why were light-skinned actors used who had to be "blackened up" to fit the roles? What is the specific rela-tionship of blackface to gender, given that the vast majority of the actors who appeared in blackface in the period were women? This was the case in two films already mentioned, as well as in the 1953 Cuban-Mexican co-production *Mulata,* in which Ninón Sevilla appeared as the title character, and in the protofeminist Mexican work *La negra Angustias,* directed by Matilde Landeta in 1948.[11] An even harder question to answer, perhaps, is why these actors routinely were made up in a way that emphasized, rather than detracted from the cosmetic effect. Did filmmakers assume that audiences would not notice the blatant artifice of such characterizations, or did they exploit filmgoers' desire to see Blackness as a temporary and cosmetic condition?

Nowhere are such patently false appearances more apparent in *Angelitos negros* than in the scene of José Carlos and Ana Luisa's daughter's birth, in which it appears that even the doll that stands in for the newborn wears blackface. In that section of the film, we see the caricature-like responses to the event of Belén's birth of her horrified mother, her perplexed but then resolutely proud papa, her anguished secret grandmother, and the complicit priest, and if we listen carefully, we can even hear the new father call his baby daughter "*hollín,*" the Spanish word for soot, and a synonym for blackface. As Mexican film critic Carlos Monsiváis has pointed out, in melodrama, characters typically emblematize specific emotions or characteristics, such as compassion, innocence, resentment, or generosity (Monsiváis and Bonfil 1994:99). In *Angelitos negros,* the way in which each character reacts to the sight of the dark-skinned baby provides a condensed history of the range of responses to Blackness and the legacy of miscegenation within the Latin-American family.

The film continues with little Belén's growing awareness of and frustration with the scorn her color produces in those around her, especially when that scorn is shown her by her own mother. At one point, she covers her face and hands in white talcum powder, telling her father, "Quiero ser blanca para que mi mamá me quiera" [I want to be white so that my mommy will love me]. In that scene, we are presented with a Hispanic or "white" Mexican child—actually the daughter of director Joselito Rodríguez—who appears in an overlay of blackface in order to portray her character, and who then re-paints herself white to try and win her film mother's affection.

In scenes like this one, complex *racechanges* of the sort Gubar has studied in North American minstrelsy and its cultural descendants are starkly evident. And if the explicit message of *Angelitos negros* is that Blackness is all right after all, the film also reveals, through the incorporation of these racechanges, that racial otherness is subject to musical performance and spectacle that can choose to highlight or conversely, hide or erase it, as the moment dictates. As José Carlos tells Ana Luisa, "a la gente le gusta verme caracterizado" (people like seeing me in blackface). But he apparently drops the blackface routine for his Latin-American tour; instead we see him performing on the Buenos Aires stage with his *rancheros,* singing *corridos* or Mexican cowboy songs. That is, he returns to the same stages where

Montaner had feared being typecast as a Black *rumbera,* and is himself typecast as a Mexican cowboy crooner, complete with the iconic sombrero.

Montaner's subsequent participation in films such as *Negro es mi color* [My Color is Black] in 1950, and *El alma no tiene color* [The Soul Has No Color] 1955, reveals a further engagement with and portrayal of Blackness in Latin-American cinema. "Rita la Única," as she was known and revered in Cuba, had already earned fame as both the voice and face of Cuban Black and mulatto sectors in earlier film and theater productions such as *Cecilia Valdés* (1935), in her musical renditions of compatriot Nicolás Guillén's Afro-Cuban poems, and in enormously popular interpretations of Afro-Cuban numbers by composers such as Ernesto Lecuona and Gilberto Valdés. But more often than not, these acts did not depend on the artifice of blackface. In the Mexican production *Negro es mi color,* however, Montaner is again painted Black to portray a sweet and long-suffering Black *nana* who softens the blow for a mother who discovers at the moment of her son's birth the "horror of a dark geneology" (García Riera 1993:260). The casting of Montaner in the parallel blackface roles of *Angelitos Negros* and *Negro es mi color* in fact suggests a Latin-Americanized version of the Southern mammy featured in such North American films as *Gone with the Wind* (1939), Hollywood productions that were well known in Mexico and elsewhere in Latin America. Manthia Diawara has signaled the fundamental quality of domesticity in the mammy figure, a quality that marks her, and thus her Blackness, as civilized and domesticated, well-behaved within the context of the family manor or the larger society. Ultimately, the movie public's desire to see stock racial characters, and its complicity with lingering stereotypes, even in a film as seemingly "anti-racist" as *Angelitos negros,* seems to confirm some of Montaner's worst fears, hinted at so many years earlier before her debut in Buenos Aires.

In *Angelitos negros* and several of its contemporary film musicals, blackface and Afro-Cuban musical performance function, finally, as signs of recognition of the racial other and as the absorption of otherness into dominant forms of national and regional identity. Through parody, substitution, or caricature, Blackness is rendered superficial and thus empty; through blackface, the Mexican or Latin-American collective subject is paradoxically whitened. As Eric Lott has suggested in his excellent work on this phenomenon in the United States during the late nineteenth and early twentieth centuries, the complex appropriations of blackface reveal "contradictory racial impulses at work" in a "mixed erotic economy of celebration and exploitation," a simultaneous activity of love and theft (1993:4–6). In another commentary from the North American context, W. T. Lhamon notes, "blackface fascination shows a miscegenated culture becoming aware of itself. It makes theatre out of mingling selves trying to understand their inversions" (1998:131). While such films were created principally as vehicles for enjoyment, and not political consciousness-raising, their highly emotive character also allowed for the peripheral display of the sad state of race relations in Mexico and Latin America. Michael Rogin writes that "the racial/ethnic social-problem film, both in its original generational-conflict and later antidiscrimination forms, thus appears as the underside of the blackface musical" (Rogin 1996:169).

Although the history of blackface performance in Latin America, both on the stage and in film, is significantly different from what occurred in the United States, certain parallels are evident. As Diawara has pointed out, "inherent in the blackface myth is a white fantasy that posits whiteness as the norm. What is absent in the Blackface stereotype is as important as what is present: every black face is a statement of social imperfection, inferiority, and mimicry that is placed in isolation with an absent whiteness as its ideal opposite" (1999:7). Within this cultural economy of racial exchange and substitution, it is possible to view Infante's beloved rendition of "Angelitos negros," as itself an appropriation of blackness, but without the face paint. In that scene, perhaps the most poignant moment in the film in musical terms, Infante places his daughter on the piano facing him, sits down and begins to sing, "Pintor, nacido en mi tierra . . ." But the chords of the piano are not enough to convey the drama of a little dark-skinned girl being rejected by her own mother and being called a "negrita" at her fourth birthday party, and the strings begin to fill out the music behind the voice. When he finishes the song, Belén asks her father, "Didn't I behave well, Daddy?" and José Carlos responds, "Yes, daughter, you aren't guilty of anything." But before Mercé tucks her granddaughter into bed, she sings "Belén" to her, a song that incorporates Black venacular and emphasizes anew Belén's racial difference and her grandmother's as well: "Con tu pasá tan alborotá, y tu bembón colorá. . ." [With your kinky hair so disheveled and your big colorful lips . . .]. Although "Belén" serves here as a *canción de cuna* or lullaby, Montaner assumes a "Black" voice and character to perform it. And though Belén is neither big-lipped nor particularly kinky-haired, she is portrayed in Mercé's mannerist lullaby as such, that is, she is blackened up through the vehicle of song, she is *performed* as markedly Black.

Given the centrality of blackface performance in its thematic and musical structure, I suggest viewing *Angelitos negros* and similar film musicals from the period not only as ambivalent vehicles for the vindication of the Black role in Mexican or Latin-American history, but also as complex negotiations of racial otherness and difference that simultaneously outline and erase the contributions of people of African descent to such histories.

Returning, in conclusion, to *Angelitos negros,* we find that José Carlos exemplifies an appreciative, fun-loving acceptance and occasional habitation of Black identity, while his wife Ana Luisa incarnates an "opposed" reaction of horror and disgust, though it is she who "in fact" inhabits a Black (but not blackened) body. The film exaggerates and weds both these reactions to Latin American Blackness, providing viewers with an offspring that inevitably bears the ambivalence of her parents' opposed perspectives.

Notes

1. For a discussion of the Miním Pingín debate, see Mexico City's *La Jornada,* viernes, 1 de Julio de 2005, accessed at http://www.jornada.unam.mx/2005/jul05/050701/a04n1cul.php.

2. A brief history of the figure is provided at http://members.tripod.com/gmoaguilera/memin.html.

3. An unusual piece of *Angelitos negros* ephemera is a collection of poetry, also titled "Angelitos negros," submitted by Gricel Montes as an M.F.A. thesis at the University of Texas at El Paso in 1997. In her preface, Montes writes that the children in her poems reminded her of the plight of the unwanted mulatta daughter in *Angelitos negros.* Although Montes gets many of the details wrong in her synopsis of the film, she claims to have chosen that title because she wanted "to specifically write about children that suffer from working under the sun and abusive/or neglectful parents" (Montes 1997:xiii).

4. While documentary information regarding the score of *Angelitos negros* is spotty, García Riera notes that many of the songs were written by Raúl Lavista and Nacho García, or by famed Cuban composer Eliseo Grenet ("Belén"). Chucho Monge also wrote "Tus ojitos."

5. All translations from Spanish, unless otherwise specified, are my own.

6. Flack's version can be heard on her album *First Take* (1969).

7. "Generalmente no se conoce en el extranjero el verdadero arte popular cubano, que se desvirtúa, se desnaturaliza. A los argentinos creo que les ocurre lo mismo con su folklore. Por eso me preocupa un poco mi 'debut', pues acaso el público espere de mí una de esas rumbas con mucho movimiento y mucha bulla de timbales, bailada por una negra. Y eso me resultaría muy pesado . . . Sin necesidad de caracterizarme, ni de cambiar continuamente de indumentaria, interpreto los tipos populares, la mulata callejera, la guajira, et., dando a cada canción el acento y el gesto que requiere. Hago un género nuevo y bien puedo decir que lo he creado, porque los autores cubanos han escrito las canciones para mí, para que yo las interprete, y siguiendo también algunas indicaciones mías. Todo esto es lo que presentaré al público argentino, y espero que le gustará."

8. *Santería* is an African diasporic syncretic religious system practiced in Cuba and other parts of the Caribbean that recognizes parallels and affinities between a pantheon of African deities or spiritual beings and Catholic saints.

9. Cuban scholar Rine Leal's contention that the actors "were mulattos and projected themselves that way on stage" does not sufficiently take into account the posturing qualities of blackface (Leal 1975:27). Nonetheless, Leal does confirm that due to its incendiary political nature in the context of Cuban independence struggles, the *bufos* had to take their show to Mexico in 1868, a development that surely had bearing on the later development of the racial melodrama in Mexico

(ibid.:31). The relationship between nineteenth century *teatro bufo* and twentieth century racial melodrama can be seem as analogous in some ways to the relationship between minstrelsy and cultural expression that Gubar labels "modernist" racechange in the United States: "Paradoxically, modernist racechange—so often subversive in its intent, so often avant-garde in its setting—finds its historical roots in exceptionally popular and virulently racist entertainments undertaken primarily by and for white men (Gubar 1997:42).

10. Podalsky posits that the practice is infrequent in the Cuban filmic tradition (Podalsky 1994:67).

11. A sustained analysis of these works should also take into account the fact that many of the films discussed here were adaptations of earlier works. *Angelitos negros* is purportedly a Mexican remake of the 1937 North American film *Imitation of Life*, which was adapted from the novel by the same name, written by the white author Fannie Hurst. Matilde Landeta acquired the rights to Francisco Rojas Gonzales' award-winning novel *La negra Angustias* to produce her film of the same name. In the opening credits to *Mulata*, the filmmakers advise the viewers that the work they are about to see was inspired by Roberto Olivencia Marquéz' "estampa negra" published in Montevideo in 1943.

Works Cited

Aparicio, Frances R. 1998. *Listening to Salsa: Gender, Latin Popular Music, and Puerto Rican Culture*. Hanover and London: Wesleyan University Press.

Arrizón, Alicia. 2002. "Race-ing Performativity through Transculturation, Taste and the Mulata Body." *Theatre Research International* 27, no. 2:136-52.

Aviña, Rafael. 2004. *Una mirada insólita. Temas y géneros del cine mexicano*. México: Cineteca Nacional, Editorial Oceano.

Diawara, Manthia. 1999. "The Blackface Stereotype" in *Blackface,* ed. David Levinthal. Santa Fe, N.M.: Arena Editions, 7-17.

Fajardo Estrada, Ramón. 1997. *Rita Montaner. Testimonio de una época*. La Habana: Casa de las Américas.

García, Gustavo. 1994. *No me parezco a nadie. La vida de Pedro Infante, II*. México: Editorial Clío.

García Riera, Emilio. 1993. *Historia documental del cine mexicano. Tomo IV. 1946–1948*. Guadalajara: Universidad de Guadalajara.

Gubar, Susan. 1997. *Racechanges: White Skin, Black Face in American Culture*. New York and Oxford: Oxford University Press.

Hershfield, Joanne. 1999."Race and Ethnicity in the Classical Cinema," in *Mexico's Cinema: A Century of Film and Filmmakers*, ed. Joanne Hershfield and David R. Maciel.Wilmington, Del.: SR Books.

Hershfield, Joanne, and David R. Maciel, eds. 1999. *Mexico's Cinema: A Century of Film and Filmmakers*. Wilmington, Del.: SR Books.

Huaco-Nuzam, Carmen. 1987. "Matilde Landeta." *Screen* 28, no. 4:96-105.

Larrea, Ramón Fernández. "Carta a Antonio Machín. http://www.puntog.com .mx/2004/20040425/IDB250404.htm.

Leal, Rine. 1975. "Prólogo." *Teatro bufo Siglo XIX. Antología*. Tomo 1. La Habana: Editorial Arte y Literatura , 15-46.

Levinthal, David. 1999. *Blackface*. Santa Fe, N.M.: Arena Editions.

Lhamon, W. T. 1998. *Raising Cain: Blackface Performance from Jim Crow to Hip Hop*. Cambridge, Mass.: Harvard University Press.

López, Ana. 1991. "The Melodrama in Latin America: Films, Telenovelas, and the Currency of a Popular Form," in *Imitations of Life: A Reader on Film &*

Television Melodrama, ed. Marcia Landy. Detroit: Wayne State University Press, 596–606. Reprinted from *Wide Angle* 7, no. 3 (1985):5–13.

Lott, Eric. 1993. *Love and Theft: Blackface Minstrelsy and the American Working Class.* New York: Oxford University Press.

Martín-Barbero, Jesús. 1993. *Communication, Culture and Hegemony: From the Media to Mediations.* Trans. by Elizabeth Fox and Robert A. White; intro. by Philip Schlesinger. London: SAGE Publications.

Monsiváis, Carlos, and Carlos Bonfil. 1994. *A través del espejo. El cine mexicano y su público.* México: Ediciones el Milagro. Instituto Mexicano de Cinematografía.

Montes, Gricel. 1997. "Angelitos Negros." MFA thesis, University of Texas, El Paso.

Podalsky, Laura. 1994. "Negotiating Differences: National Cinemas and Co-productions in Prerevolutionary Cuba. *The Velvet Light Trap* 34:59–70.

Rogin, Michael. 1996. *Blackface, White Noise: Jewish Immigrants in the Hollywood Melting Pot.* Berkeley: University of California Press.

ERIC A. GALM

Baianas, Malandros, *and Samba*
Listening to Brazil through Donald Duck's Ears

·◉·

Introduction

The Three Caballeros (1945) is a feature-length animated film by Walt Disney Productions in which Donald Duck takes a trip to Latin America. Donald is transported to various countries by opening a series of wrapped presents in a large box. During these adventures, he combines with Joe Carioca of Brazil and Panchito of Mexico, thus forming the Three Caballeros.[1] In this technologically cutting-edge film (the first production to incorporate live actors with animation), Disney uses symbols of the working classes in Mexico (*serape* blankets and *sombrero* hats) and Brazil (samba music and street vendors) to convey different messages to people throughout the hemisphere. For North Americans, these symbols are used to demonstrate that Donald has seen an authentic Latin America. For South Americans, these symbols help to send a wartime-era message of peace from the United States that is directed towards all sectors of Latin-American societies.

This film provides an excellent opportunity for the exploration of identity construction and cultural misrepresentation by Hollywood projects. Within this film, Donald Duck is presented as a cultural outsider who gains valuable access to Brazilian culture from his guide, the cigar-toting parrot, José (Joe) Carioca. Since a large portion of the Brazilian sequence of this film revolves around the northeastern city of Salvador, Bahia, Donald soon discovers that José (who has never been to Bahia himself) is as much of a cultural outsider as Donald. This moment reveals that Disney's entire construction of Brazil was derived from a brief research trip to Rio, where his animators were dispatched to study the flora and fauna at the city's Jardim Botânico (Botanical Garden), Jardim Zoológico (Zoo), and trademark cobblestone sidewalks along Avenida Atlântica and adjacent Copacabana beaches.[2]

Although this film has been analyzed from historical and gendered perspectives, the music has not been discussed.[3] Analysis of the music used in this film can shed light on how identity has been shaped through musical expression in both Brazilian cultural and broader global contexts. This analysis is also informed by biographical information about the singer and composers, as well as discussion about the Brazilian cultural figures of the *baiana* (archetypical Bahian woman of African descent) and the *malandro* (rogue).[4]

From the sixteenth to the nineteenth centuries, Brazil received more enslaved Africans than any other country. As a result, Brazil has the largest presence of African descendants in any single country beyond Africa. The northeastern Brazilian city of Salvador, Bahia, was one of the principal ports where enslaved Africans were brought to labor on sugar plantations.[5] From the colonial era to the present, Bahia has maintained a strong presence of African descendants; however, in *The Three Caballeros,* Disney has portrayed a Bahia without any Black people whatsoever.[6]

Accounts of Bahia's African presence can be seen in the writings of colonial-era chroniclers, to twentieth-century Brazilian and foreign social scientists who developed and tested theories of African retentions in the Americas. Some scholars even waged territorial battles over whose informants were more "authentic."[7] Some of Bahia's cultural and artistic African-derived expressions include Candomblé (an African-derived religion) and *capoeira* (a martial art dance game), both of which have become popularized throughout the world.[8]

The mystique of Bahia's African charms is a question that anthropologist Livio Sansone pursues in attempting to discern which elements within Brazilian society actually can be considered "African." He suggests that

the determination of "African" is mostly impressionistic. Objects, lexicon and music beat are defined as African often by superficial association and similarity, by visual observation—rather than through careful research, which is still scarce. "Looking African" or "Sounding African" is, in fact, what makes things "African"— so, a group of sturdy black men toiling at the central market of Salvador makes it an "African" market in the commentary of books for sale to tourists and traveling anthropologists alike. (Sansone 1999:18)

Therefore, for Sansone, many of the popular "African" cultural manifestations that exist in Brazil have been derived in part from a superficial gaze.[9] Aspects of this are explored in the discussion of the song "Os Quindins de Iaiá" [Iaiá's Sweets], below.

The Three Caballeros was a later product derived from American governmental policies that encompassed the era surrounding the Second World War. As tensions increased throughout the world with the possibility of war, President Franklin D. Roosevelt strengthened the Good Neighbor Policy in 1939, to alleviate tensions between governments throughout South America, and to attempt to strengthen allies within the hemisphere. One of the primary conduits of this cultural bridge-building policy was through the entertainment industry, particularly Hollywood films. As a result, icons such as Carmen Miranda began to represent a broader pan-Latin American (as opposed to only Brazilian) persona. Films produced in this style include *Down Argentine Way* (1940), *Week-End in Havana* (1941), *That Night in Rio* (1941), and *The Gang's All Here* (1943).[10]

In August 1940, the Council of National Defense (Coordinator of Commercial and Cultural Relations between the American Republics) was formed, headed by Nelson A. Rockefeller. Film producer John Hay Whitney led the motion picture division, and Walt Disney was one of the first producers to be approached under the auspices of the Good Neighbor program (*Three Caballeros* laserdisc 1991).[11] The State Department financed lavish excursions to Latin America for Disney and his staff, and commissioned several films.[12] As a result of these trips, Disney created films ranging from short-length informational agricultural and health pieces, to full-length feature productions. Three prominent films comprise the cornerstones of this project: *South of the Border with Disney* (1941), *Saludos Amigos* (1943) and *The Three Caballeros* (1945). Within these three films, we see the genesis of the animated talking parrot, José (Joe) Carioca, who is now formally promoted throughout Brazil in Disney-produced newsstand comic books as "Zé Carioca."[13] In the first of these three films, Carioca appears only as a series of "two-color pencil sketches, briefly and provisionally animated to offer a glimpse of him performing an incipient samba" (Burton-Carvajal 1994:134). The second features an extensive interaction between José Carioca and Donald Duck, in which José gets Donald drunk on *cachaça* (sugar-cane alcohol) and teaches Donald how to dance the samba, accompanied by music from Ari Barroso's "Brazil."[14]

The importance of music in relation to the Good Neighbor Policy can be seen in two letters from the United States government addressed to executives at the Music Educators National Conference (MENC) in 1941. The first letter, from Nelson A. Rockefeller of the Council of National Defense is dated April 21, 1941, and is addressed to Fowler Smith, president of the MENC, in response to a proposed program of "American Unity through Music" where a committee of MENC representatives would embark on a cultural tour and educational exchange with several Latin-American arts institutions. In this letter, Rockefeller states:

Music is so inherent a social element and such a universal language that its importance in a progress of peaceful international intercourse cannot be overestimated. It is particularly significant that, at this time, when the cultural activities of the Old World are engulfed in war, in at least part of the world there be preserved an order in which such activities can thrive. An important foundation for our scheme of hemispheric defense must be a social order in which there is balance and perspective. The American Unity through Music program can play a very important part in preserving such an order. (in Seeger 1941:12)

This theme was echoed on May 8, 1941, in a letter to the Executive Secretary of the MENC from Charles A. Thomson, Chief of Cultural Relations from the United States Department of State: "It seems to me that the medium of music can be of great value in developing that comprehensive inter-American understanding which is essential to the progress of the Good Neighbor policy" (in Seeger 1941:12).

The early 1940s also represents a time when Hollywood began to incorporate African-American actors and thematic material prominently into mainstream cinema, which were relegated previously to the separate subgenre of race films. At this time, many Hollywood filmmakers agreed with the National Association for the Advancement of Colored People to produce films that presented African Americans in realistic roles; however, it must be noted that the early 1940s was also an era when new markets were being created to appeal to segregated African-American audiences and African-American soldiers.[15] As a means to accommodate these two contrasting markets, Disney presents an all-white Bahia to help make these Afrocentric themes accessible to predominately white audiences, without entering debates of race and class in either Latin America or the United States.

Carmen Miranda and the Baiana Motif

Since Disney's portrayal of Bahia in *The Three Caballeros* is based largely upon the figure of the *baiana*, I begin with a discussion of the international construction of the Bahian figure with whom the world was most familiar, Carmen Miranda. Known as "The Brazilian Bombshell," she initially enjoyed a successful singing and recording career in Brazil, and then became an international star in 1930s Broadway musicals, and later in several Hollywood films. Her energy and enthusiasm brought life to her extravagant costumes. For North Americans, her character represented a generic Latina personality, whereas within a Brazilian context, much of her persona was culled from African-derived culture, including samba dance steps, stylized attire, and her energetic percussive delivery of lyrics. Miranda popularized many songs that were composed by working-class samba musicians from Rio de Janeiro, an area where samba crystallized into a popular music genre.

In international contexts, Miranda often played a broad range of naïve young immigrant women who blamed misunderstandings on language barriers. When Miranda sang sambas in the United States, English translations were interpreted differently from their initial meaning. For example, when Miranda sang about picking up and playing various Brazilian percussion instruments, she would sing and then self-translate: "K-k-k-Katy, *pega pandeiro, agogô e tamborim*. In English, this means 'k-k-k-Katy, you're the most beautiful girl I've ever seen'" (*Carmen Miranda: Bananas Is my Business* 1996).[16]

Miranda's famous costume is modeled after the figure of the *baiana*, an Afro-Brazilian woman whose traditional attire includes a white hoop-dress, head wrap, and expensive *pano da costa* (shawl). *Baianas* are extremely important throughout Brazil, as they represent "authentic" individuals who maintain direct connections with the roots of African-derived cultures in Brazil. The *baiana* is also a central figure in the religion of Candomblé. Miranda developed her idea for using the *baiana* motif in the film *Banana da Terra* (1938), to illustrate the lyrics of Dorival Caymmi's song "O Que É Que A Baiana Tem?" ("What Does a Baiana Have?"), which includes features such as a silk headdress, a golden necklace, and other adornments. *Baianas* are still prominently visible in Bahia, where women sell a variety of foods on the streets, dressed in traditional attire. These foods also represent dishes that specific gods enjoy within the religious context.

Disney's portrayal of Bahia revolves around this international construction of the *baiana* figure, played in the film by Carmen's sister, Aurora. Disney initially had wanted to contract Carmen for *The Three Caballeros*, but scheduling conflicts intervened, and following a successful screen test in October 1942, Aurora was the first live actor contracted for *The Three Caballeros* (*Three Caballeros* laserdisc 1991).[17] Aurora Miranda da Cunha was a formidable singer, who also enjoyed a successful singing career in Brazil. Aurora's career was launched prior to her eighteenth birthday, when she sang a song live on the radio, and subsequently received a regular job singing at a competing radio station. In the decade of the 1930s, Carmen and Aurora were the most widely recorded female singers in Brazil. Aurora began working in films in 1935, occasionally singing duets with her sister. Aurora premiered many sambas and *marchas* (marches) and has recorded 161 songs on eighty-one 78-rpm discs (Marcondes 2000). Aurora was married at twenty-five years of age in 1940, and moved to the United States, thus leaving her successful recording career in Brazil. In the 1940s, she occasionally participated in North American radio shows, live theater productions, and films. In *The Three Caballeros*, Aurora is the live actor and singer, "Iaiá" (pronounced ya-ya), a *baiana*-style vendor on the streets of Bahia.

Music Overview

The Brazil section of *The Three Caballeros* features six musical selections, consisting of three instrumental and three vocal pieces. All three songs with lyrics enjoyed success in the Brazilian music market preceding the release of the film. In this section, I present an overview of all musical selections, followed by a discussion about each of the vocal selections. The first is an introduction to the Brazil section, where Donald Duck is attracted to a wrapped present, a book about Brazil that is literally playing and moving to samba music. When Donald opens the book, a proscenium stage appears, displaying José Carioca in a one-bird show, where he is making music magically with his umbrella, switching between flute and guitar, thus establishing this Brazilian bird's musical virtuosity. The second musical selection is entitled "Baía," originally released as "Na Baixa do Sapateiro," by Ari Barroso. The third song is Dorival Caymmi's "Você Já Foi À Bahia?" ("Have You Been to Bahia?"), followed by a musical interlude that enables Donald and José to take a train trip to the imaginary land of "Baía."[18] This train music is set in the style of either an early samba composition or possibly modeled after a *choro* composition.[19] The fifth selection is another Barroso song, "Os Quindins de Iaiá," about a street vendor who is selling her sweets. This section segues into an instrumental samba fantasy, based on "Os Quindins de Iaiá," which concludes the Brazil portion of the film. This montage is underscored by a constant samba beat, and consists of live dancing, which seems to be based largely on other generic "Latin" dance numbers, featured in Hollywood musicals of the era.[20] In this mix of live footage interspersed with animation, an energetic samba dance between two men quickly turns into a *capoeira* fight, literally animated as a cockfight between birds, and each aggressive movement is highlighted by a flash of bright light and a cymbal crash. Within this scene, no actual *capoeira* movements can be discerned in either the live action or the animation. The Brazil segment concludes with Iaiá inviting Donald and José into the streets of Bahia, where the street lamps, buildings, and even the picturesque Lacerda elevator all dance the samba into the night, until the book comes to a crashing close, thus concluding the segment.[21]

Vocal Selections

The lyrics of the songs in *The Three Caballeros* feature untranslated and marginally translated Portuguese passages, as well as newly composed English versions that somewhat alter the character of the composition. These songs were all very successful in Brazil prior to their incorporation into the film. Ari Barroso composed two of the songs, "Baía" ("Na Baixa do Sapateiro") and "Os Quindins de Iayá," and Dorival Caymmi composed "Você Já Foi À Bahia?" ["Have You Been to Bahia?"].[22] Barroso and Caymmi were part of a group of younger samba composers who emerged from higher-class neighborhoods of Rio in the 1930s, and began to produce romantic sambas that highlighted harmonic and melodic aspects and placed less emphasis on rhythm. These composers set trends for the definition of popular Brazilian music until the development of bossa nova in the late 1950s. Songs like Barroso's "Na Baixa do Sapateiro" and "Aquarela do Brasil" came to be known as a subgenre of samba that Barroso called "samba *exaltação*" (McGowan and Pessanha 1998:30), a style of samba designed to sing about the beauty of Brazilian national culture.

"BAÍA" ("NA BAIXA DO SAPATEIRO")

The song "Baía" originally was composed as "Na Baixa do Sapateiro" by Ari Barroso in 1938, and was one of the most successful compositions of that year (Severiano and Mello 1997:166).[23] "Na Baixa do Sapateiro" initially was supposed to be incorporated into the film *Banana da Terra* (1938), featuring Carmen Miranda, but Barroso and the film's director, Wallace Downey, were not able to come to an agreement. Instead, Carmen Miranda suggested a young composer who had written another song about Bahia, "O Que É Que A Baiana Tem?" ["What Does a Baiana Have?"] by Dorival Caymmi. As discussed above, Caymmi's composition became the inspiration for the development of her international trademark, the exaggerated *baiana* costume. An English version of "Na Baixa do Sapateiro" was incorporated into *The Three Caballeros,* and this became so popular that one million copies of sheet music were printed in the United States in 1945 alone (Severiano and Mello 1997:166).[24]

A comparison between the Portuguese lyrics of "Na Baixa do Sapateiro," and the Disney lyrics for "Baía" demonstrates that the overall tone of the song has moved from a bittersweet agony, to a more generic romantic ideal. Barroso's original version begins by diminishing the importance of the love, by casting it off as a silly, unexplainable entity that will be sure to cause eternal suffering:

Oh, love, ai, ai
Nonsense love
that people can't explain, ai, ai
Try a little piece, oi
It will poison you, oi
And for the rest of life
Nothing but suffering, olará,
olerê

Hello Bahia, ai, ai
Bahia that never leaves
my thoughts, ai, ai
I lament, oi
In despair, oi
To encounter in this world
The love that I lost
In Bahia, I'll tell you:[25]

Bahia is portrayed as an endless agony that will never be completely resolved. In the second half of this song, which is omitted from *The Three Caballeros,* the suffering from Bahia is transformed into a story about a brief encounter between two potential lovers on the "Baixa do Sapateiro" street:

On "Baixa do Sapateiro" street
I encountered one day
The most elegant *moreno* of Bahia
He asked me for a kiss, I didn't give,
A hug, I smiled,
He asked for my hand,
I didn't want to give . . . I ran away.
Bahia, land of happiness
Moreno
I am full of nostalgia
Please, my Lord of Bonfim
Find another *moreno*
for me.[26]

Through the coy evasiveness of the protagonist combined with the use of the masculine form of *moreno,* it is clear that this song is presented from a feminine perspective.[27] Following the flirtatious encounter of the rebuffed kiss, hug, and hand, the protagonist flees, only to live in remorse, even praying to the patron saint of Salvador to create another substitute for this lost love.

The affair aspect of this song has been removed from Ray Gilbert's English, and has been replaced by the protagonist's tranquility being haunted by his past ("Someone I long to see / keeps haunting my reverie"). The lyrics of the English version are constructed in order to deliver catchy rhymes that spin in a circular manner, as opposed to the progressive development of details about the love affair.

Disney sets these lyrics in an animated romance between two doves flying over the city of Bahia. The connection with Senhor do Bonfim is retained within the overall concept, as this song is set in a lush instrumental and choral orchestration that is dripping with conventional techniques found in Hollywood and Broadway musicals, such as drops of water in a pond depicted musically by string pizzicato notes and orchestra bells. The choral harmonies sound remarkably similar to the vocal arrangement featured at the beginning of Disney's film about African-American Uncle Remus stories, *Song of the South* (1946).[28] Needless to say, this singing style and these harmonies would never be heard in a communal backyard samba celebration anywhere in Brazil. In both of these versions, Bahia is an unobtainable "other" whose longing causes eternal suffering.

"VOCÊ JÁ FOI À BAHIA?"
["HAVE YOU BEEN TO BAHIA?"]

The Three Caballeros was released in Brazil bearing the title "Você Já Foi À Bahia?" [Have you been to Bahia?], named after a song of the same name by Dorival Caymmi, composed in 1941, a song that is noted as one of the year's most successful compositions (Severiano and Mello 1997). While some biographical retrospectives have noted the connection between the title of Caymmi's song serving as the film's title in Brazil (e.g., Marcondes 2000), there is no mention that the actual song (either in English or Portuguese) was included in the film. Although "Have You Been to Bahia?" features a duet between José Carioca and Donald Duck, no credit in *The Three Caballeros* is attributed to either Caymmi or the title of the song.[29]

For the most part, the song presented in *The Three Caballeros* and Caymmi's original song are relatively the same, except the opening line of the latter is directed to a "*nega*" (woman of African descent): "*Você já foi à Bahia, nega?*" ("Have you been to Bahia, dear?") (Lisboa Junior 1990:103). During a portion of the song that is not translated into English, José Carioca splits into four identical cigar-toting Carmen Miranda–style parrots, who sing in Portuguese:

> On the balconies of the two-story houses
> Of old São Salvador [Bahia]
> The memory of the maidens
> In the time of the emperor
> Everything, everything in Bahia
> Makes people really want it
> Bahia has a way
> That no land has

This song is used as a means to shrink Donald Duck to a very small size, so that he can enter the book and be transported to the imaginary land of "Baía," where, as these lyrics suggest, one can still find women who embody desirable aspects from an idealized colonial-era Brazil. Donald undergoes another transformation within this song where language barriers seem to evaporate dramatically, regardless of his understanding of the term.

As José Carioca sings about Bahia's exotic cuisine—such as *vatapá, caruru*, and *munguzá*[30]—that is popular with the people as well as with African-derived religious deities, Donald inquires about the meaning, and José quickly moves on to the next word without explanation. The only concept that appears to be fully understood is when José Carioca asks Donald if he likes to samba. This point already has been established, since José taught Donald how to dance the samba in the preceding Disney film, *Saludos Amigos*.

Prior to the 1930s, the middle classes of lighter complexion spurned Afro-Bahian cuisine, considering foods prepared in *dendê* (palm oil) to be "unhealthy, filthy and only fit for *negros*" (Sansone 1999:22).[31] In the 1940s, a transformation took place that began to incorporate these exoticized foods into a "national" Brazilian cuisine, but with certain restrictions. "Today, palm oil is accepted by everybody, as part of daily life for the lower classes and only on special days for the middle and upper classes" (ibid.). Additional research may highlight how international media projects (like these animated Disney and Carmen Miranda–style films) might have influenced these changes that took place in 1940s Brazilian society.

"OS QUINDINS DE IAIÁ" ["IAIÁ'S SWEETS"]

"Os Quindins de Iaiá" was composed by Ari Barroso in 1941, and was a successful song from that year (Severiano and Mello 1997:200).[32] This song is about a Bahian street vendor, Iaiá, who, according to José Carioca, is selling "cookies."[33] The audience soon discovers that she is offering much more. Iaiá comes strolling down the street, singing a street vendor's song, a common sales technique that spans back to colonial-era Brazil, and can still be heard today on the streets of Bahia. She sings:

> Come get Iaiá's *quindins*
> Who wants to buy my *quindins*?

Donald immediately falls in love with Iaiá, and begins a competitive race with José to win her affection.[34] As she launches into the song, a group of percussionists surround Iaiá, whose musical instruments and costumes are nearly identical to Carmen Miranda's on-stage musicians. As Iaiá sings "*Os Quindins de Iaiá*," the percussionists energetically respond "*cumé, cumé, cumé*" (eat 'em):

Iaiá's sweets. . .
eat 'em, eat 'em, eat 'em
Iaiá's sweets. . .
eat 'em, eat 'em, eat 'em
Iaiá's sweets . . . eat 'em
Eat them because they will make you
cry
Iaiá's little eyes. . .
eat 'em, eat 'em, eat 'em
Iaiá's little eyes. . .
eat 'em, eat 'em, eat 'em
Iaiá's little eyes . . .eat 'em,
Eat them because it causes suffering
The way that Iaiá is—give me—give me
A pain—give me—give me
That I don't know—if it is—if it is
If it is or is not love
I only know that Iaiá has something
That the other Iaiás don't have . . . what?
Iaiá's sweets (repeat 4 times)[35]

This song features many creolized adaptations of Portuguese words, such as "cumé" (from *comer*—to eat), and "oin" (possibly from *olhinhos*— little eyes). Therefore, in addition to physically eating Iaiá's sweets, you are also encouraged to consume her beauty. When Iaiá sings "The way that Iaiá is," the men respond "me da," which means, "give it to me." Both Donald Duck and José Carioca accentuate this vocal response with pelvic thrusts in their dance movements. Iaiá provides contrasting interjections for each repetition at the end of each verse, as if she is selecting men like they were delicacies upon her tray. At the first "Os quindins de Iaiá," she says "ah?" as if expressing interest, after the second she refuses "ah, ah" as if to say no, and the third, she sees one she likes, and says "aaahhh," affirming that she is definitely interested.

The Disney version only uses the first verse of this song, and the second verse is briefly used to introduce another street vendor who is selling oranges in a basket resting on his head. He sings: "look at the fresh orange, look at the good tangerine."[36] Donald becomes jealous and begins to confront the orange vendor. José stops Donald and says "no, no, no, Donald, take it easy," implying that direct confrontation is not the proper way to resolve this sort of conflict. Instead, José hands Donald a large mallet, so that Donald can squash the oranges and the vendor in one blow. While Donald is swiping at the vendor, the salesman sings an untranslated passage: "And you can go with me to the church, my sweet little *baiana*," suggesting that he is interested in a long-term commitment.

The second verse of this song, largely omitted from the Disney film, merely enriches the setting of people, places and things that can be found in Bahia, followed again by a humorous concluding line that segues to the refrain:

> There are so many things of valor
> In this world of Our Lord:
> —There is the flower of midnight
> Hidden among the flowerbeds
> There is music and beauty
> In the voice of the cowboys!
> The silver of the full moon
> The fans [leaves] from the coconut tree
> The smile of the children
> The song of the boatsmen
> But I swear to the Virgin Mary
> That none of this can kill . . . what?
> Iayá's sweets (repeat 4 times)

Iaiá rebuffs the seductive advances of one of her musicians, and Donald even joins in singing Portuguese lyrics and dancing the samba with Iaiá. José cautions Donald to watch out for the musician attempting to seduce Iaiá, because he is a "*malandro*" (rogue).

In order to gain a more comprehensive understanding of the interactions contained within this scene, it is necessary to discuss some elements in more detail, such as the development and transformation of the term "Iaiá," the term *malandro,* and a comparison between the *marcha* and the samba, two genres of early-to-mid-twentieth-century Brazilian music that were popular on the streets during carnival, and continue to be popular today.

Who Is *Iaiá?*

Capoeira scholar John Lowell Lewis notes that the term "Iaiá" and its masculine equivalent, "Ioiô" were developed by enslaved Africans and their descendants in Brazil as a way to refer to the children of slave owners (Lewis 1992).[37] This device has been used in *capoeira* songs as a means to evoke imagery of slave resistance. By blaming a situation on the slave owner's child, the enslaved person can mask a situation that could have been caused by a simple accident or direct sabotage. "The manipulation of the system of production is one of the ways slaves gained some leverage over their masters indirectly, without resorting to outright rebellion or escape" (Lewis 1992:29). Moreover the actual terms Iaiá and Ioiô may have developed from a corruption of the proper terms "*senhor*" (*sinhô,* eventually becoming *ioiô*) and "*senhora*" (*sinhá,* eventually becoming *iaiá*), that an enslaved person would direct toward the masculine slave owners and their wives. Within the realm of Candomblé, the term "*Iá*" refers to "mother," and signifies maternal hierarchy in terms such as "*Ialorixa*," the woman responsible for directing the sacred proceedings (Cacciatore 1988:138).[38]

The terms Iaiá and Ioiô have been used repeatedly in Bahian-themed popular Brazilian music produced in Rio de Janeiro in the early twentieth century, where the image of Iaiá has transformed from the child of the slave owner into a seductive *baiana*, who is waiting for foreign tourists to arrive on Bahia's sacred land. Toward the end of the nineteenth century, there was a large southern migration of Bahians in search of work in the industrializing cities of Rio de Janeiro and São Paulo. Therefore, Bahia and related nostalgic themes were incorporated into the musical landscape of Rio de Janeiro's urban popular music.

As early as 1915, the song "Quem Vem Atrás Fecha A Porta" ["Who comes last shut the door"], composed by José Luis de Moraes ("Caninha"), describes an informal encounter with Iaiá on the side of a road:

> I want Iaiá to take me
> There at the edge of the road
> Be patient, Iaiá,
> Take me slowly[39]

In "O Coco de Iáiá" (Iáiá's coconut), composed by Canhoto in 1927, Iáiá is analogous to various Bahian sweet and spicy foods:

> I want to try my *iáiá*
> Sugared *doce de coco*
> I already ate the spicy
> *mungunzá*.
>
> Ah! I want to go to Bahia to
> eat *cuscus*
> Let's run away there any day
> Oh, little *baiana* you seduce
>
> It's very good, my *iáiá*
> Every little bit that you make,
> It's good to feel what you eat
> And ask for more.[40]

There is certainly a connection between Iaiá and Bahian cuisine, but "O Coco de Iaiá" reinforces her seductive qualities, as well as the resulting indigestion that arises from eating socially less than desirable foods.

The lyrics in "Sinhô do Bonfim" ["Saint of Bonfim"], composed in 1932 by Joracy Camargo, are thematically similar to Barroso's "Na Baixa do Sapateiro":

I went one time to Bahia
To see if Our Lord Bonfim. . .
Would make a miracle for me.
But Iáiá took me there. . .

I prayed every night. . .
Iáiá also prayed for the one she loved. . .
I returned to Bahia,
And again I went with Iáiá,
To tell Lord Bonfim
That we would be married within the month. . .
And contently laughing, he took her,
And gave the *baiana* to me.[41]

In this setting, Iaiá is taking the man to church to pray. Emphasizing "otherness," Iaiá prays to her god. The image of limited freedom is also reinforced, when Lord Bonfim "took" Iaiá, and "gave" her to the singer.

Iaiá and the Malandro

In the 1930s and 1940s, the *malandro* became a cultural stereotype based on a man who did not work at a steady job, and survived through exploitation and deceit of women. This stereotype emerged from the urban samba environment of Rio de Janeiro. *Malandros* hustled cash with fast-talking roadside gambling and tricks. *Malandros* often dressed in a white suit and white hat, and in Rio's popular culture, they represented a "romantic bohemian ideal" and "were proud of their lifestyle" (McGowan and Pessanha 1998:27). Lewis explains that this pride represented individual and group survival strategies that were seen as a "positive cultural value," since *malandros* were able to rely on their quick verbal or physical reactions to adverse situations (1992:49).

José Carioca is styled after a *malandro,* and his character has been described as "seductively feminine," with the ability to sell "himself with the batting of his eyelashes" (Piedra 1994:155). In order to interpret Carioca from a cultural perspective, his actions must be viewed through the perspective of *malandragem* (pursuing deception). The character of the *malandro* is a refined and dignified person who is strong and can instantly become dangerous. Above all, the *malandro* must defend his character at all costs in order to continue through life without obtaining a steady job. Moreover, if a man or a woman challenges him, he may respond either through direct confrontation, or by some alternative means that draw upon his cunning creativity.[42]

In the final section of "Os Quindins de Iayá," the *malandro* steals Iaiá's limelight by interrupting her samba party with a cortège of women, as if it is a carnival procession that is passing though the middle of the samba celebration. Although this procession is most likely used for plot advancement to move all of the characters from one location to another, it highlights a moment that provides a deeper reading of class and race within the Brazilian street carnival.

In his procession, the *malandro* is playing "Os Quindins de Iaiá," but he has transformed the musical style from a samba into a *marcha* (slow march). Therefore, he has taken her song, and by changing the vernacular, he is signifying a musical double entendre that can be projected onto hierarchical class struggles portrayed musically in the Brazilian street carnival. Through their direct association with the *marcha*, it can be discerned that the participants in the *malandro's* procession are of a higher class and are only dressed in *baiana*-style costumes for the carnival festivities. In contrast, it is firmly established that Disney's Iaiá is an "authentic" street vendor, who lives the life of the working-class *baiana*, not a carnival participant.

Prior to the 1850s, carnival in Brazil consisted of the *entrudo*, a free-for-all chaotic event in the streets, with men as the participants. Organized street processions developed over the next two decades, and in the early 1870s, the *rancho* (organized thematic procession) brought a sense of civility to the streets, modeled in the style of European parades. As a result of these more dignified forms of public expression, women began parading in 1873 (McGowan and Pessanha 1998:37). These parades featured the music of slow *marchas* (marches), and in 1899, the first piece of music composed specifically for the Brazilian street carnival was "O Abre Alas" by Chiquinha Gonzaga. Therefore, the *marcha* served to define a musical style for Brazil at a time when it was planting the seeds for the development of artistic nationalism that would not come to fruition until the development of the modern art movement in the early 1920s.

This brief sequence in *Three Caballeros* reveals class structure within the hierarchy of Brazilian musical expression. During carnival in Brazil, it is common to find both the samba and the *marcha* in public celebrations, but each genre represents a different stratum within Brazilian society. Whereas the samba is a physically energetic seductive dance, created and reproduced by a marginalized working class, the *marcha* is firmly entrenched as an expression of the middle classes. Anthropologist Roberto DaMatta compares the function of these two genres within Brazilian society. He believes that marches feature provocative physical expression, but in a much more restrained capacity:

Whereas samba is more danced than sung, the march is more spoken and sung than danced. In the march the lyrics are more important than the music because of the middle classes; in contrast, things are danced in the samba in a visceral, bodily way that is much more closely associated with the world of workers and the marginal members of the labor market, the former slaves. The march is the samba of the middle class, as it were . . . this is important, for it reveals the fascination of Brazilians with formalized modes of singing and dancing. . . . Alongside the music of the poor that is freer and made for dancing, we have a musical formula that allows us to harmonize the world in a more discreet, "spoken" way; its square, dry rhythms are more reminiscent of the large military corps. (DaMatta 1991:110 –11)

DaMatta believes that the public co-existence of these two genres promotes inclusion rather than exclusion of members from contrasting social classes. This blurring of social boundaries makes the *malandro's* actions even more intriguing, because through the process of parading in the middle of Iaiá's samba circle, he not only steals her limelight, but he also steals her musicians, who jump from the samba bandwagon to join in the new *marcha* celebration, leaving her alone. Donald Duck then comes to her rescue with a bouquet of flowers, followed by an international, inter-species exoticized kiss that launches into the final sequence of the montage, a samba fantasy that features dancing Brazilian musical instruments, live dancing sequences, allusions to *capoeira,* and an animated dancing city of Salvador, Bahia.

For North American audiences, this scene would read simply as a carnivalesque atmosphere, with an amorphous party moving from one location to another. Many Brazilians also would read this as a normal carnival-style occurrence. What is not accurate, however, is the use of the *baiana* figure dancing to a *marcha*. The music of the *marcha* was used to support the ambulant *ranchos,* which were modeled after high-society European parades. Therefore, no *baianas* were present in this genre. Also, since the figure of the *malandro* is from the samba culture that emerged in Rio de Janeiro, how has he appeared on the streets of Bahia? These two events demonstrate that Disney's vision of "Baía" has been constructed primarily of popular references from one location (Rio de Janeiro), and transplanted to another (Bahia).

Conclusion

The Three Caballeros is only one of many World War Two–era projects that were designed to promote positive relations between the United States and a potentially unified Latin America. Through the process of presenting an American "self" (Donald Duck) and his relationship to the "other" (Donald's interpretive hosts José Carioca and Panchito) as well as the "exoticized other" (all Latin-American women), Disney relied on the deconstruction of reality (as seen in the animated landscapes and cityscapes) and culture (presenting an all-white Bahia) that existed only on the screen. Animated fantasy is superimposed onto real images, such as when Donald, Panchito, and José are flying on a Mexican *serape* above the beaches of Acapulco, that are "inhabited by a remarkably homogenous species: all female, all shapely and fair-skinned, all apparently between the ages of eighteen and twenty-two" (Burton-Carvajal 1994:244), who are excited by Donald's magic carpet dive-bombing escapades. Perhaps this was a "good neighbor" message to Latin America that North Americans were not interested in taking over any countries, but they were definitely interested in the women. In the Brazil section, Disney and his staff created a glitzy Hollywood musical that drew from the spirit of songs that had enjoyed success in Brazilian society; however, most of the delicate phrases, concepts, and images evoked from the original texts were left behind on the cutting-room floor. Disney's image of Brazil was constructed in Rio de Janeiro and transposed onto the imaginary land of "Baía." Not only is Donald an outsider to this mysterious place, but his Brazilian guide, José Carioca, is as well.

This film is the result of an exchange of international conquests by Carmen Miranda and Donald Duck. Miranda spearheaded a "Latin" erotic invasion of United States popular culture, and in turn, Donald Duck celebrated his birthday by invading the Latin-American cultures that emerged from his birthday presents. Donald Duck was not just representative of an American citizen but he was also seen as an ambassador to Latin America, even being officially dubbed an "International Symbol of Good Will" in 1935 by the League of American Nations (Piedra 1994:155). Even though Carmen Miranda was seen by North Americans as an "authentic" Brazilian, she was born in Portugal and moved to Brazil at a young age, whereas her sister Aurora was actually born in Rio de Janeiro. Both singers enjoyed successful singing and recording careers in Brazil in the 1930s, but Carmen's career clearly moved into international realms following the development of the *baiana* motif in the film *Banana da Terra* (1938). In *The Three Caballeros*, Aurora did not play herself, but she reproduced an imitation of the character developed by her sister.

Through analysis of the music presented in *The Three Caballeros*, along with information that has emerged as a result of this exploration, new perspectives can be developed that further enhance interpretations of this film. For example, the exoticized *baiana* figure of Iaiá had undergone her own transformation in Brazilian popular music and culture, long before Donald Duck set his eyes on her. Iaiá's movement from a colonial-era daughter of a slave owner (or possibly an old nanny of African descent), to a seductive African-Brazilian woman, steeped in Bahian religious and culinary practices, demonstrates how a constructed identity can change over time. Iaiá as the *baiana* now plays a central role in perpetuating Bahia's mystical charms of calling to outsiders (within and beyond the country's borders) to come and visit essences of Africa in Bahia.

However, in Disney's presentation, we see a Bahia that is nearly devoid of African culture, sung and danced by musicians with light complexions and spiced with a few unexplained references to Bahian cuisine. Disney also has removed or reduced lyrics that warn against the dangers of pursuing relationships with an exoticized other. For example, in the original version of "Na Baixa do Sapateiro," the lyrics caution that if you eat exotic fruit, you will be poisoned and undergo eternal suffering. This suggestion parallels Sansone's discussion of how Bahian food (and references to African-Brazilian culture) initially was excluded, and then incorporated with limitations into the national Brazilian cuisine of the middle and upper classes (1999). Disney avoids this debate altogether and romanticizes the exotic gaze without dangers of indigestion. As a result, the revised English lyrics of "Baía" are more representative of Disney's trademark song, "When You Wish Upon a Star."

Brazil's exotic gaze has been reinforced through the use of brilliant color in the international cinema. Perhaps this image has been derived from the landscape that has been incorporated into Brazilian society. From explosively colorful flora and fauna, to the colonial-era painted buildings of Salvador, to the annual carnival costumes and floats, Brazil is an ambulant tapestry that lives in Technicolor. In fact, Salvador itself has undergone an image transformation in recent decades in order to accommodate the nationally and internationally promoted mystical aura of Bahia. In 1985, Salvador's Pelourinho district was declared a UNESCO world heritage site, a move that completely revitalized the city's historic center during the mid- to late 1990s. Streets that were shrouded in darkness in the early 1990s have now become popular nocturnal tourist attractions, accompanied by well-lit streets and a healthy security presence, as if this marginalized district had instantaneously become an extension of Disney's EPCOT global village theme park.[43]

The Three Caballeros was clearly part of Disney's experiences resulting from his three expeditions to Brazil. Although Hollywood was moving toward incorporating African-American roles and themes into mainstream productions in the early 1940s, one can only wonder if Disney's exposure to Afro-Brazilian culture inspired him to explore the music and folktales from African-American culture in the United States. Disney's Uncle Remus stories appeared on the big screen in *Song of the South* (1946), just one year following the release of *The Three Caballeros*. Regardless of the success or authenticity of Disney's wartime animated features, the long-term impact of these films continues to be felt in Brazil, where newsstands regularly sell newly published adventures of Pato Donald (Donald Duck) and Zé Carioca.

Notes

1. *The Three Caballeros* was released in Brazil under the title "*Você Já Foi À Bahia?*" ["Have You Been to Bahia?"]. There is a long-standing tradition in Brazil to re-title foreign films, including *Saludos Amigos* (1943) that was released under the Portuguese title, *Alô Amigos*. Although *The Three Caballeros* takes place in several South American locations, this chapter focuses specifically on Disney's portrayal of Brazil. Special thanks to Vincenzo Cambria, Luiz D'Anunciação, and Evanira Mendes Birdman for clarification of terms.

2. Incidentally, José Carioca was named after José, Disney's personal guide during his visit to Rio (*Three Caballeros* laserdisc edition 1991).

3. See Burton-Carvajal (1994) and Piedra (1994).

4. These terms are discussed in more detail below.

5. Although Bahia is the name for the state, the city of Salvador is also frequently referred to as Bahia.

6. See Stam (1997) for discussion on the portrayal of race in Brazilian and internationally produced films.

7. See Frazier (1942, 1943) and Herskovits (1943).

8. Candomblé is a religious practice that has developed from a mixture of influences from several African cultural groups (Yoruba, Fon, Bantú), popular Catholicism, and Brazilian indigenous cultural elements.

9. Much of this "superficial gaze" has been constructed by entities interested in promoting an authentic African culture in the Americas, such as tourist organizations and by social scientists (i.e., the 1940s Frazier/Herskovits debate previously cited).

10. This topic has been explored extensively elsewhere. See, for example, Clark (2002), Coelho (1998) and O'Neil (2005).

11. *The Three Caballeros; Saludos Amigos* laserdisc released in 1991 features all three Disney films referenced in this project, along with related information including the Disney South America travel agenda, copies of original artwork, and multimedia footage from newsreels, radio, and television shows of the era.

12. Disney denied having taken any money from the State Department due to the commercial success of *Saludos Amigos*. He claims to have "almost needed the subsidy" during the latter production stages of *The Three Caballeros*. The Brazil portion of Disney's trip lasted between August 18 and September 7, 1941. The official agenda included exploring the city and culture, making public appearances including radio broadcasts, recording regional music, and attending premieres of Disney's film, *Fantasia* (*Three Caballeros* laserdisc 1991).

13. "Zé" is a nickname derived from José. *Carioca* refers to an individual who is born and raised in Rio de Janeiro, and enjoys a relaxed lifestyle associated with living near the beach.

14. Disney does not use the full title of this composition, "Aquarela do Brasil." Barroso's first name is also often spelled Ary.

15. For an extensive discussion on the development of African-American characters in North American cinema up to the 1940s, see Cripps (1977), and from the 1940s through the 1960s, see Cripps (1993).

16. Tambourine: double-bell and small frame drum.

17. Carmen served as "technical advisor" for *Saludos Amigos* (*Three Caballeros* laserdisc 1991).

18. Disney never uses the proper spelling of "Bahia." For example, a geographical map, a sign at a train station and the actual song are all errantly spelled "Baía."

19. If this music is modeled in the style of a *choro* composition, it does not adequately represent the genre. *Choro* music is an urban instrumental art form that developed in Rio de Janeiro in the early twentieth century. The presence of conventional *choro* instrumentation, such as guitar, flute and *pandeiro* (tambourine) suggests the *choro* style, but this piece does not fully capture this complex musical tradition. For example, the *choro* composition "Tico-Tico na Fubá" [Crown Sparrow in the Corn Meal] by Zequinha de Abreu (composed in 1917 under a similar title, and recorded many times in the early to mid-1940s) may have influenced Disney. José Carioca quotes the title of this song toward the end of the Brazil segment.

20. A samba beat is constructed by alternating a light and heavy beat, with corresponding polyrhythms that pull against and resolve around these principal beats.

21. Another allusion to a musical-style interlude follows this conclusion, when Donald attempts to open his final present. Since José had reduced Donald to a small size, in order to enter the book, Donald had to find a way to return to his normal size. José said that all he needed was a little "black magic," thus reinforcing Hollywood stereotypes of African-derived religious practices. As if presenting a magic show, Carioca shows his sleeves are empty, and then launches into an untranslated, rhythmically spoken verse based loosely on lyrics of other songs that were popular in the era: "Balacubaco, tear the shreds of a vulture / A duck's foot mixed with bamboo / It would be "Tico Tico na fubá" [crown sparrow in the cornmeal] / "Tico tico," powder of a monkey / I want to see what will happen."

22. Caymmi was born and raised in Bahia, and moved to Rio de Janeiro to establish his career.

23. The title refers to a street in Salvador that bears the official name "Rua Dr. J.J. Seabra," and is popularly referred to "Baixa dos Sapateiros"[Shoemakers at the bottom of the hill] (Severiano and Mello 1999:166).

24. "Na Baixa do Sapateiro" is Barroso's second-most widely recorded work. His most popular song is "Aquarela do Brasil," which was featured in Disney's *Saludos Amigos* (1941).

25. My interpretation of eternal suffering is in reference to longing for an unobtainable "other." All translations of Portuguese lyrics and text are by Eric Galm; the original Portuguese is not included due to permission issues. Song texts about marginalized Afro-Brazilian cultures often tend to feature contractions of Portuguese words to imply a regionalized and/or an uneducated flavor. The song lyrics can be found in recently produced songbooks and other published sources.

26. *Moreno* is an ambiguous term that is used to evade discussions of race, and refers to many subtle physical characteristics that transcend skin color. These specifics may vary depending on context. See for example, Maggie and Rezende (2002). In Salvador, Nosso Senhor do Bonfim (Our Lord of Good Ending) is the patron of the city. For many Bahians, Senhor do Bonfim simultaneously represents Jesus Christ and the Yorubá deity, Oxalá. This connection is reinforced on the third Thursday of every month, when a procession of *baianas* performs a Candomblé-derived ceremony of washing the Bonfim church steps with special flowers, herbs, and oils. Mascarenhas (1982:207) cites the lyrics *"arranje um moreno igualzinho prá mim"* ["find another *moreno* just like that one for me"].

27. Since Carmen Miranda recorded the original version of this song, it is possible that the original lyrics feature the masculine Moreno, and the version changes when a male singer is delivering the song.

28. Ray Gilbert also penned the lyrics to this film's title song, "Zip-a-dee-doo-dah."

29. The "Musical Numbers" section of the opening credits only lists "Baía" and "Os Quindins de Iayá," attributed to Ari Barroso.

30. *Vatapá* is a food made from shrimp, coconut milk, palm oil, peanuts, and cashews, said to be a favorite food of certain deities (Cacciatore 1988:245). *Carurú* is made with okra, shrimp, and peanuts, and is a favorite food of the deities Xangô, Obá, and Iansã (ibid.). *Munguzá* is made from dried white corn, cooked in coconut milk and seasoned with sugar and cinnamon. This is a favorite food of the deities Oxalá and Nanã (ibid.:141). In the original version of this song, all of the responses for Donald Duck's portion are "*então vá!*" ["then let's go!"].

31. *Negro* is a Portuguese term that is generally accepted as a self-classification among some Afro-Brazilians, but it also has a negative historical connotation depending upon the context in which it is used.

32. Disney and Mascarenhas (1982) spelled this name as Yayá, however other Brazilian music sources (Lisboa Junior 1990; Severiano and Mello 1997; and Marcondes 2000) cited "Iaiá." I use the term "Iaiá" for consistency, except when citing lyrics.

33. *Quindins* are large, macaroon-style cookies made from coconut, sugar, and egg yolks.

34. Daisy Duck (Donald's significant other) is mysteriously absent from this film, thus enabling Donald to pursue Latin-American women at will. While this promotes stereotypes of North American men going abroad in search of licentious experiences, it is not a unique situation. There is a long-established tradition in American popular music in songs about American men pursuing women in Asia, Japan, and Europe, where the "girl back home" is distinctly absent (see Lancefield 2005).

35. "Cumé" could also possibly be a contraction of "como é" ("how it is"). These verses of "Os Quindins de Iaiá" are from Mascarenhas 1982, IV:65.

36. The dialect of the orange vendor is a style of Portuguese from Portugal instead of Brazilian Portuguese—he is the only individual in the Brazil segment who speaks in this manner.

37. Also spelled *iáiá* and *iôiô*.

38. Another term that bears mention is "*Iabá*," which refers to the "chief of the ritual kitchen of the *orixás*" (Cacciatore 1988:138). Yet another possible origin of the term Iaiá is in reference to an old woman of African descent who was the nanny or caretaker of the slave owner's children (Luiz D'Anunciação, telephone interview with the author, September 10, 2005).

39. These lyrics are only a small sample of references to Iaiá in the lyrics of popular Brazilian music in the first half of the twentieth century (Lisboa 1990:36).

40. *Doce de coco* is a sweetened coconut dessert. See the translation for *munguzá* in "Você Já Foi À Bahia?" listed above. *Cuscus* is a sweetened coconut and tapioca dessert. This excerpt from "O Coco de Iaiá" is from Lisboa Junior 1990:42.

41. The lyrics from "Sinhô do Bonfim" are from Lisboa Junior 1990:49.

42. Femininity also could be invoked as one of the malandro's tools of deception; therefore, this trickster could also play that role to perfection (D'Anunciação, personal communication, 2005).

43. This was also assisted by a musical renaissance in Bahia in which portions of the music recording industry were transferred away from the centers of Rio de Janeiro and São Paulo (see Perrone and Dunn 2002).

Works Cited

Burton-Carvajal, Julianne. 1994. "'Surprise Package:' Looking Southward with Disney." In *Disney Discourse: Producing the Magic Kingdom*, ed. Eric Smoodin. New York and London: Routledge, 131–47.

Cacciatore, Olga Gudolle. 1988. *Dicionário de Cultos Afro-Brasileiros*. 3rd ed. Rio de Janeiro: Forense Universitária. Orig. pub. 1977.

Clark, Walter Aaron. 2002. "Doing the Samba on Sunset Boulevard: Carmen Miranda and the Hollywoodization of American Music." In *From Tejano to Tango*, ed. Walter Aaron Clark. New York and London: Routledge, 252–76.

Coelho, José Ligiéro. 1998. "Carmen Miranda: An Afro-Brazilian Paradox." Ph.D. Dissertation, New York University.

Cripps, Thomas. 1993. *Making Movies Black: The Hollywood Message Movie from World War II to the Civil Rights Era*. New York and Oxford: Oxford University Press.

———. 1977. *Slow Fade to Black: The Negro in American Film, 1900–1942*. New York: Oxford University Press.

DaMatta, Roberto, C. 1991. *Carnivals, Rogues, and Heroes: An Interpretation of the Brazilian Dilemma*. Trans. by John Drury. Notre Dame: University of Notre Dame Press.

Frazier, E. Franklin. 1943. "Rejoinder." *American Sociological Review* 8, no. 4:402–405.

———. 1942. "The Negro Family in Bahia, Brazil." *American Sociological Review* 7, no. 4:465–78.

Herskovits, Melville J. 1943. "The Negro in Bahia, Brazil: A Problem in Method." *American Sociological Review* 8, no. 4:394–402.

Lancefield, Robert Charles. 2005. "Hearing Orientality in (White) America, 1900–1930." Ph.D. Dissertation, Wesleyan University.

Lewis, John Lowell. 1992. *Rings of Liberation*. Chicago: University of Chicago Press.

Lisboa Junior, Luiz Americo. 1990. *A Presença da Bahia na Música Popular Brasileira*. Brasília: MusiMed/Linha Gráfica Editora.

Maggie, Yvonne, and Claudia Barcellos Rezende, eds. 2002. *Raça como retórica: A construção da diferença*. Rio de Janeiro: Civilização Brasileira.

Marcondes, Marcos Antônio, ed. 2000. *Enciclopédia da Música Brasileira: Popular, Erudita e Folclórica*. 3rd ed. São Paulo: Art Editora/Publifolha.

Mascarenhas, Mário. 1982. "Os Quindins de Yayá." In *O Melhor da Música Popular Brasileira*. Rio de Janeiro and São Paulo: Irmãos Vitale Editores (IV):65.

McGowan, Chris, and Ricardo Pessanha. 1998. *The Brazilian Sound: Samba, Bossa Nova and the Popular Music of Brazil*. Philadelphia: Temple University Press, New Edition.

O'Neil, Brian. 2005. "Carmen Miranda: The High Price of Fame and Bananas." In *Latina Legacies: Identity, Biography, and Community*. New York: Oxford University Press, 193–208.

Perrone, Charles A., and Christopher Dunn, eds. 2002. *Brazilian Popular Music and Globalization*. New York and London: Routledge.

Piedra, José. 1994. "Pato Donald's Gender Ducking." *In Disney Discourse: Producing the Magic Kingdom*, ed. Eric Smoodin. New York and London: Routledge, 148–68.

Sansone, Livio. 1999. *From Africa to Afro: Use and Abuse of Africa in Brazil*. Amsterdam and Dakar: Sephis-Codesria.

Seeger, Charles. 1941. "Music for Uniting the Americas." *Music Educators Journal* 27, No. 6:12.

Severiano, Jario, and Zuza Homem de Mello. 1999. *A Canção no Tempo: 85 Anos de Músicas Brasileiras.* 4th ed. São Paulo: Editora 34. Orig. pub. 1997.

Stam, Robert. 1997. *Tropical Multiculturalism: A Comparative History of Race in Brazilian Cinema and Culture.* Durham and London: Duke University Press.

Videography

Carmen Miranda: Bananas Is My Business, 1996. Helena Solberg and David Meyer. Orig. pub. 1994.

Saludos Amigos, 1943. Walt Disney Productions.

Song of the South, 1946. Walt Disney Productions.

South of the Border with Disney, 1941. Walt Disney Productions.

The Three Caballeros, 1945. Walt Disney Productions.

The Three Caballeros; Saludos Amigos, 1991. Walt Disney Productions (laserdisc edition).

BRENDA F. BERRIAN

Diversity and Orality in Euzhan Palcy's La Rue cases-nègres

·◉·

During the mid-twentieth century, the cinema of Martinique and Guade-loupe, also known as *le cinéma antillais,* originated in Paris, France, where many of the film directors still live, study, and practice their craft as a prod-uct of the political and economic dependence between France and its over-seas departments and territories.[1] Until the present day, neither a special-ized school of film studies nor a Department of Film Studies exists on the campuses of the Université des Antilles et de la Guyane in Martinique, Guadeloupe, and French Guyane. Thus, at the end of the 1960s, the then-young Guadeloupean filmmakers—Christian Lara, Jacques Ferly, and Ga-briel Glissant—partially chose to make short films about migration and dis-placement and the effects of colonialism.

Lara, a former journalist, began his film career by representing France at the Cannes Film Festival of 1968 with *Lorsque l'herbe* [When the Grass], which criticized the replacement of field laborers with agricultural machines. This auspicious debut was followed in 1969 by *Les Stabiles* [The Stabilizers], another short documentary, at the biannual *Journées Cinématographiques de Carthage* (JCC) in Tunis, Tunisia, North Africa. Despite the showing of the documentaries at two major international film festivals, Lara really caused a stir in 1978 with *Coco la fleur, candidat* [Coco the Flower, Candidate], a 90-minute feature in Creole with French subtitles about a man who only enters electoral politics as a puppet. Yet, as soon as he discovers how much publicity the campaign will generate, he voices the disenfranchised people's concerns. Although the subject matter and the use of Creole for the first time in a Gua-deloupean movie titillated the French Caribbean audience's imagination, the 1980 controversial *Vivre ou mourir libre* [Live Free or Die] stirred up a nationalistic fervor by paying tribute to the mulatto Colonel Louis Delgrès, an opponent of the restoration of slavery and the reoccupation of Guadeloupe by Napoleonic France, who committed suicide rather than risk being captured and killed by General Richepanse's troops in May 1802.

Also interested in history and politics, Jacques Ferly, who did his professional training at the Institut de la Formation Cinématographique, terminated his studies with the 1971 *Chronique d'un retour* [Chronicle of a Return], a 20-minute black-and-white short about a disillusioned Guadeloupean who leaves France to return to his country of birth. Some of his other shorts were the 1976 20-minute, 16-mm *Liberté coupée* [Brief Freedom]; the 1977 25-minute, 16-mm black-and-white *Tambour long et joli son* [Long Drum and Pretty Sound]; and the 1981 25-minute, 16-mm color *La Charpente marine* [The Marina Construction].

Then, in 1972, Gabriel Glissant, a graduate of the Institut des Hautes Etudes Cinématographiques (IDHEC), an actor and a sound-and-light technician, released *Le Pion* [The Pawn], a 30-minute film about a Caribbean immigrant who remains in France. His next venture, *La Machete et le marteau* [The Machete and the Hammer], co-produced with Jean-Serge Breton for Z-Productions, the first film production company in the French Caribbean, was a 70-minute, 16-mm movie that examines the ambiguous colonial state of Guadeloupe during the 1970s.

After the appearance of these films and others by Caribbean directors in Paris, history was made in the emerging French Caribbean cinema with the 1983 release of *La Rue cases-nègres*, the first feature film made by then-twenty-two-year-old Euzhan Palcy of Martinique.[2] At the age of fourteen, Palcy was already tired of seeing "stupid portrayals of Black people in American movies" (Glicksman 1989:65). When her mother gave her Joseph Zobel's *La Rue cases-nègres* (translated into English under the title *Black Shack Alley*, but changed to *Sugar Cane Alley* for the American film release), she eagerly read the novel, which reflected her daily reality. Three years later, at age seventeen, she wrote the first draft of the script based on the book. In her mind, it was urgent for her to make a movie of the story. As Palcy states, "It was the first time that I had read a novel by a black man, a black of my country, a black who was speaking about poor people. In school, we never read or studied black authors. All our books were written by white Frenchmen" (Linfield 1984:43).

Zobel had written an autobiographical novel about a segment of the French Caribbean population that largely had been ignored: the Black sugar-cane laborers on whom the French colonials depended to enrich themselves under slavery and colonialism. They were also the people who benefitted the least from the effects of their physical labor. Fully aware of these facts, and desiring to be a film director, Palcy went to Paris in 1975 to earn a degree in film at the renowned Ecole Nationale Supérieure Louis Lumière and a degree in theater and French literature at the Sorbonne. While there, she established contact with Zobel and received his moral support for the making of the film.[3] Then Palcy completed the second draft of the script, for which she won a 1981 French government grant from the *Centre National du Cinéma* (CNC) for the best script to do the film.

To finance the film, Palcy drew upon this support of the $800,000 French grant. When she was about $7,000 short to complete the production of the film, Palcy approached Aimé Césaire, then mayor of Fort-de-France (Martinique), for help. Césaire, in turn, had the Fort-de-France City Council vote the sum of approximately $7,000 to help Palcy complete the film (Givanni 1992:295). When asked about the Council's decision, Césaire replied, "We thought that Euzhan Palcy's film was a national Martiniquan film that needed and absolutely deserved our support. We are glad that we were able to provide that kind of support. This kind of help, however, is not institutionalized. We are only a municipality, a city with a limited budget" (Sephocle 1992:365–66). With regards to his personal feelings about films, Césaire added, "through cinema, I believe Antilleans will gain self-assurance and comfort" (ibid. 360). To clarify his position, Césaire continued, "What we have suffered from the most, more than any other people, is really alienation. In other words, the lack of knowledge of one's self. This seems fundamental to me. The Antillean being is a human being who is deprived of his own self, of his history, of his traditions, of his beliefs. In a nutshell, he is an abandoned being" (ibid. 380). Other monetary subsidies were forthcoming from the French director François Truffaut and two young French producers.

Both Zobel's novel and Palcy's film adaptation give voice to the cane-cutters and their progeny. In the film, Palcy provides a historical re-reading of Martinican history while exploring relations between cultural and racial identity and memory. The dehumanizing effects of colonization, the quest for an education and the sacrifices of the matriarch are highlighted along with the efforts of the cane-cutters to preserve their freedom and dignity. *La Rue cases-nègres,* set in Martinique of the 1930s, is the story of José Hassam, a boy reared by his grandmother in the Black shack alleys of a sugarcane plantation in the southern part of the island. A loving but sometimes short-tempered woman, Amantine, who is affectionately called "M'man Tine," wants her grandson to obtain the education that neither she nor her late daughter (José's mother) were able to acquire so that he will be able to elevate himself from their wretched living conditions. She makes numerous sacrifices to ensure that her grandson will succeed, even moving to Fort-de-France, a city she dislikes, to supplement the partial scholarship that José has received to attend high school. The subplots include the deep bond between José and M'man Tine; his love for his mentor, the elderly man M. Médouze; a friendship with Léopold, a mulatto classmate; and a tutorial relationship with Carmen, a young man who aspires to be an actor.

Palcy's writing of a script that made her feel comfortable was not an easy task. She found it to be more difficult "to adapt a book to film than to write an original story" (Givanni 1992:298). Regardless, in her dual roles as screenwriter and director, Palcy wrote and directed a faithful interpretation of the book. However, because she took liberties by modifying the plot and characters and inserting rural and urban musical forms to pinpoint diversity, the film artistically stands on its own terms. For instance, Palcy omits Délia (José's mother) in order to idealize M'man Tine, giving the film a strong matriarchal slant. Adamant about José's not working in the cane fields like the other Black children, M'man Tine influences and instills in her grandson specific values to succeed. The energy required to raise *un enfant naturel* (a child with an absent father) is validated through M'man Tine's character, who selflessly works night and day to get her grandson out of poverty. "Mothers," remarked Césaire, Martinique's most renowned poet, statesman and playwright, "are the origin of most of our Martiniquan families . . . [Mothers] are the ones who sustain our families" (Sephocle 1992:364).

In the 1930s, many single women had to raise their children. If it were not possible for them to fulfill the caretaker's role, the grandmothers inherited the children. In tribute to these women, Palcy devotes the first scene of *La Rue cases-nègres* to the pipe-smoking M'man Tine, who is wonderfully played by Darling Légitimus.[4] Clad in a worn dress, M'man Tine appears with her hair covered by a madras scarf. One of her shoulders supports the hoe that she will use in the cane fields. After accepting her grandson's goodbye kiss, she issues instructions about the maintenance of their shack during her absence. When she reappears at the end of the work day, M'man Tine, now exhausted, has barely enough energy to acknowledge her neighbors' friendly greetings or to accept José's welcoming kiss. Muttering and humming to herself, the strict disciplinarian speaks in a harsh tone to José and strikes him when she notes that her precious sugar bowl, a gift from her deceased daughter and José's mother, has been broken. "Women in Martinique," Palcy explains, "are very kind, very lovely. But they are proud, very strong, very hard. They don't let you *see* their tenderness" (Linfield 1984:44). Despite M'man Tine's harshness and infrequent display of affectionate gestures, she has a deep love for José, who, in turn, loves her dearly and vows to take care of her when she becomes sick.

Palcy's decision to transfer some of Délia's characteristics into M'man Tine and to change the structure from three to two parts are two more modifications of the book. The first segment of the movie focuses on José's life from age five to seven with his grandmother on the *habitation* (plantation). The boy spends a carefree vacation with his playmates and is also the receiver of oral history lessons from his spiritual mentor, M. Médouze, until the old man's death halfway through the movie. The second segment covers major events from the final two parts of the book, focusing on José's primary school years and his first year of high school. Whereas José and his classmates are encouraged to do well by their upper primary school teacher in Petit-Bourg, the nearby village to the plantation, José encounters an indifference from the teachers at the high school in Fort-de-France. Moreover, through the telling of José's story and the shifting between orality and music, Palcy highlights the importance of the spoken word, the acquisition of an education, and the diversity of musical choices in rural and urban Martinique. And this explains why separate sections are devoted to these topics within this chapter.

In the beginning, the sugar-cane estate, with its fruit trees, animals, and river, is a source of delight for the children. In his role as José, Garry Cadenat announces in his first voice-over narration that he and his playmates are the masters of their freedom while they play in the Black shack alleys without adult supervision.[5] Their universe is one of innocence, tempered by harshness and amusement. They rejoice in raiding birds' nests, watching a mongoose fighting a snake, and nailing lizards to fences. Forgetful about possible parental punishment, and in an attempt to assuage a constant hunger, the children ransack Jose's shack for a hidden bowl of sugar, eventually breaking the bowl and then setting fire to Julien-douze-orteils' garden. The aftermath of the fire brings their wonderful vacation to an abrupt end, with the mulatto overseer decreeing that they must work in the cane fields with their parents. Henceforth, their childhood is cut short; their innocence gradually disappears; and they become part of the poor, dependent labor force.

The Spoken Word

José is the only child among his friends to escape working in the cane fields. During the interim between his summer vacation and the primary school year, José often visits his elderly neighbor, M. Médouze, who teaches him historical lessons about the past and philosophical lessons about the creation. Son of a father who had been transported from Guinea, West Africa, to Martinique, M. Médouze personifies the African elder in his demeanor, choice of clothing, and manner of speech. Walking as erect as he can with the aid of a walking stick, the bare-chested M. Médouze is only garbed in an earth-toned loincloth, signifying that he lives in harmony with nature. For Palcy, he is the Black Christ because he is thin, sleeps on a wooden plank, and looks like a crucified Jesus (Mbouguen 2001). Yet, using the natural environment as his open classroom, the proud M. Médouze engages in nocturnal and daytime verbal exchanges with José, his *protégé,* by relating riddles and speaking in parables.

In one of the film's longest scenes, an evening lesson occurs at the end of a disappointing payday for the cane-cutters. While the cane-cutters seek a release from their frustrations by dancing, singing, and playing the *bèlè* drums, M. Médouze, in an effort to define José's Black identity, teaches him about the cultural identity of Martinique. M. Médouze recounts tales told to him by his African father. The *vieux couper* (the old cane-cutter), for instance, tells José how his own father and other slaves had organized the 21–22 May 1848 rebellion on the plantations of Saint Pierre, only to find themselves working again for the whites a few years later. After the official abolishment of slavery, M. Médouze declares in his late father's voice, "We were free, but we had empty bellies. The whites had all the land. The law forbade them to beat us, but it didn't make them pay us enough to live on."[6] M. Médouze's verbal lesson informs José about the past and present socio-economic realities of his island.[7] As a consequence, José repeatedly falls under the spell of M. Médouze, who uses metaphor and imagery to delight his young listener.

The duality of formal and informal education defines the film's foundation because José is culturally torn between the power of the spoken word and that of the written word. However, the two contrasting forms of education contribute to the creation of his autonomous self. By studying at the colonial French school, José learns how to read and write, but his subject lessons are narrowly focused only on the mother country, that is French history, French geography, French culture, and French literature. These lessons are not as exciting as the ones with M. Médouze. By studying with M. Médouze who functions like an African *griot* (an oral historian), José is exposed to the digressive narrative style of the oral traditions. M. Médouze transmits communal values and the collective memory and history of Martinique. In addition, M. Médouze uses what Raphaël Confiant calls diurnal speech, the speech of the *griot,* to recite the history of slavery, but he mainly prefers nocturnal speech, which is characteristic of an oral storyteller (Confiant 1991:55–62).

In broad daylight, the two sit down in a lush, green field where they hear the sounds stirred by a balmy breeze and those of chirping birds. Their act of sitting on the earth coincides with M. Médouze's story about the creation and the secret of life. The old man tells José, "Don't think that water and fire are enemies . . . No! They are the forces of creation. Each needs the other to create life." The direct overhead sun beams down on them while their bodies become one with nature. M. Médouze's eloquence captivates José as he discusses the creation. In African cosmology, the spoken word is a living force. As noted by Sylvia Washington Bâ, "the Being is force. Thus life force is conceived of as extending beyond the human influence to the natural environment" (1973:46).

Later on, the awestruck José will find out that neither M. Médouze's version of the creation nor his history of Black resistance to slavery will be taught in the French colonial classroom. In a systematic fashion and through legislation and colonialism, as described by Frantz Fanon, the French colonial government is "not simply content to impose its rule upon the present and the future . . . By a kind of perverted logic, it turns to the past of the oppressed people, and distorts, disfigures, and destroys it" (Fanon 1961:210). Knowing this and having attended French schools herself, Palcy strongly believes that the elderly, represented by M. Médouze and M'man Tine, are the true guardians of her people's memories to pass on cultural beliefs to the youth. Relying on her personal belief and knowing that the *griot's* function in African society is to pass down historical lessons, Palcy wisely chose the Senegalese actor, Douta Seck, to play M. Médouze with great dignity.[8]

Garry Cadenat does likewise in his role as José. For example, during a classroom scene about a vocabulary lesson, José displays his virtuosity with verbal aesthetics. When asked by his upper primary teacher to differentiate between cackling and singing, his face lights up as soon as he figures it out. Having absorbed M. Médouze's teaching, José is perceptive enough to compare the relationships between human beings and their singing to those of animal noises and nature. José points out how the word "sing" is used for people when they express music. He also mentions how much his grandmother enjoys smoking her pipe and singing. Then he speaks about the way the hen cackles after she lays an egg. His imaginative and poetic way of talking impresses M. Roc so much that the teacher encourages José to compete for a scholarship to study at the *lycée* (high school) in Fort-de-France.

Bèlè *and Other Rural Music*

The rural repertoire of *bèlè* drumming originates from African customs and represents the powerful contribution that the enslaved ancestors have made to the specificity of French Caribbean identity. In fact, the Martinican *tambou bèlè* originates from the ancient Fon of Dahomey (now called Benin). This drum was carried to the Caribbean by the Africans on the slave ships. Others were made after the Africans' arrival in Martinique to use for festive and religious occasions or for funerals. The rhythms emitted from the drum cast a spell upon its listeners and produced spontaneous dance movements. Concerned about this spiritual awakening, which was anathema to their religion of Catholicism, and wanting to counteract the effect and power of the drum, the colonial French government officials, plantation owners, and Catholic priests led a campaign to construct a negative image of traditional African culture among the African slaves (Berrian 2000:209). As early as 1654, an ordinance was passed forbidding song and dance gatherings once it was learned that the drum was a form of communication. In 1685, the article to the *Code Noir* extended the ban to all French colonies. It was common to flog with whips slaves who were caught playing the drum or to brand them with the *fleur-de-lis*.

To avoid punishment, the cane-cutters resort to the playing of the *bèlè lisid* drum and the *ti bwa* (two hard wooden sticks used to mark the rhythm) on weekends and in the evening. It is through music, dancing, and songs that they communicate their resistance to being dehumanized and poorly paid. In a 1989 interview, Palcy stated, "The best, most deeply felt music, in 90 percent of the cases, comes from countries where this is the only solution to express the people's suffering" (Aufderheide 1989:31). In Palcy's film, after open confrontations between the workers and the management on payday, the *bèlè* drum is summoned to call the spirits for help. Drinking rum while sitting around the fire, the men sing and dance the *ladja* (the battle dance), so common among the folk dances in the south of Martinique. The *ladja* is composed of four elements: the single soloist, the dancers, the drum, and the *ti bwa*. The highly acrobatic fight-dance is performed by two men to the sound of the drum. The *kriyé* (soloist) and the chorus sing in reponsorial style while the skilled drummer follows closely each of the dancer's movements. Since some of the cane-cutters already had engaged unsuccessfully in verbal exchanges with the *gerec* (overseer) about their meager wages, they dance the *ladja* while Julien-douze-orteils' voice soars in the night, forging a relationship among the cane-cutters and the ancestors, whose spirits are in the air and in the ground. The soloist turns words into a living force, establishing an organic relationship between the *bèlè* drumming and himself. Along with the interactive drumming, dancing, singing, and the call-and-response among the cane-cutters, Julien-douze-orteils also sings almost at full volume, almost at the top of his voice, until his voice becomes incantatory.

Quite fittingly, Eugène Mona, the singer and flutist who plays Julien-douze-orteils, was a spiritual man aligned to the earth.[9] For him, music existed as a companion to natural impulse and the emotions expressed in his voice dictated the rhythm (Berrian 2000:120). In an earlier scene, when the cane-cutter Ti Coco was chastised by the overseer for urinating in the fields during working hours and fined fifteen cents for being lazy, Julien-douze-orteils observes the exchange. After realizing that Ti Coco was not viewed as a man but as a beast, Julien-douze-orteils sarcastically sings in a rough timbre of voice: "Whitey's in his easy chair / Black man burns in the sun / Ti Coco pisses / Boss man comes along." By giving voice to the injustice and pointing out grievances of the oppressed, protest singing is used as a psychological and physical strategy of resistance, particularly when Julien-douze-orteils and the other workers mock and ridicule the overseers. Their zombification of intense and repetitive physical labor is temporarily halted. When they sing in call-and-response during the harvest, they simultaneously move and sing at a faster pace to earn more money for their labor.

The ritual *ladja* in which the men engage at nightfall resembles the Afro-Brazilian art of *capoeira* (a fight for the liberation of Blacks and a reaffirmation of Black identity).With the *ladja* dancing and singing in the background, M. Médouze tells José about his impending death:

> When I will be dead,
> When my old body is buried,
> Then I'll go to Africa,
> But I can't take you along.
> We'll all go back to Africa one day.
> Don't you worry.

As soon as he makes this announcement, the drums' rhythms rise in tempo and the dancers go into a frenzy, Shortly thereafter, José find M. Médouze alone and dead in the canefields. Since custom dictates that the deceased Médouze be integrated and absorbed into the spiritual world, the cane-cutters gather for a wake outside his shack while the bereaved José sits inside next to M. Médouze, who is laid out on his wooden plank. Having no living family members, M. Médouze is represented by José as a de facto grandson, and a few yards away, men and women sing and listen to tales about the deceased by another cane-cutter M. Saint-Louis.

With the exception of José, who is a child, M. Médouze's death is marked by the adults with happiness and celebration, not nostalgia and sadness.[10] To accomplish M. Médouze's wish to return to Africa, his fellow workers oblige by helping him through the transition from the visible into the invisible world. Through the *bèlè* rhythms that invigorate a spiritual link to Africa and the communal dancing within a circle, the mounting tension and the urgency of the journey are expressed rhythmically. To prepare the ancestral spirits for M. Médouze's arrival, M. Saint-Louis, played by the *parolier* Joby Bernabé, skillfully arouses the crowd.[11] His recitation, in a call-and-response style, is accompanied by the *bèlè* drums and the *ti bwa*.

For those who did not hear the *lambi* [conch shell], the *bèlè* drums are played to bring them to the central meeting place.[12] Once the people are assembled, the formulaic ritual storytelling interjection of "Hé cric" and the response "Hé crac" are uttered to set the stage for M. Saint-Louis, who addresses his neighbors with the following observations:

> Ladies and gentlemen.
> The cane fields ate Monsieur Médouze's life.
> So he went to die in the cane fields.
> He laid down his hide and his old opossum's bones.
> May his soul rest in peace in all the days to come.
> Always, for time immemorial. Amen!

The wake song is a connection between music and spiritual consciousness. With his chant, rhythm, and refrains, M. Saint-Louis encourages his people to give the words *un sens inoui* [an extraordinary sound]. Celebrating the communion of man with nature, he also reflects upon human spiritual identity by using his voice with the intonation of two *bèlè* drums. M. Saint-Louis' role as the storyteller is therefore integral to the existence of the community and to the relationship between the living and the dead. Most of all, M. Médouze's spirit is channeled through the singers and the storyteller M. Saint-Louis to help his transition to Africa.

In addition to the *bèlè*, the sound of the flute is heard more than once among the Black shack alleys. The first time the *toutoun-bamboo* [bamboo flute] enters the soundscape is when the weary cane-cutters straggle home after a long day of work. The sky is reddened by the moon; the stars are beginning to twinkle; and a slow, drawling melancholy tone comes forth from the flute. The next time the flute is heard is when José looks for the missing M. Médouze. Associated with *les mornes* [the mountainous hills] of northern Martinique, the bamboo flute is played by Max Cilla with a light, vibrato-laden tone in a semi-sad melody.[13] Called *le père de la flute des mornes* [father of the mountainous flute], Cilla usually performs melodies with an introspective of joy and peace, but, in this case, he blows a sweet, clear, plaintive melody laden with sensitive shadings to express José's fear at not finding M. Médouze at home.

To cast aside some of the fatigue and fear, singing is used whenever a moment of struggle and deep tribulation is invoked. A literal strategy of survival, a protest song is uttered by the male and female laborers when Léopold, José's best friend who replaces George Roc, the school teacher's nephew, is caught trying to steal the overseer's ledger to expose how the books had been doctored to deny the cane-cutters their rightful wages. A harsh punishment by the *gendarmes* [armed policemen] is enforced by tying Léopold's hands to a rope on a horse that drags him along the dirt road. Such an humiliating experience reveals the contradictions of the mulatto experience. Or as Haseenah Ebrahim maintains: "Palcy creates a new character Léopold to illustrate the liminal political and social position occupied by the mulatto in Martinican society" (2002:149). Privileged in Martinican society as compared to the Black working class but also called "a whitey's nigger" in a work song sung in the film, Léopold had been scolded by his *béké* father (a white descendant of the French planter), his mulatto mother, and the Black maid for consorting with Black children.

Shortly thereafter, Léopold's allegiance to his father shifts when he overhears his mortally wounded father saying that he will not bestow his family name of de Thorail upon his mulatto son, for it is reserved only for whites. Leaving home like a runaway, Léopold aligns himself immediately with the cane-cutters who raise their machetes and hoes in an attempt to stop his public punishment. When their action does not force the *gendarmes* to cease the dragging, the laborers who witness Léopold's punishment express their support of the boy and sing their opposition to his treatment, "Martinique, you are suffering. / Life is fading away."

As the lyrics are sung in the film, a woman's voice is heard beneath that of the male voices. The musical structure takes on an importance because the viewer is directly drawn into the workers' angst as the camera pans a long shot of Léopold's back and close-ups of the workers' faces. The final stanza is devoid of satire but clearly articulates the workers' suppressed feelings: "Money and justice are what's needed to end our suffering / Life has become impossible in this land / Yet life could be easy." Justifiably, Palcy comments: "I feel the poor black boy is luckier than Léopold, the mulatto, because José has his people, black people with him to love him, to help him. He has M'man Tine, Carmen, all of them. But Léopold is alone" (Linfield 1984:44).

Urban Music

The terms "rural" and "urban" are indicative of more than just a geographical origin; they also contain sociological and historical implications as related to a tripartite ethnic and class division. Historically, Martinicans are multi-ethnic descendants of Arawaks, Europeans, Africans, and East Indians. Colonized by the French in 1635, given statehood in 1946, and obtaining regional status in 1974, Martinicans speak French and Creole and primarily draw upon French and African traditions. For example, their musical productions and choice of instruments are primarily representative of the French and African dichotomy. So the urban music of the 1930s, which consisted of the *biguine, contredanse, quadrille,* and *mazurka,* drew most of its components from European traditions. The primary instruments associated with the dances were the accordion, clarinet, piano, and violins. Dancing during this era of violent social conflicts was done either separately or in quadrille sets.

In terms of social elevation, the mulatto offspring of master-slave relationships constitute an intermediate class between the *békés* and the peasants. Living in the capital of Saint Pierre before the Mount Pélée volcanic eruption in 1902 and later in Fort-de-France, mulatto children were exposed to classical European music and taught how to play the piano, while the *békés* played the violin. Yet in the rural area where poor Black children of sugar-cane, banana, or pineapple workers were raised, Blacks were exposed to *bèlè* drumming, bamboo flutes, work, plantation, and funeral songs, and *ladja* dancing. In 1940, some unidentified French Caribbean soldiers composed "Nèg ni mové mannyé" [The Black Man Has Bad Manners], a satirical song whose second verse addresses the availability of instrumental choices among the three racial groups: "*Béké ka jwé violon / Mulat ka jwé piano / Nèg ka bat gwo tanbou*" [The Béké plays the violin; the Mulatto plays the piano; and the Black beats the big drum]. The song naturally struck a nerve with its double-entendre language about the three social classes and racial categories (Berrian 2000:110). This song was an example of harmonic duality, illustrating the demarcation between rural and urban music along racial lines, which were to be blurred in the latter part of the twentieth century.

Daughter of a pineapple-factory personnel manager, Palcy grew up with her five siblings in Martinique during the 1950s and 1960s, knowing about the musical divisions along class and racial lines that narrowed by the end of the twentieth century. Consequently, to emphasize the racial and social stratification that is well exposed in *La Rue cases-nègres*, Palcy ensures that the musical score will coincide with location and class. From the 1930s to the 1950s, the *biguine* was the most popular music performed by French Caribbean bands until music from neighboring islands began to infiltrate the local scene. To revive the *biguine's* waning popularity in the mid-1960s, four students at the Lycée Schoelcher, where José eventually studied, founded a band initially called the Merry Lads during the late 1960s.[14] The band's later choice of the name Malavoi refers to a rare variety of sugar cane of a rich sugar content, which was a means of survival and nourishment to slaves during the era of slavery (Berrian 2000:32–33). By coincidence, Palcy contacted the popular band with its symbolic name about composing the musical score for her film about sugar-cane workers.

Known for its nostalgic promotion of French Caribbean music, Malavoi, featuring Paulo Rosine on the piano, plays an instrumental *biguine soutillante* to accompany a collage of postcards during the beginning of the film.[15] Drawing the spectators' immediate attention to the diversity of Martinican culture, the opening credits of *La Rue cases-nègres,* which replicate the historical context of the 1930s, are superimposed over the postcards in subdued sepia tones of beige and brown. The pictures, produced by French photographers, are those of island life: government buildings, a circle of people, a church, a school, a sugar-cane mill, a factory, the streets around the savanna, and an oxen-drawn cart. The postcards, which express the material and cultural values of the colonialists, were a popular form of information.[16] They were bought by French tourists and colonists to mail to their friends and families back in France to acquaint them with a skewed vision of the Caribbean colony. Therefore, before the narration of the film begins, Palcy delves into the plight of the colonized by adding a political dedication: *Pour toutes les cases nègres du monde* [For all the world's Black shack alleys].

Duplicating the sound of a pianola, Rosine plays a couplet in a moderate tempo and a repetitive refrain to the accompaniment of violins and other instruments. This theme music enters the narration two more times, during Mlle Flora's scenes and in the closing credits of the film. In the second part of the film, the viewer meets Mlle Flora, the cashier in the ticket booth, when she is generous enough to inform José about available housing in Fort-de-France. To support her kind offer, the thematic *biguine* is played softly in the background. However, another variation of the *biguine* is played when Mlle Flora renounces the entire Black race out of shame and anger after seeing a Black stealing a wallet. To expose her negativity about her own people, the cashier's preference for whiteness is mirrored in the movie posters of *Dracula, The Jazz Singer,* and *Cleopatra* that serve as a backdrop. Dracula is a blood-sucking vampire; the jazz singer makes himself up in blackface to imitate a Black man; and Cleopatra commits suicide. To intensify Mlle Flora's inferiority complex, the *biguine* consists of a piano that sounds like a thin echo and of a melody that is minimally repeated.

Malavoi also performs an instrumental *mazurka,* featuring a clarinet solo, when José goes to the city by riverboat to sit for the qualifying exam and to the cinema on the savannah in Fort-de-France. When José and M. Roc travel across the bay to Fort-de-France, the *mazurka* with the clarinet solo is played as José stops in wonder to gaze at the new sights: cars, the Bibliothèque Schoelcher, open-air cafés, and the Palais de Justice. Having no choice but to leave his self-enclosed, nurturing world with M'man Tine, José enters the unknown. Symbolically, José is the lone clarinet, wondering if he possesses the intellect to pass the exam and the courage to be the only

Black outsider in his class of mulatto and *béké* boys. Just as one comes to a full stop to twist the body to the left while dancing the *mazurka*, José figuratively does likewise. After all, he has M. Médouze's carved wood totem to protect him and M'man Tine's love and support.

The *mazurka*, considered by Dominique Cyrille to be emblematic of the cultural specificity of Martinique, flourished in the early decades of the nineteenth century. According to Cyrille, "the European-derived mazurka was deemed to be a genre of the mulatto class and supposedly a threat to the black identity" (2004:241). However, at the end of the twentieth century and the beginning of the twenty-first century, under the growing influence of *Créolité* as a synthesis of all the various cultures that make up the French Caribbean, musicians began to cross the territorial boundaries, blending rural and urban music across the island.

The third kind of urban music is the instrumental combination of the accordion and the maracas, first heard when Carmen, a young adult friend of José, arrives on a sunny day in Petit-Bourg on the *Albatros* riverboat. Not content with his monotonous job as a riverboat pilot and encumbered by being a fluent Creole speaker but only a passable French speaker, Carmen understands that his path toward a better future will be through learning how to read and write in French. With José as his onboard tutor, Carmen painstakingly traces his letters, but the waves slap against the boat, causing his handwriting to slant downward while he writes the letter "U." In jest, since he hears the accordion music in the background, José comments, "Your 'U' is dancing the *biguine*," and Carmen asks, "Is it really dancing the *biguine*?" Just like the accordion music is repetitive, so to is Carmen's task to write his letters over again at Jose's command. Symbolically, the daylight and music coincide with Carmen's movement toward an assimilation into French thought. During his second lesson at night when he encounters José finishing his homework, Carmen reaches under José's papers for his exercise book. Elated to learn that his French has improved, and happy about his progress, Carmen reveals his dream of being a Hollywood actor. As a half-literate, hard-working Black man, Carmen knows that he will have to migrate abroad; so his struggle with French is intentionally linked to satisfying his dream.

The next time accordion music is heard on the film's soundtrack is when M. Saint-Louis hesitantly informs M. Roc, the upper primary teacher in Petit Bourg, that his daughter Tortilla will not be taking the qualifying exams to attend the *lycée* in Fort-de-France. Normally a very forceful man, M. Saint-Louis, with his head bowed, haltingly explains that Tortilla's earning power is badly needed. To punctuate the sadness shown on Tortilla's face and the disbelief on José's, the barely audible accordion music, which is not an accessible instrument for the cane-cutters, is aligned symbolically with the city and M. Saint-Louis' economic and gender-based decision. The inhale and exhale, expanding and squeezing of the accordion's pressure bellows also duplicate the four characters' breathing upon hearing the sad news.

European Music

Through two additional characters, Léopold and his mother Honorine, Palcy presents a multilayered film by connecting the complexity and irony of the mulatto's position in Martinique to that of an African American based in France. When Léopold returns home from school, he finds his mother Honorine proudly listening to "J'ai deux amours" [I Have Two Loves], the latest song from France. Unbeknown to her, "J'ai deux amours," whose music was composed by Vincent Scotto and whose lyrics were jointly written by Henri Varna and Géo Koger, was composed for Josephine Baker, the African-American music-hall singer and dancer. Baker sang "J'ai deux amours" for 481 performances for *Paris qui remue* [Swinging Paris], the 1930–1931 revue at the Casino de Paris and recorded it, along with five other tunes from the show, for Columbia Records. A very talented performer who could not rise to her artistic potential in the United States because of her race, Baker, at age nineteen, relocated to Paris to dance almost nude in *Revue Nègre* at the Théâtre des Champs-Elysées in 1925. Marketed as an exotic, she found French acceptance for her physical attributes, artistic talent, and later spy activities with the French Resistance during World War II.

Every time Baker sang "J'ai deux amours / Mon pays et Paris" [I have two loves / My country and Paris] in France, she probably thought about her own "cross-cultural linguist and racial dilemma" (Pauly 1993:249). She initially loved both the United States and France, but, as her years abroad lengthened, she identified more with France. Singing the melancholy song in a thin, soprano voice, Baker's rendition often reminded the French audience that she was the exotic foreigner. Eventually, "J'ai deux amours" became Baker's theme song about a nostalgic longing for her homeland and Paris, even though its original context was about an African woman in love with a French colonizer who invited her to go to Paris with him. Although the African woman wanted to go to Paris, her answer was "No" because her people would not allow her to betray them. Thus, she was torn between two loves: the French colonizer who represented Paris and her people who symbolized her country. Or, as noted by Phyllis Rose, "On the one hand racial and national identity, on the other romance, sex, and swinging Paris"

(Rose 1989:147). Like Baker, Honorine was torn between two loves. In her case, though, it was her love for a white man and her desire to obtain legitimacy for her son.

The Charleston music composed by Slap-Cat is performed when José visits Carmen at the home of his *béké* employer on the Route de Didier after a heated exchange with his high school teacher.[17] Since Charleston music and its dance were considered to be risqué during this time period, the music coincides with Carmen's risky affair with his employer's wife. The cocky Carmen gives José a tour of his mistress' bedroom and jokingly brags about their sexual relationship while lounging on the bed. Needless to say, José is not impressed. Instead, he is annoyed because Carmen is oblivious to his state of distress. Having helped Carmen with his French lessons, José is hurt that the self-centered man fails to observe his own need to vent.

The Formal Education

The material and cultural values of Martinicans are demarcated as Palcy uses cinematic juxtaposition to create meaning out of cultural, political, educational, and socio-economic conflicts. The contrast between the lifestyles of the Blacks and mulattoes is marked. Unlike Léopold, who lives in isolation in a villa and is told repeatedly by his mother, father, and maid not to play with *les petits nègres* [the little Negroes], José resides in a closely knit neighborhood with an abundance of friends. Even a female adult neighbor comes to his defense when the mulatto overseer falsely accuses José of being lazy and sneers at him. Léopold's white cement house, which is richly furnished, sports a fenced-in front veranda, and contrasts with José's two-room wooden shack with its dirt floor and its wallpaper of used newspapers. While Léopold has a choice of freshly squeezed juices to drink, José has only water. While Léopold has more than one suit to wear to school, José owns only one suit, which he takes great pains to keep neat and clean. While Honorine is the well-kept mistress of a *béké* planter, the rape victim M'man Tine rouses her tired body on a daily basis to work for a *béké* planter in order to provide for herself and her grandson.

Since diversity is the underlying framework of the *La Rue cases-nègres,* the characters are torn between two worlds: African- and French-imposed influences. The lighter-skinned Blacks, as Herndon notes, "occupy some professions while the lower classes are mostly darker skinned blacks who produce the wealth but do not see the profits" (1996:202). In the film, Palcy also uses the primary and secondary schools as a strategy for exploring the crises and tensions associated with intra-racial prejudice. The racial dichotomy and the dilemma of cultural multiplicity in colonial Martinique are more complex than white versus Black; it is also mulatto versus Black. In fact, José's experiences in the cane fields and his attendance of school will allow him to gradually see a topography of oppression (Kandé 1994:40). Luckily, his past lessons with M. Médouze are a countervailing force to that of the school and French colonial culture, so that José is able to move from one geographical/cultural space to the other with the fluidity of a hybridized identity (Ebrahim 2002:148).

One banner in a teacher's classroom at the primary school in Petit-Bourg is especially symbolic: *L'instruction est la clé qui ouvre la deuxième porte de la liberté* [Education is the key which opens the second door of freedom]. In another classroom, school children sing, spell, and recite: "*Les Gaulois sont nos ancêtres*" [Our ancestors are the Gauls]. The exercise confirms how the children's cultural identity is devalued, if not erased. While the teacher is either lecturing about the French vocabulary or reading aloud from the students' essays in the enclosed classroom where José is located, the viewer listens closely to what the invisible students are singing. The English-speaking viewer perhaps thinks they are reciting an idyllic song; the conservative French-speaking viewer most likely nods in approval.

Through the medium of repetitive music and spoken voices, the students chant the same sentence over and over until it becomes a sing-song litany with one message layered upon the other. This device of overlapping the sounds of the invisible students' voices with that of the teacher in José's high school classroom serves as a prelude to what is to come. In this regard, José submits a moving composition about M. Médouze's death and his wretched condition as a cane-cutter. The nameless teacher, known as M. Jean-Henri in the novel, accuses him of plagiarism. However, José's early success in the primary school and the reinforcement of his self-worth by M'man Tine and the late M. Médouze have made him secure and courageous enough for him to contradict the teacher. Shocked and hurt by the unwarranted and false accusation, José incurs the teacher's wrath by engaging in a heated exchange with the teacher before his classmates until he rushes out of the classroom.

In contrast to the *lycée* teacher, M. Roc (played by the stage actor Henri Melon), in an earlier scene, had encouraged good scholarship in his Petit Bourg classroom. He hoped to send ten Black students to the same *lycée*. A strict disciplinarian, he would grab the boys by their ears to stop their fighting on the school's veranda and sharpen the tip of a wooden stick used to beat the students. Yet, when the telegram about the students' scores for the *Certificat d'Etudes Primaires* exam arrives, the mulatto M. Roc crosses class and racial barriers by going to see José and M'man Tine in the Black shack alley to relate the good news that José has passed. Totally absorbed in his happiness for José, M. Roc displays no awkwardness when he enters the shack. Moreover, class and color differences are temporarily ignored through the formal education because the goal has been attained, confirming M. Roc's effective teaching skills.

Therefore, the mulatto teacher's spontaneous and stereotypical chastisement of José at the *lycée* completely catches the boy by surprise. Used to three teachers (M'man Tine, M. Médouze, and M. Roc) who had been very supportive of him, José, the only dark-skinned student in the high school class, stands up for his rights, declaring that he is the author of the essay. To further empower José, Palcy steps in by modifying the portrayal of the unnamed teacher. In Zobel's book, the teacher M. Jean-Henri does not apologize to José. However, in the film, the teacher atones, paying a visit to M'man Tine who confirms that M. Médouze had existed. With a subtle shift in power relations, the fastidiously dressed teacher in his white suit and straw hat with a black band stands beneath the doorway while M'man Tine, garbed in her work dress, looks down upon him from the top step. To repair the damage his spoken words have done to José, the teacher humbles himself, thereby countering his ingrained prejudice against darker-skinned people. Recognizing that José is a gifted and honest student, and in M'man Tine's presence, the teacher tells José that he possesses the talent to become a very good writer. And to prove his newly acquired belief in José, he successfully approaches the bursar about granting the boy a full scholarship. Furthermore, the teacher's act of kindness also allows M'man Tine to quit working for the first time in her life.

The Film's Reception

For Palcy, "the power of film is incredible to change people's minds, open their eyes, their vision of the world" (Glicksman 1989:65). The French colonial policy was one of cultural and psychological domination. Schoolchildren were encouraged to identify with French culture and history to reinforce their loyalty to France and to undermine challenges to the colonials' authority. As illustrated in the film, José is exposed to the geography of France and Alphonse Daudet's nineteenth-century writings about childhood in the folkloric French countryside, while the folklore of Martinique is ignored. Having gone through the same system, Palcy emphasizes that "this education belongs completely to the white world and does not correspond to the reality of the world of the black child" (Micciollo 1983:33).

In this vein, Palcy validates Creole by inserting it in the film's dialogue, thereby demonstrating the aesthetic reality of orality in the rural community.

As Abiola Irele notes, one sees in "orality a common relation to the world and the imagined consciousness" (1990:252). Although Zobel wrote his autobiographical novel in French with some Creole words, Palcy imaginatively sprinkles liberal amounts of Creole expressions throughout the film through the tales, the proverbs, the children's games, the meta-natural religious system, and especially the cane-cutters' work songs and dances. This infusion of vernacular language and music makes the film more realistic because this language and music are an integral part of island life. "Since cinema is a work of truth," Césaire explains, "it is possible that, as literature, it will express itself sometimes in French, sometimes in Creole, because Martiniquans use the two languages, sometimes in turn, sometimes at the same time. In a same sentence, can be found both French and Creole figures of speech, and, in a conversation in French, a Creole sentence can appear" (Sephocle 1992:362). This technique of interchanging Creole and French is illustrated particularly with Julien-douze-orteils and the children and the market women who sell their wares.

La Rue cases-nègres premiered in Fort-de-France in June 1983. For over a month, it was difficult for Martinicans—who bought more than 125,000 tickets—to get into the sold-out theater to see the film because half of the population came to see themselves. Palcy insists that Césaire, who she calls her first godfather, helped to prepare the Martinican audience for her film. Having built his reputation as a *négritude* poet and playwright as well as a mayor and statesman, Césaire helped to establish SERMAC (Service Municipal d'Action Culturelle), a cultural institution that is still active in the center of Fort-de-France. After opening in 1975, SERMAC organized activities in the arts, dance, music, and folklore. Workshops on various aspects of Martinican culture were offered every weekend. Even though people were skeptical at first, they began to realize its importance, for the classes and workshops helped to break down many complexes. When June Givanni asked Palcy about Césaire's support, she remarked:

thanks to this kind of cultural work that Césaire was able to instill in Martinique an affirmation of a new sense of culture and race identity. I believe this prepared the way for people in Martinique to receive my film, *Rue Cases-nègres [Sugar-cane Alley]*, with the enthusiasm and pride they did. Without this kind of cultural work to make people aware and to accept and be proud of themselves and their culture, they would have never been able to accept this film. (Givanni 1992:294–95)

La Rue cases-nègres marked a change in the French Caribbean film industry, culminating in the founding of the Association for the Promotion and Development of Caribbean Cinema (APDCC) in 1985 by the Martinican Suzy Landau in collaboration with representatives of the other islands. The APDCC efforts resulted in the founding of the *Images Caraïbes* film festival, which was held twice in Fort-de-France, in 1988 and in 1990. The two festivals promoted the work of local and neighboring film directors. Since then, other film festivals to promote Caribbean films have taken place annually in St. Barthélémy, Barbados, and Jamaica.[18] At the opening of the tenth Salon du Livre de l'Outre-mer [Overseas Book Fair] on October 14, 2003, a special *soirée* [evening affair] was organized at the Cinéma des Cinéastes in Paris with Palcy and Zobel in attendance to commemorate the twentieth anniversary of the release of *La Rue cases-nègres*.

The film's twenty-two years of popularity can be attributed to the ability of a majority of the viewers to identify with José's struggles to maintain a sense of himself in the French colonial classrooms. They were also most likely raised by a hard-working, proud grandmother like M'man Tine. At the end of the film is another tribute to a deceased elder. José tenderly and carefully uses his bare hands to wash his deceased grandmother's hands and feet, the two extremities upon which she had relied so much to raise him. The washing is part of the preparatory rites and the ceremonial gesture for her burial. Sure of himself, José closes the film with a last voice-over, announcing that, "M'man Tine has gone to Africa with M. Médouze. Tomorrow I'll return to Fort-de-France and I'll take my Black Shack Alley with me." This powerful, self-affirming message is reinforced by alternating the *bèlè* and the thematic *biguine* with a final panoramic view of the green cane fields.

The viewers' identification with José, M'man Tine, and M. Médouze adheres to what constitutes a point of view in Third World Cinema, which Teshome H. Gabriel says, "is not a reflection of the consciousness of subjectivity of a single subject (a protagonist/hero); rather, the central figure in Third Cinema serves to develop an historical perspective on radical social change" (Gabriel 1982:7). Palcy follows the format in *Siméon*, her third feature, released in 1992. Labeled a fable and a musical and filmed in Guadeloupe and Paris, *Siméon*, told from the viewpoints of the ten-year-old Orélie (Lucinda Messager) and the adults Isidore (Jacob Desvarieux) and Siméon (Jean-Claude Duverger), is about the spirit of *zouk* music, the liveliness of French Caribbean people, and the power of myth and dreams. Isidore, a mechanic but also a singer and guitarist in a small town in Guadeloupe, shares a dream of introducing a new brand of music to the world with Siméon, his music instructor. However, Siméon drinks too much rum one night and falls to his death. Knowing the Creole legend that a person is not dead if a part of him is in someone's possession, Orélie, Isidore's daughter, sneaks into the room where Siméon is laid out in his coffin and cuts a lock of his hair to keep as a memento. This enables her to communicate with Siméon's spirit so he can help her father to realize his dream. As a result, Isidore goes to Paris and eventually forms the group Jacaranda, which achieves the success that he and Siméon always wanted.

The making of *Siméon* gave Palcy the opportunity to mix the important elements of what she considered to be the French Caribbean experience: orality, bodily gestures, dance, and music. "*Siméon*," she said, "has social, cultural, political and sociological dimensions." Her aim was to bring together Martinicans, Guadeloupeans, and *négropolitains* (French-born Blacks) in Paris, because the three groups share the same history of colonialism, assimilation, departmentalization, and regionalism as French overseas territories. Desiring to reappropriate and to reaffirm French Caribbean music and culture, Palcy approached several members of Kassav', the popular *zouk* band that symbolizes pan-Africanism with Martinican, Guadeloupean, French, and African musicians, to act and perform in the film.[19] They each accepted and the film pulsates with the slick, sophisticated, layered sounds of *zouk* dance music with Creole lyrics.[20]

Kassav's insistence on singing in a mixture of Martinican and Guadeloupean Creole positions them squarely within Palcy's desire to break down political and cultural barriers because "orality functions as a counter discourse to assimilation, regionalism and departmentalization" (Berrian 2000:40). Two songs heard in *Siméon* are "Mwen alé" [My Departure] and "Mwen viré" [My Return], whose lyrics were written by Jocelyne Béroard, the only female soloist for Kassav', and featured on Kassav's CD *Tekit izi* (1992). In the theme song, "Mwen alé," Isidore sings about his mixed feelings upon leaving Guadeloupe for France to launch his musical career. He states that he does not want to die far away from his country of birth. Later, Béroard, who plays the role of Roselyne, sings "Mwen viré" with Kassav' about Isidore's desire to leave the greyness of Paris in order to feel some sun on his skin. Then, at the end of the film, Kassav' introduces *zouk raggamuffin* with "Levé Tèt Ou" [Hold Up Your Head], a song with energetic horns and steel drums about being proud of one's accomplishments. Through hard work, good marketing, and numerous performances of his music, Isidore returns to Guadeloupe in triumph with the Jacaranda band.

Although Palcy won a Special Jury Prize at the 1993 Brussels Film Festival and awards at the film festivals in Milan and Montreal for *Siméon*, the French Caribbean public did not know what to make of the film. When the trailers showed that Kassav' was in the film, the public thought that they would see a film about the band's history and personal life stories. To their disappointment, it was a fictional story about Isidore, Siméon, and Orélie. Even one of the Kassav' band members admitted that he regretted being in the film in spite of the band's award of a French gold record for some of the movie's music on *Tekit izi*. Nevertheless, in May 2004, at the Cannes

International Film Festival, Palcy announced that *Siméon,* whose script she wrote, was her favorite film because it was a mixture of genres and a synthesis of everything she had done by merging the present with the past.

Film Music, Production, and Distribution

Following in Palcy's footsteps is Guy Deslauriers, a Martinican who began his career in film in the early 1980s while working as Palcy's assistant for *La Rue cases-nègres.* He frequently returns to the past for inspiration and material for such films as the 1994 *L'Exil du roi Béhanzin* [The Exile of King Béhanzin] and the 2000 *Le Passage du milieu* [Middle Passage]. The former is about the king of Dahomey, who was exiled by the French colonial government to Martinique; the latter about the horrors of slavery. Deslauriers' latest film *Biguine* (2004) looks back at the origins of the *biguine* during the late nineteenth century through the characters of Hermancia and Tiquitaque in the town of Saint-Pierre, the first capital of Martinique until its destruction in a volcanic eruption in 1902.[21] Labeling Saint-Pierre "*le ventre de la Martinique*" [the stomach of Martinique], Deslauriers states that the city signified the confrontation of huge fortunes where wealthy people enjoyed the opera and literary salons and the miserably poor left the countryside to search for a better lifestyle in the city (Dicale 2005).

The narrative point of view, music, and song lyrics play a dominant role in Palcy's and Deslauriers' films as well as in French African films. Entering into the narrative development, both music and lyrics enhance the overall meaning of certain scenes. Often, they function as commentary and this technique of narrative layering is also a stylistic feature of French African film to demonstrate how music accompanies oral storytelling. For example, Palcy's featuring of a child's point of view for *La Rue cases-nègres* and *Siméon* has been adapted by the Senegalese Ben Diogaye Bèye with a slight twist for *Un amour d'enfant* [A Childhood Love]. Children are the main actors and adults play secondary roles. The daily antics of and the conversations among five school-age friends between the ages of ten and twelve at the Ecole Ste Marie in the city of Dakar, Senegal, are prioritized. Opening with the lush, sensual music of Wasis Diop, a Senegalese composer-musician-singer and brother of the late filmmaker Djibril Diop Mambety, *Un amour d'enfant* (2004) relates the tale of Yacine and Omar, who fall in love only to be separated because Yacine's father loses his job as a result of the World Bank's economic policies of structural adjustment. Relocating to Saint Louis, a town in the northern part of Senegal, with her parents and siblings, Yacine insists that her love for and friendship with Omar will endure when they talk to each other while looking at a full moon. As the film closes, Diop's voice is heard over the shots of the Saint Louis bridge and Yacine's comments to her mother about marriage. Therefore, the narration, music, and lyrics all serve as a bridge between the present and the past, childhood and adulthood.

As a baby on a blanket on the grass, Palcy was surrounded by noise and nature, birds and the wind. From babyhood to adulthood, she grew up loving to sing, eventually composing children's songs for two albums with EMI Productions. She also composed some of the lyrics and the original dialogue for *La Rue cases-nègres,* particularly the conversation when José defines the difference between cackling and singing and the lyrics sung by the cane-cutters in support of Léopold. In other words, the film is in homage to the women, men, and children of Martinique. Under Palcy's direction, the ringing of the cathedral's bells, the sounds of a honking car horn, and the changing of a car's gears are heard in the narrow street scenes of Fort-de-France. The sounds of oinking pigs, bleating goats, and crowing roosters are also interspersed in the rural scenes. Instead of ringing a bell to signal the end of the school recess, a man in a gray uniform beats a side drum with sticks until all of the students return to class.

Minimal scenes are devoted to the *békés* because the main focus is on the Black cane-cutters. Low-slung shots of the children predominate along with close-up shots of adults gathered together in relation to their surrounding to stress collectivity. The film earned a total of seventeen awards, including a 1984 French *César* for Best First Work, the *Lion d'argent* for Best First Film and the Best Actress award for Darling Légitimus at the 1983 Venice Film Festival, and the First Prize Critic Award at the Houston Film Festival. An enormous hit in the French Caribbean, the film was also well received in France. *La Rue cases-nègres* had a successful commercial release in the United States with Orion Classics, and still continues to be shown in universities and sold in video stores. The film was made in French, with some Creole, to satisfy the French grant requirements, since there is no infrastructure in the French Caribbean to support film productions. But, to twist things around, a postcard campaign to advertise the film from Martinique to France became a hit among Martinicans and *négropolitains.*

With a clear focus on orality and musical diversity, *La Rue cases-nègres* has exposed viewers across the world to a range of French Caribbean music—*biguine, mazurka, bèlè,* and *ladja*—as well as European music. In addition, Palcy uses music in *La Rue cases-nègres* and *Siméon* to make several psychological points about the effects of duality and to make specific moments more effective. Simultaneously, the music underlies psychological problems and accentuates the drama in certain scenes to create a far greater degree of intensity. Her former assistant Deslauriers does likewise in *Biguine*. The music also enters directly into the plot and subplots of the film, adding a third dimension to the spoken words and the visual images. By paying attention to such details, Palcy has made a film that can "touch people, awaken their conscience in a sense of change, a revolt in a positive sense, and then move them to struggle peacefully for a better life, to come see themselves as people with dignity."[22]

Described as a woman with a mission to represent Black people in films, Palcy has spoken openly about the constraints imposed upon her by the Centre National du Cinéma (CNC). When she was awarded the CNC grant for *La Rue cases-nègres*, the stipulation was for her to hire a French technical consultant. A common practice is for foreign directors to approach French friends who are directors to sign the CNC form, because they most likely do not show up on the set. Luckily for Palcy, Truffaut offered to be her assistant on the film (for the first time during his lengthy career). He intervened again when the French producer insisted that she had to cut some scenes from the final copy of *La Rue cases-nègres* because it was longer than one hour and thirty minutes. Compliant, but hurt and complaining that the soul of the film had been removed, Palcy turned to Truffaut for advice. Enthusiastic about the film, he met with the producer, demanding that the scenes be reinserted. "The next day," according to Palcy, "the scenes were reinserted and a catastrophe was avoided" (Mbouguen 2001). Now, to avoid seeking CNC funding and to consider other options, Palcy has founded her own company, Saligna Productions.

Palcy, along with other Caribbean and African directors, expends a lot of energy acquiring financial backing for her films, which explains the three-year or longer gap between films. She realizes that her films and those of other Caribbean and African directors are primarily shown at international film festivals and on foreign university campuses rather than in the few movie theaters in their own countries. African directors contend with the slow process of post-production and editing, the shortage of money for foreign subtitles, and ill-equipped local personnel. Furthermore, there is no circuit for distribution after their films are completed. More importantly, the import and distribution of their own movies in their respective countries are still controlled by the French-owned Compagnie Franco-Africaine de l'Audiovisuel (CFAA). A large holding company of banks including Crédit Lyonnais and the Caisse Populaire, CFAA controls African cinema or what Emmanuel Sana glibly calls the French "game reserves" (1996:152).

Moreover, the lack of economic and technical infrastructures and distribution necessary for an autonomous industry plagues the French Caribbean and Africa. For instance, Sana thinks that French African films are "foreigners in their own countries" (ibid.:148). Yet French Caribbean as well as African audiences want to see films that represent them. The arrival of 100,000 Martinicans to see Deslauriers' *Biguine* and the sold-out theaters in Martinique and Guadeloupe for *La Rue cases-nègres* prove their interest. In March 2005, as the international patron of the Images of Black Women Film Festival in London, England, Palcy remarked, "We have to find ways, we Blacks of the Diaspora to do films, to construct bridges and to produce without being cut from the rest of the world."

By circumventing the obstacles, Palcy surely accomplishes her goal of emphasizing the complexity of cultural affirmation in her films. In *La Rue cases-nègres*, there are five interpolated voice-over narrations by José. The first occurs at the beginning of the movie, three during the film, and the last at the end of the film. They provide a cohesive structure for the film, reflecting the continuity of Martinique, its land, and its laborers. Edouard Glissant writes, "music, gesture and dance are forms of communication, just as important as the gift of speech. This is how we first managed to emerge from the plantation: aesthetic form in our cultures must be shaped from these oral structures" (Glissant 1981:248–49). In addition, Palcy thoughtfully intersperses real feelings, discerns hidden subtexts and juxtaposes a diverse assemblage of musical genres from the countryside and the city through diversity and orality.

I am grateful to Jacqueline-Brice Finch for her comments that greatly improved this essay.

Notes

1. To read more about the history of French Caribbean films, consult Osange Silou's *Le Cinéma dans la diaspora africaine: les Antilles françaises*. Bruxelles: Organisation Catholique Internationale du Cinéma, 1991.

2. Five films that were released before *La Rue cases-nègres* were Willie Rameau's *J'ai une île dans ma tête* (1977); Jean-Paul Césaire's *Derive ou la femme jardin* (1977) and *Hors des jours étrangers* (1978); Constant Gros-DuBois' *O Madiana* (1979); and Michel G. Traore's *Mizik de Rez de Chaussée Nèg* (1981).

3. Zobel appeared as a priest for a brief moment in the movie.

4. Born Mathilde Paruta in Le Carbet, Martinique, in 1907, Darling Légitimus was seventy-six years old when she received the *Lion d'or* for best female actress at the Festival de Venice in 1983 for her role as M'man Tine. From the 1930s until her death in 1999, Légitimus was involved actively with movies. She had even danced in *La Revue Nègre* with Josephine Baker, posed for Pablo Picasso, and starred with Marlon Brando in *Last Tango in Paris* (1972). In 2002, her grandson, Pascal Légitimus, also an actor and filmmaker, released *Darling Légitimus, ma grand-mère, nôtre doudou* (Darling Légitimus, My Grandmother, Our *Doudou*), a 52-minute documentary about his grandmother's life.

5. Garry Cadenat was a young boy enrolled in elementary school when Palcy discovered him; it was the first experience in cinema for him and the other children. Today, he works for a local television studio in Martinique.

6. The U.S. English subtitles are by Helen Eisenman.

7. Although Martinicans are French citizens, their minimum wage is lower than that of the French based in France.

8. Aimé Césaire recommended the Senegalese actor, Douta Seck, to Palcy for the role of Médouze. Seck previously had acted in Césaire's play *La Tragédie du Roi Christophe* [The Tragedy of King Christopher].

9. Eugène Mona popularized the *ladja* on the performance stage. The barefoot singer was very popular for his songs about drug abuse, political corruption, and the psychological state of the exploited Black man during the 1970s and 1980s until his untimely death at age forty-eight.

10. M. Médouze's death is a reminder of Amadou Hampaté Ba's famous quotation, *En Afrique, un vieillard qui meurt est une bibliothèque qui brûle* (In Africa, when the elder dies, a library goes up in flames).

11. The performance poet, Joby Bernabé, who is a native of Saint Pierre, Martinique, sings a capella and has released several compact discs on which he recites tales and his own poems about spiritual identity and the communion of men with nature to musical accompaniment.

12. During the slave uprisings on the plantations, the *maroons* (runaway slaves) had used the *lambi* as a form of communication.

13. In 1996, Max Cilla composed music for Julius Amedée-Laou's *Monsieur Zobel,* a play in homage to Joseph Zobel that premiered at the Municipal Theatre of Fort-de-France.

14. During the 1930s, the Lycée Schoelcher was the only high school for French Caribbean students, serving Martinique, Guadeloupe, St. Martin, and French Guyane.

15. Under Rosine's leadership, Malavoi rose to new heights, performing often at Caribbean and international venues until Rosine's untimely death from cancer at age forty-five in January 1993.

16. See Ménil 1992:167. Between World Wars I and II, there was a great boom in sending "penny" postcards to show where one had visited. Ménil explained that the only images that Antilleans had of themselves was from the outside and from that which was "sent."

17. As reported by Palcy to Berrian, Slap-Cat was a popular white group based in Paris during the late 1970s and early 1980s.

18. In April 1996, the St. Barth Caribbean Film Festival/*Cinéma Caraïbe* was founded to showcase Caribbean cinema with films by Caribbean filmmakers or with Caribbean themes. Two of Palcy's films (one of which was *La Rue cases-nègres*) were shown. The actress/producer Sheryl Lee Ralph, in association with the Jamaica Tourist Board, launched the annual Jamaican Film and Music Festival in November 1999. Inaugurated in 2002, the Barbados Festival of African and Caribbean Film takes place every October to recognize the importance of visual media to the Caribbean region and the processes and procedures of distribution, spectatorship, and criticism. All three film festivals are still active.

19. Having sold over a million records worldwide, Kassav', a band founded in the late 1970s, has had a major impact on the Caribbean and world music industries.

20. *Zouk* is a fusion of West African highlife, Congolese *soukous*, Haitian *compas*, Dominican *cadence*, Trinidadian *calypso* and *soca*, and African-American blues and jazz.

21. Micheline Mona, the niece of the late Eugène Mona who was Julien-douze-orteils in *La Rue cases-nègres,* plays the role of Hermancia in *Biguine.*

22. On October 14, 2004, at the Yari Yari conference in New York, Palcy also acknowledged that her paternal grandmother taught her a lot, so she always wanted to film the elders' presence and legacy.

Works Cited

Aufderheide, Pat. 1989. "A Different Freedom." *Black Film Review* 53:6–10, 31.
Bâ, Sylvia Washington. 1973. *The Concept of Negritude in the Poetry of Léopold Sédar Senghor.* Princeton, N.J.: Princeton University Press.
Berrian, Brenda F. 2000. *Awakening Spaces: French Caribbean Popular Songs, Music and Culture.* Chicago: University of Chicago Press.
Confiant, Raphaël. 1991. "La littérature créolophone des Antilles-Guyane." *Notre Librairie* 104, no. 2:55–62.
Cyrille, Dominique. 2004. "Sa Ki Ta Nou [This Belongs to Us] Creole Dances of the French Caribbean." In *Caribbean Dance from Abakuá to Zouk: How Movement Shapes Identity,* ed. Susanna Sloat, 221–44. Gainesville: University of Florida Press.
Dicale, Bertrand. 2005. "La Biguine retrouvée: Quand le cinéma retrace avec rigueur la genése d'un genre musical." 17 January. http://www.rfimusique.com/siteFr/aticle-15320.asp.
Ebrahim, Haseenah. 2002. "*Sugar Cane Alley:* Re-reading Race, Class and Identity in Zobel's *La Rue cases-nègres.*" *Literature Film Quarterly* 30, no. 2:146–52.
Fanon, Frantz. 1961. *Les Damnés de la terre.* Paris: Maspéro. *The Wretched of the Earth,* trans. Constance Farrington. New York: Grove Press, 1965.
Gabriel, Teshome H. 1982. *Third Cinema in the Third World.* Ann Arbor: University of Michigan Research Press.
Givanni, June. 1992. "An Interview with Euzhan Palcy." In *Ex-Iles: Essays in Caribbean Cinema,* ed. Mbye Cham, 286–307. Trenton: Africa World Press.
Glicksman, Melanie. 1989. "A Tempest: Euzhan Palcy's 'Dry White Season.'" *Film Comment* (September–October):64–69.
Glissant, Edouard. 1981. *Le Discours antillais.* Paris: Seuil. *Caribbean Discourse: Selected Essays,* trans. J. Michael Dash. Charlottesville: University of Virginia Press, 1981.
Herndon, Gerise. 1996. "Auto-Ethnographic Impulse in *Rue Cases-Negres.*" *Literature Film Quarterly* 24, no. 3:261–66.
Irele, Abiola. 1990. "Orality, Literacy and the African Imagination." In *Semper Aliquid Novi,* ed. Jánus Riesz and Alain Ricard, 251–63. Tübingen: Gunter Narr.
Kandé, Sylvie. 1994. "Renunciation and Victory in *Black Shack Alley.*" *Research in African Literatures* 25, no. 2:33–50.
Linfield, Susan. 1984. "*Sugar Cane Alley:* An Interview with Euzhan Palcy." *Cinéaste* 13, no. 4:43–44.
Mbouguen, Hervé. 2001. "Euzhan Palcy, réalistrice de 'Rue Cases-Nègres,' première partie." http://grioo.com/info 3564.html.
Ménil, Alain. 1992. "*Rue Cases-Nègres* ou les Antilles de l'intérieur." *Présence Africaine* 129, no. 1:96–110. Originally published as "*Rue Cases-Nègres* or the Antilles from Inside." In *Ex-Iles: Essays on Caribbean Cinema,* ed. Mbye Cham, 155–75. Trans. Oumar Kâ. Trenton: Africa World Press.
Micciollo, Henri. 1983. "Rue Cases-Nègres." *Cinéma* 298, no. 10:31–34.
Pauly, Rebecca M. 1993. *The Transparent Illusion: Image and Identity in French Text and Film.* New York: Peter Lang.
Rose, Phyllis. 1989. *Jazz Cleopatra: Josephine Baker in Her Time.* New York: Doubleday.

Sana, Emmanuel. 1996. "African Films Are Foreigners in Their Own Countries." In *African Experiences of Cinema*, ed. Imruh Bakari and Mbye B. Cham, 148–56. London: British Film Institute.

Sephocle, Marie-Line. 1992. "Interview with Aimé Césaire." In *Ex-Iles: Essays on Caribbean Cinema*, ed. Mbye Cham, 359–69. Trenton: Africa World Press.

Silou, Osange. 1991. *Le cinéma dans la diaspora africaine: Les Antilles françaises*. Bruxelles: Organisation Catholique Internationale du Cinéma.

West, Joan W., and Dennis West. 2003. "Euzhan Palcy and Her Creative Anger: A Conversation with the Filmmaker." *French Review* 77, no. 6:1193–1203.

Zobel, Joseph. 1950. *La Rue cases-nègres*. Paris: Présence Africaine. *Black Shack Alley*, trans. Keith Q. Warner. Washington, D.C.: Three Continents Press, 1980.

Filmography

Un amour d'enfant, 2004. Dir. Ben Diogaye Bèye. Dakar: Les Productions lion rouge.

Biguine, 2004. Dir. Guy Deslauriers. Paris: Kréol Productions.

L'Exil du roi Béhanzin, 1994. Dir. Guy Deslauriers. Paris: Swift Productions.

Le Passage du milieu, 2000. Dir. Guy Deslauriers. Issy Les Moulineaux: Les Films du Raphia. Distributed in the U.S. by HBO Home Video under the title *The Middle Passage*.

La Rue cases-nègres, 1983. Dir. Euzhan Palcy. Paris Sumafa/Orca/N.E.F. Distributed in the U.S. by Orion Classics under the title *Sugar Cane Alley*, 1984.

Siméon, 1992. Dir. Euzhan Palcy. Paris: Saligna Productions/ President Films.

MARTIN STOKES

Listening to Abd al-Halim Hafiz

·◈·

This chapter concerns Egyptian film music of the mid- to late 1950s, specifically that of crooner and film star, Abd al-Halim Hafiz. Abd al-Halim was born in the province of Zagazig in 1929. He studied oboe in Cairo at the Arab Music Conservatory, found his way into recording and radio in the early 1950s, and into the film world a little later (making some sixteen musical films). He enjoyed the patronage of Gamal Abd al-Nasser as a singer of political songs at state-sponsored anniversaries of the revolution that deposed the king and brought the "Free Officers" to power on July 23, 1952.[1] He died in 1977, an ailing, bilharzia-wracked figure, to massive public mourning.[2] Abd al-Halim's music lives on in Egypt and elsewhere in the Arab world through state patronage, through intelligentsia-inspired nostalgia, and, currently, through the activities of media corporations, taking advantage of an eminently exploitable resource. And, in less obviously observable ways, he continues to be held in broad popular affection, both in Egypt and in many parts of the Arab world.

The durability of the popular Arab film musical "heritage" has inspired important questions and influential theorizations both within and outside the Arab world. In particular, the role of popular film in mediating broader experiences of modernity, in shaping both Arab and Egyptian nationalism, and in nourishing an—at least incipiently—democratic public life have been stressed by Walter Armbrust (1996), Joel Gordon (2002), Viola Shafik (1998), and others. Their work constitutes my own point of departure, to which I add a question that has not, I believe, been squarely addressed. To what degree does it matter that *music* and *musicians* are central to so many of these films? That those sitting in movie theaters, or, these days, watching at home on television or video, were hailed not just as people skilled in the conventions of narration and pictures in motion, but as listeners, steeped in Arab music history and the skills and pleasures of interpreting voices, styles, genres, the play of musical form and nuances of instrumental artistry?

The issue has broader ramifications. If, as Frankfurtian and post-Frankfurtian media theory has insisted, the social productivity of mass media is conditioned by "lexes" particular to them; that they are, in other words, conditioned by the "structure of reading that a particular medium requires and allows" (Mazarella 2004:359), how might we go about identifying and critically engaging with the structures of listening that musical film both "requires and allows"? And how might we then go about considering the role of listening in the context of the broader social transformations wrought by states in pursuit of modernity, nationalism, and democratic public life?[3] These are somewhat abstract questions, with resonance in other parts of the world. But the Egyptian experience, even when grasped with the clumsy eyes and ears of an (admiring) outsider, such as myself, might add nuance, as well as some empirical specificity, to these questions. Where Frankfurtian and post-Frankfurtian media theory assumes Western experience as a norm against which all else is read and usually is deemed lacking or deviant, there is something to be gained in, quite simply, starting elsewhere and grasping modernity, and the familiar questions that cling to it, "otherwise" (c.f. Chakrabarty 2000).

In the remainder of this chapter, I want to pursue the question of listenership in Egyptian film musicals in response to three pieces of writing I have found productive and thought provoking in this context, each of which I will introduce with a quotation. Two relate specifically to modern Egypt, allowing me to say something of what I know about the conditions of film production, the position of musicians, composers, and arrangers in the general scheme of film production, and what seems to have been involved in the musical making and reception of these films. I should stress at the outset, with other scholars of Egyptian film in these years, that the material at hand is scanty (see Vitalis 2000) and add that my own expertise is far from complete. One can only hope that archival material will come to light and life once this rather ambiguous moment in Egyptian cultural history comes into clearer focus. The third quotation opens the door to some broader questions about listening, ethnography, and mass mediation, which may bear on how we consider music in film genres more broadly.

The flourishing (Egyptian) film industry captivated the fancy and imagination of the populace, not just in Egypt but throughout the Arab world, where the current songs were on every lip, and where a faithful audience of urbanites from taxi drivers to porters memorized the dialogue of popular films and gave a running commentary to the new viewers. (Zubaida 2002:19)

Zubaida's celebration of the secular and cosmopolitan cultural spheres of Cairo and Alexandria in the 1930s and 1940s challenges those who are inclined only to see state power and religious authority in Middle Eastern public life. He depicts not only lively cultural interactions across the colonial divide, but also within the colonized elite, bourgeoisie, and urban working classes. The contributions of Bela Bartok, invited to the Arab musical congress in 1932 and Edward Evans-Pritchard, lecturing on primitive religion at Cairo University are duly mentioned, but Zubaida comes to rest, in this paragraph, on a nice depiction of popular Arabic-language cinema, not only as shared cultural property, but a distinct vector for communication and interaction across classes and between strangers. Taxi drivers and porters memorize the dialogue and pass on their expertise to the "new viewers," who they imagine, like them, to be animated by the possibilities for chat and banter that movies inspire, and, like them, to be steeped in a shared Egyptian cinema lore, a commonality that overrode, however temporarily, all other differences.

Zubaida's depiction of this golden age also hints at the decline that was to follow, a decline that, despite the "current songs on every lip," has been associated in the minds of many with the rise of Egyptian movie musicals. These began with Mohammed Abd al-Wahhab's *al-Warda al-Bayda* [The White Rose] of 1933, a light romantic comedy involving star-crossed lovers. The nine films in which Abd al-Wahhab either starred or appeared as a musician between 1933 and 1963 established a formula to which his contemporaries and rivals, including Umm Kulthum, Farid al-Atrash, Layla Murad, Huda Sultan, and later, Abd al-Halim Hafiz, were highly indebted.[4] The Egyptian film industry hit its productive stride in the-mid 1940s.[5] Nasser, the argument goes, was interested in cinema merely as propaganda, however. As a consequence, he stifled creativity and failed to provide proper infrastructural support. This resulted in an exodus of talent and an under-resourced industry, increasingly dependent on a small stable of stars, and a dwindling stock of ideas and storylines, in which song-and-dance numbers increasingly substituted for real creativity. The economic austerity and political catastrophes of the 1960s hammered a further nail in the coffin of Egyptian cinema. The introduction of television and, later, the VCR in the 1970s accompanied a fundamental reorientation of the Egyptian public sphere, part and parcel of Sadat's *infitah* ("opening") of the Egyptian economy to foreign trade and investment. This put broadcast media in the hands of (often) Saudi Arabian-based conglomerates. Media consumption shifted from the public to the private space, a means no longer of radical social transformation, but a pernicious and deadening conservatism.[6]

The decline narrative can be read in various ways. Revisionists would stress that the roots of the crisis were systemic and deeply rooted even in the 1930s and 1940s. What happened in the 1950s, the period in which film musicals such as those of Abd al-Halim Hafiz predominated, was simply a working through of underlying contradictions inherent in this system. Vitalis for example, suggests that many accounts of Egyptian cinema neglect the crucial role of Hollywood cinema in Egyptian society throughout the "golden years" of the 1930s and 1940s, a role that created a space for the local industry, but damaged its long-term prospects. As Vitalis points out, Hollywood needed its overseas markets. During the 1940s, approximately 40 percent of the large Hollywood studios' revenues came from overseas. Universal had established itself in Cairo in 1926, followed by MGM, Twentieth Century Fox, and Paramount, owning their own movie theaters (the Royal, Metropole, Triumph, Roxy, Olympia, and Diana among them) in Cairo and Alexandria. These catered mainly to English-speaking foreigners. The American Embassy, the State Department, and the Motion Pictures Association of America and the Motion Pictures Export Association lobbied energetically and effectively to keep these cinemas in profitable business. They had to negotiate the occasional hostility of the Young Egypt movement, the Wafdist vanguard, and the Muslim Brothers and also deal with British censorship. They also had to cope with efforts to establish and protect a national film industry. Misr Studios was founded in 1935, owning its own production plant and movie theater. Yusuf Wahbi, who ran it, worked hard and successfully to extract concessions from the Hollywood-owned theaters (such as requirements to show at least one locally produced film per year). After the coup of 1952, Nasser authorized the creation of a National Film Center in 1957, whose efforts to promote local production and inspire a revolutionary cinema, however, cannot be said to have been at all successful. The figures for production, attendance, and functioning theaters went into decline and never fully recovered.

As Vitalis shows, a rather complex balance of power prevailed during Abd al-Halim's film career, in which Hollywood called the shots. This state of affairs prevailed until Nasserite legislation, later in the 1950s, began to make life difficult for the movie companies. By the 1930s, Hollywood had a Cairo-based apparatus in place to ensure regular profits from (elite, European) audiences across the Arab world. Dominating this niche, it had relatively little interest in branching out into Arabic-language film, which flourished in a space that Hollywood was for the most part able to control to its own advantage. The local industry's financial and institutional footing was always shaky, despite the boom-time of the war years. Each Hollywood film typically made 8,000 LE in Egypt alone, all costs having been covered by the time it reached the overseas markets: Hollywood could afford to show a large number of films and turn them over quickly. By contrast, the local industry operated on a fine margin. A typical Egyptian film would cost about 20,000 LE and would only just recoup these figures at the box office.[7] Films were few in number and turned over in movie theaters rather slowly, at least by comparison with the Hollywood films. The state enterprise Misr Studios functioned below capacity, relying on rental income from its production plant and the showing of foreign films at its one downtown movie theater. With the establishment of the National Film Center, things went from bad to worse. Although figures are hard to establish, it seems clear that local cinema, viewed as a whole, struggled to remain profitable. The number of functioning cinemas and films in production declined rapidly from a high point at the end of the 1940s.[8]

Two questions arise when we consider Abd al-Halim Hafiz's film musicals in the context of "decline." How might we understand their extraordinary commercial success and how do we understand their enduring cultural significance? Like his predecessors (and later business associates Mohammed Abd al-Wahhab and Farid al-Atrash), he starred in films that involved remarkable talents as writers, directors, actors, composers, musical arrangers, and instrumentalists who were, by the mid-1950s, experienced and very much in their stride. Egyptian cinema could still exploit the buzz of wealth, social mobility, and excitement bought by the war years. Cinemas were established firmly in the urban imagination not just as places to watch films, but to attend concerts and other events, places to see and be seen.[9] The films told stories that chimed subtly with the anxieties and excitements of the time, of young love prevailing despite the will of the old order and the tired patriarchs who preside over it, of wit, humor, and charm overcoming the adversity of fate, stories that now seem to brim with the anticolonial, nationalist, and revolutionary sentiments of the day. The continuity of Abd al-Halim's films with those of the past was cultivated and palpable, inviting the kind of intertextual referentiality that made Egyptian cinema tick from the very outset. Thus Abd al-Halim's first film role, Ustaz Galal in *Lahn al-Wafa* of 1955, reprises Mohammed Abd al-Wahhab's Ustaz Gallal in *al-Warda al-Bayda* of 1933.[10] Abd al-Halim's success surely owes something to the ability of the movie companies of his day to exploit a lively set of formulae and an energetic culture of cinema-going, despite straitened circumstances.

This doesn't fully explain why Abd al-Halim's light shone with such a peculiar intensity during those years. It may have been that the straitened circumstances of the mid- to late 1950s meant that there was little room at the top for more than a very small handful of successful companies and stars. If Mohammed Abd al-Wahhab, Layla Murad, Umm Kulthum, Farid al-Atrash, and Asmahan could share the musical cinematic stage a decade earlier, from 1955 onwards, it would seem that there may have been only room for one. Companies working with Abd al-Halim could rely on a smoothly running and highly talented "machine," involving a stable of composers who took on rather specific jobs (Munir Murad, Kamal al-Tawil, and Mohammed Mougi in particular), music arrangers (Ali Ismail and Andreas Reider), musicians (particularly Ahmed Fuad Hassan and the Firqa al-Masiyya, and Ali Ismail and Andreas Reider's jazz bands). Most of these had known Abd al-Halim since their youth, and had forged close musical relationships with one another as contemporaries at the Ma'had al-Musiqa al-'Arabiyya in Cairo in the late 1940s. Their work in cinema constituted just one element of complexly interdependent careers, divided between "day jobs," work in the radio, the commercial recording market, and live performance.[11] Abd al-Halim, a dominant force, was clearly at the center of a large network of musicians. He could be relied on to make the music "happen" in film productions efficiently, dominating an industry facing a shrinking market and rising production costs.[12]

One can readily understand why the Egyptian movie companies of the mid-1950s might have been so dependent on the charisma and the technical and organizational skills of a small number of musicians. By the late 1950s, they were able to flex their muscles, seeking a percentage share in profits, rather than one-off fees, and a greater degree of control of the production process. In 1959, Abd al-Halim bought his way into Aflam al-'Alam al-'Arabi, with whom he made *al-Banat wa al-Sayf* in 1960. It was, according to his biographer Magdi al-Amrussi, his frustrations with his dealings at this time with Cairophon, the state-run sound recording enterprise, which pushed him further in this direction (1994:81). Abd al-Halim had signed a contract with Cairophon for which they had offered LE 400. He asked for LE 2,000, plus 20 percent of the profits. Cairophon, by all accounts, readily agreed to the fee, but refused the percentage. Abd al-Halim then formed a partnership with Mohammed Abd-al Wahhab and Magdi al-Amrussi, adding a sound-recording and distribution arm to Aflam al-'Alam al-'Arabi, and renaming the company Sawt al-Fann. Abd al-Halim continued to manage his business through Sawt al-Fann until his death.

One can get a sense of how and why Abd al-Halim was quickly able to occupy such a powerful position in the Egyptian film and recording industry. This does not, however, fully explain the extraordinary appeal of the movies in their own time, or their resonance since.[13] Why are the songs still sung, and the stories of the films recalled by so many with such pleasure? Any account of the enduring popularity of these films must take into account their musical content. Rather than seeing the music as part of a general dumbing-down process, as the conventional "decline" narrative insists, I would argue that the musical content of Abd al-Halim's films was sophisticated, subtle, and intimately related to the powerful narratives of nationhood, modernity, and revolution circulating elsewhere. The audiences assumed by these films were, very evidently, not only knowledgeable and well versed in Egyptian movie history, particularly movie musical history, but intelligent listeners. The films assumed, and rewarded, an extensive knowledge of the conventions of Arab classical music, of Western classical and popular genres. They demanded, and played on, a subtle awareness of the debates and arguments being fought over Arab music, between traditionalists and modernists, between purists and cosmopolitans; they evoked discussions concerning the role of microphones and the effects of mass media, over conflicting interests in the music business, over the legitimacy of dance. They were, in other words, not simply films containing music that people loved; they were films *about* music.

The experience of this imagery (in film) was analogous to the mass rituals of reading novels and newspapers that Benedict Anderson identifies as an important means for knitting together "communities" of anonymous strangers. But more than the newspaper or novel, this film and others like it were intensely reflexive. *The Flirtation of Girls* was not really about anything other than itself. (Armbrust 2000:315)

Armbrust's discussion of *Ghazal al-Banat* [The Flirtation of Girls], Anwar Wajdi's classic from 1949 starring singers Layla Murad and Mohammed Abd al-Wahhab, engages many of the themes of his earlier study of Egyptian cinema (Armbrust 1996). Cinema in Egypt, he argues, did much of the work of novels and newspapers in Anderson's well-known account of print media in shaping a public, one preoccupied by the question of national belonging and the place of their nation in the world. The particular and peculiar formations of Egyptian national experience can be understood through, and with a proper regard of cinema, he argues; particularly its ambiguous frame of reference (Egyptian or Arab nationalism?), its formulation of a "split vernacular," in which language both unified and maintained abiding tensions between more and less legitimate cultural strata, its functions in a largely illiterate society. Armbrust brings the social and political significance of popular cinema into focus, complicating the claims of those overly focused on "art" cinema in the production of national and modern identities, particularly in a postcolonial context.

Reflexivity is a constant refrain in Armbrust's account of Egyptian cinema. This was cinema about itself, engaged in endless intertextual games and overt acknowledgement of the conditions of viewing, listening, and movie fandom. In *Ghazal al-Banat,* for instance, the characters reprise, in a spirit of high satire, roles they had already played earlier in their career. Al-Rihani reprises his role as Kishkish Bey from the days of the theatrical Franco-Arab reviews as the old man thwarted in love. Layla Murad's very first appearance with Abd al-Wahhab in *Yahya al-Hubb* (1938) is recalled. Abd al-Wahhab's advice to al-Rihani at the end directly evokes the plot and Abd al-Wahhab's sorry state at the end of *al-Warda al-Bayda.* In the through-the-looking-glass, story-within-a-story world the characters eventually enter in *Ghazal al-Banat,* the owner of the mansion, where the crazy resolution of the plot takes place, is Yusuf Wahbi, famous actor, director, and playwright. Anwar Wajdi, the director and playwright, was also Layla Murad's husband, who had co-starred with her in numerous romantic comedies. Dense intertexuality and reflexivity, Armbrust stresses, was central to the pleasure of Egyptian popular cinema, and central to its social processes and effects.

This insight can be extended to the place of music and musicians in Abd al-Halim's films. First of all, we should put Abd al-Halim's musicals in their context. Mohammed Abd al-Wahhab's first film musical, *al-Warda al-Bayda* of 1933, shows a genteel aristocrat fallen on hard times, whose musical struggles to define a route between tradition and modernity parallel his struggle to define his social and amorous relationships with the beautiful daughter of a vulgar but wealthy family. Umm Kulthum's films, by all accounts less successful at the box office than those of Abd al-Wahhab, but still well-known nonetheless, use musical scenes to dramatize the struggle between the innocent and the exploiters, the licentious and the decent, in settings that were often historical fantasies, yet clearly bore on contemporary moral concerns about the place of music and musicians in Egyptian life. Farid al-Atrash's films, which dominated Egyptian cinema in the years immediately preceding Abd al-Halim's rise to fame, dramatize the quest for an authentic musical modernity in various ways. In *Akhir Kizba,* for example, he travels with his troupe to Cairo to find the sheikhs who will help him in the task, tracking them down to a café where an ecstatic *dawr,* the culmination of the traditional *wasla* (suite) is in progress. Abd al-Halim's first film of 1955, *Lahn al-Wafa,* has the young singer bringing to fruition the musical dream of his estranged adopted father, a distinguished maestro. His character takes the name of Mohammed Abd al-Wahhab's hero in *al-Warda al-Bayda.* In this as in many other ways, the films of Abd al-Halim clearly were designed to be placed in a certain context: a history of

Egyptian musical films that narrate the making of Egyptian, and, more generally, Arab music.

Abd al-Halim's films dramatize some rather specific conflicts and tensions within this field. Western popular music is dangerous (as in *al-Wisada al-Khalia*, 1957), but correctly handled, it also can make Arab music modern and cosmopolitan (*Maw'id Gharam*, 1956). Musicians must be revolutionary, but must also be true to the past, as well as the street (*Lahn al-Wafa*, 1955; *Sharia al-Hobb*, 1958). Poor performance by singers and musicians can reduce the efforts of the most intelligent composer and poets to cheap and tawdry entertainment; performing musicians and audiences must be educated, too, if music is to move "forward" (*Dalila*, 1956). Singers need to balance the intimate aesthetics of enchantment (*tarab*) with the demands of studios, concert halls, and other disenchanted modern spaces (*Maw'id Gharam*, 1956).[14] Stardom treats men and women differently (*Ma'abudet el-Jamahir*, 1967). Decency is always under duress, with quite different effects either side of the gender divide.

One particular element of musical reflexivity is at issue in all of these films: how music (and sound more generally) circulates under conditions of mass-mediation. Films lend themselves to this kind of reflexivity, as Michel Chion (1994) has argued. The processes of assembling a story on celluloid involves separating sound from dramatic action and reassembling it in a complex process that has elicited, from various filmmakers, subtle narrative play on the relationship between diegetic and nondiegetic sound. At the most general level, twentieth-century mass-mediation technologies separated bodies and voices in ways that fascinated, absorbed, and perplexed producers and consumers. This splitting has gendered implications, as Chion's analysis of thrillers suggests. Women's voices are separated from and reconnect with their bodies on screens in ways that differ from those of men's voices. The questions this raises for female spectatorship are complex and fascinating (see Hansen 1991 for an extended discussion).

Abd al-Halim's films exemplify many of the general points in Chion's analysis. They are almost obsessively absorbed by the question of how voices circulate around public space, not only on radios and televisions, but in cafés, on streets, and around houses, between young and old, informed and uneducated, men and women. In a nicely subversive joke at the expense of Umm Kulthum in *Dalila*, Dalila's ancient mother wants to tune in to (we assume) the Thursday Umm Kulthum program, but the radio is broken.[15] Abd al-Halim, always on the alert for an opportunity to fool around, goes into the next room and speaks through a hole in the wall behind the radio set, announcing the number and faking an Umm Kulthum song with his oboe and own voice. Her mother appears not to notice the joke being played; Dalila and Abd al-Halim are in stitches. A popular image of Abd al-Halim, an image that recurs in a large number of his films, involve a circulating voice, whether cycling around Cairo, or circling the world as he shoots to fame (see Gordon 2002).[16] Entire plots revolve around messages overheard or missed, on encounters in crowed and noisy spaces where verbal messages cannot be exchanged, on voices present but bodies far removed in space, of messages left and picked up either too soon or too late. It is impossible to watch an Abd al-Halim movie without constantly being struck by the preoccupation of those who made the film with the properties of voices circulating around (and between) public and private spaces: their speed or slowness, the ease or difficulty with which they circulate, the extent of their emotional or coercive impact. To a point, one might say, this preoccupation is contiguous with the more general phenomenon noted by Chion, and shared, to a degree, by Hollywood and other film musicals, known—at least to the elite—in Abd al-Halim's Cairo.

Some rather more specific issues are at play, though. Alongside a preoccupation with the making of music and the making of the musician is a preoccupation with the act of listening. In this one might detect echoes of a much longer concern in Arab culture with the legitimacy of music, and the conditions and contexts in which listening might most productively and appropriately take place. However, the central questions being posed in these films are distinctly modern. If "traditional" performance contexts enable and sanction a particular, socially validated kind of emotionality through close feedback loops connecting performers and audiences (*tarab*), does mass-mediation produce deviant listening and listeners? Is *tarab* possible under modern conditions? What are the alternatives?

In most regards, concert life and mass-mediation never proved too detrimental to *tarab*, as Racy (2002) demonstrates. However idealized the small-scale event (the *jalsa*) might have been in Arab society, something of its intimacy and subtlety and something of its intricate social protocols could be reproduced on stage or in recordings (where the appreciative comments of listeners often were included in the final cut). At issue, one might say, is not the problem of modernity per se, but, rather, an anxiety about what *can* happen under modern conditions; specifically, musical emotion produced and consumed in conditions of solitude and isolation. Without the intricate but rigorous checks and balances of *tarab*, in which emotion circulates, but is also regulated, sanctioned, and socialized, the modern subject is incapable of withstanding the psychically destabilizing effects of music well-known to Middle Easterners through scholarly and popular Islamic traditions.

Abd al-Halim's *Maw'id Gharam* of 1956 might be read not just as a dramatized confrontation of two very different ways of being a modern Arab musician, but of being a modern Arab listener. The film is worth describing in a bit of detail. It conforms in many respects to Joel Gordon's (2002) characterization of revolutionary melodrama in this period, marketed, as it was, as a "love story," full of the "noblest human sentiments" (*qissas 'atifiyya tanbid fiha anbal al-ahasis al-insaniyya*) (*Akhir Sa'a*, 1957), but also clearly a parable about the social responsibilities of the artist. It is a story of how love for a serious young female journalist (Nawal, played by Fatin Hamama) transforms the carefree life of an urbane young man (Samir, played by Abd al-Halim) into one of social commitment and responsibility. Having heard him singing to her, Nawal encourages Samir to consider taking up a career in music, to do something serious with his life. At the very point that Samir's career takes off, Nawal succumbs to an illness, which confines her to a wheelchair, though, through complicated narrative mechanisms, this information is kept from Samir. This provides an opportunity for a rival to Samir's affections to enter the scene, the stiffly upright and decent Dr. Kamal, played by Imad Hamdi. He takes responsibility for looking after Nawal, though with a growing realization that she really loves Samir. Samir finally declares his love and returns from Beirut, where he is on tour. Dr. Kamal arranges a trip to the Gulf for Nawal for hospital treatment, secretly arranges for the lovers to be reconciled at Cairo Airport, and gracefully steps out of Nawal and Samir's life.

How does musicianship and listenership figure in this film? The emotional epicenter of the film falls shortly after the halfway point, framed by two large musical numbers that configure musicianship and listenership in two contrasting ways. In the first, Samir is launching his career as a musician. A few fragmentary scenes show him hard at work with an orchestra, and before we know it he is giving his first concert, in the al-Andalus gardens in downtown Cairo. We hear an up-tempo number with a foxtrot feel, in melancholy *maqam* (mode) Nahawand, with some gracefully descending chromatic phrases.[17] It is typical of many of Kamal al-Tawil's songs for Abd al-Halim: modally clear and rhythmically robust, with an instantly identifiable tune and verse/chorus structure. The refrain in the lyrics, by Ma'amun al-Shinnawi, ask *"beyni wa beynak eh?"* [what is there between us?] If there is a hint of ambiguity here, it is dispelled in the scene we observe. Nothing seems to come between Samir and his admiring listeners. The voice circulates effortlessly and the camera tracks its movements, playing over a well-drilled orchestra, a well-groomed audience listening quietly but with obvious pleasure, and the attentive talent scouts from Beirut nodding to one another with professional interest. Nawal, sick, is at home in bed, but is shown briefly, listening with friends to the live broadcast of the concert on the radio. A scene, in other words, of disciplined musical production, mediation, and consumption. This is definitely what Nawal had in mind for Samir, and, one might say, for Arab culture more generally.

The moment this musical number comes to an end, the plot is thrown into turmoil. Samir is offered a contract by the Beiruti entrepreneurs. He does not realize the extent of Nawal's illness at this stage, or the full nature of her relationship with Dr. Kamal. So at this point he is torn between his career and his affection for Nawal. But the matter is decided when he sees Nawal and Dr. Kamal together in the latter's car. He quickly jumps to the understandable conclusion, accepts the Beirut deal, and phones Nawal reproachfully from the airport. All of this takes place within a few minutes of screen time. The sounds of the last song are still ringing in our ears as the next one strikes up, and the contrast could not be more pronounced.

A crash of drums and a dramatic orchestral flourish introduces a concert hall scene. A serious and disciplined orchestra sets to work, once again. But, fairly quickly, we realize from the music that something is amiss. The long instrumental introduction meanders. Quasi fantasia gives way to something that sounds as though it is going to be a tango, and then settles on a relentless and featureless motoric rhythm. Modally, a fluctuating D natural/D flat suggests that a conflict between Nahawand (with a lower five-note grouping of C-D-E flat-F-G) and Kurd (with a lower four-note grouping of C-D flat-E flat-F) is not going to be resolved.[18] Nahawand is only established along with a sudden shift in tonal center from C to G in the final *qafla* (cadence). Experienced listeners will detect at once all of the hallmarks of the work of Abd al-Halim's other main composer, Mohammed Mougi, with its wrenching changes of musical affect, its emotional excess, its rhetorical bombast and lachrymosity.[19]

So far, neither audience nor singer is in evidence. The camera dwells at length on the huge orchestra, instrument by instrument, section by section. Finally, the singer appears, the camera moving down rather oddly over his head, so Samir seems to rise up in front of the orchestra as he sings the opening lines of the song, "Law Kunt Yawm Ansak" [If the day were to come and I were to forget you]. The camera remains on his face as he sings the opening verse. Samir is clearly already a star: here he is in Lebanon, with massive forces at his disposal and broadcasting live to the entire (Arab) world. And yet Nawal's betrayal clearly has crushed him. He has achieved success, but at a terrible price. The song meanders, even by the standards of Abd al-Halim's "dark night of the soul" songs. The Nahawand/Kurd ambiguity persists. A central section introduces another set of tone colors (woodwinds) and a contrastive tonality. The ends of the verses cleverly dovetail with the opening line of the choruses, both musically and lyrically; there is no clear transition. Though one can interpret it in terms of the *mazhab*/refrain structure of popular Arabic song of the time, Mougi has set out to write a song that will disorient listeners, to pose musical questions that can't easily be resolved.

And the dramatic focus, at this moment, is indeed on the listener. During the long orchestral sections, we switch from Samir in Beirut to Nawal listening in Cairo, alone in her room, confined to her wheelchair, tears streaming down her face. The camera moves closer and closer to Samir's face as he sings; during the instrumental interludes, it moves closer and closer to Nawal. First her wheelchair-bound body dominates the frame, then her face, then a teardrop forming on her eye. This slow-motion, dual-focus zoom is broken when the song ends. Dr. Kamal walks through the door as the announcer tells the listeners that they have been listening to Samir live from Beirut. In a guilty panic, Nawal jerks forward on her chair and switches off the radio.

The contrast with the first scene of listenership is marked. The first is collective; this is solitary. In the first we see couples, professional folk, friends and strangers, present at the concert and elsewhere. Here we see only Samir and Nawal. In the first, we see an audience visibly following the music, nodding, tapping their feet, exchanging appreciative glances. Though disciplined and a little passive (and not quite the *tarab* audience described by Racy and others), they are clearly very much part of the musical scene. Here, Nawal is lost in her own misery, and hardly seems to be listening at all. The contrast is emphasized by the contrast in musical styles. In the first, we hear music that is palpably modern, but which reaches out to and engages with audience expectations and conventions. The conventions at play here are rooted in *tarab* and *turath,* but they also assume a familiarity with the American dance styles and genres of the 1940s and 1950s. In the second, we hear a music that follows its own unruly and whiny emotional outbursts wherever they take it. Long sections of it can be heard as *mawwal,* classical vocal nonmetered improvisation, or as the long "*bidun misura*" (nonmetered) sections, in which singer and unison strings move together at the opening of long concert songs (*ughniyya*).[20] But a listener with some knowledge of the rhetorical flourishes of nineteenth-century Western orchestral art music also seems to be assumed.

The contrast is also emphasized by the relationship between what we see and what we hear in the two scenes. In the first, we start off diegetically: What we see is what we hear. When the accordion strikes up the "Woody the Woodpecker" instrumental hook, we see the accordion and the accordionist. When Abd al-Halim starts singing, we see the singer. From that point on, sound and visual image part company. Abd al-Halim's voice accompanies the camera as it circulates, across the orchestra and the audience, and across the faces of listeners at home. The conjoint movements of camera and voice depict—within the conventions of the story—ideal conditions: modern music and listeners constituting an organized, modern, disciplined public in and through the act of listening to this voice. The second depicts conditions that are far from ideal: modern music, certainly, but music that fails to generate any significant social solidarities. We see one singer and one listener, trapped in their own misery. The movement of the camera emphasizes the point. When Abd al-Halim is singing, we see his body, and eventually only his face. It is only when the orchestra is playing that we cut to Nawal. (Eventually we only see her face, too.) If, as Chion suggests, the technique of moving voices toward and away from the bodies visually represented on screen can be put in the service of particular dramatic and expressive ends, a contrast between the two scenes seems to be established here in precisely these terms. In the first, the voice circulates; in the second, it doesn't. In the first, it is depicted generating community; in the second, social atomization.

Walter Armbrust suggests that reflexivity and self-referentiality are general properties of popular Egyptian cinema, and of particular resonance in the rather specific colonial conditions in which an Egyptian modernity was being fashioned in the 1930s and 1940s. Abd al-Halim's films are clearly no exception, although they complicate the picture in certain ways. The madcap, helter-skelter, humorous reflexivity of *Ghazal al-Banat* is rather distant from Abd al-Halim's films. In *Maw'id Gharam*, for instance, as we have seen, Samir is asked to consider a musical career as a means of putting his talents, his leisure and his wealth to productive social effect, and thus win the love of Nawal. The (rapid) scenes in which Abd al-Halim is shown learning his craft and honing his musical skills before his first appearance in public are clearly not intended to be comic or fantastic. Rather, they assert that music is socially productive, socially self-constitutive *work*. One might want to distinguish, then, reflexivity as a kind of subversive, excessive humor operating in a colonial context (Armbrust's characterization of *Ghazal al-Banat*) from reflexivity operating in a revolutionary context, promoting a rather sober message about the artist in the service of the community. It is also worth noting that musicianship in the films of the older generation (Mohammed Abd al-Wahhab, Farid al-Atrash, Umm Kulthum) is usually a sign of actual or potential social marginality, a problem to be overcome or an issue to be negotiated on the route to respectability, decency, and social approbation. In Abd al-Halim's films, it is usually the reverse. Music—properly modern music—is a social virtue.

Abd al-Halim's films seem to echo their predecessors, but also inject new concerns and preoccupations. The revolutionary context is important. Nasser's political power, to an extent unprecedented in Egyptian society, was mediated by the sound of his voice. This was a voice full not only of political power and persuasion, but of subtle emotional inflection and a certain kind of intimacy: a voice both public but also *close*. This was a public, one might say, in which the central institution was not the book, or the newspaper, or even the cinema, but the *microphone* (see Stokes, forthcoming). Gamal Abd al-Nasser and Abd al-Halim were linked closely in this regard. Like Nasser, Abd al-Halim, too, had a voice that exploited the microphone for its powers and effects.[21] His films, though, spell out the anxieties associated with this new technology of public address and mobilization. How does one guarantee the emotional effects of one's voice when those listening to it are not co-present, their reactions not gauged and calibrated, their feedback not at hand to help the speaker or singer shape his/her rhetoric, his/her improvisatory flow? In a dyadic scene of listenership, how is the listener to be protected, to be safeguarded from powerful emotions that burn too powerfully when not appropriately collectivized? Can mass media be relied on to reproduce, in other words, the kind of constructive emotional circulation of *tarab* culture?

Ethnographic approaches to mediation are potentially powerful because they do not have to rely primarily on speculative abstraction to render visible those potentialities that are constitutive of, and yet disavowed in, any social order. Given a well-chosen field site, an anthropologist has access, as events unfold, to the precarious relationship between determination and indeterminacy that structures mediation in the flow of social practice. Nonethnographic critical theorists of the media may strive to rescue or redeem these potentialities by projecting them into a radical future or mourning them in a receding past. But anthropologists enjoy the empirical benefits of being in the thick of it while not succumbing to the plain empiricism that characterizes instrumental and applied analyses of culture, globalization, and mediation. (Mazarella 2004:359)

One can sense the ways in which Abd al-Halim renders visible (and audible) potentialities constitutive of, and yet disavowed in, the Egyptian social order. If, for example, the dominant discourses of Egyptian social life since Nasser have been male-oriented, revolutionary, and laying a high store on wit and good humor, Abd al-Halim's appeal to women (often commented upon in his lifetime), and the current of melancholy, tearfulness, and sentimentalism that runs through his films and music, strike a very different note. One needs to ground these intuitions, though. Can one aspire to a critical ethnography of Abd al-Halim Hafiz, in Mazarella's terms? Can one avoid the dangers of projecting one's sense of such "potentialities" onto a radical future, or mourning them in a receding past? What would constitute a "well-chosen field site" in this case, where the artist in question is dead and gone, his business interests dispersed, his voice and image omnipresent, but fleeting and elusive? How can one place oneself "in the thick of it" when one only has fragments, memories, silences? The difficulties involved in such a project are all too obvious.

Things can be "done," of course, despite—and in some cases because of—these very difficulties. Less plugged in to local networks of expertise and habits of scholarly deference and dependency, I found myself, a newcomer to Egyptian studies in 1999, able to notice and ponder at least some of the quirks, blind spots, disavowals, and silences that accumulate in the discourses surrounding such major cultural icons. Struggles to follow colloquial language, whether in conversation, watching films, or listening to recordings, occasionally could free me (in moments of exhaustion and frustration) to attend to nuances of language use before they had become fully naturalized, normalized, and "understood" in routinized ways. They also enabled me to consider how stories are being told, points being made, and emotional effects produced *beyond* the linguistic, narrowly conceived. It is precisely in these moments, one might argue, that one can get a rather direct access to the "precarious relationship between determination and indeterminacy" of which Mazarella speaks, a relationship one must surely understand if one is to get a sense of the complex social life still lived by Abd al-Halim Hafiz, his music, and his films in Egypt today.

I will conclude with a brief analysis of sites characterized, I believe, by just such a "precarious relationship between determination and indeterminacy." One concerns the public memorialization of Abd al-Halim Hafiz over the last decade. Abd al-Halim's music gradually was removed from the airwaves during Anwar Sadat's rule as a legacy of a Nasserite policy. His nationalist anthems, such a prominent feature of the Egyptian mediascape in the latter part of the 1960s, disappeared after Camp David and Sadat's peace with Israel. Hosni Mubarak succeeded Sadat in changing circumstances, characterized by growing popular support of the Palestinian intifada, and the decline of oil revenues and migrant remittances that previously had propped up the state and mitigated the effects of economic liberalization on the poorer sections of society. This produced an ambiguous and highly conflicted nostalgia for Nasser and the signs and symbols of his era, prominent among which was Abd al-Halim Hafiz. Celebrations of Abd al-Halim Hafiz's death, previously a matter of journalistic reminiscence, took a more official and overtly serious tone. Highbrow newspapers began to join in the celebration with scholarly, rather than anecdotal and gossipy articles. The Cairo Opera celebrated anniversaries of his death with gala performances of songs he had made famous, and singers who had, to my eyes and ears, carefully studied not only Abd al-Halim's voice but also his mannerisms and general demeanor on stage. Cairophon, the state recording company, began to distribute Abd al-Halim's *wataniyat* (nationalist anthems) alongside those of Mohammed Abd al-Wahhab and Umm Kulthum. Official celebrations of the half-century of the revolution in July 2002 involved a sound-and-light show over the Nile in downtown Cairo, in which "Sura Sura," Abd al-Halim's nationalist anthem of 1967, to words by Salah Jahin and music by Kamal al-Tawil, was played repeatedly on the public address system.

And yet this official recuperation has in some regards been a rather cautious and selective affair. Cairo contains a number of statues of Umm Kulthum and Mohammed Abd al-Wahhab, though none, at the moment, of Abd al-Halim Hafiz. Large new museums and research centers have been dedicated to Umm Kulthum (on Roda Island) and to Abd al-Wahhab (at the newly renovated State Conservatory near Ramses Square), though none have to Abd al-Halim Hafiz. There has been a disproportionate emphasis in the official recuperation of Abd al-Halim's political songs and the long concert songs sung at the end of his career. Only a relatively small proportion of his many film songs get sung in state-sponsored performances at the Cairo Opera and by state-sponsored ensembles elsewhere. Why this ambiguity and selectivity? On the one hand, I would venture, one sees a state anxious to recuperate the pride, glamour, and excitement of the Nasserite era, though equally anxious to distance itself from its social radicalism. On the other is a nostalgic intelligentsia, combing the past for recognizably "high cultural" signs of a vigorous political modernism that might yet be regained. The film songs and the film career have no obvious role to play in this recuperation, but they cannot be entirely forgotten, as long as the rest of his career is being celebrated. Hence an ambiguous, cautious, and highly selective top-down recuperation of Abd al-Halim that has focused disproportionately on his political songs, and the long concert songs of his late career. This ambiguity has been explored subtly in a number of recent films that have evoked the image (and soundtracks) of Abd al-Halim Hafiz, notably Muhammad Khan's *Zawjat Rajul Muhim* of 1987, and Khayri Bishara's *Ice Cream fi Glim* of 1992 (see Gordon 2002).

Another such site is the highly public struggle over the fate of the recording company that Abd al-Halim established with Mohammed Abd al-Wahhab and Magdi al-Amrussi, Sawt al-Fann. The Abd al-Halim trust, established by family members, contested Amrussi's right to exploit the large catalogue that Sawt al-Fann had built up over the years, including not only many of the early Abd al-Halim recordings, but many of those of Mohammed Abd al-Wahhab, as well. The dispute rumbled on through the Egyptian press throughout the later 1990s and the early 2000s. At the same time, EMI, who had garnered the rights to Abd al-Halim's film songs and many of his later concert songs through the efforts of John Deakin in their Dubai office, were busy exploiting a relatively new market in CDs, both in the Arab world and among Diasporic audiences in Europe and the United States. Internet music providers were simply helping themselves. New legislation in 1998 opened the doors for the large transnational media corporations, Sony, AOL Time-Warner, and Vivendi, who quickly moved into Egyptian media markets. A newly formed conglomerate, the Arab Company for Arts and Publishing (known in Egypt as the "Funun") seized the moment, buying up the distribution rights to some nine hundred Egyptian films and a number of large recording companies, amongst them Sawt Libnan (which owned the rights to Farid al-Atrash's recordings) and Sawt al-Fann (Faulks 2001:74). Their aggressive expansion into Arab media markets (which included their purchase of the large entertainment complexes owned by the Renaissance Group and the Osman Group in Egypt, and the al-Masa chain in the Gulf, as well as launching their own film production company) eventually landed them in financial trouble. In 2004, they were bought out by Rotana, a major Saudi media conglomerate owned by al-Walid ibn Talal. Egyptian film critics launched a campaign to stop the sale of "heritage" to foreigners. The Egyptian government recently responded by proposing a law to protect cinematic and musical heritage (Awad 2004:235).

If there is a broad shift here as far as Abd al-Halim's music is concerned, it is from larger to smaller (and less controllable) commodity forms, and from circulation in public places (in movie theaters) to circulation in private places (in the home, on television, CD and DVD). This has been enabled by political and technological developments common to many parts of the world, in which miniaturization and privatization have gone hand in hand. However, the process has not gone without commentary or dispute in Egypt. As we have seen, Sawt al-Fann's claims to Abd al-Halim's music were disputed by family members. Local lobbies have protested the free circulation of his music on the internet, and its expropriation by foreign capital. The state has made half-hearted efforts to address these concerns to make a show of protecting heritage and cultural patrimony, all the while seeking to promote (selected aspects of) Abd al-Halim's legacy for its own political purposes, as described above. Here at least, though, Abd al-Halim's film music, in the smoky and jazzy original versions orchestrated by Ali Ismail and Andreas Reider, are being given a new lease of life, thanks to the widely available EMI film soundtrack CDs. Although both state and corporations have struggled to control Abd al-Halim's legacy in recent years, no one version of this legacy yet predominates.

Finally, one can consider the musical spaces in which Abd al-Halim's songs still circulate. A newcomer to Cairo will quickly notice the sound of Abd al-Halim's voice, if he or she has been taught how to recognize it, more or less everywhere. One hears it on cassettes in taxicabs, on a popular state radio program (the *Idha'a al-Aghani*) often tuned into by shop and stall owners, and thus all over the streets of Cairo, and on late-night TV movies on the state channel, often on Thursdays as the weekends begin and families relax together in front of their televisions. As already mentioned, one heard his *wataniyat* on the radio and television with increasing frequency as the fiftieth anniversary of the revolution approached. Concerts of classical *takht* music at official downtown venues such as the Cairo Opera and the Gumhurriya Theater include renditions of songs that Abd al-Halim made famous sung by young conservatory-trained singers. It is easy to lay one's hands on publications of his song lyrics and musical notations, particularly those published by the Dar al-Sharq al-'Arabi, designed with educational intent (Fakhouri n.d.). Although I know relatively little about vocal training in Cairo, I can attest to the fact that learning classical instrumental music, one quickly encounters the quirky and winding instrumental introductions to Abd al-Halim's songs as exercises in teaching not only *turath*, but also *maqam* and instrumental technique. Abd al-Halim's music is, in a sense, monumental: deeply internalized and naturalized as part of the legitimate cultural order and as materially tangible as a historic mosque or a portrait of the president. In another sense, it is a pedagogical resource: something to be studied, dissected, picked over, discussed, and appreciated by people seeking to gain serious musical knowledge, a knowledge that will produce new things as well as simply reproduce the past.

Abd al-Halim's film songs linger in the memory of musicians in Cairo, though, in ways that cannot be entirely reduced to their monumental or pedagogical status. A personal anecdote will serve to illustrate. At the end of the summer of 2004, during one of the minor (pre-Ramadan) Qandil festivals, one of the various Ministry of Culture sponsored ensembles was to perform a concert of religious music at a small downtown venue. I attended out of curiosity, partly because I thought it might offer an interesting contrast to the larger concerts of religious music I had been to earlier that week. It was poorly advertised and even more poorly attended. Most of the "audience" turned out to be part of a state radio recording crew, who were setting up their equipment and doing sound checks for nearly an hour after the concert was supposed to have started. Evidently the point of the exercise was the production of a radio concert to be aired at some subsequent point.

Within seconds of starting the concert proper, a buzz, a bang, and a yell from the mixing desk, followed by the acrid smell of burning plastic, suggested that this was not to be. An hour passed, the audience melted away, technicians were summoned, and the musicians kicked their heels. I made small talk and waited to see what would happen, having nothing better to do. It was at this point that the accordion player, sitting on the stage on his own, quietly struck up the accordion phrase that starts "Beyni wa Beynak Eh?," the Abd al-Halim film song from *Maw'id Gharam* discussed above. A handful of musicians joined him, singing along quietly to the end of the song. Another Abd al-Halim song from the movies followed, and then another and yet another, each attracting a different singer and a handful of instrumentalists who wandered on and off the stage. They sang quietly, but were listened to by those left in the concert hall, attracting smiles and applause at the end of each. The songs continued for about an hour and half. Soon it was midnight. The director, who seemed to me to have made a point of not joining in, listening to, or responding to the music on stage, apologized and sent everybody on their way.

The event said much to me about the complex ways in which Abd al-Halim is remembered today: a demonstration of musical chops and memory to peers; a sardonic and humorous evocation of a secular age in increasingly religious times; a kindling of social warmth in an anonymous modern space; a whiling away of time when the apparatus of officialdom breaks down. Where Abd al-Halim's music serves official purposes, monumentalizing *turath*, bringing musicians in conservatories and audiences in the large state-sponsored downtown concert halls into the disciplinary force field of Arab modernism, it serves unofficial purposes as well, in everyday spaces on the fringe of officialdom (for officialdom is omnipresent), spaces shaped by daydreams, boredom, frustration, humor. It is a curious and powerful property of Abd al-Halim's film music that it can shape such different kinds of cultural memory. Some, as we have seen, are very much determined by the apparatus of power and cultural legitimacy in Egyptian society. Others are more elusive, hinting at critique and a vision of how things still could be.

I am most grateful to John Deakin (formerly of EMI), Martin Hart (of widescreenmuseum.com), Ziyad al-Tawil (son of Kamal al-Tawil), and Zakariya Amir (former recording engineer in Studio 49, Cairo Radio) who provided me, in interviews and e-mail correspondences, with much of the information that appears in these pages. I am indebted to Joel Gordon, Charles Hirschkind, Ron Inden, and Farouk Mustafa for patient feedback, thoughts, and encouragement as this project has progressed. If I haven't always been able to respond adequately here, I hope to in the future. I pursued some of this research, and did much thinking about it, on a fellowships generously provided by the Howard Foundation and by the Franke Institute for the Humanities at the University of Chicago. I use common and recognizable English orthography for Egyptian names as far as possible, but the IJMES standard for transliterating written Arabic elsewhere.

Notes

1. Gamal Abd al-Nasser (also transliterated as Jamal abd al-Nasir), led the "Free Officers" in the coup of July 23, 1952, installing one of their number, Muhammed Naguib, as President. Naguib was eventually deposed, and Nasser, then vice-chairman of the Revolutionary Command Council, took over as President until his death on September 28, 1970. Land reform, the nationalization of resources and industry, and the development of pan-Arab socialism were early goals, though by the later 1950s, Nasser was absorbed by the suppression of dissent, and the collapse of public confidence after the catastrophic 1967 war against Israel. His rule took an increasingly authoritarian cast, and the later years were marked by increasingly close ties with the Soviet Union. He was succeeded by Anwar Sadat, a fellow Free Officer, who chose a diametrically opposed route: rapprochement with the West and Israel, and an "open door" (*"infitah"*) to foreign investment.

2. Bilharzia, otherwise known as schistosomaisis, is a parasitic disease picked up in water, often by wading or swimming. It gradually debilitates those who have caught it, affecting digestive and urinary systems, liver, and spleen, ultimately causing nervous system lesions and fibrosis. The disease is associated with poverty in Egypt; even in decline and death, Abd al-Halim was an emblematic figure.

3. The question has been broached in Egypt by Charles Hirschkind (see, for example, Hirschkind 2001), and, at a general and theoretical level, in Viet Erlmann's recent collection (Erlmann 2004, containing essays by Hirschkind, among others).

4. I draw from (and refer readers to) Walter Armbrust's detailed discussion of Mohammed Abd al-Wahhab (in Armbrust 1996, particularly chapters two and four) and the filmography that appears in a footnote (1996:238, f.n. 4). Abd al-Wahhab was a noted *oud* (lute) player, composer, and film star, born in 1907. He died of heart failure in 1991. His film career wound down in the 1950s; composition, including for his famous rival, Umm Kulthum, increasingly occupied him. For his longevity and continued activity as a singer and composer right up to his death, he was know as across the Arab world as the "musician of generations."

5. Armbrust mentions that about nine hundred films were made in the heyday of the musical, which is to say the period stretching between the mid-1940s and the early 1960s (2002:237). Of these, approximately one-third might be described as musicals.

6. For a useful account of the history of the introduction of electronic media technologies in Egypt, see Boyd 1999. The "conventional" narrative being evoked at the end of this paragraph draws—perhaps a little crudely—on Ezzedine (1966)

and on Shafik for the impact of television (see particularly 1998:27). Ezzedine (1966) is emphatic on the subject of the ruination caused by film musicals. Both are particularly concerned with the domination of singers in the industry, the growing hegemony of their poor taste, and the high fees they were commanding. Shafik also finds little to praise in the musical cinema of this period. On the introduction of television, Abu-Lughod offers some important nuances. Recent television soaps effect an "emotionalization of the quotidian" (2005:124) thoroughly bound up with the nation-state project in Egypt. But their political effects are complex and hard to predict from their overt messages. Soaps like *Hilmiyya Nights,* which dominate much Egyptian television programming today, are thoroughly imbued with the ideologies of national development and Arab socialism held dear by the media elites who script and produce them. But they are also complicit in the religious conservatism and consumerism ushered in by Sadat's *infitah* (economic "open door" policies) of the late 1970s. Soap morality, whilst individuated, is also squarely located in domestic networks and other collective environments. As a political force-field, they are often conflicting and contradictory.

7. Abd al-Halim's final film, *Abi Fawq al-Shajjara,* reputedly cost LE 168,000 to make in 1967, an intermediary stage between the figures for the 1950s and those of today, where Shafik suggests a figure of LE 750,000, of which up to LE 300,000 will be spent on actors. A constant here is the high cost of securing the services of stars, leaving little for other production costs.

8. Vitalis (2000) and Shafik (1998) indicate annual production of some 49 films per year late in the 1940s, showing in some 315 movie theaters in Egypt.

9. On cinemas as sites of modern self-fashioning in other contexts, see Larkin 2002 and Hansen 1991.

10. Amrussi mentions that Mohammed Karim, respected director of the first Egyptian film musical, Abd al-Wahhab's *al-Warda al-Bayda,* had Abd al-Wahhab very firmly in mind when he was crafting the Abd al-Halim character for *Dalila;* Abd al-Halim, apparently, dug his heels in and insisted on doing things his way (al-Amrussi 1994:291).

11. Mougi was, in 1956, still a schoolteacher (Mahir 1956). Hassanayn (1995) mentions his rising stock as a film-music composer, earning EL 600 for the two songs he often would compose for Abd al-Halim's films in this period, each of which would typically have six songs, divided up between Kamal al-Tawil, Mohammed Mougi, and Munir Murad.

12. Cinemascope technology was an important contributor to these rising costs. *Dalila* was Abd al-Halim's first experiment with Cinemascope. Briefly, Cinemascope involved an apparatus by which film images were compressed in the making of the film, and then expanded to fill a broad screen in new, specially designed movie theaters. The costs and licensing fees were, by all accounts, prohibitive. The movie apparently was a flop (al-Amrussi 1994:291), and his next several movies reverted to the old system. Perhaps the local industry was not yet ready to make the leap. Perhaps, too, audiences were slow to appreciate the new aesthetic of Cinemascope, appropriate for epics in which one could watch action and sound moving around on the big screen, captured by a more or less stationary camera and stereo recording, but less appropriate for intimate dramas, in which head shots and close-ups of facial expressions were important, and much could be made, dramatically, of a relatively mobile camera (as my analysis of *Maw'id Gharam* here suggests).

13. In what sense were the films "successful"? This is extremely difficult to establish in a quantative sense. Otherwise uncritical biographers (for example, al-Amrussi) comment that *Dalila,* his first Cinemascope film, was not a success,

though whether this means that numbers were low, or that it attracted adverse comments in the press is hard to tell. Likewise, *Abi Fawq al-Shajjara* apparently showed for a full year in the Diana cinema in downtown Cairo when it was released in 1969, though it is difficult to say whether this also means that it showed for a corresponding long period of time elsewhere. Certainly, leafing through the pages of the popular press of the 1950s, *Ruz al-Yusuf, Kawakib, Akhir Sa'a,* articles on Abd al-Halim start to proliferate very soon after 1955, and advertisements and promotional pieces on his films begin to predominate. They were, at the very least, successful in capturing media space, whatever the details of their reception.

14. On *tarab*, see, notably, Racy 2002. Racy describes the intimate art of "enchantment" in Arab classical music, involving knowledge of "heritage" (*turath*), *makam* (modes), *qaflat* (cadential patterns), the unwritten rules of ensemble playing and accompaniment, improvisation (*taqasim*), and the intricate protocols of the musical gathering, involving musicians and listeners, the latter, in key regards, co-authors of the musical event. *Tarab*, as defined by Racy, describes the key aesthetic goals of urban art music practice in the major urban centers of the Arab Levant, between Cairo and Aleppo from, roughly, the later nineteenth century to the present day. On the complex imbrications of *tarab* and modernity in Syria, see Shannon 2006; on sentimentalism and "the limits of enchantment" in the Arab world, see Stokes 2007.

15. It is worth mentioning that by this stage, the great diva Umm Kulthum had consolidated her hold of the national media, assuming, among other things, the presidency of the powerful Musician's Union in 1945. This gave her significant control over broadcasting, and facilitated her own increasing domination of the airwaves (if not cinema, a space she effectively ceded to Muhammed abd al-Wahhab, Farid al-Atrash, Abd al-Halim Hafiz, and others). By the time of Abd al-Halim's film, her Thursday evening live concerts were already an institution. See Danielson 1997.

16. Note the song "Gabbar" in *Ma'budet al-Jamahir* of 1965. Abd al-Halim's rise to fame is tracked, during the course of the song: As the press rolls, larger and larger audiences appear in a montage in front of him and a globe spins in the background.

17. The opening tag apparently was inspired by the theme tune to *Woody the Woodpecker* (interview, Ziyad al-Tawil, September 2003).

18. These four- and five-note pitch-sets are often referred to theoretically as tetracords and pentacords, or as *jins* (plural *ajnas*) in Arabic, a version of the ancient Greek *genus,* from which they derive. Each constitutes a specific and recognizable affect in the Arab musical universe, and movement between them constitutes an important form of musical signification. For a detailed and clear account, see Marcus 2002.

19. These long, meandering instrumental introductions are by no means unique, but have a distinct aesthetic function and purpose in Abd al-Halim's films. See Stokes 2007, focusing on the finale of *Lahn al-Wafa* (1955) for more discussion of a similar instrumental opening, this time by Riyadh al-Sunbati (a composer associated closely with Umm Kulthum, who only worked on this one Abd al-Halim film). The kinship between these rambling modernist fantasies and the instrumental music of some of Abd al-Halim's subsequent nationalist anthems are to be noted, and discussed, in a preliminary way, in this article.

20. The first of these long concert songs is often considered to be Umm Kulthum's celebrated collaboration with Abd al-Wahhab, *Inta 'Umri,* of 1964. With repetitions and improvisations later in life, concert versions of this song could last over two hours, containing within it most of the elements of the classical Arab suite form (separate songs, instrumental numbers, solo and chorus items, and vocal

and instrumental improvisations, all connected by *makam*). See Danielson 1997:136–37.

21. Abd al-Halim's use of the microphone was often the topic of commentary and satire, if one is to judge by the cartoons that appear in *Ruz al-Yusuf* and *Akhir Saʿa* at the time. Umm Kulthum, by contrast, could manage without, and made much of her power to fill a concert hall with her unaided voice (Danielson 1997). For a detailed discussion, see Stokes (forthcoming).

Works Cited

Abu-Lughod, Lila. 2005. *Dramas of Nationhood: The Politics of Television in Egypt.* Chicago: University of Chicago Press.

al-Amrussi, Magdi. 1994. *Aʿiz al-Nas.* Cairo: al-Tabʿa al-Rabʿia.

Armbrust, Walter. 1996. *Mass Culture and Modernism in Egypt.* Cambridge: Cambridge University Press.

———. 2000. "The Golden Age Before the Golden Age." In *Mass Mediations: New Approaches to Popular Culture in the Middle East and Beyond,* ed. Walter Armbrust, 292–327. Berkeley: University of California Press.

———. 2002. "The Impact of the Media on Egyptian Music." In *Garland Encyclopedia of Ethnomusicology.* Vol. 6, *The Middle East,* ed. V. Danielson, Scott Marcus, and Dwight Reynolds, 233–41. New York: Garland.

Awad, Sherif. 2004. "Sex, Cries and Video Tape." *Egypt Today* 25, no. 9 (25th Anniversary Issue):230–35.

Boyd, Douglas. 1999. *Broadcasting in the Arab World: A Survey of the Electronic Media in the Middle East,* (3d Edition). Ames: Iowa State University Press.

Chakrabarty, Dipesh. 2000. *Provincializing Europe: Postcolonial Thought and Historical Difference.* Princeton, N.J.: Princeton University Press.

Chion, Michel. 1994. *Audio-Vision: Sound on Screen.* New York: Columbia University Press.

Costello-Branco, Salwa al-Shawan. 2001. "Performance of Arab Music in 20th Century Egypt." In *Garland Encyclopedia of World Music,* Middle East, Volume 6, ed. Virginia Danielson, Scott Marcus, and Dwight Reynolds, 559–62. New York: Garland.

Danielson, Virginia. 1997. *The Voice of Egypt: Umm Kulthum, Arabic Song and Egyptian Society in the Twentieth Century.* Chicago: Chicago University Press.

El-Charkawi, Galal. 1966. "History of the U.A.R. Cinema (1896–1962)." In *The Cinema in the Arab Countries,* ed. Georges Sadoul, , 69–97. Beirut: Interarab Centre of Cinema and Television.

Erlmann, Viet, ed. 2004. *Hearing Cultures: Essays on Sound, Listening and Modernity.* Oxford: Berg.

Ezzedine, Salah. 1966. "The role of Music in Arabic Films." In *The Cinema in the Arab Countries,* ed. Georges Sadoul, 46–53. Beirut: Interarab Centre of Cinema and Television.

Fakhouri, Jozef. n.d. *Abd al-Halim Hafiz: Iʿdad wa Tadwin,* (two volumes). Beirut: Dar al-Sharq al-Arabi.

Faulks, Ben. 2001. "Whose Property?" In *Egypt Almanac 2001: A Yearly Review of the Egyptian Scene.* Wilmington: Egypto-file.

Gordon, Joel. 2002. *Revolutionary Melodrama: Popular Film and Civic Identity in Nasser's Egypt.* Chicago: Center for Middle East Studies.

Hansen, Miriam. 1991. *Babel and Babylon: Spectatorship in American Silent Film.* Cambridge Mass.: Harvard University Press.

Hassanayn, Adil. 1995. *Abd al-Halim Hafiz: Ayamna al-Hilwa.* Cairo: Amadu.

Hilmi, Hassan. 1966. "The Industry in the U.A.R. 1955–58." In *The Cinema in the Arab Countries,* ed. Georges Sadoul, 166–67. Beirut: Interarab Centre of Cinema and Television.

Hirschkind, Charles. 2001. "The Ethics of Listening: Cassette Sermon Audition in Contemporary Cairo." *American Ethnologist* 28, no. 3: 623–49.

Larkin, Brian. 2002. "The Materiality of Cinema Theaters in Northern Nigeria." In *Media Worlds: Anthropology on New Terrain,* ed. Faye Ginsberg, Lila Abu-Lughod, and Brian Larkin, 319–36. Berkeley: University of California Press.

Mahir, Ahmad. 1956. "Qissat al-Malahhin al-Rabi wara Umm Kulthum." *Akhir Sa'a* (no number):20–21.

Marcus, Scott. 2002. "The Eastern Arab System of Melodic Modes in Theory and Practice: A Case Study of Maqam Bayyati." In *The Garland Encyclopedia of World Music,* Volume Six: *The Middle East,* ed. Virginia Danielson, Scott Marcus, and Dwight Reynolds, 33–45. New York: Routledge.

Mazarella, William. 2004. "Culture, Globalization, Mediation." *Annual Reviews of Anthropology* 33:345–67.

Racy, Ali Jihad. 2002. *Making Music in the Arab World: The Culture and Artistry of Tarab.* Cambridge: Cambridge University Press.

Shafik, Viola. 1998. *Arab Cinema: History and Cultural Identity.* Cairo: American University of Cairo Press.

Shannon, Jonathan. 2006. *Among the Jasmine Trees: Music and Modernity in Contemporary Syria.* Middletown, Conn.: Wesleyan University Press.

Stokes, Martin. 2007. "Adam Smith and the Dark Nightingale: On Twentieth Century Sentimentalism." *Twentieth Century Music* 3, no. 1:1–18.

———. Forthcoming. "Abd al-Halim's Microphone." In *Music and the Play of Power: Music, Politics and Ideology in the Middle East, North Africa and Central Asia,* ed. Laudan Nooshin. London: Ashgate.

Vitalis, Robert. 2000. "American Ambassador in Technicolor and Cinemascope: Hollywood and Revolution on the Nile." In *Mass Mediations: New Approaches to Popular Culture in the Middle East and Beyond,* ed. Walter Armbrust, 269–91. Berkeley: University of California Press.

Wahab, Munir Abdel. 1966. "The Industry in the U.A.R. 1964–5." In *The Cinema in the Arab Countries,* ed. Georges Sadoul, 168–70. Beirut: Interarab Centre of Cinema and Television.

Zubaida, Sami. 2002. "Mass Media and the Arab Public Sphere." *ISIM Bulletin* 40.

Filmography

Maw'id Gharam, 1955. Gamal Elleissi Films, Cairo.

Discography

Aghani Film "Maw'eed Gharam"/Songs from the Film "Maweed Gharam." Abdel Halim Hafez, Soutelphan 1995/EMI Arabia 1996 0946 310597–2 8.

PART THREE

·◉·

COMPARATIVE VISTAS

·◉·

MARK SLOBIN

Comparative Vistas

·◉·

Take One: Knots and Figures

Listening carefully to films from many sources, it slowly becomes clear that certain striking musical moments are not unique: They reappear in movies across time and space. Why does this happen? One reason might be that innovation spreads quickly. If one production team comes up with an effective way for music to make a difference, others will pick up on that ingenuity, as a part of craft. Tradition is as important to filmmaking as to any other creative form. As film historian Robert Stam puts it, "any text that has 'slept with' another text . . . has also slept with all the other texts that that other text has slept with" (Stam 2005:27). But the possibility also looms that people independently draw on similar expressive and technical materials. A convergence of minds and resources can produce similar results. This chapter isolates moments across the film world that collectively form familiar patterns of sound effect and affect, as a way of opening the ears to the ethnomusicology of film.

Some resonant nodes form a *narrative knot*. Music and storyline are like threads from two different balls of brightly colored yarn. Filmmakers weave them together, and sometimes tie knots to fasten the narrative, as well as the viewer's attention. Example: characters—often an emotionally engaged couple—sit in a concert hall and listen to performed music, often classical. Something happens to the relationship. Another example: a group of children sings, making a narrative point about innocence or experience. Third example: an early model of phonograph suddenly appears in a community unused to this device. These calculated concatenations combine the way that music works socially and the need for narrative structure. They can occur in very related and very unrelated films in a variety of cinema systems, and these three examples are just isolated members of a large family of narrative knots, or just "knots" in the discussion below.

A knot can appear in wildly different cinemas, yet be extremely specific in both form and meaning. To take a widely comparative example, in more films than one might imagine, set in the earlier twentieth century, the gramophone makes a sudden intervention into the space of the action, always rural. In each case, it symbolizes the power of the ruling class or colonizers and/or the onset of modernity. The first instance, already cited in the first chapter of this volume, comes in *Bird of Paradise,* the early Max Steiner score of 1932, where the American sailors charm the native islanders with the magic of the record-player. Later films include *Spices* (India, 1986), *Tree of the Wooden Clogs* (Italy, 1978), *White Sun in the Desert* (USSR, 1964), and *The Stone Wedding* (Romania, 1972). *Spices* features an extended scene in which the despotic and cruel tax farmer, who extorts the natural and human resources of a village, commands his servant to bring out a gramophone for the pleasure of the local worthies. The servant drops and breaks a record, and the villain beats him savagely.

Tree of the Wooden Clogs shows poor peasants bringing their grain to the landlord's courtyard for weighing. They will be cheated. Inside the manor house, the decadent members of the ruling class put on a record of an opera aria, which floats down to the peasants. *Stone Wedding,* from the socialist era, tells the tale of a pre-socialist, middle-class country wedding at which the bride runs away with the charming folk musician. In the middle of the festivities, a gramophone is carried out ceremoniously and the well-dressed but rustic bourgeoisie switch from live vernacular music to a canned, citified waltz that marks their sense of class. *White Sun of the Desert* is a semi-satirical, semi-nationalist look at the early 1920s, when the fledgling Soviet army suppressed guerillas in Central Asia. The main plot device that deflects the movie from being a pure Soviet product is the sudden appearance of a group of women described by the screenwriters as "an abandoned harem," a group of wives of a rebel leader. The good-hearted Soviet officer protects them chivalrously. To bring them up to speed with the twentieth century, he produces a gramophone, which first puzzles them, then sets them to dancing.[1]

All of these unrelated appearances of the gramophone knot share a common outline: The unfamiliar playback device appears ceremoniously, as a semi-sacred object representing a distant, technologically advanced urban lifestyle with strong implications of class or colonial power. Since it would be not be feasible to tease out the possible intertextuality of this image—which director was watching what?—we can only suppose that the conditions of modernity make it possible for a wide range of global filmmakers to think of tying the same knot. It economically offers a compact image

Figure 1. Enter the gramophone: the subalterns' first contact with the phonograph, their master's voice. *Spices*, 1986.

that bundles the visual and the sonic, and this very condensation makes it a metaphoric motor to drive the narrative in the desired direction.

Another approach to knot analysis proposes a pairing of just two very closely matched scenes in radically different films and cinema systems. One case study leads back to square one: Max Steiner, the inventor of many a knot. One of his best-analyzed works is the score for *Now, Voyager,* a "women's movie" and Bette Davis vehicle of 1942—indeed, a whole book is devoted to it (Daubney 2000). Charlotte, the heroine, overcomes her dictatorial Boston Brahmin mother through the help of a psychiatrist. While on a liberatory cruise, she has an affair with Jerry, a married man with a despotic invalid wife and mentally unstable daughter, Tina. Back in Boston, Charlotte becomes engaged to society man Elliot, but pines for Jerry. Eventually, she empowers Tina, which becomes her life's mission. Self-sacrificingly, she rejects both Jerry and Elliot.

At one point, the elite society group dutifully leaves a cocktail party to hear the Boston Symphony. Charlotte sits between impassive Elliot and passionate Jerry, who asks to stop by Charlotte's house later. She agrees. Throughout this small scene, the orchestra—whom we see first, but very briefly—is playing Tchaikovsky's *Pathetique* symphony, featuring the particularly pathos-drenched main theme of the first movement. The music continues into the next scene, as Charlotte awaits Jerry. It recurs later, playing over the radio, when Charlotte breaks off the engagement with Elliot. Kate Daubney understands the Tchaikovsky theme as belonging to Elliot's world, since Elliot has no other theme and because "Charlotte's commitment to Elliot prevails at this point" (Daubney 2000:69)

The concert-hall knot in *Now, Voyager* recurs in movies across a long stretch of time and in various climes, and can be thumbnailed this way: the coupling of romantic involvement, or at least sensuality, with the space of the classical concert hall. One thinks of Cher and Nicolas Cage bonding while watching *La Bohéme* at the Metropolitan Opera, or even the Schlegel sisters in *Howard's End* getting fatefully entangled with a working-class man while listening to Beethoven. Various examples of this knot refocus the analysis of Charlotte's moment at Boston's Symphony Hall. The moment is more deeply involved with the attraction between her and Jerry than with wooden Elliot, who responds neither to the music nor to Charlotte in the scene. It is those two who are setting up a tryst during the music. So while Daubney may be right in thinking of the Tchaikovsky as an emblem of Elliott, thinking in knots suggests there's more at work. Here, the comparative approach might help, since looking outside the specific film can offer more perspective. A strikingly parallel instance of the concert-hall knot occurs in an obscure, early post-Stalinist Soviet film, *Neokonchennaia povest'* (1955, dir. Fridrikh Ermler). The heroine is a hard-working doctor-healer who is also struggling to find private happiness. Early in the film, she goes out with an older colleague to Leningrad's (now St. Petersburg's) Philharmonic Hall, where the orchestra is playing precisely the same theme and symphony as in *Now, Voyager.* The Soviet film dwells on the heroic conductor and passionate orchestra much longer than does the Hollywood movie. Elizaveta is enraptured with the music. She turns her gaze in one direction and sees a young couple who are completely enthralled and who murmur "beautiful." She looks the other way and sees her date fast asleep after a night of hospital rounds. Her crestfallen closeup shows that she will have no further romantic interest in this man; he is a cultural failure.

The Leningrad-Boston comparison and contrast is telling. In the Steiner world, the image of the symphony musicians seems more perfunctory. The society folk have no intrinsic interest in Tchaikovsky—it's purely a ritualized visit to the classics—but the composer's passion moves the lovers to carry on their forbidden liaison. The Soviet version stresses individual happiness as part of a collective agreement, under the conductor's baton and the aegis of high culture. This commonality lies in the understanding that this music, by itself, carries an immense emotional charge that goes from the musicians to the listeners, and that it pushes couples together, at least ideally. Elliot and the dozing doctor can be rejected as both passionless and culturally insensitive. As a node of musical meaning, the concert hall knot adds extra value, beyond what the dense and motif-laden Steiner score, or its orchestral counterpart in the Soviet film, does by itself to detail emotion and push the plot.

The concert hall knot relies on the power of classical music, which makes an appearance in so many ways in so many films globally that just looking at its use in knot-tying seems insufficient. Another term addresses a broader category of comparativism: the *figure*. Figures are far more general, as well as being extremely pervasive within and across cinemas. The term appears here in two senses given by the *Oxford English Dictionary*, one literary and one musical. In literary terms, particularly in rhetoric, a "figure" "is adopted in order to give beauty, variety, or force to a composition," and this is certainly the case for the world of film music. The term "rhetoric" is important here, meaning the power of persuasion.[2] For "music," the *OED* gives "any short succession of notes, either as melody or a group of chords, which produces a single, complete, and distinct impression." This is very close to what this chapter advances in terms of film-music figures.

There are master-figures that generate whole sets of figures. A good example is the peculiar power and status of Western classical music, which makes it a fertile figure-producer. Take the conflict or contrast between classical and popular music. Hollywood worked this over extensively in the 1930s. In her trenchant analysis of the Hollywood film musical, Jane Feuer highlights the classical-popular music competition as a key theme: "those musicals which do raise the classical/popular conflict to a central position in the films plot always show the triumphant victory of the popular style" as part of Hollywood's "*rhetoric* of affirming itself by applauding popular forms," tied more deeply to a self-celebration of America's vibrancy versus European "old-world" obsolete decadence (Feuer 1993:56; italics added). This figure moved beyond the musical into the fiction film, once it became an available resource. Such large-scale narrative-building relies on subsets of specific knots and general figures that help maintain coherence within and across numbers of films. In Europe, where classical music retains a certain authority that is ebbing in the United States, filmmakers keep mining this figure's narrative gold. For example, Agnes Jaoui's critically acclaimed debut film *Le Gout des Autres* ("other people's tastes," 2000) opens with a celestial classical female choir accompanying a businessman's mundane drive in a car. Eventually, he will shift from his more pop tastes to classical consumerism, while the high-culture characters in the film will drift into more mainstream tastes. Music metaphorizes class relationships. At a screening, when I asked Jaoui why that choir opens the film, since it has no narrative value yet, she confirmed that she needed to have viewers hear the contrast between character and music so she could work it out systematically. The classical pop–duel figure is alive and well, seventy years after the supercultural pioneers set it up. Below, a case study of classical music in Soviet film describes how this tension illuminates the dark corners of a tightly controlled cinema system.

Many music-plot nodes offer filmmakers versatility in advancing their rhetoric. One that is as old as sound cinema is the appearance of singing children in a film. In movie after movie, this figure does a particular kind of work. It is perhaps more tightly knit than some others, since we possibly can trace its origins and relationships over time, intertextually. Maybe it began life in the opening of Fritz Lang's *M* (1931). That film narrates the career and downfall of a serial child-killer. The opening shot reveals children in a round, chanting out a rhyme about "the chopper-man will get you," only to stop, when admonished by a mother. One of those children will fall prey to the stalker. Lotte Eisner, who knew Lang well, says he was aiming at a "newsreel" documentary effect in this sequence, shot from above, suggesting a detached look and a social indictment of the courtyard's poverty (Eisner 1976:116). But the fact that the children are singing (with organ-grinder accompaniment) opens up an area of affect that only music can provide. These poor kids are innocent, but also prescient: This is a two-pronged figure, which perhaps explains its durability.

Over forty years later, in *Apocalypse Now,* a totally unrelated project at all levels, a three-second sound of chanting schoolchildren in a Vietnamese village precedes the horrific helicopter attack by the Wagner-playing American choppers, setting up a musical contrast of peace versus horror, and local vernacular versus mainstream, here figured as classical music. Through cinema history, childhood innocence, expressed through song, is touching yet transient. Yet the knowing way in which the children sing in *M* endures as well. In *Hush, Hush, Sweet Charlotte* (1965), the children are moved even further forward than the opening shot, to a position just before the credits. They mock the title character as someone who chops off hands and heads; their tune becomes the main title music, so infuses the score. And there are countless examples of the possibly evil intent of singing children, from classically based films like *The Turn of the Screw* through horror movies.

Close attention to the singing-children figure sheds light on the solution that John Williams found for Steven Spielberg's challenge in *Schindler's List* (1993): how to give voice to a scene embodying the terror and helplessness of the youngest Jewish victims of the Holocaust. Here, it is worth considering Williams's range of options and noticing the ideological angle of the one he settled on. One historically accurate choice might have been a vernacular children's chorus. In many Nazi-run ghettoes such as the one pictured in the film, people kept schools running, in a desperate struggle for normalcy, including regular performances of music and theater. Williams avoided this ethnographic solution. He also chose not to write his own music. Rather, he piped in an offscreen children's choir. They sing the best-known, beloved Yiddish song, "Oyfn pripetshik," usually thought to be a folksong, but actually composed around 1900 as a nostalgic village scene. The *Schindler* team made the crucial decision to hire an Israeli children's choir to deliver this sentimental song. Knowledgeable listeners might notice the kids' lack of familiarity with Yiddish. This anachronistic performance—there was no Israel during World War II—matches the film's teleological slant, which situates the Holocaust as a prelude to the re-location of Jewish life to Israel. In the final scene, the vintage-looking sepia filmstock that the movie has been stuck in yields to present-day color as the Jews that Schindler saves arrive in the State of Israel. An Israeli anthem, "Jerusalem of Gold" drives home this Zionist message. The *Schindler's List* situation reveals how musical figures get grounded in the specifics of each film, including ideology.

The figure- and knot-hunting sketched out above aims to sharpen the ears and to suggest new patterns of comparative film analysis. Of course, since there is no way of assembling all the filmed examples of singing children or flute-playing Indian heroes, one can't build and test universally valid hypotheses. Some figures are so commonplace that large-scale mapping is highly unlikely. Take the broadest possible figure, the appearance of the piano. Sifting through all the examples you can think of, and adding suggestions from your friends, you can easily come up with dozens of examples. Sorting through even this unsystematic survey does reveal patterns, since figures fall into families. Some have to do with race relations, if the piano stands in for African American music culture. Others stay strictly within the bounds of polite society, referencing upper-class spaces and customs. A third set of examples belongs to the popular music world in all its shadings. Then there are whole films in which the piano is a star, such as *The Piano*, or has a crucial cameo role, as in *The Pianist* or *The Piano Teacher*, or, as Lawrence Kramer notes in *The Portrait of a Lady*, not to mention the biopics of pianists, composers, and songwriters (2000). The instrument emerges as one of those controls against which the independent variables of each film can stand out in sharp relief, allowing for further steps in the ethnomusicology of film music.

As a master figure-generator, classical music offers an endless source of comparative insights into global film music.[3] Taking just one composer, Beethoven, and a handful of examples sets up a broad field of figural studies. That composer casts a large shadow over many a movie, as he has over Western music in general. As Alexandra Comini says, "By the end of the nineteenth century, this larger-than-life legend of the deaf composer whose music sounded new spheres provided a mythic answer to society's nostalgic yearning for a *cultural* rather than political or military hero . . . [and the idea] that 'redemption through art' was available to all" (Comini 1987:14). The coverage below figures Beethoven as cultural hero in film music, to both good and bad effect. It begins in the Soviet Union and extends through Yiddish film, race film, and even a blaxploitation movie, to explore and summarize the approaches that this chapter offers.

This story starts in 1931, when Stalin sent director Gregory Alexandrov (along with Sergei Eisenstein) to Hollywood to learn how the capitalists entertain the masses. Stalin took a strong interest in the details of filmmaking and licensed the creation of the Soviet musical. He watched American movies incessantly and involved himself in all phases of production and critique. Alexandrov was ready for Hollywood's rush of excitement and expertise. Through the 1930s, he created four indelible screen musicals, which the citizenry viewed dozens of times, since the choice of popular home-grown films was always slim. They tend to feature singing more than dancing since, as Maria Enzenberger has pointed out, the rhythm of work supplanted Hollywood's emphasis on dancing as the collective form of rhythmic unison (1992). In one of the Alexandrov classics, Stalin's favorite film, *Volga-Volga,* the "simple" village heroine, Strelka the letter carrier, feuds with her mannered boyfriend Alyosha, who runs a classical music band. Their romance centers on the elitist-popular dichotomy. She writes a pop song—anonymously—which becomes a big hit at the Moscow festival they travel to. On their long upriver ride, he tries in vain to pose Beethoven as a standard-bearer of music:

Alyosha: We are bringing Beethoven, Mozart, Schubert, Wagner. Who are you bringing?
Strelka: Aunt Pasha and Uncle Kuzmin!
Alyosha: What a comparison! Uncle Kuzmin and Beethoven.
Strelka: Just think—Beethoven could have been somebody's uncle too!

It is not Western cinema's fascination with Beethoven's nephew (Mitchell 2004:16–32) that lies behind this dialogue; rather, it is the figure of the duel between classical and popular music that both Soviet and American cinema loved to exploit, each for its own reasons. But in the USSR, more was riding on Beethoven than the American interest in glamorizing pop at the expense of classical music. Bringing Beethoven into the family was not a likely move in a Hollywood musical. This sequence in *Volga-Volga* points to the greater ambivalence of the Soviet side, which had a different version of the culture wars. The folksiness about Uncle Kuzmin and Beethoven covers a serious internal dispute surrounding the viability of high culture in the USSR.

An historic film of the same period, *Chapaiev* of 1934, the year of the first Alexandrov musical, addresses this issue more seriously. Far from being a musical (though loaded with important musical moments), *Chapaiev* chronicles the heroic life of a Red cavalry leader during the civil war that consolidated Soviet power. It has been described as the most popular socialist-realist film ever made. The makers of *Chapaiev* were responding to a call from film boss Boris Shumyatsky for larger-than-life Soviet film heroes. He wanted to create a "Red Hollywood" that would include a star system as well as heroic and musical movies. With the character of Chapaiev, they struck gold. The hero "penetrated into popular culture and everyday life in a way that few other screen characters have done," even becoming the topic of endless (sometimes antigovernmental) jokes (Taylor 1993:77). Most of the music stresses the communal, folk-like atmosphere of the Red camp, with a pervasive aura of collectivism that rises from their idealistic, sometimes dreamy songs. The songs are "fakelore," part of a vast repertoire of assumed vernacular music written for films or mass songs. The enemies, the Whites, get only one musical moment, the one that introduces Beethoven. Borozdin, their commander, is in his headquarters. Elegant, with a gleaming bald pate, Borozdin is playing Beethoven's *Moonlight Sonata* on a grand piano, dramatically lit, a polar opposite to Chapaiev's folksy digs and unadorned voices. Borozdin is "accompanied" by his orderly, who shuffles around the parquet floor in grief while polishing it with rags attached to his shoes. His brother has just been executed on Borozdin's order. It is altogether a very compelling scene visually and sonically, and certainly one of the oddest of the many filmed appearances of the *Moonlight Sonata*.

What are we to make of this remarkable counterpoint to the Reds' dominance of the filmscore? Borozdin, says Peter Kenez, "is perhaps the most successfully drawn negative character in socialist realist cinema," his "multidimensional" side being shown by his being a "cultured" piano player (1992:176). Here culture—that is, bourgeois high culture—equals Beethoven, specifically in the guise of the composer's reflective, "moonlight" side. Usually, the Reds preferred their leader Lenin's favorite piece, the more revolutionary *Apassionata Sonata*. Beethoven was on the approved list of cultural imports, yet here it is the villain who is displaying the foreign composer's talents to a Soviet audience. This reveals a deep ambivalence about an enemy who possesses an apparently admirable cultural capital while being inhumanly indifferent to suffering. Indeed, Shumyatsky sent out an order to make counterrevolutionary protagonists less attractive, accounting for the flatness of much subsequent socialist-realist cinema. So a great deal of cultural debate was being reflected in the gleaming grand piano and Borozdin's cueball head. It seems that Commini's idea that Beethoven represents "redemption through art" is relative and contextual; it is his sense of dominance as a cultural hero that resonates here.

Beethoven makes a surprising appearance twenty years later in the film whose Tchaikovsky scene was explored above, *Neokonchennaia povest'*. The composer makes a cameo appearance in the movie's climactic finale. The doctor-heroine Elizaveta has been trying therapy on a prominent architect who mysteriously has lost the use of his legs. He secretly adores her and refuses other treatment. To cap their coy, implicit romance and to advance his return to city planning for the good of the state, he asks her to play the piano while he tries to stand up on his own two legs. In a culturally revealing shot, we see the grand piano in the force field of two personalities. At one end sits the Soviet heroine, at the other, a prominent bust of Beethoven. Elizaveta does not play the *Moonlight Sonata* like Borozdin, but rather resorts to resolute Soviet music (written for this film-score), which the orchestra amplifies for the movie's final shots outside on the balcony. The camera pans out to the city, which needs to be revived and erected like the city planner himself. The triumphant music swells as the couple finally gets a closing clinch above the classical architecture of St. Petersburg. Here "redemption through art" is very relevant. So is Richard Taruskin's assessment of the overall impact of Beethoven's image as "the lonely artist-hero whose suffering produces works of awe-inspiring greatness that give listeners otherwise unavailable access to an experience that transcends all worldly concerns" (Taruskin 2005:649). The appearance of the bust on the piano in a film otherwise dominated by Russian Soviet culture does give viewers "otherwise unavailable access," since Elizaveta does not actually *play* Beethoven.

Why not? Perhaps people were still avoiding "cosmopolitan" thinking in 1955, when Stalin's shadow still hung over the social landscape. Or maybe it's just that all the music in the film, including Tchaikovsky, has to be Russian to work. But the physical, brooding, almost shamanic presence of Beethoven, through his effigy on the piano, seems stronger, and provides a continuous and powerful trace of the ambivalence of Soviet culture toward Western aesthetics. Analyzing *An Unfinished Tale*, Josephine Woll writes that "the musical score reveals nothing, since the music is either classical (Tchaikovsky at the concert), traditional (folksongs with [a] patient's family), or generic Soviet anthems [a song of students in the street])" (Woll 2000:27). Woll is making the valid point that by 1955, things should have moved on. Soon after this film, the guitar-playing kid supplanted classical music as Khrushchev's "thaw" pushed the cinema to reach out to the needs and tastes of the younger generation. This parallels the new rock scores of Hollywood films of the late 1950s. The way Beethoven blocks the way in 1955 signals classical music's persistent power to offer dominant values, even under a nationalist version of socialism.

Following down the trail opened by the figure of Beethoven opens up comparative vistas.[4] Around the corner from Soviet cinema, we come upon Beethoven making a surprising cameo appearance in a Yiddish film. As mentioned above, this subcultural cinema was based in the United States, but also in Poland until 1939 and even in the Soviet Union. So the Yiddish-language film lived at the margins of the Russian/Polish culture zone. Most films were made by American immigrants who recreated Eastern European small-town life on film sets built in New Jersey. One 1940 film, *Der vilner shtot-khazn* [The town cantor of Vilna] introduces the *Moonlight Sonata* in a telling way. It recounts the semi-legendary history of the famous nineteenth-century cantor Strashunsky, who vaulted over ethnic boundaries by switching from sacred song to opera. This cultural turncoat suffered terribly and died young. In an intriguing scene, the script implicates the great Polish composer Moniuszko (1819–1872) in the cantor's downfall. We see him inviting the Jewish sacred singer into a cozy parlor for evenings of music appreciation. As J. Hoberman puts it, "in a scene presided over by a bust of Beethoven, [Strashunsky] succumbs to the *Moonlight Sonata* and eagerly accepts the composer's offer to teach him how to read music . . . Strashunsky feels that he is suffocating in [his hometown] Vilna and dreams of visiting Warsaw" (1991:271). Eventually, the cantor goes on stage to sing in Monsiusko's national Polish opera, *Halka,* and flirts with a Polish countess. The experience ultimately destroys him, as he is torn between ethnicity and assimilation. At the end, he expires melodramatically while singing in a synagogue for Yom Kippur in a vain attempt to return to his people. It is precisely Beethoven, the foreign composer who healed the ailing Soviet architect, who brings about Strashunsky's ruin through sheer elemental power and prestige. Here the general figure of Beethoven is compressed into a quite specific narrative knot, as in the Soviet film: the bust on the piano as the agent of a personal turning-point. In the terms of this chapter, then, Beethoven is a very general literal and metaphoric figure, who can appear in many different guises and contexts, but mainly as a representative of European classical music and high culture. The bust of Beethoven on the piano as a catalyst, as in both the Soviet and Yiddish films, tightly ties music and storyline together.

Despite their vast differences, the Soviet and Yiddish cinemas were cultural cousins. Both Russians and Russian Jews composed their culture as marginals, viewed by the Euro-American mainstream as semi-members, at best. Richard Taruskin has illuminated the inferiority complex of Russian composers, who were treated as exotic peripherals by the European classical culture controllers (Taruskin 1997). The Jews fell into something of a similar category. Even when both Russians and Jews integrated into the

European musical system in the early 1900s (e.g., Stravinsky and Mahler), they could not shake their outsider status. So these two appearances of Beethoven in the 1930s to 1950s era converge at some points. Together, they suggest that knots and figures might be window-prying tools for climbing into the domain of global film music.

Figures come in sets. Another 1930s' culturally peripheral film draws on Beethoven. *Ten Minutes to Live* (1932) was directed by Oscar Micheaux, the great innovator, poet, and moralist of early African-American cinema discussed earlier. In a dramatic moment early in the movie, the imperiled heroine is trying to escape a stalker from her hometown by visiting her aunt in Westchester County. As her taxi pulls up to the house, Beethoven's *Fifth Symphony* underscores the action. Inside, suspense music follows her up the stairs. In a bedroom, she undresses, as jazz slinks into the soundtrack. Smoking in her negligee, she tries to relax. Suddenly, something catches her attention. As she rises to peer out the window, where she spots the stalker, Beethoven returns, then vanishes as she goes downstairs to figure out her next move.

Why Beethoven? is a logical question, but one with no clear answer. Partly because it's free music, part of the reason Yiddish film also relied on the classics. Subcultural cinemas are often badly underfunded. But there might be more. Think about the clear contrast between the cultural space inside and outside of the house. Micheaux sees the street as a male-dominated, threatening hubbub of metropolitan life and crime. Beethoven lends a certain trademarked heaviness to this arena, and perhaps suggests that Black people are not in charge of city life. Perhaps the feminized interior, a space of pleasure and ease voyeuristically viewed by the filmgoer, goes along with in-group jazziness.

To take the African-American film experience of Beethoven a bit further, Micheaux's approach in *Ten Minutes to Live* might be put in perspective by viewing a surprising Beethoven scene from Frank Capra's *The Negro Soldier*

(1943), part of the Hollywood director's wartime series that starkly defined America and its enemies. A scene of an African-American conductor leading a massed performance of Beethoven's *Ninth Symphony,* the ultimate emblem of brotherhood, serves as visual counterpart to the narrator's rising rhetoric about "Negro" progress. Beethoven's innate Germanness, which might seem like a problem in a film decrying Nazi values, brings us back to the ambivalence around *Chapaiev's* enemy Borozdin playing the *Moonlight Sonata.* But for Capra, the upward mobility value of the high-culture music outweighs the resident-alien status of the composer. Beethoven remains the heavyweight champion, despite the earlier footage of Black boxer Joe Louis knocking out the German boxer Max Schmeling.

The African-American connection continues with a wildly divergent example of Beethoven. In *Scream, Blacula, Scream* (1973) one of Hollywood's "blaxploitation" movies, Blacula, once an African king, but now living as a vampire in New York due to an evil white plot, is ill at ease in his mansion. Cultivated, as are most onscreen vampires, he sits down to his grand piano. Under a full moon, he begins to play, but then suddenly rejects the *Moonlight Sonata* in favor of reflecting on his African roots. His setting matches the upward mobility of Beethoven, yet the subcultural pull drives him away from the classics. Instead, much of the film is drenched in Caribbean and African sounds. Even without a detailed analysis of the ideology of blaxploitation films, it does seem that even for Hollywood, by 1973 Beethoven as mainstream icon could only serve as a fleeting reference within a play of multicultural symbols that has more to do with target markets than with the creation of unified narratives. By the 1990s, the composer's name became best known as a St. Bernard in the *Beethoven* dog movies.

Finally, what figures of Beethoven emerge in Germany itself, the heartland of high culture? Even there, it is an open question whether Beethoven is universal or national, transparent or ambivalent as a cultural symbol. Caryl Flinn's probing of classical music sources in the New German Cinema of the 1970s and early 1980s puts its finger right on this sore point. It was a time when young filmmakers "freely pillaged existing music, which it then put to very different uses" (Flinn 2000:128). Flinn cites films by Kluge and Fassbinder in which Beethoven is a prime source for postwar cinematic improvisation on German themes. "Music," says Flinn, "can put the past into new contexts, moving it forward instead of only facing backward" (ibid.:138). She is pointing to a particularly German situation. In this national cinema, classical music is not the imported or even threatening cultural baggage found in the Soviet, Yiddish, and African-American examples. Instead, it figures as a core component of the national narrative.

Beethoven in particular, and above all the *Ninth Symphony* that these directors quote, stands at the very center of German identity. Recognizing reality, younger filmmakers deployed this hallowed music to subvert and reconstruct both past and present. Fassbinder, in *The Wedding of Maria Braun,* makes sure that the symphony "falsifies any sense of acoustic continuity . . . and suggests that the piece's ability to unify in other regards—say, as a token of national culture—is equally counterfeit" (ibid.:128). There will be no busts of Beethoven in Fassbinder's ethnographic view of postwar German settings.

Before moving on to other comparative vistas, one more thought about locating figures. In addition to hunting them worldwide, one can also map them within a single cinema system. India offers a wealth of helpful examples. We have seen that within the Euro-American film world, classical music yields an endless supply of possible metaphoric and literal-minded connections between narrative and music. In older Indian films, and to some extent still today, specific domestic musical resources set up an automatic viewer response that can take the form of knots and figures. Take a 1980s' Hindi film like *Geet.* It opens with an audience watching a dance performance of the early life of the deity Krishna, when he appeared as a naughty boy teasing sexy shepherdesses. We hear and see the flute prominently. Later, the actress-heroine, tired of male harassment, goes to the Himalayas for a break and falls in love with a flute-playing folk shepherd. The Krishna resonance echoes strongly, as did this particular knot for a long time in Indian film, for example in a very different 1980s' Hindi film, *Disco Dancer.* The hero, a lower-class fellow who has risen to disco stardom, is constantly attacked by his rival's thugs. After one such kung fu episode, framed by the hero's mother calling on Krishna to help her son, the scene switches to an elaborate staged disco number invoking Krishna, culminating in the disco dancer posed upon a huge flute spread across the stage. Like the piano in the West, the flute in India has provided a rich source of narrative knots, as musical instruments do crossculturally, for example in Sumarsam's analysis of Indonesian cinema in this volume.

To take two other Indian examples, in the Tamil cinema of South India, anytime the *nagaswaram* (a long oboe) surfaces in the soundtrack, we know a wedding is afoot. Citing yet another local instrument, Regula Qureshi has written eloquently about how the *sarangi,* a poignantly played fiddle, instantly evokes intense emotion in movies: "the solo sound of the filmi *sarangi* has become the aestheticized voice of sadness on screen" (Qureshi 1997:28). In fact, this recent role for the *sarangi* has stopped its decline as a concert instrument, a fine example of the power of film music to project—literally—into the wider music culture. Qureshi observes that the instrument's attraction for Hindi film is tied not only to local sensibilities, but also to Western influence: "the *sarangi*'s projection of a delicate and feelingfully expressive solo sound also owes something to the generalized sound image of the violin that came to dominate the film music studios from the 1940s onward, along with other Western instruments" (ibid.). From the strictly analytical perspective, I tend to think of the *nagaswaram*-wedding connection as a knot, a permanently paired duo that fits a variety of plotlines. The *sarangi* sensibility, though, can be applied so broadly to fit multiple moods that it seems more like a figure, which adds "beauty, variety, and force" to the film and its score.

This short study of figures and knots has revealed the crisscrossing, zigzagging lines of ideology and aesthetics that have linked world film music for decades. These rhetorical and structural figures form some of the pathways linking the world cinema nervous system. Fertile figures of the imagination, they outline a localized, yet global set of sound strategies that continue to resonate today. For devices such as these never really disappear; they just change shape to fit new temporal and social surroundings.

Take Two: Ornament and Intermediary

This section takes another, more speculative angle on comparativism. It scans the broad theoretical horizon of Oleg Grabar's seminal art history work, *The Mediation of Ornament* (Grabar 1992).

Based solidly on his lifelong work on Islamic art, Grabar moves out toward general principles that have a comparative thrust. He is interested in going beyond just deciphering the "codes" that a work of art embodies, even though this is the normal job of the art historian (and, often, the film studies scholar): first to identify maker, style, period, and function, then to analyze how those combine in a specific object to embody local social and aesthetic codes. But Grabar is more interested in how the types of what he calls "ornament" have a life of their own as they flash directly into the viewer's eye and heart. He calls them "intermediaries." They enact "an order of perception, and, therefore, of reality between the viewer and the object":

Codes are indeed used to build and represent whatever artists sought to make and viewers and users decode artifacts to deal with them appropriately. But the zone of intermediaries which I have studied differs from codes by its *independence from the specifics of a work of art*. At best, it could have been part of a code to the maker, but it becomes an intermediary of "pleasure" to the viewer. (Grabar 1992:237; emphasis added)

This sounds intriguingly like music's controlled, yet indeterminate, relationship to film narrative. It also brings to mind that huge gap, never bridged enough by film studies, between what filmmakers and composers think they are doing and the ways that viewers shape their own experience. How do intermediaries work?

[They are] agents that are not logically necessary to the perception of a visual message but without which the process of understanding would be more difficult . . .
 These intermediary agents facilitate or even compel access to the work of art by strengthening the pleasure derived from looking at something . . .
 They are like catalytic agents for chemical reactions. (ibid.)

Grabar is saying that there are components of artworks that stand free of whatever their producers put into them and that catalyze the viewer's response. He thinks this process is pleasurable, and it is not fixed in its potential for interpretation. He finds ornament both persuasive and subversive, because it offers us pleasure: "ornament is the ultimate mediator, paradoxically questioning the value of meanings by channeling them into pleasure. Or is it possible to argue instead that by providing pleasure ornament also gives to the observer the right and the freedom to choose meanings?" (ibid.:237).

To back up his informed intuitions, Grabar draws on a huge range of examples, mostly from Islamic art, but also European and Asian. He identifies four intermediaries that, as ornament, open up meanings beyond what the artwork is nominally "about": writing, geometry, nature, and architecture. He resorts to an invented term, *terpnopoietic*, or "providing pleasure." "The four examples I have used—writing, geometry, architecture, nature—function as intermediaries rather than as concrete designs because they evoke . . . in viewers well-defined emotions or stances . . . and throughout sensory pleasure, that terpnopoietic condition central to the arts" (ibid.:230). *Nature* pleases the eye, in the plant and animal forms that surround, frame, and animate many artworks: "it recalls meanings without compelling them. It transfers the decision of how to understand a work of art to its viewer or user" (ibid.:207). About *architecture*, he writes:

Architectural images colored other topics, feasted on them, cuddle them, at times perhaps even overwhelmed them, but they always remained separated from the reality or the truth of whatever it was they adorned . . . architecture is a true ornament in the sense I have been developing in these essays. Without it, life loses it quality. Architecture makes life complete, but it is neither life nor art. (ibid.:193)

In addition to serving as a boundary, the architectural element also compels attention to the main subject, focuses on it, provides it with its frame and, so to speak, gift wraps it for the viewer (ibid.:186).

Writing—for example, the exquisite calligraphy of Arabic script—goes beyond its task as a cultural code of everyday life: "All these moments of time or areas of space—Far East Asian, West Asian, Mediterranean, European—picked up writing, a vehicle for the transmission of something else than itself, and transformed it into a neutral means to an end or into an end in itself in which meaning could become transfigured into free form" (ibid.:117).

Grabar's insights can work as a powerful analogy for how music relates to film, in four ways: (1) the idea of ornament as an aspect of the artwork that is not logically necessary, but enhances understanding; (2) the sense that ornament recalls meanings, or questions the value of meanings; (3) the concept that ornament transfers the decision of how to understand a work of art to its viewer; and (4) the feeling that ornament mediates by channeling response into pleasure. "Music" can stand in for "ornament" or for one of Grabar's intermediaries. Writing on film music tends to deal less with pleasure than with utility: How does a composer help clarify narrative structure or underpin emotion? Perhaps the terpnopoietic power of film music could use more attention. Another advantage is that Grabar's comparativism shifts the analytic gaze away from Hollywood.

Films have places where music stretches on behind a fixed scene for a very long time, acting like the geometric, natural, calligraphic, or architectural frameworks in Grabar's crosscultural examples. A glaring example of dedication to this approach occurs in the standard pre-internet pornographic film. Centered on naturalistic depiction of intercourse, this genre avoids the personal and emotional aspects of the action, even when it is home-movie directors who are creating the scenario. The core trajectory towards a rise in tension, leading to a climax, does need to be supported by underscoring. A bland "wallpaper" music marks time through a steady beat, and carries on throughout an entire episode. Here music as ornament recalls Grabar's sense that intermediaries "facilitate or even compel access to the work of art by strengthening the pleasure derived from looking at something" in ways he did not intend, but which offer an extreme example of film music as ornament. Ordinary narrative films offer rich resources for following up on music's work as an intermediary. Below, I offer six moments of long sequences with static musical commentary, in the work of radically different directors, aesthetically and culturally: Hitchcock, Forman, Egoyan, Kiarostami, Varda, and the Soviet director Nikolai Ekk.

In Hitchcock's *The Birds,* the camera scans the skies to chart the gathering of winged villains intent on attacking small-town California humans. Well into the story, the glacial heroine Melanie drives her roadster up to a one-room schoolhouse, intending to bring home the daughter of the family to which she has become bonded. The schoolteacher asks her to wait, so Melanie sits outside smoking while the children sing. Out of her view, the evil birds gather on the playground equipment; eventually, they will swoop down on the defenseless children, to the accompaniment of Bernard Herrmann's ingenious, electronic aviary action music. The waiting-and-gathering scene is long, nearly four minutes. Throughout, the kids go on singing a simple American folksong for many more verses—twelve—than it is customary to sing such tunes. The viewer does not really ask why the teacher insists on holding the kids so long when the situation might be dangerous, so the song plays an important role. It is chantlike in its repetitions of this structure: text line, nonsense words, text line, longer string of syllables as a refrain: "risselty-rosselty/hey johnny jossity/rhetrical prosody/risselty-rosselty/now now now." This metrical, accented redundancy sustains an almost hypnotic effect against the short shots of the anxious, smoking, waiting woman and the stealthily gathering birds. This scene from *The Birds* presents an extended encounter between the human and the animal worlds, both of which take their time, instead of flitting by in the normal shot-countershot rhythm. To make a musical analogy, the overall feeling is like a Bach passage where a strong pedal point is held against the working out of a fugue.

Why is there source music in this scene instead of an orchestral effect? Why is there any sound at all? The implied narrator wants us to feel the tension mount until the attack releases it, so a portentous and scary silence might have operated just as well. What was the filmmaker thinking? Nothing about the music, according to an "authorized and illustrated look inside the creative mind of Alfred Hitchcock," which contains the director's own account and drawings of the scene, from his notebooks: "These actions are pretty straight-forward as indicated by the script. It's a matter of how interesting we can [make] Melanie sitting there smoking. There isn't much she can do. We have the voices of the children in the background. The audience's interest, naturally, are in the gathering of the birds behind her" (Aulier 1999:410). It is useful to know that Hitchcock thought of "the voices of the children" as ornament, which adds richness to the simple suspense device of the gathering birds. Perhaps he was thinking of the moment in the long chain of narrative knots based on singing children, discussed earlier in this chapter. He seems to care less about the musicality of those voices, or their cultural content, areas that have stayed out of the spotlight of film studies, focused as it is on the great man's thinking.

The film's composer, Hitchcock's longtime collaborator Bernard Herrmann, enriches our sense of how moments like the schoolyard scene came about. In interviews, he always said that Hitchcock left decisionmaking to the composer about a need for music in a particular scene. If Herrmann said "we need it," Hitchcock might respond "Oh good, then I'll make the scene longer, because if you were not going to have music, then I would have to contract it" (Herrmann 1980:122). It is this elasticity that draws my attention. As Herrmann himself says, music "changes time values. What you think is long may be only four seconds, and what you thought was very short may be quite long. There's no rule, but music has this mysterious quality" (ibid.:121). Even Herrmann is baffled: "this use of cinematic music is so mysterious that I can actually say, after surviving 60-odd films, that I don't know much about it myself. I know *instinctively* about it, but I don't know intellectually" (ibid. 1980:135). At the same time, the way the children's chant marks time is extremely precise, and has a long history in sound cinema. It is surely not true, as Hitchcock said in his notes, that all of the audience interest is in the birds; we have seen the children singing, and their imminent danger lingers in the mind. As long as they sing, they are safe. They doggedly repeat not a mathematics lesson, but an American folksong. This cultural grounding stands out visually as well, with the American flag and the portrait of George Washington in the classroom's establishing shot.

The everyday, vernacular atmosphere of the moment clashes sharply with the surreal suspense that the birds engender. This is rare for *The Birds*, with its stress on claustrophobic psychologizing of the lead characters. Most readings of the film say that the birds metaphorize a dysfunctional family romance. The music inserts a sense of community that underlies the town's response to the menace. In this context, "risselty-rossolty" can stand a closer look.[5] At the time of the Hitchcock film, the song was being integrated into the American folk-music revival movement at a number of levels by the multitalented Seeger family. Charles and Ruth Crawford Seeger were using it as a "worker's song" by 1937, with Ruth even writing a set of symphonic variations on the tune. Pete Seeger was singing it as a children's song and a banjo-teaching item. Ethnomusicologically viewed, then, the song's appearance in *The Birds* offers cultural added value in addition to its function as a framing device, carrying "ornament" away from its purely accessory function. Music, as a poignantly expressive element of a knot—singing children—can move beyond its role as a plainly colored tile in the narrative mosaic, particularly when it is culturally grounded, here as American folksong. Like Grabar's artworks, the ornament of music mirrors, renews, and repositions meanings from earlier designs. But unlike his carved and painted figurations, the visual and musical world of film unrolls in a precise, real-time way, usually leaving little if any time for contemplation and second thoughts, for a breathing space to think over earlier experience and crosscutting reference. In this sense, the music acts as ornament the way Grabar thinks of it: It "recalls meanings without compelling them. It transfers the decision of how to understand a work of art to its viewer or user."

Figure 3. George Washington, the flag, and "rissolty-rossolty:" the knot of singing children, American style. *The Birds,* 1962.

A scene from Milos Forman's *The Loves of a Blonde* (1968) differs wildly from the Hitchock example. In his slight but brilliant tale, Forman sums up the social situation of late socialist Czechoslovakia through the simple story of a provincial working girl. She hears a cool-jazz pianist at a factory dance, is seduced by him, and follows him to his family's apartment in Prague. He's not home; it's late. His parents, rather surprised, let her in and carry on an agitated discussion about their son's life, ignoring her, while the television set plays throughout a scene that lasts several minutes. The TV relentlessly rehashes a catalogue of kitsch culture of the socialist age, with repeated banal songs. As in *The Birds,* this sound backdrop of *Loves of a Blonde* stands out by its sheer length and homogeneity. As Grabar says of one of his intermediaries, architecture, it "compels attention to the main subject, focuses on it, provides it with its frame and, so to speak, gift wraps it for the viewer." At the same time, it leaves the viewer with the problem of just what the gift is. The chatter and music babble of the television is both unwatched by the characters and unseen by the audience. Beyond wrapping the comic scene of the squabbling parents and confused blonde for the viewer-listener, the relentless kitsch, like the singing children, carries on a parallel discussion with the viewer, who must register and reflect on its meanings even as it unfolds. Czech viewers would have recognized the shows instantly and would have had to juggle their response to the television and the scene. Foreign viewers, such as the Cannes jury that awarded Forman a prize, would have had to make their own decisions about meaning. The presence of state television in the very private context of the family kitchen marks *Loves of a Blonde* with its moment: central Europe of the 1960s to 1980s. State-supported but also state-monitored, this flavorful film system thrived on parallel tracking of social realities, particularly the domineering public sphere and the fragile private world. In this context, music as ornament can carry real weight.

The third citation of music as ornament and intermediary comes from Atom Egoyan's *Calendar,* cited earlier for its Vivaldi quotation. Egoyan is telling a visually disjunct story, mixing footage from different time segments that are being made or reviewed by the characters, shots of Armenia and repetitive scenes in Canada, grainy video and high-resolution film—in short, the film is the very model of today's innovative, independent, diasporic/ethnic filmmaking. Egoyan's couple are both Armenian-Canadians, struggling with identity and each other. The protagonist, a photographer who has been working on an assignment on location in Armenia to produce a calendar of ancient churches, becomes increasingly estranged from his wife, who has grown close to the local guide. She stays in Armenia and our anti-hero ignores her calls. The film opens with interspersed credits and scenes of the couple still abroad, all accompanied by an ethnographically Armenian sound, the traditional slow duo of *duduk* pipe and drum. The viewer sees the Armenian countryside from a car window through the viewfinder of the photographer-protagonist as well as the cinematographer's lens. There is a two-minute segment displaying a large herd of sheep that slows down the travelers' progress; there is no dialogue. The film offers no similar sequence in its remaining short seventy minutes, so it is a singular scene. The camerawork roughly matches the cycles of relaxation and tension that we hear in the drumming as the pipe plays on, but the music does not.[6] Since the music remains unchanged, the shot cannot be interpreted as just one of the protagonist's playbacks, which dot the film as he reviews his videotapes, fast-forwarding at will. The director takes the camera away from the hero, so to speak, and it is the sustained, pulsing music that makes the scene effective. The *duduk* is understood as the soundtrack of Armenian culture, the core instrument. The intense rhythmicism of this long take strikes me as another example of music as a sensual intermediary. Only at the end of the film does the sheep scene get its full narrative weight, when its memory is cited by the protagonist's estranged wife as a turning point in her understanding of her husband's odd detachment. But we have seen it as a highly charged, emotional event. Here, as in so many fusions of film and music, the resulting experience yields drama and layers of meaning that add up to more than just a parallelism of sight and sound.

Do these three moments of music as ornament offer "pleasure?" Perhaps not, in the obvious terpnopoietic sense that Grabar seems to demand. But he has anticipated this wrinkle; pure "pleasure" is not so much in play as the more basic quality of what he calls "sensory attraction":

> The other way to consider intermediaries is to say that sensory attraction (or repellence) in whatever shape is built into the very existence of an artifact. It is part of its reality, of its truth, and its only peculiarity is that it is an attribute whose range can vary as widely as human emotions and feelings can be dissected and analyzed. Reality and ornament . . . are always mixed with each other. (Grabar 1992:235)

For each of the three scenes I've cited, a certain reality—threatened, defenseless childhood innocence, life as bickering accompanied by kitsch, the pastoral landscape as embodiment of emotion—intermingles exquisitely and effectively with a calculated ornamental quality to make these filmed moments evocative and complex. Music as ornament goes beyond the bounds of narrative support to enhance viewing pleasure.

It seems appropriate, given Grabar's reliance on Islamic, often Iranian, objects for his speculation, to take the next, contrasting example from a filmmaker of the region. Abbas Kiarostami is one of the luminaries in a constellation of recent Iranian directors who have evolved a new national cinema under difficult conditions. As has often been noted about their work, they have responded with a fascinating creative outburst to limiting factors such as the absence of nudity (even a woman's bare face), sex, violence, or open criticism of the authoritarian religious rulers of post-1978 Iran. The musical dimension of these filmmakers' output has received scant attention compared to the intense visuality and innovative narrative style of their exposition. Without generalizing, it does seem that music also has a very particular ornamental function in some of these films, which are located outside the grid of the superculture. Several Kiarostami films feature long, repetitive stretches of characters driving through arid landscapes, often on complex quests with uncertain outcomes. Sound is extremely important, appearing with the fine precision that the director gives to dialogue, visual composition, and editing. Often natural and human sounds alternate or overlap in apparently meaningful ways.

In *A Taste of Cherry* (1996), music's appearance is so sparse that its rare intervention draws attention. The protagonist, voluntarily trapped in his car, scours a desolate landscape seeking someone to help him with his impending suicide. Fairly far into the film, he encounters a lonely Afghan refugee security guard on a desolate construction site. They have a long, meaningful if terse discussion that is one of a series of such set pieces, all set to light natural or industrial sounds. But in this case, the scene is accompanied throughout by an Afghan popular song, its somewhat echoed, diffuse resonance implying a radio or cassette player we never see. Why is this scene, unlike the others, musically ornamented? The particularity of the tune tends toward an ethnographic answer. The isolated, displaced Afghan looks for support through song, which simultaneously implies a community and a culture behind his severe isolation. Kiarostami balances this scene with the only later appearance of music, in the town down the endless, tortuous dirt road, where we see a human collective whose everyday energy unsettles the protagonist's solipsistic searching. But the urban soundscape is fragmented, not as relentlessly continuous as it was for the Afghan, just serving as one element in a mix rather than as a pure framing device. This type of intricate intermediary work for music very nearly parallels some of the ancient Iranian artifacts that Grabar analyzes, with their sparse patterns on pottery that make something complex out of a functional domestic object.

The ending of *A Taste of Cherry* totally jars the viewer. Just as we are wondering whether the protagonist has survived his determined effort at self-destruction, the entire narrative collapses. We see a film crew at the site, and understand that the whole story was a film within a film. There is music for this shocking scene, and it continues through the closing credits: "St. James Infirmary," a classic New Orleans blues that talks about finding "my baby" cold and dead at the morgue. I will not venture a facile interpretation about what Kiarostami is up to by tacking this raucous ending onto an unsettling, cryptic, and emotionally wearing movie that raises deep existential issues. At the least, the music here acts as an ornamental frame to everything seen before. The moment literally underscores an ambiguity that music, as intermediary, offers with its sensory load. In Grabar's sense, it shifts the burden of meaning straight to the viewer. It also offers the pleasure of sonic release after the claustrophobic near-silence of the soundtrack.

The sense of film music as ornament emerges sharply, almost starkly, in other movies that are precisely structured like Egoyan's and Kiarostami's. A fine example is Agnes Varda's early film *Le Bonheur* ("Happiness," 1965). Varda cuts the simple narrative into concise scenes that mirror each other, to match the tale. François is a model husband, a carpenter with an attractive wife and small children. He takes up with an equally desirable postal worker who becomes his mistress. He tells his wife the situation; she immediately drowns, perhaps a suicide. The film ends as he reshapes the same idyllic life with the mistress as new wife and mother. The opening scene of the first family on a Sunday in the park is matched by the closing scene of the refigured family, identically situated. Many sequences are in balance, often in roughly three-minute lengths. The music is as restricted as the rest of the cinematic elements, consisting entirely of two Mozart selections, apart from a couple of moments of source music that briefly define a community beyond the closed-in wife/mistress, family scenes that dominate the movie. *Le Bonheur's* opening and ending rely on a fugal passage from a wind quintet, and the balance rests on a wind arrangement of the first movement of the clarinet and string quintet. Varda segments the quintet into sections that musically match the scenes' beginning and end, rather than fading out or crossing over. With a musical palette of such limited color, small variations take on large implications. The fugal passage shifts from a wind quintet instrumentation to a string orchestra timbre for the ending sequence, offering a new sonic richness while preserving repetition. Throughout, the music is quite pronounced, and on the newly restored video version approved by the director, is sometimes reasonably loud, so we are meant to feel its impact.

What that impact might be is elusive. *Le Bonheur's* objective stance to the plot is deliberately designed to elicit a strong audience response, which in fact it received—the film provoked outrage and controversy: What *is* she saying about love and relationships and morality anyway? The mediation of music as ornament stands out in relief. The music packages the scenes, making it seem that their length is cut to the music, were it not for the fact that the clarinet quintet is subtly abridged to fit the visual sequence.

Grabar's "gift-wrapping" is operative here, but so is his insistence on the way ornament allows for multiple readings of the object. In the case of film narrative, the "object" is much more multifaceted than for the architectural or artifactual objects of the art historian. For a film like *Le Bonheur,* where music is more structural than affective, music's work as intermediary only gains in importance. The severity of the scholastic, fugal opening and closing section seem particularly designed to constrain the feeling of complicity with the narrative that classic film music is supposed to produce. Varda is playing with pleasure, using nature and eroticism to attract, but pacing and music to rein in the response, particularly through an almost austere version of Mozart. But this type of commentary does little to explain or define what is ultimately a mysterious alchemy between the music, the visual sensuality, and the narrative that give this particular film its distinctive quality. Very divided viewer response to the story confirms the director's deliberate choice of clashing and overlapping intermediaries, with the music having a powerful ambiguous ornamental role.

Varda, in a televised interview, makes plain why she chose Mozart, when, in a response to a query about her choice of music, she says: "From the first film, from 1954, I asked for good, real musicians . . . [music is] not just soap to fill the hall." About *Le Bonheur*, she specified: "I chose Mozart—good, yes?—because . . . it was the best example. [It's happy, it's lively, but], behind, you feel death coming."

Now, just because the filmmaker knows what lurks behind Mozart does not mean that the audience gets the message. The varieties and gradations of the Mozart performances add dimensions beyond the simple point of darkness behind light. The structural framing built by the change from one of the two pieces to the other also adds possible meanings. But what we do learn from Varda is that for her, the music fulfills her mission more effectively than other parameters, since there is no other component of the action that makes us feel that "death is coming." Indeed, the wife's demise is totally unforeseen, and then erased quickly from the narrative. The soundtrack for *Le Bonheur* makes the case for music's power as an intermediary form. As ornament, it surrounds and sustains, but it also enriches and amplifies in ways that go well beyond mere support.

A final example of music as ornament and intermediary pushes the terms away from aesthetic ambivalence toward concrete social reality. A Stalinist film can certainly do this kind of work. Ekk's *Putyovka v zhizni* ("The Path into Life," 1931), a politically correct tract, still has the rough edges of the years just before socialist realism was officially defined and promulgated. The film tells us about the "lost" street boys of 1923, a period of massive restructuring after the horrendous civil war. Organized Dickens-like by an underworld clique, the boys work as pickpockets outside the train station. The authorities sweep up the boys, who then become the subjects of a new social-engineering plan. In a distant, commandeered monastery, party cadres train the boys as shoemakers to make them model, useful citizens. The boys' leader is Mustapha, a Turkic ethnic who represents the assimilation of national groups into the Russian-led soviet system. After victories and setbacks, the commune triumphs, but only after Mustapha is killed by his old underworld boss, who tries to sabotage the railroad the boys have built.

Two contrasting moments of ornament stand out in *Putyovka v zhizni*. A carefully crafted high winds-and-harp glissando passage stands in for a snow storm, instead of the source sound that was becoming technically possible to strip in. In this early sound film, Ekk is relying on the conventions of silent film and theater, extending an old-fashioned sense of ornament. What is newer as a device is the intermediary of an invisible male chorus that enlivens the boys' work twice, first for shoemaking, then for railroad building. These moments are openly ornamental in the sense of upfront framing and enhancing of the message of the artwork. The movie is loaded with tight male interaction of the type that today's cultural theory would label not just homosocial, but homoerotic. The singing men behind the scenes of the hardworking boys, shirtless and muscled on the tracks, speak of the need for concerted struggle. Here, music as ornament marches into areas of ideology and command. The songs are exhorting and shaping the boys even as they support the visual image. They stand in for the full weight of the social pressure that is turning boys into men before our very eyes. The rhythmic yet rigid chorus helps to pave "the road to life" that is the film's title. This literal-mindedness goes far beyond the Hollywood model, pushing the limits of the idea of film music as intermediary. In the high-pressure environment of Stalinist cinema, "background" music jumps into the front seat, steering the viewer's attention toward safe ideological locations. Ornament goes beyond gift-wrapping the scene, to arm-twisting. The refusal of multiple meanings focuses extreme concentration on the music itself. In fact, the many repeated hearings of these single-minded songs etched them into the brains of soviet viewer-listeners and are to this day rehearsed as powerful nostalgia long after the regime has faded into distant memory.

This chapter has been an exercise in rethinking film music through making an analogy from other disciplines, especially literary theory and art history.[7] I hope that readers will think of many other ways to expand the vision of film music from single-film, single-composer, and single-cinema studies to a broader, more inclusive, comparative perspective.

Notes

1. Suitably, the Russian gramophone plays the extremely well-known song "Stenka Razin." It tells the tale of a Cossack leader who has taken a beautiful Persian princess as booty and is enjoying her on his boat while floating down the Volga. His men mutter that he "has become a woman," so to appease them, he throws the princess into the Volga. This rejection of the appeal of the oriental erotic woman suits the scene of *White Sun in the Desert,* where the good officer fends off the sexual appeal of the Asian maidens in favor of the vision he keeps seeing of his faithful Russian girlfriend in a birch forest.

2. Claudia Gorbman recently has pointed out the way that film-music studies have concentrated heavily on analyses of aesthetics, scanting a necessary look at rhetoric. As a corrective, she points to "the academic study of such multimedia forms as television music and computer music," which has "forsaken the aesthetic approach to go full bore into music's rhetorical dimensions, its functions and

effects" (Gorbman 2004:15). Her approach echoes this volume's call for a broader look at all forms of "film music," in whatever medium, to seek out its culture-based methods of persuasion, as part of an ethnomusicological perspective.

3. A whole chapter could be devoted to ways of looking/listening to classical music's appearances in film. One approach not taken in the body of this chapter would be to track the same piece of music across cinema space and time. I have done this a little for Vivaldi's *Four Seasons,* which was first recorded only in 1942 in Europe and 1948 in the United States (Eicheler 2005:32), so has a fixed point of entry for both filmmakers and audiences. It might have come into play first with Renoir's *The Golden Coach* (1959; Leahy 2003:54), and it spread widely. There are deeply ironic versions, such as the opening of Wajda's *Landscape after a Battle* (1970), which shows the liberation of a concentration camp in 1945, with the prisoners running out into the snow to the sounds of "Spring," or, more playfully, as the score for a working-class barroom brawl in Guedigian's *Marius et Jeanette* (1997), a film in which the piece also functions as romantic support. To editorialize for once, I find Guedigian's use of Vivaldi in tune with his generally patronizing attitude towards the working class. In the Tamil film *Mouna Ragam* (1989), the *Four Seasons* plays on the husband's home-office stereo as part of the furniture of modernity, paired with the wife listening to the Beatles in the up-to-date kitchen. It is an arranged marriage and they are incompatible, but both are decidedly upper-class and modern. Alan Alda's decision to title a film *The Four Seasons* (1981), and doggedly have the music shadow the lives of a set of couples throughout the year, offers a different, perhaps more American point of view on the piece's utility and cultural context. By contrast, Atom Egoyan's deadpan insertion of the piece in his "accented cinema" film *Calendar* (discussed below for other reasons) might represent an individualist director's approach. His conflicted Armenian-Canadian protagonist entertains a series of international call girls, for whom he pours wine against a background of appropriate and neutral recorded musics, including the Vivaldi.

4. The reliance on Beethoven's authority never ends. In a scene recalling the earlier uses discussed here, Ingmar Bergman's *Saraband* (2003) shows a painting of Beethoven looming over the shoulder of the domineering grandfather, who is trying to dictate the career path of his cellist granddaughter. As throughout Bergman's work, Bach offers a kindlier, or at least more spiritual, omnipresent authority, even supplying the film's title here through the single-minded use of a solo cello saraband that echoes those works' appearance in his earlier movies. In a 2005 interview, Bergman said "my prophets are Bach and Beethoven, they definitely show another world" (http://movies.monstersandcritics.com/new/article_1028000, July 1, 2005).

5. It is tempting to keep on interpreting, but further exegesis belongs only in a footnote, which can contemplate the intense misogyny of the "Risselty-rossolty" text as a possible extra layer of meaning for the screenplay's deep conflicts about women's roles. The song's narrator says he "married me a wife" who "swept the floor (and combed her hair) but once a year" and "churned the butter in dad's old boot/and for a dash she used her foot/the butter came out a grisly grey/the cheese took legs and ran away." Part of my reluctance to interpret comes from the fact that the soundtrack keeps the words indistinct, so one would have to assume that audiences knew the song, which is possible, or rely on a sense of subliminal understanding.

6. This lack of synchronization of sound and image has been noted as a special quality that music has in films, as in Nicholas Cook's analysis of another car-driving sequence, in *Psycho.* Cook notes the way the filmscore and the windshield wipers stay on different rhythmic planes as the obsessed heroine drives away with the

embezzled cash, and he sees this as "complentarity" (as cited in Gorbman 2004:18) and a way to dig into the character's psyche, rather than the action, actually a rather conventional use of music in classic Hollywood practice. By contrast, Egoyan's evasive *duduk*-and-camera duo tells us nothing at the moment about character, and packages the scene, in Grabar's terms, for the viewer to unwrap. Ornament is not complementarity.

Other car-driven film intros come to mind, such as *Gerry* (Gus Van Sant, 2002), which opens—without title or credits—with shots of two young men in a car on a desert highway, accompanied for seven long minutes without dialogue by a sparse chamber music sound of the minimalist composer Arvo Pärt. As in *Calendar,* the music rhythm and the camera rhythm are not in sync.

7. Other analogies might also be developed from the discipline of art history. The work of Michael Baxandall (whom I have borrowed from previously—Slobin 1993:90) on the role of shadow in Western painting comes to mind. He scrupulously scrutinizes shadow, which we may or may not notice, as a way of getting at a crucial issue: the relationship of *attention* to the social life of artworks. Attention is so critical to how viewers relate to film music that it is worth listening to Baxandall when he says "Attention is such a diffuse or tentacled concept that it touches most areas of visual perception, and shadow is certainly one of those areas; so much so that one may question whether attended and unattended shadows are the same thing; or (to put it another way) whether shadows survive attention" (Baxandall 1995:vi). Substitute "music" for "shadow" to see where this line of inquiry could lead: What happens when a viewer's focus shifts in and out of musical consciousness? Also, how does music play across film surfaces to influence interpretation, the way shadows act in paintings? For example, in *Crash* (2005), a scene involving Iranian-American characters is underscored by a mournful Iranian-language song, but the song spreads across subsequent scenes to create an extended emotional resonance that is quite different than the usual "sound bridge" way of extending a piece of music to provide transition. It blocks or reshapes our ways of attending to those unrelated scenes along lines suggested by Baxandall for shadow.

Works Cited

Aulier, Dan. 1999. *Hitchcock's Notesbooks.* New York: Avon.

Baxandall, Michael. 1995. *Shadows and Enlightenment.* New Haven and London: Yale University Press.

Buhler, J., C. Flinn, and D. Neumeyer, eds. 2000. *Music and Cinema.* Hanover and London: Wesleyan University Press.

Cameron, Evan William. 1980. *Sound and the Cinema: The Coming of Sound to American Film.* Pleasantville, N.Y.: Redgrave.

Comini, Alessandra. 1987. *The Changing Image of Beethoven: A Study in Mythmaking.* New York: Rizzoli.

Daubney, KIate. 2000. *Max Steiner's "Now, Voyager": A Film Score Guide.* Westport, Conn.: Greenwood.

Dyer, R., and G. Vincendeau, eds. 1992. *Popular European Cinema.* London and New York: Routledge.

Eichler, Jeremy. 2005. "The Masterpiece that Took 200 Years to Become Timeless." *New York Times,* February 27.

Eisner, Lotte. 1976. *Fritz Lang.* New York: Hill and Wang.

Enzenberger, M. 1992. "'We Were Born to Turn a Fairy-tale into Reality': Svetlyi put' and the Soviet Musical of the 1930s and 1940s." In *Popular European Cinema,* ed. R. Dyer and G. Vincendeau, 87–100. London and New York: Routledge.

Feuer, Jane. 1993. *The Hollywood Musical*. Bloomington: Indiana University Press.

Fischer, Lucy. 1985. "Applause: The Visual and Acoustic Landscape," in *Film Sound: Theory and Practice*, ed. J. Belton and E. Weis, 232-46. New York: Columbia University Press.

Flinn, Caryl. 2000. "Strategies of Remembrance: Music and History in the New German Cinema." In *Music and Cinema*, ed. J. Buhler, C. Flinn, and D. Neumeyer, 118-41. Hanover, N.H.: Wesleyan University Press.

Gorbman, Claudia. 2004. "Aesthetics and Rhetoric." *American Music* 22, no. 3:14-26.

Grabar, Oleg. 1992. *The Mediation of Ornament*. Princeton, N.J.: Princeton University Press.

Hermann, Bernard. 1980. "Bernard Hermann, Composer." In *Sound and Cinema*, ed. E. W. Cameron, 117-35. Pleasantville, N.Y.: Redgrave.

Hoberman, J. 1991. *Bridge of Light: Yiddish Film between Two Worlds*. New York: Museum of Modern Art and Schocken Books.

Kenez, Peter. 1992. *Cinema and Soviet Society: 1917–1953*. Cambridge: Cambridge University Press.

Kramer, Lawrence. 2000. "'But She Knew Schubert': Music, Desire, and the Film Image in Jane Campion's Portrait of a Lady." Paper delivered at the annual meeting of the American Musicological Society.

Leahy, James. 2003. "A Slap of Sea and Tickle of Sand: Echoes of Sounds Past." In *Soundscape: The School of Sound Lectures 1998–2001*, ed. L. Sider, D. Freeman, and J. Sider, 54-72. London and New York: Wallflower Press.

Mamoulian, Rouben. 1980. "Rouben Mamoulian, Director." In *Sound and Cinema*, ed. E. W. Cameron, 85-97. Pleasantville, N.Y.: Redgrave.

Mitchell, Charles P. 2004. *The Great Composers Portrayed on Film 1913 through 2002*. Jefferson, N.C., and London: McFarland.

Qureshi, Regula. 1997. "The Indian Sarangi: Sound of Affect, Site of Contest." *Yearbook for Traditional Music* 29:1-38.

Slobin, Mark. 1993. *Subcultural Sounds: Micromusics of the West*. Middletown, Conn.: Wesleyan University Press.

Stam, Robert. 2005. "Introduction: The Theory and Practice of Adaptation," In *Literature and Film: The Theory and Practice of Adaptation*, ed. R. Stam and A. Raenga. Oxford: Blackwell.

Taruskin, Richard. 2005. *The Oxford History of Western Music*, volume 2. Oxford: Oxford University Press.

———. 1997. *Defining Russia Musically*. Princeton, N.J.: Princeton University Press.

Taylor, Richard. 1993. "Red Stars, Positive Heroes and Personality Cults." In *Stalinism and Soviet Cinema*, ed. R. Taylor and D. Spring, 69-89. London: Routledge.

Woll, Josephine. 2000. *Reel Images: Soviet Cinema and the Thaw*. London and New York: I. B. Tauris.

Film Sources

Many Soviet films, though not necessarily all those discussed above, are available at www.facets.org and www.kino.com, which are also prime sources for Central European and many other world cinema movies.

Contributors

·◈·

Abdalla Uba Adamu is professor of Science Education and Curriculum Studies, Department of Education, Bayero University, Kano, Nigeria. His main research focus is the "glocalization" of Muslim Hausa popular culture, particularly in literature, video films music, and knowledge-sharing, which were explored in his recent work, *Passage to India: Media Parenting and Changing Popular Culture in Northern Nigeria* (Kaduna: Informart Publishers, 2005).

B. Balasubrahmaniyan is a vocal artist of South Indian Karnatak Music, which he studied under several teachers, including T. Viswanathan and T. Brinda. In 2006, he received his Ph.D. degree from the University of Madras for his dissertation on the nineteenth-century Tamil opera *Nandanar Caritram* by Gopalakrishna Bharati. He has taught South Indian Music at Wesleyan University since 2003.

Brenda F. Berrian, author of *Awakening Spaces: French Caribbean Songs, Music and Culture* (University of Chicago Press, 2000), is professor of Africana Studies, Women's Studies, and English at the University of Pittsburgh. She is also the author of essays, interviews, and bibliographies about Caribbean and African women writers and South African music.

Greg Booth is a scholar of South Asian music and culture. He is the author of a recent book on brass wedding bands as well as articles on *tabla* and the oral tradition. His current research focuses on the music, musicians, and culture of the commercial Hindi cinema.

Eric A. Galm is Assistant Professor of Music and Ethnomusicology at Trinity College in Hartford, Connecticut. He was a Fulbright Fellow in Brazil in 2000–2001, and holds degrees and performance certificates from Wesleyan University, the University of Michigan, Tufts University, the Escola Brasiliera de Música, and Universidade Federal do Rio de Janeiro.

Joseph Getter is a doctoral candidate in Ethnomusicology at Wesleyan University, and teaches at Southern Connecticut State University. He learned South Indian music primarily from the late T. Viswanathan, and has appeared in concerts in India and Indonesia as well as throughout the New England region.

Marilyn Miller is Associate Professor of Latin American and Caribbean Studies in the Department of Spanish and Portuguese at Tulane University. She has published on topics related to music, poetry, translation, slavery, and the intersection of these themes. Her first book, *Rise and Fall of the Cosmic Race: The Cult of Mestizaje in Latin America,* was published in 2004 by the University of Texas Press.

Mark Slobin is Professor of Music at Wesleyan University and the author or editor of fourteen books on musics of Afghanistan, Eastern European Jews in North America, and on the theory of subcultural musics.

Martin Stokes is Associate Professor of Music and Director of the Center for Middle Eastern Studies at the University of Chicago. He is the author of *The Arabesk Debate: Music and Musicians in Modern Turkey* (Oxford, 1992), and is currently working, with Joel Gordon, on a critical biography of Abd al-Halim Hafiz.

Sumarsam is a graduate of the Indonesian National Academy of Music and holds a Ph.D. from Cornell University. He is the author of *Gamelan: Cultural Interaction and Musical Development in Central Java* (University of Chicago Press, 1995) and is Adjunct Professor in the Music Department at Wesleyan University.

Sue M. C. Tuohy teaches Ethnomusicology, Chinese Studies, and International Studies at Indiana University. She has published on topics such as Chinese nationalism and folklore, the musical dimensions of nationalism and other forms of social-political transformation, and early Chinese film music. She also has conducted ethnographic research, beginning in 1983, on the relations among music, festivals, and social life in western China.

·◉·

INDEXES

·◉·

Index of Film Titles

Page numbers in *italics* refer to tables or illustrations.

Index of Personal and Geographic Names

Page numbers in *italics* refer to tables or illustrations.

Prakash, Kemchand, 92, *101*
Prasad, Madhava, 100, 118
Prawirodirjo, Sentot, 230
Preminger, Otto, 38, 43
Prokofiev, Sergei, 10
Puerto Rico, 248

Quaresima, Leonardo, 160
Qureshi, Regula, 350-51

Racy, Ali Jihad, 318, 331n14
Raden, Franki, 224, 232, 235-36, 238n18
Raengo, Alessandra, 38
Rafi, Muhammad, 105
Raguvanshi, Shankar, 92-97, 100, *101*, 103-5, *104*, 108, 110
Rahman, A. R., 107, 122-26, 128, 131, 134-35
Rai, Aishwarya, 135, *137*, *141*
Raja, Karthik, 127
Raja, Yuvan Shankar, 127
Rajadhyaksha, Ashish, 118
Rajam, S., 123
Rajeswari, M. S., 128
Rajkumar, S. A., 127
Ralph, Sheryl Lee, 306n18
Ramamoorthy, T. K., 123
Ramanathan, 127
Ramchandra, C., 90, *101*
Rameau, Willie, 305n2
Ram-Laxman, 106
Rani, Bulo C., *101*
Ratnam, Mani, 108, 135
Ravi, 96, *101*, 103-5, *104*
Ray, Satyajit, 115
Reagan, Ronald, 36
Reddy, H. M., 115
Redroad, Randy, 73, 74-75
Rehman, A. R., *101*
Reider, Andreas, 314, 326
Ren Jingfeng, 205n3
Renoir, Jean, 363n3
Ren Qingtai, 205n3
Rhoma Irama, 218-19
Richie, Lionel, 58
Rihani, Naguib al-, 316
Roberts, Julia, 27
Robeson, Paul, 44-45, 47, 61n2
Rocha, Glauber, xvii
Rockefeller, Nelson A., 260-61
Rodríguez, Ismael, 242
Rogers, Roy, xiii, 26
Rogers, Shorty, 41-42, 44
Rojas Gonzales, Francisco, 256n11

Romay, Titina, 245, 250
Roosevelt, Franklin D., 260
Rose, Phyllis, 295-96
Rosenblatt, Yossele, 68-69
Roshan, 96, *101*
Roshan, Rajesh, *101*, *104*, 106
Rosine, Paulo, 292-93, 306n15
Rosza, Miklos, 4, 10
Rotella, Carlo, 45
Ruan Lingyü, 189, 199, 200-203
Ruby, Jay, 179
Russia, 344-47, 361-62, 362n1

Sadat, Anwar, 311, 324, 329n1, 329-30n6
Sahai, Malti, 93
Said, Edward, xv
Sana, Emmanuel, 304-5
Sangare, Oumou, 170, 173
Sansone, Livio, 259
Sargam, Sadhana, 128
Sayan, 77
Sayles, John, 48-51
Seck, Douta, 287, 306n8
Seeger, Charles, 355
Seeger, Pete, 355
Seeger, Ruth Crawford, 355
Sekhar, R. K., 124
Sen, Dilip, *101*
Sen, Hiralal, 114
Sen, Krishna, xv, 225, 236
Sen, Sameer, *101*
Senegal, 302-3
Sequiera, Peter, 89
Sevilla, Ninón, 251
Shafik, Viola, 309, 329-30n6
Shakira, 74
Shamshad Begum, 90
Shankar-Jaikishan, 92-97, 100, *101*, 103-5, *104*, 108, 110
Sharma, Madhulal Damodar, *101*
Shata, Mamman, 171
Shinnawi, Ma'amun al-, 319
Shore, Howard, 12, 60
Shumyatsky, Boris, 345
Sidibe, Aichata, 173
Sigur Ros, xvi
Simone, Nina, 58
Singh, Ram, 89
Singh, Uttam, 106
Sivakumar, 125
Sivan, Papanasam, 122-23
Skinnie, Pope, 173
Skyhawk, Sonny, xi

Vargas Dulché, Yolanda, 242
Varna, Henri, 295
Vasudevan, Malaysia, 128
Vasudevan, Ravi, 118
Vaughan, Sarah, 61n2
Vaz, Antonio (Chic Chocolate), 90
Verdi, Guiseppe, 123
Vidyasagar, 127
Vincendeau, G., xii
Virmani, Ashish, 87, 99
Vishal, 107
Viswanathan, M. S. ("MSV"), 123, 128, 129, *141*
Viswanathan, T., 121
Visweswaran, R., 125
Vitalis, Robert, 312
Vivaldi, Antonio, 357, 363n3
Vyas, Avinash, *101*

Waadkar, Dattaram, 94
Wagner, Richard: in *Apocalypse Now*, 342; film score orchestral style and, 7; influence on Korngold, 34n1; influence on Steiner, 5, 16, 34; post-supercultural system and, 58
Wahbi, Yusuf, 312, 316
Wajda, Andrzej, 363n3
Wajdi, Anwar, 315-16
Waldman, Leybele, 70
Walt Disney Productions, 258-61, 266, 274-76, 276nn11-12
Wang Renmei, 189, 199
Wang Wenhe, 207n24
Waxman, Franz, 29
Wayne, John, 19-20

Webber, Andrew Lloyd, 125
Weiss, Florence, 71
Welles, Orson, 61n4
West, Kanye, 173
White, Armond, 56-57
Whitney, John Hay, 260
Wildcat, Tommy, 75
Willemen, Paul, 118
Williams, John: intertextuality in, 27-28; *King Kong* as musical precursor to, 9; *Schindler's List* filmscore, 342-43; *Star Wars* filmscore, 56-57; stylistic milieu of, 60
Winders, Wim, 75
Woll, Josephine, 346

Xiao Youmei, 189, 207n18
Xia Yan, 196-200
Xia Yu, 204

Yakasai, Alee Baba, 163
Yang Hansheng, 198-99
Yesudas, K. J., 127
Yuan Muzhi, 199
Yuen Biao, 194

Zhang Shu, 207n24
Zhang Yingjin, 205n7
Zhang Zhen, 206n11
Zhao Dan, 188, 196, 199
Zheng Junli, 207n24
Zhou Xuan, 188, 203-4
Zobel, Joseph, 282-83, 298-300, 305n3
Zubaida, Sami, 310-11

MUSIC/CULTURE
A series from Wesleyan University Press.
Edited by Harris M. Berger and Annie J. Randall
Originating editors: George Lipsitz, Susan McClary, and Robert Walser

The 'Hood Comes First:
Race, Space, and Place in Rap and
Hip-Hop
by Murray Forman

Wired for Sound:
Engineering and Technologies in Sonic
Cultures
edited by Paul D. Greene
and Thomas Porcello

Sensational Knowledge:
Embodying Culture through Japanese
Dance
by Tomie Hahn

Voices in Bali:
Energies and Perceptions in Vocal Music
and Dance Theater
by Edward Herbst

Traveling Spirit Masters:
Moroccan Gnawa Trance and Music in
the Global Marketplace
by Deborah Kapchan

Symphonic Metamorhoses:
Subjectivity and Alienation in Mahler's
Re-Cycled Songs
by Raymond Knapp

Music and Technoculture
edited by René T. A. Lysloff
and Leslie C. Gay, Jr.

A Thousand Honey Creeks Later:
My Life in Music from Basie to Motown—and Beyond
by Preston Love

Songs, Dreamings, and Ghosts:
The Wangga of North Australia
by Allan Marett

Phat Beats, Dope Rhymes:
Hip Hop Down Under Comin' Upper
by Ian Maxwell

Carriacou String Band Serenade:
Performing Identity in the Eastern
Caribbean
by Rebecca S. Miller

Global Noise:
Rap and Hip-Hop Outside the USA
edited by Tony Mitchell

Popular Music in Theory:
An Introduction
by Keith Negus

Upside Your Head!:
Rhythm and Blues on Central
Avenue
by Johnny Otis

Coming to You Wherer You Are:
MuchMusic, MTV, and Youth Identities
by Kip Pegley

Singing Archaeology:
Philip Glass's Akhnaten
by John Richardson

Black Noise:
Rap Music and Black Culture in Contemporary America
by Tricia Rose

The Book of Music and Nature:
An Anthology of Sounds, Words,
Thoughts
edited by David Rothenberg
and Marta Ulvaeus

Angora Matta:
Fatal Acts of North-South Translation
by Marta Elena Savigliano

Making Beats:
The Art of Sample-Based Hip-Hop
by Joseph G. Schloss

Dissonant Identities:
The Rock 'n' Roll Scene in Austin, Texas
by Barry Shank

Among the Jasmine Trees:
Music and Modernity in Contemporary
Syria
by Jonathan Holt Shannon

Banda:
Mexican Musical Life across Borders
by Helena Simonett

Subcultural Sounds:
Micromusics of the West
by Mark Slobin

Music, Society, Education
by Christopher Small

Musicking:
The Meanings of Performing and
Listening
by Christopher Small

Music of the Common Tongue:
Survival and Celebration in African
American Music
by Christopher Small

Singing Our Way to Victory:
French Cultural Politics and Music
During the Great War
by Regina M. Sweeney

Setting the Record Straight:
A Material History of Classical
Recording
by Colin Symes

False Prophet:
Fieldnotes from the Punk Underground
by Steven Taylor

Any Sound You Can Imagine:
Making Music/Consuming Technology
by Paul Théberge

Club Cultures:
Music, Media and Sub-cultural Capital
by Sarah Thornton

Dub:
Songscape and Shattered Songs in Ja-
maican Reggae
by Michael E. Veal

Running with the Devil:
Power, Gender, and Madness in Heavy
Meteal Music
by Robert Walser

Manufacturing the Muse:
Estey Organs and Consumer Culture in
Victorian America
by Dennis Waring

The City of Musical Memory:
Salsa, Record Grooves, and Popular
Culture in Cali, Colombia
by Lise A. Waxer

ABOUT THE EDITOR

Mark Slobin is a professor of music at Wesleyan University. He is a former president of the Society for Ethnomusicology and Society for Asian Music and author of
books including *Subcultural Sounds: Micromusics of the West* (Wesleyan University
Press, 1993) and *Fiddler on the Move: Exploring the Klezmer World* (2006).